animals&men
THE JOURNAL OF THE CENTRE FOR FORTEAN ZOOLOGY

THE NUMBER OF THE BEAST
Issues 6 – 10 of *Animals & Men* magazine
April 1995 – July 1996

Edited by Jonathan Downes

Scanned back issues of Animals & Men by Oliver Lewis
Typeset by Jonathan Downes,
Cover and Layout by Mark North for CFZ Communications
Using Microsoft Word 2000, Microsoft , Publisher 2000, Adobe Photoshop CS.

Photographs © 2001 CFZ except where noted

First published in Great Britain by CFZ Press

CFZ Press
Myrtle Cottage
Woolsery
Bideford
North Devon
EX39 5QR

© CFZ MMVI

All rights reserved. Without limiting the rights under copyright reserved above, no part of this publication may be reproduced, stored in or introduced into a retrieval system, or transmitted, in any form of by any means (electronic, mechanical, photocopying, recording or otherwise), without the prior written permission of both the copyright owners and the publishers of this book.

ISBN: 978-1-905723-06-5

PREFACE

It must have been eleven years ago that I first became aware of the Centre for Fortean Zoology. Since then many things have happened, which made me more and more involved with the activities of the organization. So how did I become interested in it all?

To cut a long story short, it was my grandfather - who incidentally went to school with the science fiction author and forteanist Eric Frank Russell - who first introduced to me as a child to the magical realms of local folklore and even more so when I would watch with my brothers and sister the re-runs of the films animated by Ray Harryhausen that my fascination with mysteries, monsters and ghost really began.

During school I became interested in natural history, and would often venture around the countryside with my friends or parents observing and studying the local wildlife through the seasons. It wasn't till later that I learnt about the study of Cryptozoology, that the fusion of both interest could co-exist. It was in the final years at college, before I was introduced to the CFZ journal *Animals & Men*, at that time everyone was into *The X-Files*, UFOs and aliens, so it was difficult to find any magazine apart from the *Fortean Times* that covered any aspect of Cryptozoology in depth. Through an advert in Rip Hepple's *Nessletter*, I discovered a small publication home produced by Craig Harris called the *Crypto Chronicle*. Bearing in mind this is before Internet forums and message boards, I thought finally a cryptozoology fanzine. I had always like producing my own magazines in the past, and I thought this may be a good way to do some illustrating for a subject I like, so I decided I would offer my support and supply him with some useful artwork to put in the magazine, however it was short lived, and Craig had to call it a day.

Craig forwarded all his subscribers to Jonathan Downes, who had already by that time produced four copies of *Animals & Men*, and thus started my introduction to the CFZ. It wasn't till much later, that I received a letter from Jonathan, asking if he could use any of the artwork I sent Craig in his journal, I was more than happy to contribute my skills to the journal. It wasn't till issue nine - after the tragic death of the resident cartoonist, `Mort` - that Jon offered the position of resident artist and cartoonist [1] and as one would say the rest is history.

Mark North
(Assistant Director of The CFZ/ Art Director)
Weymouth
Dorset
7th December 2006

---

[1] EDITOR'S NOTE: It wasn't quite that simple. Jane Bradley, our first cartoonist, had died tragically in an alcohol related car accident, and `Mort`, who - like me - was bipolar, had killed himself, and so I warned Mark that if he *was* to become our cartoonist, the role was very similar to that held by drummers in *Spinal Tap*. Little did I know, that over a decade later, he would be a permanent fixture here at the CFZ. Well done dude.

INTRODUCTION

Over Christmas 2002 I read the authorised biography of my hero Gerald Durrell. It was both heartening, and slightly distressing to find out quite how much we had in common. I do not wish, for one moment to suggest that I am equal to him. Durrell was undoubtedly a giant amongst men, and was undoubtedly one of the greatest naturalists of the past 300 years. His achievements rank with those of Linneaus, Fabre, Attenborough and Scott, and in comparison my humble efforts to enrich the sum total of man's knowledge about the natural world pale so far into insignificance that there is no real comparison. However, like Durrell, I hope that the sum total of my work will have made some difference to the world in which we live. On a personal level, however, we are far more similar. We have similar vices and are haunted by similar demons.

I was saddened when I read the account of his divorce from his first wife. The circumstances were very similar to that of my own divorce in 1996. When I read how he tried - for quite understandable reasons - to rewrite the history of his great organisation and attempted to expunge the very significant role, which his first wife had held it in its formation, I was determined not to do the same thing. In writing this, the introduction to the second volume of reprints of *Animals & Men* I have to cover, not only the years when the Centre for Fortean Zoology started becoming a real force to be reckoned with, rather than a back bedroom publication written for and by hobbyists, but the years when my own marriage fell apart.

Like Durrell, it is hard for me not to draw the inference that my single-minded obsessiveness with making the Centre for Fortean Zoology a success, contributed in great part to the dissolution of my marriage. I formed the Centre for Fortean Zoology in 1992, and launched the first issues of its journal in 1994. Jan has gone on to do other things, and again, I'd like to pay tribute to the immense volume of work that she put into the CFZ during the first few years of its existence. Unlike Alison, Jan and I parted company happily and amicably, and she ceased direct involvement with the CFZ purely because of pressure of other commitments.

It was issue six of the journal, which really took us on to a new level. The first five issues (which are collected together in *Volume One: In the Beginning*) were essentially a magazine finding its feet, finding its identity, and working harder to create a foothold within the fortean zoological community. Issue 6 was the first magazine to contain any groundbreaking fieldwork, and in many ways set the seal on how the CFZ would operate over the next decade. It included a number of topics that would - in many people's eyes - become synonymous with the Centre for Fortean Zoology over the years to come. It included the first accounts of "Gavin's" sighting of the Owlman of Mawnan, and also the first contributions from the notorious Tony Shiels.

It also included the first expedition report from the man who was eventually to become our honorary life President: Colonel John Blashford-Snell. It set the tone for the future of the magazine - a potent mix of hard science, meticulous fieldwork, and surrealchemy. The twin icons of the distinguished Colonel and the notorious Wizard were to spur the CFZ on to greater and more impressive feats over the years.

animals&men

THE JOURNAL OF THE CENTRE FOR FORTEAN ZOOLOGY

It was with this issue that we also began making inroads into the zoological establishment. Chris Moiser - a man who over the years has become a close friend and trusted ally - came on board with this issue as did Clinton Keeling (another contributor who is no longer part of the CFZ family.) It is probably Tony Shiels, however, who had the greatest effect on the CFZ during the years between 1995 and 1997. He taught me to see the world through different eyes, and in many ways it is true to say that he had as great an effect on me as I approached middle-age, as Gerald Durrell had done when I first read his books as a small child. The story of Tony's and my alcohol-fuelled adventures can be read in my book *The Owlman and Others*, and I am happy to say that we are still friends today.

However, I have no wish to rewrite history. If it hadn't been for the support of my first wife, Alison, the Centre for Fortean Zoology would never have gone off the ground, and all of us involved with the project today - over 10 years after its first inception - owe her a debt of gratitude for her encouragement and hard work during the early days. We are no longer in contact with each other, and it is probable we never shall be again, but it would be wrong of me not to pay tribute to her in this introduction. Another person, no longer involved with the CFZ is Jan Williams, who - again - was pivotal in launching the magazine. Without those two women, there would be no CFZ. .

Three other people, but for whom there would be no CFZ, appeared on the scene towards the end of this volume: Mark North, an artist from Weymouth started to contribute cartoons, an impoverished young student from Leeds called Richard Freeman appeared in the letters pages, and a certain Graham Inglis - at that time the roadie for my notorious art-rock band - began receiving the credit for his carrying out similar duties for the CFZ. It is difficult, seo many years after issue 10 was published, to imagine the Centre for Fortean Zoology without either of these two extraordinary, eccentric, and very gifted men.

On July 28th, 1996 my marriage effectively ended. What I did not realise at the time, was that my unexpected and completely unwanted change in circumstances would, in time, lead to the Centre for Fortean Zoology actually becoming what I had always claimed it had been - the most important, the biggest, and the best Cryptozoological research organisation and the world.

Slainte Mhor

Jon Downes
(Director of The CFZ)
Exeter
Devon
22nd July 2001

ISSUE 6
APRIL 1995

animals&men

THE JOURNAL OF THE CENTRE FOR FORTEAN ZOOLOGY

This was one of the pivotal issues of the magazine. It contained an article by John Blashford-Snell, the explorer who was to become our Hon. Life President, upon the death of Bernard Heuvelmans. It also contained my first work on the Owlman of Mawnan - a zooform entity, the search for which had taken up the previous twelve months or so of my life, and which was to - some years later - result in *The Owlman and Others*; still my most popular and best-known book. It was the first time that any of my collaborations with The Wizard of the Western World had made it to print, but it was not to be the last...

animals&men

THE JOURNAL OF THE CENTRE FOR FORTEAN ZOOLOGY

Animals & Men
The Journal of The Centre for Fortean Zoology

The Nepalese Elephants-Expedition Report; The Owlman of Mawnan-new evidence; Mystery Hominoids in Africa..

Issue Six   Incorporating "The Crypto Chronicle"   £1.75

animals&men
THE JOURNAL OF THE CENTRE FOR FORTEAN ZOOLOGY

Animals & Men   Issue Six

CONTENTS AND CREDITS

This issue of Animals & Men was put together by the following band of Animals and Men:

Jonathan Downes: Editor and Fall Guy.
Jan Williams: Newsfile and Catfish.
Alison Downes: Ornithological Administratrix.
Lisa Peach: Art, Typing Tea and Ferrets.
John Jacques: Sole Representation and Psi-cop.
Graham Inglis: Video (we are the road crew).
'Mort': Cartoonist par excellence.

Consultants

HONORARY CONSULTING EDITOR
    Dr Bernard Heuvelmans
SURREALCHEMY   Tony 'Doc' Shiels.
ZOOLOGY: Dr Karl P.N.Shuker.

Regional Representatives

KENT   Neil Arnold.
BELGIUM   ABEPAR.
NORFOLK   Justin Boote.
N.YORKS   Alaister Curzon.
WILTSHIRE   Richard Muirhead.
LANCASHIRE: Stuart Leadbetter.
SUSSEX: Sally Parsons.
CUMBRIA AND LAKELANDS: Brian Goodwin.
HOME COUNTIES: Phillip Kibberd
SOUTH WALES/SALOP   Jon Matthias.
DENMARK   Lars Thomas/Eric Sorenson.
EIRE   Tony 'Doc' Shiels.
SPAIN: Alberto Lopez Acha.
FRANCE: Francois de Sarre.
MEXICO: Dr R.A Palmeros.
SCOTLAND: Tom Anderson.
WEST MIDLANDS: Dr Karl P.N.Shuker.
GERMANY   Hermann Reichenbach/Wolfgang Schmidt

The Centre for Fortean Zoology
15 Holne Court
Exwick, Exeter.
Devon EX4 2NA

0392 424811

Contributors this issue:
Col John Blashford-Snell, Neil Arnold, Tony 'Doc' Shiels, 'Gavin', Eric Sorenson, Francois de Sarre, Dr Karl P.N.Shuker, Stephen Shipp, Tom Anderson, Alan Pringle, Clinton Keeling, Neil Nixon,

4 ISSUE SUBSCRIPTION RATES
UK/EIRE £7.00
EEC £8.00
EUROPE Non EEC £8.50
REST OF WORLD: £10 (surface Mail)
REST OF WORLD £14 (Air Mail)

Payment in UK Currency, Cheque drawn on UK bank, IMO, Eurocheque. Cheques payable to A&J DOWNES or THE CENTRE FOR FORTEAN ZOOLOGY

CONTENTS
p.3 Editorial
p.4 Apology
p.5 Newsfile
p.11 Blashford-Snell in Nepal.
p.13 Big cat sightings in Kent
p. 15 OWLMAN SPECIAL
p.21 Sabre Toothed Tigers
p.22 Crypto Rock
p.23 Hominoids of Africa
p.26 Bibliography of Books on Cryptozoology
p.29 King Kellas
p.30 Letters
p.31 Errata
p.32 The British Nandi Bear.
p 34 A-Z of Cryptozoology
p.35 HELP
p.36 Book and Video Reviews
p.37 Periodical reviews
p.39 Nervous Twitch
p.40 Cartoon

ANIMALS & MEN is published four times a year and is typeset and assembled by diverse poultry using an antiquated AMIGA A500, Pagesetter 2, D Paint v.4, and Penpal. Oh for a 486.

THE GREAT DAYS OF ZOOLOGY ARE NOT DONE.....0.

Dear Friends,

After another eventful three months here we are with another issue of 'Animals & Men'. 'Eventful' is not probably an adequate word! We ran a stall at the Fortean Times "Unconvention '95", where I met a lot of people that I had wanted to meet for a long time, (and managed to persuade quite a few of them to subscribe to/write for us. If you weren't there, and I have to admit to being a little surprised by the lack of familiar faces (or names on ID badges), then I strongly urge you to go next year. The word is that next year's event will be bigger and better and probably in a new venue.

Another event which promises to be a very exciting one, and incidentally another one at which you will be able to find a contingent from The Centre for Fortean Zoology plying our wares is Zoologica. It is organised by the zoologist and former zoo-keeper Clinton Keeling and has been described as being for Animals what the Chelsea Flower Show is for horticulture.

Also much deserving of our gratitude are my good friends Mike and Liz who put us up in their flat in South Norwood when we went to London for the FT Convention. Graham, the roadie, who threw caution to the wind and worked extremely hard all weekend despite a broken leg (itself broken under bizarre fortean circumstances-but that is another story), to Tom Anderson who has, even by the standards of our regional representatives worked far beyond the call of duty, and once again to Steve Browning the DJ from the land of the Bunyip and the Thylacine, who once again gave me air time on his severely entertaining show for Gemini Radio in Exeter.

The small screen has also been beckoning your editor. Some of you may have seen me on The James Whale Show in May and readers in the Westcountry TV area may be interested to know that I have contributed six segments to a ten part TV series called 'Mysterious West'. The series is being shown from the 11th August and should, though I say it myself be well worth watching, if only for the sight of me hugging the lovely Ruth Langsford during a discussion about the Golden Frogs of Bovey Tracey.

Finally, subscribers will find a questionnaire with this issue. I would be very grateful if you could fill it in and send it back to us. A large chunk of our readership are true forteans and another chunk of our readership are zoologists, and yet more are something in between it will help us improve our service if we know what subjects particularly interest you and what subjects, if any leave you completely cold! Issue seven will be out in October but until then....

Best wishes,

animals&men

THE JOURNAL OF THE CENTRE FOR FORTEAN ZOOLOGY

Animals & Men   Issue Six

APOLOGY BY JAN KINGSHOTT

I refer to my previous article, entitled *'Witness reliability in Big Cat Sightings'*.

In this article I made reference to a Bodmin Police Officer and I claimed that he had declared himself a big cat expert. It has been brought to my attention that the officer concerned has himself never made such a declaration. I therefore wish to totally withdraw this remark. I further claimed that he frequently saw these animals and that they were described by him as black. I now also accept that he has only seen them four times and that he described them only as dark coloured.

I also wish to point out that the officer concerned is a long serving member of the police service and I have no reason whatsoever to doubt his integrity or credibility and I must point out that he has confined his study to his off-duty time.

I wish to make a total withdrawal of my comments relating to this mans involvement and to apologise for any embarrassment or distress caused by my article and the reference to him and his involvement. In the writing of this article I accept that I did not approach him personally but I relied on press and documentary reports shown on television. These were not totally accurate and I accept fully that I should have made further research.

No slur, offence or derogatory allegations were intended and if this was taken to be so, then I fully withdraw any such inference.

EDITORIAL APOLOGY

The Editor would like to add his own regrets for any embarrassment, either professional or personal caused to the officer concerned who is, as far as the editor is aware, above reproach.

Public Domain Software for the Amiga Computer.

Thousands of titles available at less than £1.00 a disk including post and packing. Utilities, slideshows, word processing, educational, comms, demos and more than 1000 games. Over 5,000 disks contain everything you could ever need for your Amiga. Send a blank disk and a stamp for a free copy of my list which includes free games and utilities.

B. Goodwin, 6 Peter St., Whitehaven, Cumbria, CA28 7Q8.

Animals & Men — Issue Six

NEWSFILE

MYSTERY CATS

Compiled by JAN WILLIAMS (of no fixed abode) with the occasional interruption from THE EDITOR (of no fixed hairstyle) ....

Hereford and Worcester

A cow belonging to farmer Norman Edwards of Pembridge, near Leominster, was found in the early hours of the morning with deep slashes on its rump. Local vet John Horlock said 'There is no doubt this animal was attacked by a big cat.' There were four clawmarks 18 inches long and about 1.5 inches apart on each side of the cow. A pawprint 4 inches wide and 5 inches long is being examined at London Zoo. (Daily Mail 2.5.95)

Oxfordshire

A large black cat, described as four times the size of a normal cat, was seen on the outskirts of Witney in the last week of May. The witness was out jogging at 5 am, and watched the animal for 10 minutes as it walked round a field. The report follows other recent sightings at Stonesfield, Charlbury, and Fawler. (Oxford Times 2.6.95)

Buckinghamshire

Exotic cats have joined the concrete cows of Milton Keynes. Amateur naturalist Andrew Walpole saw a brown 'jungle cat' at Shenley Church End on the western outskirts of the city in mid-May. A labrador-sized cat was seen last year 'skulking under a bush' in Conniburrow, close to the huge shopping complex of Central Milton Keynes, and another was reported chasing deer in Brickhill Woods, close to the Bedfordshire border.

Deep aggressive growls 'like a cat defending its territory' disturbed a peaceful April afternoon in Dunsmore on the edge of the Chiltern Hills. The growls alerted residents Rod and Val Hamer to the presence of an Alsatian-sized black cat in a tree amidst thick undergrowth near their garden. The animal climbed head-first down the tree as they watched, jumping the last few feet and stretching like a domestic cat after it landed.

Mr Hamer found a clump of underfur on the bark which he sent to the Natural History Museum. Museum staff are still trying to identify the fur, but say it is definitely not from a puma. Both black and sandy-coloured cats have been seen in the area in recent months. (Bucks Herald 27.4.95)

A cat-flap is on the cards at Chalfont St. Giles. Following a police search for a 'tiger' in the grounds of Bucks College Campus in the town, the Buckinghamshire Advertiser has set up a 'Beast Hotline' and is offering £100 reward for a photo of the Bucks Beast.

One hot-line sighting came from Leslie Hockman of nearby Chalfont St Peter who says the beast scratched bark off a tree in his garden at 1.40 am. 'Then it went to the toilet under my fir tree.'

animals & men

THE JOURNAL OF THE CENTRE FOR FORTEAN ZOOLOGY

Animals & Men — Issue Six

Reports of the 'tiger' concern a ginger or orange coloured cat about 2 and a half feet tall which, according to the Advertiser, 'confirm police suspicions that the animal fits the description of a cheetah or a leopard'. Great - a definite identification at last! *(Buckinghamshire Advertiser 31.5.95)*

Yorkshire

The death of a sheep on a common in York has been blamed on a big cat which was seen in the area several times last year. (Northants Chronicle and Echo 5.4.95)

LAKE MONSTERS Etc...

SOMETHING ELSE FROM LAKE BALA!

Two brothers from London encountered a strange creature during a fishing trip on Lake Bala, Gwynnedd, in March. 'It was very calm and we were about to finish when we noticed something coming up to the surface about 80 yards from the boat. At first we thought it was a tree trunk. Then it straightened up and towered 10 feet in the air. It had a small head and a long neck, like pictures of the Loch Ness monster.'

'Teggie' - from the Welsh name for the lake,' Llyn Tegid - has also been seen by local people, but they tend to keep quiet about it. In a sighting made 20 years ago, lake warden Dafydd Bowen described the creature as 'grey, about eight feet long, and looked like a crocodile with a small hump in the middle'.(Sunday Telegraph 26.3.95)

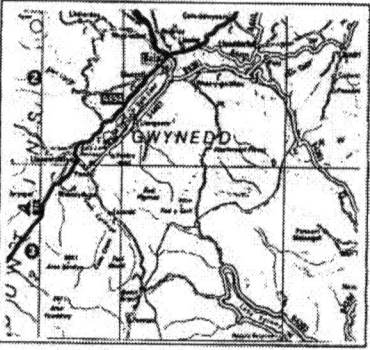

NORTH WALES SHOWING LAKE BALA

GREETINGS FROM ASTBURY PARK ...

A mysterious creature appeared at Astbury Mere Water Park, near Congleton, Cheshire, at the end of May. Park Director John Evans was alerted to the animal by a member of the public, who said he had seen a 'crocodile' enter the water. A sceptical Mr Evans went to the spot, and found some boys throwing stones at a lizard-like creature. The animal was lying on the lake bed, but was visible through the clear water. Mr Evans described it as 2'6 - 3 feet in length, greenish-brown in colour, with a long tail, feet and a lizard-like head. Park staff donned wet-suits and attempted to capture the animal, but it eluded them, and has not been seen since.

The Mere, a flooded gravel pit, has only been in existence

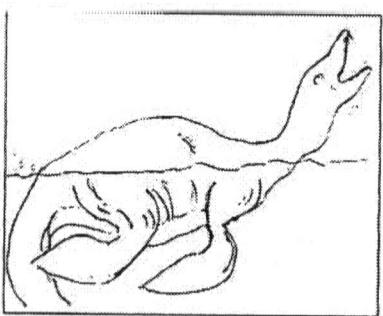

'TEGGIE' (AFTER THE SUNDAY TELEGRAPH).

for about 15 years, and no rivers or streams flow into, or out of, it. It seems likely the creature is a pet which has been dumped in the park, possibly a caiman or monitor lizard.*(Congleton Chronicle 2.6.95)*

CENTENARIAN CROC CROAKS

Kolya, a crocodile kept in Russia for more than 110 years, died in Yekaterinburg in February, having survived two world wars, a revolution, and a civil war. His skeleton will go on display in the local museum. (Yekaterinburg is of course the town where the last Tsar and his family were kept prisoner prior to their execution and I am sure that there is a quasi-fortean piece of surreal synchronicity in there somewhere but I can't find it. Ed).*(BBC Ceefax 16.2.95)*

NEWS FROM NESS

The Weekly World news, an American 'tabloid' newspaper notorious for (and I have to be careful what I say this ish) their 'interesting' approach to the news recently claimed that the Loch Ness monster became beached on the shores of the lake and *'died in agony'*. This provoked great protest from the Scottish Tourist Board and from the Aberdeen Press and Journal (undated I am afraid). The story was illustrated by quite a convincing picture of what appears to be a beached whale on which a seals head has been superimposed surrounded by refugees from a 1950's beach party movie.

Back in the real world. 21 year old Strasbourg monster hunter Thierry Regall made sonar contact with what appears to be a 'classic' Nessie type object in Loch Dochfour, which is linked to Loch Ness. He claims that he was 'lead' to the spot where the contact was made after his friend and colleague Again, David Adler (also from Strasbourg), a *'keen astrologer and clairvoyant'*, used a pendulum and a map of the loch to find "Nessie's" exact whereabouts. I have no dates but the story comes from the Aberdeen Press and Journal.

OTHER STRANGE CREATURES

WOMBLING FREE

Police and park rangers equipped with tins of dog food and a football goal net, hunted and captured two wild boar reported by a woman walking her dogs on Wimbledon Common, South London.*(The Times 24.11.95)*

LOOSE MOOSE

A 400lb female moose was running wild in Montreal last July. Police failed to catch the animal, believed to be looking for a mate. Sergeant John Green said *'If they follow a scent, it's pretty hard for them to stop'*.*(BBC Ceefax Newsround 6.7.94)*

THIS WEEK'S SPECIAL OFFER ...

A four-foot-lomg iguana was found wandering round the Tesco car park at Quedgley, Gloucester, in April. Shoppers called in Ministry of Defence police (anyone else remember that TV series 'V'?), and the reptile was taken to a local wildlife rescue centre.

In Winlaton, Tyne and Wear, a torpid toad tumbled from a lettuce which had been in Joan Veitch's fridge for a week. Officials from English Nature identified it as a Natterjack toad, rare in Britain, and suggested it had been shipped in the lettuce from Spain or France. *(Daily Mail 19.4.95, 29.5.95, BBC Ceefax 17.4.95)*

RED AND YELLOW AND PINK AND GREEN ...

Conservation groups and research bodies in Britain have been inundated with reports of frogs in a variety of unusual unusual colours. White, cream, pink, yellow, peach, and red frogs have appeared. Naturalists agree that these are albino frogs, lacking black pigment, but are arguing as to whether there are more odd-coloured frogs than normal, and, if there are, what the reason is.

Mark Nicholson of the Cornwall Wildlife Trust (see Issues 1 and 4 for previous reports of the Trust's research), said he believes there is an increase, caused by warm weather which has allowed tadpoles lacking the black pigment normally necessary to absorb warmth to survive to adulthood. Clive Cummins of the Institute of Terrestrial Ecology, said there is no evidence to show that such frogs are becoming more common, but, if they are, it could be due to intense ultra-violet light disrupting their DNA, echoing press reports earlier this year which suggested that the cause was the ubiquitous hole in the ozone layer.

Is this just a British phenomenon? If so, the ozone layer theory seems unlikely, and the cause is either a localised one, or the result of research/publicity bringing more witnesses forward. Have any of our overseas readers heard of similar reports in their areas? *(Sunday Times 4.6.95)*

A&M reader Darren Naish from Hampshire reports that several yellow frogs have been seen in his garden in recent years and enclosed a photograph of what is undoubtedly the most canary yellow frog I have seen yet. Unfortunately the quality is not good enough to print satisfactorily. We are still looking for photographs and specimens (living or dead) of these strange amphibians. In issue one we showed that in the West Country at least there is a long folkloric tradition to suggest that these frogs are not a new phenomenon which in turn suggests that the hole in the ozone layer is not a direct cause! Darren Naish also describes other deformed and abberrant frogs from his neighbourhood. Again specimens and photographs are urgently required!

ZOO NEWS

Marwell Zoo have released two Przewalski's Horses on scrubland at the Defence Evaluation and Research Agency near Farnborough, Hampshire, as the first step towards re-introducing the species to Mongolia.

Animals & Men — Issue Six

A pair of Sand Cats (subspecies Felis margarita harrisoni) at London Zoo have produced four kittens. London is one of only two European Zoos to keep Sand Cats, which are endangered throughout their range. Males of the species have the curious distinction of barking like a dog.

Woburn Safari Park celebrated its 25th Anniversary with the opening of Rainbow Landing - a walkthrough aviary where visitors can feed nectar to Rainbow Lorikeets which fly down to the hand. The Lorikeets (all captive bred) were trained by Berwick Productions - the company which trained 'The Birds' in the Hitchcock film! (*Daily Mail 31.5.95, 10.6.95*)

Six blonde hedgehogs born at the Secret World animal rescue centre, East Huntspill, Somerset, appear to be very rare chinchilla mutants, rather than albinos. Their spines are pale cream, but their eyes are dark blue, not pink. Staff member Debbie Muir said the parent hedgehogs (also blue eyed blondes) were both rescued from Wiltshire - the female two years ago, and the male this year. Secret World intend to release the four surviving hedgehogs on Alderney, in the Channel Islands, which is noted for its population of albino hedgehogs. They believe this will increase the brood's chance of survival, and hope one of the airlines will sponsor the hedgehogs' flight.

PLAGUE OF RATS

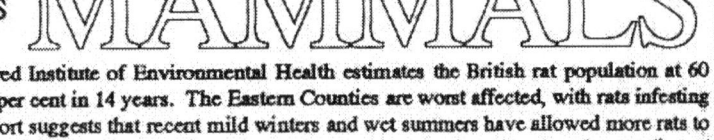

A report from the Chartered Institute of Environmental Health estimates the British rat population at 60 million, an increase of 39 per cent in 14 years. The Eastern Counties are worst affected, with rats infesting one in six homes. The report suggests that recent mild winters and wet summers have allowed more rats to survive. The Institute is calling for improved methods of control to be introduced and co-ordinated nationally. Spokesman Hilary King said 'Action is desperately needed'. The answer must be obvious to our readers - *Alligators in the Sewers!* (*Daily Mail 7.6.95*)

AQUATICSLOTH

The fossilised remains of a five million year old sloth like creature have been found on the Peruvian coast. It lived in the Pliocene and as the bones were found alongside the remains of fish and crocodiles it has been assumed that it lived at least a semi-aquatic existence. *Aberdeen Press and Journal 18.5.95*

DIRTY STINKIN' RAT...

Two Chinese soldiers have captured a two foot long, 8 lb rat with claws like a cat and a tail as thick as a man's thumb, reported the *Aberdeen Evening Express*, who got their story from the Xinhue news agency. It is not clear whether the creature which is reported to have had an eight inch tail and sharply protruding teeth belongs to any known species.

IRISH HARES

The Irish Government released 28 wild hares onto Bull Island in the estuary of the River Liffey in a bid to restore a population reduced to single figures by hunting. Such experiments often have interesting results.

Animals & Men
Issue Six

For example it is generally believed that there is a small but viable population of the Mountain Hare living on the Lizard peninsula in Cornwall after the wrong species was reintroduced by sportsmen. *Aberdeen Press and Journal (undated)*.

PAWS FOR THOUGHT — PRIMATES

Witch Doctors are believed to be responsible for cutting off the front paws of several baboons living in mountains above Cape Town in South Africa. *'It's highly likely their paws have been cut off for muti (magic potions)'*, said Ecologist Wally Petersen. *Aberdeen Press and Journal (Undated)*.

SEXY APE

An ape of an unspecified species, enraged when a domestic servant fought off its sexual advances was pacified by being thrown a banana to eat, the Kuwaiti daily al-Watan newspaper reported. *Aberdeen Press and Journal (Undated)*.

SPONGY FLESH EATERS — NEW SPECIES

A flesh eating sponge has been found in the depths of the ocean. French divers found it in a cave deep beneath the Mediterranean. The creature, known as Asbestopluma, uses its tentacles to grab its victims which are digested by a labyrinth of cells. The news report reassured us all that it does not seem to like the taste of humans. *Teletext ITV News 26.1.95*

DID WE MISS ONE?

No new species from Vietnam last issue - were the survey team on holiday? Now comes news of a black muntjac captured near the Vietnam/Laos border and being held in a Laos menagerie. DNA samples have been taken from the animal, which is smaller than the Giant Muntjac, and results are awaited, but it looks like this is number 7. I'm running out of fingers ...

ENDANGERED SPECIES — FINALLY

Why is it, that whenever some poor, (often but not always either foolhardy or mentally ill) individual gets hurt by a captive carnivore it always seems to be by one of the rarest sub-species? When the schizophrenic at London Zoo was mauled it was by an Asiatic Lion which is almost extinct in the wild. The keeper at Howletts Zoo who was recently killed was killed by a severely endangered Siberian Tiger and in the last issue we mentioned a Sumatran farmer killed by a sub species of tiger which is practically extinct in the wild state. The Daily Express on the 4th May 1995 gave a graphic description of the wounds suffered by Carl Hogben who was stupid enough to climb into the cage of a pair of Persian Leopards, a race of *P.pardus* which is far from being the most common.

Newsfile Correspondents: Richard Muirhead, Tom Anderson, Sally Parsons, Dr Karl Shuker, C. Sumner, RAJ Williams.

Expedition Report:
In search of the Nepalese Humped Elephants...

The first that most of us heard of the peculiar Elephants of Western Nepal was in Karl Shuker's 1993 book, *The Lost Ark*. He printed pictures taken on an expedition lead by the semi legendary British explorer, Colonel John Blashford-Snell. Since leaving the Army Blashford-Snell has run the extraordinarily successful *Discovery Expeditions* from his base in Dorset. He lead an expedition to Nepal during February and March 1992 where in the Bardia region in the west of the country he discovered a remote valley where the local people had reported seeing 'giant elephants'. Two such beasts, both adult bulls, named 'Raja Gaj' and 'Kuncha', were discovered and photographed. The shoulder heights were estimated as being eleven feet and three inches which is taller than the biggest specimen of the Asiatic Elephant ever recorded.

This however was not the most exciting feature of the two giant beasts because as Dr Shuker wrote:

"Each bore two very large domes on its forehead, and a distinctive nasal bridge-features not exhibited by normal Indian Elephants but which were characteristic of a primitive extinct elephant called the Stegodon".

Stegodons were not only the ancestors of the three surviving species of Elephant but also of the mammoth, a beast usually considered by all but the most hopeful cryptozoologists to have been extinct for at least five thousand years.

Earlier this year Blashford-Snell returned to Western Nepal with the help of five tame elephants, expert local naturalists and trackers, and a fourteen person team, to discover more about these colossal beasts. The team had just a week to track down the two elephants, who wander in an area of one thousand square kilometers of tropical, dry, deciduous forest and grassland. Eventually footprints of one of the Elephants, (who eventually turned out to be Raja Gaj), were found in a dry, sandy river bed, not far from the camp, but they were several days old, and large, though the elephants were, it was, in the words of the expedition's press officer, like 'looking for a needle in a haystack'.

Picture Copyright Discovery Expeditions

In March 1995 the expedition base near Shaftsbury in Dorset released a statement which included the following exciting news:

..."The two elephants were eventually sighted, resting in the shade of some trees near a village that they had been raiding for food. Raja Gaj had lost part of his right tusk and the team were able to get close enough to note that there were no lashes on his eyelids, compared to the long, thick matt of lashes on the Indian domestic elephants, nor was there hair on his tail"

The expedition is hoping that tests on the cells from the elephant's gut which are adhering to dung samples will indicate the genetic origin of two massive tuskers. Hopefully we will soon know the precise relationship that these two beasts have both with each other and with the species of Asiatic Elephants as a whole.

The team carried out other zoological work, during their stay. They sighted several groups of elephants new to the area, some with very young calves, and began compiling a census of individuals which will allow future population growth and migrations to be monitored.

The descriptions of their adventures circulated upon their return to the United Kingdom are impressive and full of fun:

"The wild elephant roam freely in the area, and a few of the team members, investigating on foot in the forest, had to frighten off a large tusker who charged and stopped just ten feet in front of them. Pilkington image intensifiers were used to monitor their nocturnal movements and the night air was always full of elephant trumpeting matched by the calls of the expedition's elephants. Two wild young males plucked up courage one evening and paid the camp a visit to investigate the local talent, but the 'domestic' ladies who were approached failed to fall for their charms".

The expedition was also lucky enough to photograph a small school of the virtually extinct Gangetic Dolphin. These mammals whose natural habitat is the warm waters of the Ganges, Brahmaputra and Indus rivers breed in the gorges on the upper reaches of the Karnali. Due to damming of the river, however, they are now trapped, unable to get down to the warmer waters and it is feared that they may die out completely. Although the species was named as long ago as 1801, it is relatively little known. The following description is taken from 'The Encyclopedia of Sea Mammals' by D.J.Coffey (Rainbird, London 1977).

"The dark grey or dark brown body shades to a pale grey or pale brown belly. The animal grows to a maximum of 2.4 metres and weighs well over 45 kg. The beak is long and well defined. The flippers are very large, spade like appendages. It has a wide, notched fluke and two ridges running along the back, and one from the anus to the tail to assist stability. The eyes are extremely small and said to be structurally degenerate causing the animal to be blind. The large, rather elongated cervical vertebrae allow flexibility and the neck can be differentiated externally".

Picture Copyright Discovery Expeditions

The animals, live off fish, freshwater crustacea and other invertebrates, possibly sifting through the mud with their beaks in order to find them. They are hunted sporadically by the local tribes for food, but are seldom filmed or photographed. After many other adventures, with dung samples safely on board the team returned to Britain and the cryptozoological world, is, as I am writing, waiting with moderately baited breath to discover whether these are merely the two largest elephants in Asia or whether they are in fact a surviving pair of Stegodonts.

Big Cats in the Garden of England.
by
by Neil Arnold

Exmoor, Surrey, Bodmin. Famous not just for the beauty of their countrysides. Each of these places is the unlikely habitat for various species of big cat. Now, we can add Canterbury, Deal and the surrounding areas to this list, for by the end of 1994 the big cat reports from locals and farmers were mounting up. Black creatures bigger than any feral dog were seen, together with smaller grey cats.

Unconvinced town folk were proven wrong when a number of sheep were slaughtered in the fields of Wingham, Eastry and Dunkirk. The sheep were victims of a clean kill with puncture marks to the throat but not a bone broken. The skin was stripped and licked clean.

Pad marks were found and local investigators tracked the cats. A family were traced to Woodnesborough, Deal and photographs were taken. The pictures are not too clear, however, and although experts have claimed that the picture showed a big cat I am not convinced. This, however does not rid me of my belief that large predators are roaming East Kent. Maybe if the creatures are left alone in the wild and protected they may become as famous as the beasts of Bodmin and Exmoor. It does seem as though the big cat situation is now being taken more seriously and there are even those who wish to capture them.

The obvious theory about the origins of the Kentish big cat phenomenon is that they are escapees from Howletts Zoo in Canterbury. Thorough checks on the captive creatures have shown that none have escaped. The cats, could, of course have come from much further afield. They can travel miles in a single night and so they haven't necessarily escaped from nearby zoos or private collections. There are, however, those who believe that more than fifty years ago a wealthy family had their own collection of of big cats. The family came from the Ashford area, and the big cats may either have escaped or may have been released due to the families inability to keep them due to their size. This is the case with many big cats kept as pets. This also applies to other animals which have been released by people unwilling or unable to pay for a license.

There have been over thirty sightings of the East Kent creatures and the paw prints suggest that there is more than one 'panther'. Whilst they continue to maul flocks of sheep one woman claims that a large black cat snatched her dog for its supper! The ridiculous thing is that after this savage incident, local newspapers and 'experts' are still offering rewards to anyone who can prove the existence of the 'beasts'. Others give advice about what to do if confronted by a 'panther'. Glamourising such a situation may end in fatal consequences for anyone who feels clever enough to track and disturb the animal.

A few sightings of big cats have been notched up in the Deal and Dover area. The sightings have mounted up over the last few months whilst the sightings elsewhere are scattered. The more recent sightings have occurred in the Canterbury region. It appears that the mystery predators may be living in the Deal area but venturing elsewhere at night. It seems unlikely that all the creatures spotted could have been escapees from private collections and it also seems unlikely that animals that may have escaped from zoos in the past are still running wild! The last big cat to escape from Howletts Zoo was tracked after a few months. There is, however always a chance that people are deliberately releasing these animals from private collections.

Animals & Men — Issue Six

The Sightings.

A large black cat was sighted in Wingham by a man walking his dog. It was night-time but the witness had a powerful torch and within the beam he saw a large, black, cat that bounded off. The man's dog apparently ran after the mystery animal which is unusual because many reports tell of dogs which are stricken with fear.

A Wingham farmer also spotted a black cat which was much larger than a dog. He was positive of his sighting and noticed the very long, sleek, tail. This sighting took place in the morning.

Sightings stretched as far as Faversham when a fisherman spotted a large, black cat near a lake. Another reliable report from the same area was of a large black cat seen by three people.

These reports were made to newspapers and to so called experts who seem to see it their duty to frighten the locals rather than inform them. Claims that the animals will strike if you run from them cannot be good for the area.

It seems obvious that these creatures are breeding and that the population can only increase. Mentions of hybrid cats are common and this could explain the different descriptions made by people who have caught a glimpse of the animals. It certainly appears as though the creatures are spreading and that there may come a time when we have to accept them as part of our wildlife.

A few years ago, on the Isle of Sheppey, a black cat was seen. This proves that the recent spate of sightings are not new for the area. A number of large cats have been spotted over the years and many were not reported. This is the case with many strange sightings. If large cats ARE being seen in Edinburgh, Devon, Derbyshire, Norfolk, The Isle of Wight, and even Australia, then why not Kent? There is enough countryside for these creatures to make their home. We can no longer doubt the presence of such creatures in our own back yards. There are enough eye witness sightings with which we can confront the sceptics. Maybe there will be some clearer photographs of the elusive creatures-the one taken by Dave Riches, who has been tracking the animals, is very unclear!

My conclusion and final theory is that whereas some of the cats may have been released from collections in the area, some may have come from far away. There may be no way of telling where they have come from but they should be left alone. We can't track down every individual, for there appear to be far too many, and with all the potential interbreeding there may be a lot of new and very interesting animals. Of course, people are going to claim their rights to walk through the meadows and fields of the Kent countryside, but its fair to warn them to 'watch your step'. The last time someone allegedly tried to track such a 'panther', they had their rib cage scratched. These cats are not human flesh eaters. They are as frightened of us as we are of them. It may be hard for some people to get used to the idea of big cats roaming the area but they are going to have to get used to it! Nature is for man AND beast.

No-one in the Deal and Canterbury areas has yet mentioned the possibility that the cats are spiritual entities like the Celtic Black Dogs, Mothman and other weird apparitions associated with Devon and Cornwall. To many this may seem a crazy theory, but although these cats appear as physical creatures which can apparently kill sheep, one should always keep an open mind in a case such as this, and the case is not yet closed. The mystery thickens!

THE DOCTOR AND THE OWLMAN
by Jonathan Downes

The Owlman of Mawnan is possibly the strangest zooform manifestation to have been reported from the British Isles. The sightings of an entity described variously as a feathered 'bird man', and a giant owl, took place between 1976 and 1978, and have confounded fortean researchers ever since. In conversation with Graham McEwan the legendary fortean Tony 'Doc' Shiels, admitted to being baffled by the whole episode, and even wondered whether the sightings had been all a hoax [1] 'Doc' Shiels is, himself, one of the biggest imponderables in the entire matter. Unfortunately, despite his exalted position as 'Surrealchemist in Residence' to 'Animals & Men', his self admitted claims to being a cheat, a thimble-rigger, a charlatan and a mountebank [2], cast some doubts on his veracity as a provider of source material.

Mark Chorvinsky, the Editor of the excellent 'Strange' magazine devoted much of issue eight to part one of an in depth investigation of "Doc's" contribution to the canon of cryptozoological evidence. The articles casts great doubt upon the veracity of the 'Mary F' photographs of the Falmouth Bay Sea Serpent. The inference was that the rest of the series would ask similar questions about the validity of "Doc's" Loch Ness and Irish Lake Monster photographs, but for various reasons they were not published. "Doc" wrote to me in October 1994 [3] but was typically oblique when I questioned him about the 'Strange' Magazine feature and essentially said nothing at all with a deep chuckle.

I think that when Mark Chorvinsky, who I have never met, described "Doc" as a 'magical wolf amongst fortean sheep' [4], he was not far from the truth. After all on a record we have just made "Doc" admits: *'I don't believe in the Loch Ness Monster even though I've seen the shagger and photographed it...'* (5) In his October letter [6] "Doc" told me to always remember that his attitudes" *(in connection with almost anything) are strictly surrealchemical",* and I sincerely believe that it is this bizarre mixture of art and science, of performance and invocation which provides the key to "Doc" and his work as a whole. "Doc" admits that his evidence is prejudiced, but as he says it is no more prejudiced than any other monster hunters [7].

A great deal of 'Monstrum' concerns "Doc's" relationship with a young Scottish Witch called Psyche. In an earlier book [8], "Doc" suggested how easy it would be to 'invent' a witch called 'Psyche', and to launch her as a media star within the worlds of forteana and stage magic:

"I think that I mentioned that Psyche was a Scots lassie so she would have a certain rapport with Nessie of Loch Ness. There would be great publicity value in Psyche offering to visit the Loch and trying to 'call up' the monster from the deep. She could claim to have done it successfully on a previous occasion...when no spectators were around...and even to have a photograph as 'proof' of this. A Photograph? Gosh!!!"

Sounds familiar?

Mark Chorvinsky and others (8) suggest that the 'Mary F' photographs, and the 'Patrick Kelly' photograph of the 'Lough Leane Monster' may have been faked by Shiels using a plasticene model affixed to a plane of glass. They may well have been, but equally they may well have not. Luckily, for believers in the Falmouth Bay beastie, there are witnesses who cannot, as far as I am aware be traced back to Shiels. It has

THE JOURNAL OF THE CENTRE FOR FORTEAN ZOOLOGY

Animals & Men   Issue Six

been suggested, however that every single 'Owlman' report can be directly linked in with the man that has been described as 'The Wizard of the Western World'[(9)].

That is until now! We have recently obtained what is, as far as I am aware, the only post 1978 sighting ever to have been published, and also the first sighting by a male witness. Most importantly, however it is the first sighting which cannot be traced back to "Doc" Shiels. This provides unexpected and very valuable corroboration to the Shiels collected Owlman stories, to Shiels himself and by inference to his work with other zooform phenomena such as Morgawr. In the ongoing battle between the rationalists and the surrealists I strongly suspect that it is the surrealists who will have the last laugh!

I have interviewed the witness and I feel certain that he is genuine. In the testimony which follows I have not identified him. I guaranteed him anonymity because this was the only way in which he would allow us to use his testimony.

We also have two unpublished drawings of the owlman phenomenon and coincidentally my postbag recently contained an article by the good doctor about owlman which we commissioned from him a year or so ago, and which was accompanied by a photograph and a note, asking us whether a serious magazine dealing with Cryptozoology printed pictures of naked witches. We don't as a rule, but in this case...why not? we thought.

REFERENCES

(1) McEWAN G. 'Mystery Animals of Britain and Ireland', (Robert Hale, London 1986).
(2) CHORVINSKY M. Ed. 'Of Dragons and Dreams', (Strange Magazine No. 8 pp 16).
(3) SHIELS Tony 'Doc', personal correspondence with Editor 7.10.94
(4) CHORVINSKY M. Ed Op. Cit. pp.5
(5) AMPHIBIANS FROM OUTER SPACE LP TRACK: 'Invocation of my daemon brother' (1995)
(6) SHIELS Tony 'Doc', 'Monstrum;a wizard's tale'. (FORTEAN TOMES; London 1990). pp.103.
(7) O'SIAGHAIL N. 'THE SHIELS EFFECT;A manual for the psychic superstar' (LYNN/RAVEN;New Jersey 1976).
(8) CHORVINSKY M. Ed. Op. Cit pp 10.
(9) SHIELS Tony ~Doc~ 'Monstrum' Op Cit.

MY SIGHTING OF OWLMAN BY 'GAVIN'.

(We were given 'Gavin's' address and details by a fellow cryptozoological researcher who had been in contact with 'Gavin' about something completely unrelated to feathered humanoids. Gavin had told him in passing that an ex-girlfriend of his had seen 'something' in the region of Mawnan Smith in Cornwall, and as we are presently researching material for a TV series could 'Mysterious West' we contacted him. We had a long conversation about his girlfriend's experience and three days later we received a letter from him. This article consists of excerpts from this letter.)

You asked if I had seen the creature. Thrown off guard, confused and suddenly alarmed, I had to reply 'No'. Well that was the lie - I DID SEE IT, as did my girlfriend at the time, Sally. (S from now on). Referring the whole experience onto S's shoulders was a route I took some time ago, and I hope that you will understand why. Mawnan owlman is a ridiculous thing that only a bizarre attention-seeker will even pretend to have seen. I am ANGRY that I have seen this creature. The whole thing is so stupid. But because I have seen this - AND I KNOW WHAT I SAW I am prepared to discuss the event intelligently.

-16-

Animals & Men — Issue Six

I am anxious not to be identified, and the idea that what I say might be on TV scares the heck out of me! I will return to this issue later, but here are the details of, and the story behind, the sighting!

I have it written down in an old diary, and thus don't need to recall the sighting. I never recorded S's version of events - do bare in mind that we were standing next to one another at the time of the sighting - but my intention was to relay the details as if it were her account. Maybe that way things didn't seem so personal. Though the sighting, particularly the details of the creature, are recorded quite well, things are not so for the exact location, time etc. So that is from memory.

Well, the event occurred late in the 1980's, probably in '88 or '89. It was on a ?camping (sic) to Mawnan, or thereabouts. I cannot remember the site or anything else helpful. I believe the area was near the sea, but can't be sure. S and I went for walks early in the evening, returning not long after it was completely dark. This was probably in June or July, so that would be fairly late. I remember small lanes and paths, a large church and lots of big trees. We had a torch and I was shining its beam across trunks about fifteen feet off the ground. I am fairly sure that the animal was standing in a large conifer tree and the illustration we made after the sighting (but not till we got home actually) does depict the animal in a conifer tree, but I'm not that sure now. Here is the actual sighting as written down in my diary:

"Every couple of hours we would walk along the fringe of the wood. This was the third time that evening and it was beginning to get dark. From a distance trees looked black but closer up the branches and trunks could be seen. We saw the animal at about 9.30 P.M. It was standing on a thick branch with its wings sort of held up at the arms. I'd say that it was about five feet tall (but please read on). The legs had high ankles and the feet were large and black with two huge 'toes' on the visible side. The creature was grey with brown and the eyes definitely glowed. On seeing us its head jerked down and forwards, its wings lifted and it just jumped backwards. As it did its legs folded up. We ran away"

As you can see from the illustration we had a pretty good idea what it looked like. We didn't know what to do about it, and essentially vowed never to tell anyone. I last saw S about two years ago and talked about it then. She was as unkeen to share the information then as she was earlier, and I promised I wouldn't tell anyone about her involvement, but I could *'do what I liked'* with my interpretation. I respect this and have never disclosed any information about her.

Seeing this creature really changed my life. It not only formed a 'springboard' for a personal interest in paranormal creatures, it also opened a different way of looking at the world. S seemed to have forgotten the whole thing, and it certainly didn't make things any different for

Animals & Men — Issue Six

I've read all the available literature on this, or similar creatures. Shortly after the event - I emphasise AFTER - I was fortunate enough to chance upon Bord and Bord's *Alien Animals*. Here was, of course, it all again. I remember reading their chapter *'Giant Birds and Birdmen'* at least six times successively. The thing that struck me, and still does, were that all the witnesses were, (as far as I know) teenage girls. At the time of the sighting, S (and I) were between 12 and 13 years of age.

What is Owlman? I think that it's like a ghost, and no way is it a real animal. More to do with the human mind than the world of zoology. Several years ago I began having 'nasty' dreams featuring similar creatures - they were always malevolent but not generally harmful. There's dreams for you. I particularly remember one when I had to hunt and kill a man with a bow and arrow and I was being watched by a BLACK AND WHITE owlman standing at the base of a birch tree. I tried drawing owlman again after this, and, as I was obviously better at drawing animals than previously, was much happier with the result. I enclose a photocopy of this latter interpretation which has caused me to change some of my ideas about the original sighting.

Firstly I don't think that it was as big as I (and S) originally described: closer to 4 feet than 5. As can be seen from the newer drawing, I found satisfaction in different config- urations of the legs and thorax. S and I had agreed early on that the creature had 'bird legs', but

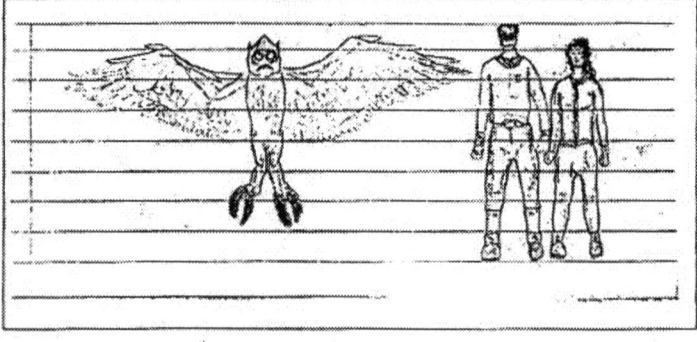

we never could agree on the feet. I am sure that they were like black pincers, or what your hands look like if you keep digits two and three pressed together and separate from four and five (which are also pressed together). S, though, said that she didn't see separate 'digits' and the feet were like clogs or bulky shoes of some kind. I remember reading in another Bord and Bord book, probably *Ancient Mysteries of Britain*, that owlman was probably just an owl after all. Even at the time of the sighting I was extremely familiar with owls, (and other birds) and had even seen several in the wild. This creature was DEFINITELY a great deal bigger than any owl (even the biggest owls in the world - the Eurasian eagle Owls - do not approach four feet in height), and, as we were sure we knew what the head looked like, it didn't really resemble an owl except superficially.

I do not mind this information being used in any way, just as long as it is not explicitly linked to myself. I hope to eventually become involved in some branch of science, and having a name tarnished by an event such as this really would not be a helpful thing. My family would also be against me, as I have already had enough trouble from my involvement with things cryptozoological/paranormal. Therefore, as I am sure you understand, I would like anonymity and complete confidentiality as regards the personal aspects of this letter. A Pseudonym, quite unlike my real name, would therefore be most appropriate. I thank you for your understanding and cooperation, and hereby give you full permission to use the relevant material, obviously with the above conditions.

THE CASE.... FOR OWLPERSON

by Tony 'Doc' Shiels

In 1927, at the Manoir d'Anjo, Verengeville-sur-Mer, Andre Breton hunted owls and wrote Nadja. Around this time, Max Ernst made a series of surreal 'Bird Monuments'; and Salvador Dali sent a letter (to Lorca) in which he confessed that he was 'painting a very beautiful woman, smiling, tickled by multi-coloured feathers.

A bizarre loploplot was being hatched.

Breton, (obsessed by eyes) should not have been shooting the hooting owls. Look what happened to John Fane Dingle - after he 'shot a crop-eared owl' - in the Richard Hughes poem:

> *"Corpse Eyes are eerie,*
> *Tiger eyes fierce.*
> *John Fane Dingle found*
> *Owl-eyes worse".*

Ending

> *"Owl-eyes, without sound*
> *- pale of hue*
> *John died of no complaint*
> *with owl-eyes too".*

In 1933, the Loch Ness Monster and King Kong became world famous; and Max Ernst created his superb collage 'novel' - Une semaine de Bonte - full of monstrous hybrids, including birdmen and bird women, in a variety of dramatic/erotic situations. Also in 1933, Andre Breton met the surrealist seer, Victor Braunder, for the first time. Like Breton, Brauner was obsessed with eyes.

Loplop, 'Bird Superior', cock-a-doodled magical sigils on eggshells. Peculiar pit-patted onto Parson's Beach, Cornwall. Deep in the Helford something stirred.

In 1937, Max Ernst visited Cornwall with Leonora Carrington. They conjured cryptozoological curiosities. Sky clad surrealist witches were involved. Morgawr the sea-serpent was seen, H.P.Lovecraft died. Fern-Owls chirred in the Mawnan woods.

When whippoorwills call and evening is nigh....

In 1976, Max Ernst died, and a 'big feathered bird-man' was seen hovering over Mawnan Old Church. Dover publications produced an edition of 'Une Semaine de Bonte'. I licked an ice-cream cone, performed prestidigitations with pears, and met some young girls who had seen the strange Owlman of Mawnan.

Animals & Men

Issue Six

Owlman has been described as being 'big as a man with a nasty owl face, big ears and big red eyes'. It had wings, grey feathers, and feet 'like big black crab claws'. Owlman could rise straight up vertically with hardly any movement of the wings. It was only ever seen by young females so far as I know.

For ten years, from 1976 to 1986, in cahoots with a group of witches, I attempted to invoke the Owlman employing the techniques of Shamanic surrealchemy. From time to time the conjourations may have worked. Some very strange things certainly happened during that period. I am sure that Max Ernst/Loplop had something to do with these happenings. My Owlman experiments ceased around Halloween 1986, when tricking and treating at Mawnan Old Church upset the ecclesiastical authorities. It was a hoot.

In 1994, something which is now known as 'The Case' captured my attention. Shortly after Paddy's day I flew from Shannon and soon found myself in London where the game was afoot and strix trix were in the city air. Somehow, it started with a crossword clue, a bag of pears, a Picasso exhibition, and the initials G.S - which could represent 'Great Strigiform'. The pears proliferated and bottles of perry soon appeared. A vaguely Fortean person asked me if Owlman was really male; was it a cock or a hen? I recalled a dream, involving Max Ernst in which I had decided that Owlman was not a cock. But then, cocks popped up everywhere, along with more pears, perry and ice cream cones. One of the young girls who saw Owlman in 1976 was called Barbara Perry. The winged thing was also encountered by the Greenwood Sisters (G.S). I thought about Hen's Teeth and Mr Punch. They were already part of The Case.

I am writing this paragraph in Ireland, on Monday morning, May 1st 1995; after an exhausting 'Eve of Bealtaine' night of conjourations and libations. Owl-eyed Dingle from the poem came to mind at some point in the proceedings. This, in turn, made me think of Dingle, Co Kerry, and the famous Giant Squid (G.S), driven ashore there in 1673. Today, one of my daughters who lives quite close to Dingle, telephoned me to announce the news that another Kerry Kraken had been netted. Something 'owl-eyed' could have invoked it.

Tony "Doc" Shiels, Corofin, 1995.

PACKED SABRES
by Eric Sorensen

There seems to be a general consensus of opinion that Sabre-toothed cats preyed on the big plant-eaters, and that they were perhaps the only carnivores who had the ability to bring down the really big carnivores. They would thus have had the monopoly on this source of meat. But How? The usual comment on the big species of Sabretooth focuses on the weaponry or 'firepower', of the individual specimen with a few comments on stabbing technique. I think that these speculations must be close to the point, by necessity, but I object to the standard illustrations which depict a lone specimen, indirectly implying, by correlation to other cats, that it had solitary habits.

IF they preyed on megaherbivores, then a couple of tons of meat for one or two sabretooths would be wasteful over-kill, severely limiting the possible number because so much meat would be lost. One or two hunters would be at much greater risk of injury. The logical solution is pack hunting, like lions or wolves minimising risk and optimising prey size to feed an entire pack for a few days. We must therefore visualize a fearsome pack of sabretooths circling and stabbing an enormous victim like an elephant.

Social behaviour can explain the fact that we have found skulls with broken canines, with the broken end worn, revealing survival that would probably have been difficult outside a pack. One might theorise that this particular individual killed smaller prey, but the Smilodon, at least, was not built for speed.

Some people have argued that because Smilodon heavily outnumbers the Californian Lion at the La Brea Tar Pits in Los Angeles, it must have been the smaller brain size or 'primitiveness' that caused them to fall in. Wolves, however, animals which we consider to be very intelligent, are equally well represented. We could simply argue that this is a sign of success, because the two species were simply so numerous.

Survivor chauvinism is a dangerous tar trap to fall into, but it has been taught for a hundred years. 'This one survived therefore it is more advanced' is just a circular statement. As long as we do not know what killed a lot of powerful, healthy animals, caution is recommended. Survival could just as well be regarded as luck.

After all the geological periods are defined by sudden global change, extinction and collapse of ecosystems. Catastrophism is on the way back!

I have seen sabretooth skeletons in Paris and Los Angeles. What struck me in L.A was the fact that Smilodon, mounted along side the Californian Lion,

BOOKS ON FORTEANA, NATURALK HISTORY, INSECTS, PET KEEPING AND EXOTIC ANIMAL HUSBANDRY, MYSTERY ANIMALS ETC ALWAYS WANTED. CASH PAID.

TELEPHONE 01392 424811

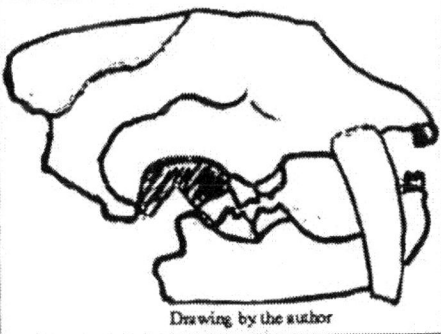
Drawing by the author

-21-

Animals & Men

Issue Six

is smaller, roughly 150-200 kilos compared to the lion which is really big at, perhaps, 300 kilos. At a distance I thought that it was a bear! The shoulder blade of the Smilodon was about half the area of that of the lion, so the powerful forelimb, that we see amongst lions and tigers can not have been a weapon of Smilodon. It was so successful and numerous, however, that I think that it was the ultimate killing machine...but not the biggest. The few thousand years which separates them from us, is nothing compared to their total existence of many millions of years with other carnivores, and they must have been known and feared by man. The fact that they survive as a Cryptozoological phenomenon is testimony to this, and whenever we deal with animals which are supposed to be extinct, but which remain in the memory, we must remember that the preservation of a specimen is a very rare event, and that the last fossil or sub-fossil is only the most recent known to science, and probably never the last that ever existed. Sadly, yet tantalizingly, therefore some of our cryptozoological subjects may have only left us within the last few hundred years, and perhaps even as recently as last year!

NOW That's WHAT I CALL CRYPTO!

Crypto-rock is a rare and strange beast. Encounters with the great crypto cuts are about as common as midnight meetings with the Thorganby Lion. But, if you plan your expedition with care, know what you're looking for and display patience then you might find the cuts that make up the legendary 'Now that's what I call Crypto' album.

Jonathan Richman and the Modern Lovers - Abominable Snowman in the Market.

Richman displayed an underground attitude to rival the Velvet Underground until a mental backflip in the mid seventies put him into career reverse with a propensity for infantile lyrics and scratchy acoustic guitar. The man is a born cult hero and as befits his role this cut is one of several in the Richman portfolio dealing with cryptozoology and UFO's. Lyrically it concerns the appearance of an 'Abominable Snowman' in a supermarket. This leads to several complaints from housewives before Richman concludes that basic mediation will solve this situation,...'Now, we've got to talk to this Abominable Snowman...Man!' Musically its basic fifties rock and roll, twenty years late, with plenty of treble on the guitars. Somewhere between light doo wop and Buddy Holly on mind expanding drugs.

The track is on the 'Jonathan Richman and the Modern Lovers' album. The original Beserkeley records release turns up occasionally in record fairs. Rev Ola should have a few copies of their CD release available. It was also compiled onto '23 great recordings by Jonathan Richman and the Modern Lovers' which has recently surfaced for the knock down price of £5.99 on CD.

EDITORIAL NOTE: "Uh Road Runner once, Roadrunner Twice, I'm in Love with the feeling now"....

PHENOMENAL BOOKS
14 Gresham Road, Thornton-Cleveleys
Blackpool FY5 3EE
01253 854617
Free Catalogue.

Egyptology; Archaeology; UFOs; Cosmology; Mysteries; Religon; Mysticism; Eastern Thought and Philosophy; Parapsychology; Popular Science; Psychology; New Age; Occult....

THE MYSTERIOUS HOMINOIDS OF AFRICA
in the light of Modern Research.

by Francois de Sarre

The survival of various-sized hairy hominoids in the large, scarcely explored African forests may not be particularly surprising, since fossil records, in Ethiopia and elsewhere, are pointing out that the black continent was once inhabited by a series of human like creatures, and new species of large mammals, like the Okapi, the Mountain Gorilla and the Giant Forest Pig, have recently been discovered in Africa by Zoologists.

The aim of the present article is not to list the hitherto still unrecognized hominoids of Africa as they are known from the numerous eyewitness reports throughout the whole continent. The interested reader may refer to Bernard HEUVELMANS' book *'Les Betes humaines d'Afrique'* (which has still not been translated into English). I intend, in this paper, to present the newest discoveries on fossil australopithecines, and to link them with the sightings of hidden hominoids in Africa for classification purposes.

APE OR HUMAN?

In Aramis, Ethiopia, the recent discovery of the fossil of a creature that appears to be closely related to a chimpanzee, re-opened the old controversy about man's origins. (*Nature, 371, 1994*). Australopithecus ramidus, as it was called by Tim WHITE, dated from about 4.5 million years ago. Some authors would have given it the generic name of Pan, but in contrast to Chimpanzees the fossil skull presented a disposition characteristic of bipedality. The occipital hole (foramen magnum) where the spinal column enters the skull, was next to the base of the skull. In apes the hole is further back which leads us to suppose that ramidus walked erect.

The teeth of ramidus were covered with thin enamel, like those of Chimpanzees, demonstrating fructivorous habits, but the small canines look very human like! The articulation of the elbow suggests that ramidus could easily climb up, around, and through branches. The fossils of Australopithecus ramidus are accompanied by fossils of fauna indicative of a forest environment. Many authors now suggest that the bipedal, upright, stance is an ancestral feature that has been lost by the apes....

Henry GEE, assistant editor of Nature, also emphasizes: *'Erect posture will thus be seen as a primitive feature that the Chimpanzees have lost, rather than an advanced feature that the hominids have acquired'.* In this way, *Australopithecus ramidus* represents a kind of *'missing link'* between an early terrestrial biped and the quadrupedal chimpanzees of today. The theory of Initial Bipedalism, indeed, already claimed that the different types of fossil hominoids and the various monkeys and apes are vestiges of mans ancestral line rather than his predecessors! (de SARRE 1994). This theory is now sustained by palaeontological data. The discovery of the new fossil provides powerful support for this interpretation, but there are other facts which confirm this point of view.

WAS 'HOMO' HABILIS A QUADRUPED?

Skulls of *Australopithecus africanus*, 'Homo' habilis and *Homo erectus*, were examined with the help of the modern technology of Computer Tomography Scanning. The morphology of the osseus ear labyrinth gives us information on the locomotory behaviour. The only species able to demonstrate 'modern' human morphology, and thus to have the ability of bipedal gait is *Homo erectus*. In contrast, the semi circular canals in the skulls of Australopithecus resemble those of the extant great apes!

A. Africanus thus presents a locomotor repertoire combining facultative bipedalism as well as arboreal climbing. In one specimen assigned to 'Homo' habilis the canal *dimensions show similarity with the canal proportions in large cercopithecoids.*

The authors Fred SPOOR and Bernard WOOD suggest that the specimen of habilis that they examined (Stw 53) relied less on bipedal behaviour than the common australopithecines! 'Homo' habilis may well be a combination of several quite different creatures. The australopithecines were apes. They only retained a relictual bipedality, just like today's chimps! If Homo erectus was indeed an obligatory biped, the other hominoids of Africa which are known only from fossils, usually had quadrupedal habits. To some observers they appear to be apes rather than hairy humans.

DWARFS OR LITTLE FURRY MEN?

Surely Africa still harbours unknown hominoids. That is, hominoids, presently undescribed by the zoologist. Many such 'cryptids' are described as 'small men', like the Agogwe of Tanganijka reported by William HICHENS in 1937. Others are naked or have a scarce pilosity. They often have a splendid mane, or at least long hair. They have a bipedal gait and are about three feet tall. As Bernard HEUVELMANS has explained, the African pygmies have downy hairs upon their bodies. Maybe smaller and hairier pygmies exist in remote parts of the deep forest?

In several of the neighbouring countries, where they only survive in people's memories legends continue to surface about these small men. In other countries such as Zimbabwe (formerly Rhodesia), they are widely mythicised and considered as goblins or other spirits. My personal opinion is that Africa's little furry men, including those resembling 'Australopithecines', are in fact 'Infra-Pygmies'; tiny human creatures who live in the Equatorial forests, outside the areas known to be populated by man.

THE BIG HAIRY 'APE MEN'.

Large hominoids are reported from different places, like Kenya ('Nanauner'), or Zaire ('Kikomba'). They look like very pilous and muscular men. They have long hair which sometimes hides their faces. The main difference between them and human beings is that they have no forehead at all. They are said to walk with an erect bipedal gait, and sometimes they will hold a stick in one hand. They are said to be aggressive. The best identification that we can suggest would surely be Homo erectus or Pithecanthopus, rather than one of the more robust Australopithecines such as Louis Leakey's 'Zinj'. These appear, in the light of modern research to have been tree dwellers, which would make them hardly distinguishable, to the casual eye witness at least, from a normal Chimpanzee. Although Pithecanthropus ('Ape-Man'), as described by Eugene DUBOIS in 1894, is not the best piece of nomenclature for a wild, hairy, man, who really has nothing to do with the apes, it should ideally replace the generic name Homo which should be reserved for the round skulled humans of the sapiens type. I would therefore identify the larger unrecognised hominoids of Africa with surviving forms of Pithecanthropus erectus, originally a savannah form, who has recently taken refuge in the rain or mountain forest, which is usually inaccessible for men. The survival of living specimens the pithecanthropus into the present day would not be so surprising. 'Young' fossil remains are attributed to this species; the famous fossil of the 'Rhodesian Man of Broken Hill' is considered to be no more than 13,000 years old! The descriptions of the large hominoids of Africa correspond well with the way that we suspect that Pithecanthropus lived and behaved. The only difference being that the fossils do not show the typical long hair reported from the living specimens, because hair does not have the ability to form fossils!

REFERENCES.

GEE Henry (1995): *'Uprooting the human family tree'*. NATURE, vol. 373: 15, 5th January.
HEUVELMANS Bernard (1980): *'Les Betes humaines d'Afrique'*. Plon, Paris.
HICHENS William (1937): *'African Mystery Beasts'*. DISCOVERY, 18: 369-373.
de SARRE Francois (1994): *The Theory of Initial Bipedalism on the question of human origins*. BIOLOGY FORUM, 87 (2/3): 237-258, Perugia.
SPOOR Fred et al. (1994): *'Implications of early hominid labyrinthine morphology for evolution of human bipedal locomotion'* Nature 369:645-8 23/6
WHITE Tim et al)(1994) *'Australopithecus ramidus, a new species of early hominoid from Aramis, Ethiopia'*. NATURE, vol. 371: 306-312, 22 September.

"The Descent of Man" by François de Sarre.

Animals & Men   Issue Six

A BIBLIOGRAPHY OF CRYPTOZOOLOGICAL AND ZOOMYTHOLOGICAL BOOKS
by Dr Karl P.N.Shuker and Stephen Shipp.

PART ONE

(EDITORIAL NOTE: This was originally intended to be run as a single article, but I should have known better than to ask a well known book dealer to collaborate with the countrie's formost Cryptozoologist and a notorious bibliophile, to boot, and expect a result of anything less than astronomical proportions. The article will now be run as a series over the next four or five issues)

For the most part this list is self explanatory, but the following comments assist in defining its precise form and scope.

Works included generally have a minimum length of 32 pages, and concentrate upon cryptozoology (undiscovered animals) and/or zoomythology (mythological animals). Space limitations preclude inclusion of the countless 'general mysteries' books in existence that contain chapters or sections dealing with cryptozoological subjects. Equally, no attempt has been made to provide a complete listing of cryptozoological books, as this would be little short of impossible, especially in relation to foreign language publications. Books clearly written specifically for children are not included.

First UK edition (generally hardback), and most recent UK edition are given for each book. Details of English Language editions published outside the UK are given only in certain instances when these predate their UK counterparts. Last but not least: Books have been deemed eligible for inclusion in this bibliography by virtue of their subject; we have made no attempt to select or discriminate upon the basis of their scientific merit. We leave that perilous task, gentle reader, to you!

Section One: Cryptozoology.

GENERAL CRYPTOZOOLOGY
(including 'mainstream' wildlife books with significant cryptozoological content).

ALDERTON, David, *Breakfast with a Bigfoot* (Beaver: London, 1986).
AYLESWORTH, Thomas G., *Science looks at Mysterious Monsters* (Julian Messner: New York, 1982).
BARLOY, Jean-Jacques, *Les Survivants de l'Ombre* (Arthaud: Paris, 1985).
BILLE, Matthew A., *Rumours of Existence* (Hancock House: Blaine, 1995).
BORD, Janet and BORD Colin, *Alien Animals* (Elek: London; rev. edit., Panther: London, 1985).
BROOKESMITH, Peter (Ed.), *Creatures from Elsewhere* (Orbis: London, 1984).
BURTON, Maurice, *Living Fossils* (Thames & Hudson: London, 1954).
CARRINGTON, Richard, *Mermaids and Mastodons: A book of Natural and Unnatural History* (Chatto and Windus: London, 1957).
.CLARK, Jerome, & COLEMAN, Loren, *Creatures from the Outer Edge* (Warner: New York, 1978).
COHEN, Daniel, *A Modern look at Monsters* (Tower: New York, 1970).

COHEN, Daniel, *Monsters, Giants and Little Men from Mars: An Unnatural History of the Americas* (Doubleday: New York, 1975).
COHEN, Daniel, *The Encyclopaedia of Monsters* (Dodd, Mead: New York, 1982; UK edit., Faber & Faber: London, 1985).
CORDIER, Umberto, *Guida ai Draghi e Mostri in Italia* (SugarCo Edizioni: Milan, 1986).
EBERHART, George M., *Monsters: A Guide to Information on Unaccounted-for Creatures* (Garland: New York, 1983).
FARSON, Daniel, *The Hamlyn Book of Monsters* (Hamlyn: London, 1978).
GARNER, Betty S., *Canada's monsters* (Potlatch: Hamilton, 1976).
GOULD, Charles, *Mythical Monsters* (W.H.Allen: London, 1886).
GRANT, John, *Monsters* (Apple Press, London, 1992).
HALL, Mark A., *Natural Mysteries: Monster Lizards, English Dragons, and Other Puzzling Animals* (M.A.H.P.: Bloomington, 1989; 2nd Edit., 1991).
HEALY, Tony & CROPPER, Paul, *Out of the Shadows: Mystery Animals of Australia* (Pan Macmillan Australia: Chippendale, 1994).
HEUVELMANS, Bernard, *Sur la Piste des Betes Ignorees* (2 Vols) (Plon: Paris, 1955).
HEUVELMANS, Bernard, *On the Track of Unknown Animals* (Rupert Hart-Davis: London, 1958; abridged edit., Paladin: London, 1965; unabridged edit. reprinted with new intro., Kegan Paul: London 1995).
HEUVELMANS, Bernard, *Les Derniers Dragons D'Afrique* (Plon: Paris, 1978).
HOLIDAY, F.W., *Creatures From the Inner Sphere* (Popular library: New York, 1973).
HOLIDAY, F.W., and WILSON Colin, *The Goblin Universe* (Llewellen: St Paul, 1986)
JOLY Eric, and AFFRE, Pierre 'Les Monstres sont Vivant' (Grasset, Paris 1995).
KEEL, John, *Strange Creatures From Time and Space* (Fawcett: Greenwich, 1970; 1st UK edit., Spearman: London, 1975).
KEEL, John, *The Complete Guide to Mysterious Beings* (Doubleday: New York, 1994).
KRUMBIEGEL, Ingo, *Von Neuen und Unentdeckten Tierarten* (Kosmos: Stuttgart, 1950).
LANDSBURG, Alan, *In search of Myths and Monsters* (Corgi: London, 1977).
LAYCOCK, George, *Strange Monsters and Great Searches* (Piccolo: London, 1976).
LEE, John and MOORE, Barbara, *Monsters Among Us: Journey to the Unexplained* (Pyramid: New York, 1975).
LEY, Willy, *The Lungfish, The Dodo, and The Unicorn: An Excursion into Romantic Zoology* (Modern Age: New York, 1941; UK edit., Hutchinson: London, 1948).
LEY, Willy, *The Lungfish, The Dodo and The Unicorn* (Viking, New York, 1948).
LEY, Willy, *Dragons in Amber: Further Adventures of a Romantic Naturalist* (Viking: New York, 1951).
LEY, Willy, *Salamanders and Other Wonders* (Viking: New York, 1955).
LEY, Willy, *Exotic Zoology* (Viking: New York, 1959).
McEWAN, Graham J., *Mystery Animals of Britain and Ireland* (Robert Hale: London, 1986).
MACKAL, Roy P., *Searching for Hidden Animals: An Enquiry into Zoological Mysteries* (Doubleday: Garden City, 1980; UK edit., Cadogan: London, 1983).
MARCHANT, R.A., *Beasts of Fact and Fable* (Phoenix House: London, 1962).
NEWTON, Michael, *Monsters, Mysteries, and Man* (Addison-Wesley: Reading, 1979).
NOLANE, Richard D., *Sur les Traces du Yeti et Autres Animaux Clandestins* (Dossiers Vaugirard: Paris, 1994).
RANDLES, Jenny, *Mind Monsters: Invaders from Earth's Inner Space?* (Aquarian Press: Wellingborough, 1990).
ROGO, D. Scott & CLARK, Jerome, *Earth's Secret Inhabitants* (Tempo: New York, 1979).

Animals & Men

Issue Six

SANDERSON, Ivan T., *"Things"* (Pyramid: New York, 1967).
SANDERSON, Ivan T., *More "Things"* (Pyramid: New York, 1969).
SHIELS, Tony ('Doc'), *Monstrum!* (Fortean Tomes: London, 1990).
SHUKER, Karl P.N., *Extraordinary Animals Worldwide* (Robert Hale: London, 1991).
SHUKER, Karl P.N., *The Lost Ark: New and Rediscovered Animals of the 20th Century* (HarperCollins: London, 1993).
SHUKER, Karl P.N. (Consultant), *Man and Beast* (Readers Digest: Pleasantville 1993).
SHUKER, Karl P.N. et al. (Consultants), *Almanac of the Uncanny* (Readers Digest: Surry Hills, 1995).
SOULE, Gardner, *The Maybe Monsters* (Putnam: New York, 1963).
SOULE, Gardner, *The Mystery Monsters* (Ace: New York, 1965).
STEIGER, Brad, *Monsters Among Us* (Para Research: Rockport, 1982).
STONE, Reuben, *Monsters and Mysterious Places* (Blitz: Enderby, 1993).
TASSI, Franco, *Ananali a Rischio* (Giorgio Mondadori: Milan, 1990).
TAYLOR, David, *David Taylor's Animal Monsters* (Boxtree: London, 1987).
THOMAS, Lars, *Fantasi og Virkelighed i Naturen* (Liberdan: Hillerød, 1987).
THOMAS, Lars, *Mystiske Dyr* (3 vols) (Andersen Bogservice: Vanløse, 1989).
TRUZZI, Marcello & GREENWELL, J.Richard (Consultants), *(Mysterious Creatures* (Time-Life: Amsterdam, 1988).
WENDT, Herbert, *Out of Noah's Ark* (Weidenfeld & Nicholson: London, 1956).
WILKINS, Harold T., *Monsters and Mysteries* (James PIKE: St Ives, 1973).

MYSTERY CATS AND OTHER MAMMALIAN CARNIVORES.

BEER, Trevor, *The Beast of Exmoor: Fact or Legend?* (Countryside Productions: Barnstaple 1984).
BERESFORD, Quentin & BAILEY, Garry, *Search for the Tasmanian Tiger* (Blubber Head Press: Sandy Bay, 1981).
BORGAARD, Per, *Mysteriet om Spøgelseknttene* (Gyldendal: Copenhagen, 1993).
BOTTRIELL, Lena G., *King Cheetah: The story of the Quest* (Brill: Leiden, 1987).
BRIERLY, Nigel, *They stalk by Night* (Yeo Valley Productions: Bishops Nympton, 1989).
BRODU, Jean-Louis & MEURGER, Michel, *Les felins-Mystere: Sur les Traces d'un Mythe Moderne* (Pogonip, Paris, 1984).
CALDWELL Harry R., *Blue Tiger* (Duckworth: London, 1925).
CAMPION-VINCENT, Veronique (Ed), *Des Fauves dans Nos Campagnes: Legendes, Rumeurs et Apparitions* (Imago: Paris, 1992).
CHEVALLEY, Abel, *La Bete du Gevaudan* (Gallimard: London, 1936).
DOWER, Kenneth C.G., *The Spotted Lion* (William Heinemann: London, 1937).
FRANCIS, Di, *Cat Country* (David & Charles: Newton Abbot, 1983).
FRANCIS, Di, *The Beast of Exmoor* (Jonathan Cape: London, 1993).
GUILER, Eric R., *Thylacine: The Tragedy of the Tasmanian Tiger* (Oxford University Press: Melbourne, 1985).
McBRIDE, Chris, *The White Lions of Timbvati* (Paddington: London, 1977).
McBRIDE, Chris, *Operation White Lion* (Collins/Harvill: London, 1981).
MARSHALL, Robert E., *The Onza* (Exposition Press: New York, 1961).
MENATORY, Gerard, *La Bete du Gevaudan* (Imprimerie Captal et Fils: Mende, 1976).
O'REILLY, David, *Savage Shadow: The Search for the Australian Cougar* (Creative Research: Perth, 1981).

ROBERTS, Andy, *Cat Flaps! Northern Mystery Cats* (Brigantia: Brighouse, 1986).
SHUKER, Karl P.N., *Mystery Cats of the World: From Blue Tigers to Exmoor Beasts* (Robert Hale: London, 1989).
STEIGER, Brad, *Bizarre Cats* (Pan: London, 1993).
WRIGHT, Bruce S., *The Ghost of North America* (Vantage Press: New York, 1959).
WRIGHT, Bruce S., *The Eastern Panther* (Clark, Irwin: Toronto, 1972).

KING KELLAS?
by Tom Anderson (Scottish Correspondent).

Mr and Mrs Jaffrey, accompanied by their grand-children, were driving up a rutted farm track in Strathdon, Aberdeenshire at a sedate five miles an hour. Six metres in front of them, a large black cat crossed the track. They stopped. It was five feet from muzzle to tail, (which was two feet long), and covered in 1.5/2" long fur. Estimated height was two foot plus. After crossing the track it drew alongside the car and surveyed the occupants before moving on. The legs were described as 'stuck on the corners', and too slender for the torso. So sure was the witness that she had encountered a laboratory escapee that she contacted the university. They vehemently denied any 'gene juggling', on cats at least; we know of trials involving goats and llamas. Relatives of the witness saw an identical, (but tawny) cat carrying a rabbit on a shingle beach at Slains, just north of Aberdeen. Slains Castle, of course, was the inspiration for Stoker's castle Dracula - how Fortean can you get?

Friends of Mrs Jaffrey, who own land at Strathdon, have seen the melanistic cat cross a field of cows with calves at foot. The cows total lack of interest in its presence shows at least one generation of familiarity. Although definitely feline, the nearest comparison this (and other witnesses) can make is 'lurcher-like'. The same animal, in two colours, has been seen on the northeast coast, highlands and Tayside in Scotland. The distances confirm three colonies at least, of an animal more gracile than the normal puma type. You will not be surprised to learn that Mrs Jaffrey 'usually kept a camera in the glove-box but for some reason it wasn't there when she needed it'. I would add that the above is an 'expert witness' and has a familiarity with foxes and wildcats that would shame some naturalists.

Editorial Note: A few weeks after we received the above article from Tom Anderson we received another letter from him....

"As a postscript to last month's interview with Mrs Jaffrey and her very detailed description of a cat in Strathdan, it would seem obvious what she and her relatives had seen on both occasions. Her description could only describe one animal (apart from the five foot long, two foot high) part. The next day I sent her a set of photos of what I thought she'd seen along with some background to fill in the details. Twenty four hours later she telephoned to say that this was exactly what she had seen. They were, of course, photographs of the Kellas Cat, and not being set against a scale for comparison, she had no way of knowing that they showed a cat at least fifty percent smaller than hers. We now have three 'King Kellas' sightings in a triangle measuring sixty miles each side. I don't know about you but I can't see a wildcat being the progenitor of this.

Yours confusedly,

Tom".

LETTERS TO THE EDITOR

THE LAST WORD ON THE 'BEAST OF BALA'.

Dear Mr Downes,

...two points of interest - The black and white Ruffed Lemur mentioned on page 10 of 'A&M No 5' came from a private collection near Lake Bala owned by a Pete Drummond and his wife Sue. They take in all sorts of waifs, strays and unwanted zoo specimens. I have not visited the collection myself but 'believe' the stock to be well cared for. How the lemur escaped and how long it was out is unknown to me.

Secondly, the shark attack mentioned on page 11 states that California's last attack was in 1989. Well, I visited San Diego in April 1994 and there had recently been a fatal shark attack. This was even mentioned in Fortean Times a few months ago because the victim had only just beaten Leukaemia.

Keep up the good work.

Alan Pringle,
Welsh Mountain Zoo
Clwyd.

I HAVE NO IDEA WHAT HEADLINE TO PRINT HERE...

Hello again Jonathan,

...I assume most people in England are acquainted with Alice In Wonderland:

A CRYPTO CAROL

Dear Father, I must go, so long
I'm big and Alien do I belong?
I hope you will understand
I must find my wonderland,
against you no malice
like my sister Alice.

Dear kitten, John, avoid the Lewis gun,
be elusive, run, please dodge son,
hunting rabbits, a lot, in the grass,
you can be shot, through the looking glass,
lay low for a while.
Go to Cheshire, smile.

Eric Sorensen,
Copenhagen.

EDITORIAL MESSAGE

The Editor welcomes letters on any subject of interest for publication. In the interests of space, letters are sometimes edited. The Editor would also like to stress that on these pages, as in the magazine as a whole, opinions expressed are not necessarily those of the editor, the editorial team or the magazine, but are those specifically of the author or correspondent. In the interests of free speech, and a frank exchange of views and information opinions will not be censored unless, in the editors view, by printing them we would be laying ourselves open to legal action

A CALEDONIAN COLLECTION

(excerpts from letter dated 5th May)

.... Update on shark specimen found in Millburies Loch in Elgin. A somewhat disgusted assistant curator told me that it was only a jawbone, fairly modern, and totally un-fortean.

Re the ever increasing volume of tosh being printed about Loch Ness. Nobody has yet mentioned the Cambell factor. Water Bailiff, local stringer for a national paper, he was extremely superstitious, his mother supposedly having second sight. Singlehanded he revived interest in the story due to his interview being shown widely in North America. This lead to a vast influx of tourists going north where they had previously stopped at Edinburgh. As a leading citizen of Inverness put it *'Forget Columba, its Alec Cambell who should have been beatified'*.

As you say this one will run and run. I await in dread the first mention of that other great beast of Inverness-shire A Crowley esq.

As recently as fifteen years ago an elderly relative of my wife, married to a shepherd in Glen Calvie in Easter Ross told me of 'things' being seen at his house, Boleskine. 1995 it may be but the old ways are still deeply held in northern Scotland. Anyone reading Dinsdale, Holliday etc might be better occupied with Muerger!

I shall end with a cautionary tale of free enterprise.

The Macallan-Glenlivet distillery at Craigellachie draws part of its water supply from an open concrete tank built into a cliff. As it started to get chocked by grass, Chinese carp were introduced to clear it. This worked a treat. The carp grew extremely large and bred furiously.

The sale of the fish turned into a profitable sideline for the lads until an otter scoffed all the carp and terminated the Christmas Fund!

Regards,

Tom Anderson,
Aberdeen.

ERRATA

To 'Witness Identification in Big Cat sightings' by Ian Kingshott. (A&M5)

Following from the paragraph which says... "Having said this, so called 'experts' from local zoos and wildlife parks continue to categorically affirm that the large melanistic cat seen on Bodmin Moor last year was a 'female black puma'..."
The following paragraph should be inserted...

"Such experts should obviously have a valid opinion due to their experience in the field. If big cat experts cannot recognise a certain species of cat then who could? Therefore, although the prospect of a black puma being the identity for the black cats is unlikely due to the rarity of such an entity, it is still a possible solution. However, when considering witnesses who are not experts in their fields, the prospect for error, whether intentional or not, has far more relevance. Therefore, the manner in which a witness is questioned can have important bearing on the versions of events and descriptions of the animals he provides".

animals&men
THE JOURNAL OF THE CENTRE FOR FORTEAN ZOOLOGY

CARTOON BY 'MORT'

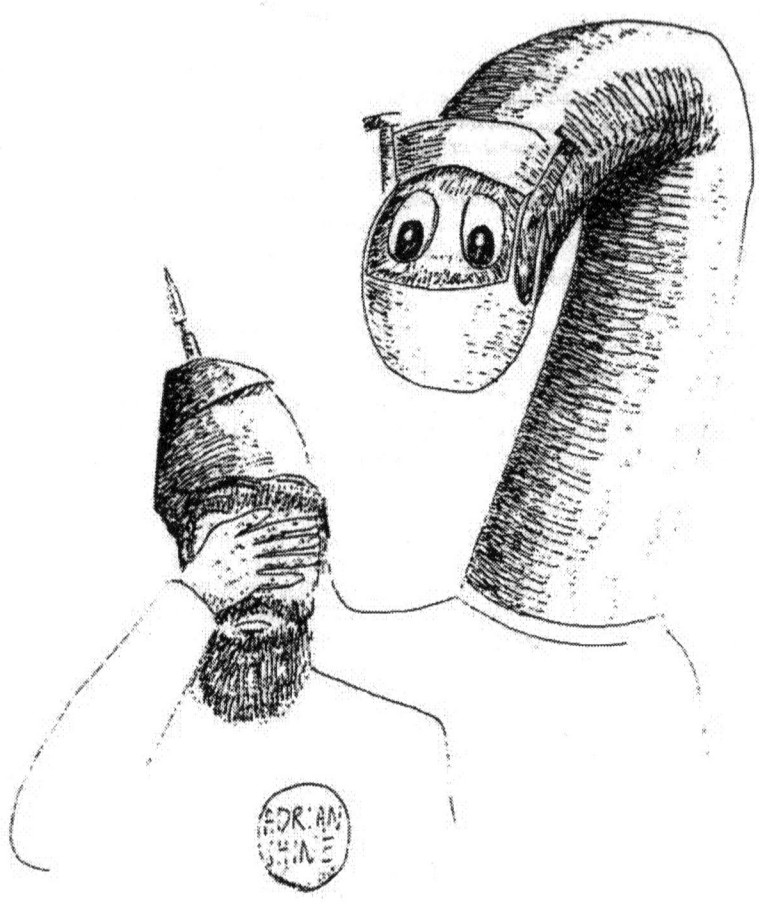

Typeset by The Artist formerly known as "HEN"
ISSN1354-0637

ISSUE 7

JULY 1995

animals&men

THE JOURNAL OF THE CENTRE FOR FORTEAN ZOOLOGY

This issue contained one of our first major pieces of field work - the research into the mysterious cat skull which had been found at Golitha Falls on Bodmin Moor. Tony Shiel's figurative fingerprints can be found all over this issue - the surrealchemical wordplay of what he called "The Case" was writ large across this issue. Ironically it was also the first issue to be sold at *Zoologica* - the now defunct annual exhibition organised by veteran zoologist Clinton Keeling who was also to be a major player in the CFZ universe over the next few years. With this issue we had established strong footholds both within the fortean and zoological communities.

Animals & Men
The Journal of the Centre for Fortean Zoology

Mystery Whales .. The Bodmin Skull .. On Collecting a Cryptid .. Strangeness in Scotland

Issue Seven £1.75

animals&men

THE JOURNAL OF THE CENTRE FOR FORTEAN ZOOLOGY

Animals & Men   Issue Seven

This issue of 'Animals & Men' was put together by the following band of Animals and Men:

Jonathan Downes: Editor
Jan Williams: Newsfile (wot no catfish?)
Alison Downes: Administratrix
Lisa Peach: Artist
Mort D Arthur: Cartoons
John Jacques: Sole Representation
Graham Inglis: 'We are the road crew'

CONSULTANTS
Dr Bernard Heuvelmans
(Honorary Consulting Editor)
Dr Karl Shuker
(Cryptozoological Consultant)
C.H.Keeling
(Zoological Consultant)
Tony 'Doc' Shiels
(Surrealchemist in Residence)

Regional Representatives
West Midlands: Dr Karl Shuker.
Mexico: Dr Lara Palmeros
Spain: Angel Morant Fores
 & Alberto Lopez Acha
Germany: Wolfgang Schmidt
 & Hermann Reichenbach
France: Francois de Sarre
Wiltshire: Richard Muirhead
Scotland: Tom Anderson
Kent: Neil Arnold
Sussex: Sally Parsons
Hampshire: Darren Naish
Lancashire: Stuart Leadbetter
Belgium: ABEPAR
Norfolk: Justin Boote
North Yorks: Alistair Curzon
Cumbria: Brian Goodwin
Home Counties: Philip Kiberd
S Wales/Salop: John Matthias
Denmark: Lars Thoma and Eric Sorenson
Eire: The wizard of the Western World

CONTENTS
p.3 Editorial
p.4 Newsfile
p. 12 'A Caseful of Cougars' by J.Downes
p.16 'On collecting a Cryptid' by Grover Krantz
p.19 'Cryptocetology' by Darren Naish
p.28 'Strangeness in Scotland' by Mark Fraser
p.30 'Bibliography of Cryptozoological and Zoomythological books - part 2' by Dr Karl Shuker and Stephen Shipp
p.36 'Letters to the Editor' from Eric Sorensen, Janet Bord, Darren Naish, Clinton Keeling and M.Playfair
p.38 Book Reviews
p.41 Now thats what I call Crypto
p.42 Periodical reviews
p.44 Cartoon

FOR REASONS OF SPACE, HELP, NERVOUS TWITCH, AND THE A-Z HAVE BEEN HELD OVER TO THE NEXT ISSUE IN JANUARY 1996

'Animals & Men' is published Quarterly by STP Communications and The Centre for Fortean Zoology.

THE CENTRE FOR FORTEAN ZOOLOGY
15 HOLNE COURT,
EXWICK
EXETER,
DEVON
U.K.
EX4 2NA

Telephone 01392 424811

The Great Days of Zoology are not done.

Dear friends,

Welcome to issue seven, the fourth of the year. We are about a fortnight late because we wanted to wait until the new books by Karl Shuker and Bernard Heuvelmans were released. We have also found a way of cutting our printing costs so, at least for this issue, we have added an extra four pages without increasing the cost. We now have twelve pages more than we did a year ago.

The results of our readers poll were interesting. It seems that the 'Animals & Men' readership is equally divided between zoologists and forteans, and it also seems, (encouragingly for us), that even the most academic zoologists have a sneaking interest in things weird and vice versa. What was noticeable, however, is that whereas most of the readers who replied were satisfied with the balance between popular and academic a significant minority wanted to see a greater academic bias in the magazine.

We have taken this on board with the start of a major new series on Cryptocetology, as well as some other research papers planned for inclusion over the next year. We have also, however decided to produce an annual collection of longer, and more in depth material. The first volume; "THE CFZ YEARBOOK 1996" is now available. It costs £10.00 and is over 180 pages long with 53 figures and 22 maps. We hope that this will be a success and that we shall publish a similar collection in time for Christmas each year.

With this issue we also welcome the eminent cryptozoologist Grover S.Krantz who has written an article for this issue. We would also like to like to welcome Clinton Keeling, the veteran zoologist and zookeeper to our editorial consultants panel. The panel now consists of three zoologists and a wizard, which seems just about right to us.

One of the biggest problems that we have at the CFZ, even with the publication of our new book, is assimilating, and recycling the sheer volume of information which comes through our office. This means that there is no room in this issue, the Hooded Seal that ended up in Cornwall, the indian spiders on the south coast or the mysterious carcasse found at Mount Edgecombe in Cornwall (it turned out to be a dog).

Morgawr has also turned up again, (seen by Gertrude (G.S) Stephens in September), and also in the Falmouth area, an unnamed American student saw the Owlman of Mawnan, only weeks after we published a new eyewitness account in the last issue. More on these and other stories next year.

The next issue will be out in January, so until then, all of us at 'Animals & Men' wish you a Happy Christmas and a peaceful New Year. 1996 will be a year to look forward to.

NEWSFILE

COMPILED AND EDITED BY OUR RESIDENT NEWSHOUND JAN WILLIAMS

NEW SPECIES

CHINESE BEARS

Chinese scientists exploring a nature reserve in the province of Shaanxi have discovered two previously unknown species of the Giant Panda with grey or white fur.

As described in Dr Karl Shuker's 'The Lost Ark' (Collins 1993) white bears are depicted on ancient Chinese manuscripts and have previously been captured in Shennongjia, a similarly mountainous region of Hubei Province, south of Shaanxi.

The bamboo-shoot diet of normal Giant Pandas is in dispute. Xinhua, the Chinese Press Agency, referred to dozens of cases where pandas have killed calves and goats in recent years, following a report in Beijing newspaper 'Benhui Bao' of a panda observed eating a sheep in Sichuan province. Since pandas are considered good luck symbols and protected by law, the shepherd held back his guard dogs and allowed the animal to continue feeding.

Less restraint was shown by a gang in nearby Gansu, where police confiscated three Giant Panda skins and arrested 12 people for peddling them. Police said the gang was the largest they had broken up in the area, involving 37 people in Gansu and Sichuan.(Die Welt 5.8.95, 15.8.95, Aberdeen Press and Journal 2.8.95)

HORSE-HEADED SNAKE

Marine biologists have discovered twenty new species of ocean creatures in an area of murky water southwest of Tasmania. The water is saturated with mud from the hills of the Southwest National Park. One animal has the body of a snake and the head of a sea-horse, and others are described as resembling creatures from Science Fiction movies.(Westfalenpost 7.6.95)

ELUSIVE TORTOISE

In 1963, Australian John Cann found tortoise hatchlings in Sydney pet stores. Cann was unable to identify them and the retailers refused to say where they came from. Eventually Cann was able to locate the supplier who was incubating eggs which he had collected from the Mary River, Queensland.

Animals & Men — Issue Seven

The new species has been named the Mary River Tortoise 'Elusor macrurus' (Elusor meaning 'to escape notice'). Its characteristics include a laterally flattened tail which, in the male, is larger than any previously known chelid and can be up to 70% of the carapace length. (The Vivarium)

LIZARDS AND AMAZONS

A species of all-female lizard has been discovered in the West Indies and South America. The lizards reproduce without male contact, laying unfertilised eggs that develop into identical females for generation after generation. It appears they derive from hybrids of two species that reproduce normally.

Herpetologist Charles J. Cole and colleagues at the American Museum of Natural Hiostory identified the parents of the species by unravelling its genetics, as Gymnophthalmus underwoodii.(The Vivarium/ National Geographic Magazine)

TINIEST PRIMATE RETURNS

The world's tiniest primate - the Pygmy Mouse Lemur - has been restored to full species status as a result of fieldwork by Jutta Schmid and Peter Kappeler of the German Primate Centre. The lemur (Microcebus myoxinus) was first described in 1852, but has been considered by many to be a sub-species of the larger Grey Mouse Lemur (Microcebus murinus).(New Scientist 15.7.95)

CHINESE WILDMAN EXPEDITION

A thirty-strong expedition, led by Professor Yuan Zhengxin of the Institute of Vertebrate Palaeontology and Paleoanthropology in Beijing, and Wang Fangchen, secretary-general of the recently-formed Committee for Research on Rare and Strange Creatures, spent two months searching for evidence of the Wildman in the isolated Shennongjia mountain range in Hubei Province.

The results of this preliminary exploration were not very encouraging, but the search did produce some potential evidence in the form of teeth found in a cave and described as 'larger than human teeth', and hair samples consisting of long thin strands of red fibre.

Tourist officials in the Shennongjia Natur Reserve have posted an 80,000 dollar reward for the capture of a live wildman. A dead specimen will bring 8,000 dollars, while 1,500 dollars is being offered for authentic hair and droppings. Wang Fangchen reacted angrily: 'This kind of hunt should be absolutely prohibited. It is uncivilised action. Maybe there is only one wildman left, and it could mean the end of that wildman's life'.(Minneapolis-St Paul Star & Tribune 15.7.95, The Times 8.4.95, Daily Mail 5.8.95)

TUATARA PUZZLE

The New Zealand Department of Conservation is investigating the origin of a tuatara found on the north-

Issue Seven

-eastern coast of North Island. The large healthy male was discovered by two medical students at Tutukaka, near Whangerei.

The lizard-like tuatara is the sole surviving representative of the rynchocephalians, which flourished 150 million years ago. They exist only on islands in Cook Strait and off the north-east coast of New Zealand, although fossil specimens have been found on the mainland.

Tuataras are strictly protected by the New Zealand Government, but reputed to fetch tens of thousands of pounds on the black market. The animal is probably a smuggled escapee, but conservation officials are checking the more exciting possibility that a previously undiscovered colony exists on the mainland.(The Times 27.5.95)

BEAR IN DOLOMITES

For the first time in 160 years, a brown bear has been seen in the Dolomites. Mountain trekker Armando Veceglio-Galeno saw the animal near the Italian mountain town of Cortina D'Ampezzo. 'The bear was 30 metres in front of me, rose on its hind legs and made a terrifying sound', Galeno reported.

The last known bear in the Dolomites was killed in 1830, though tracks were found in 1876.(Westfalenpost 5.6.95)

'WILD BEAST' OF THE ALPS

Swiss police and Italian border guards armed with night-sight equipment hunted a marauding 'beast' in the Alpine valley of Val Ferret in August. The animal, resembling a German Shepherd dog, but with longer hair and dark fur with light spots, is said to have killed about 70 sheep, twenty on one single occasion. (Westfalenpost 24.8.95)

GRUNTS FROM THE LOCH

Strange sounds were heard from the depths of Loch Ness in July. Scientist Bill Bolton from the survey team and five tourists aboard a miniature submarine near Abriachan on the west bank of the loch heard sounds described as 'like a grunt - a very deep grunt', detected by the sub's transducers.

'We first heard the noises in the same area a few weeks ago and ignored them,' said Mr Bolton. 'On three or four separate occasions we heard the noises in an area of about a square mile.'

Allan Whitfield, another member of the scientific team, said: 'I have frequently heard the calls of sea mammals. But this was odd and it certainly poses a few interesting questions'.

It would be premature to attribute the grunts to the monster, and neither scientist is prepared to so. However, it should perhaps be noted that grunts have been associated with Nessie on a previous occasion.

Animals & Men — Issue Seven

In a rare land sighting in April 1923, Alfred Cruickshank reported a creature with a twelve-foot humped body and 10 - 12 foot tail beside the Invermoriston road. as he drove past the animal it made a grunting noise. In contrast to the classic long-necked Nessie pose, this creature's head seemed to be set close to its body. *(Sunday Telegraph 30.7.95)*

MYSTERY CATS

SOMERSET

Film of a large black cat at Pawlett, near Bridgewater, was shown on Sky TV on 9th August. Wayne Broad saw the animal in a field near his home and took 3 minutes of camcorder footage showing the cat sitting and walking. He later filmed a domestic cat in the same place and from the same distance (200 yards). The domestic cat barely showed above the stubble. *(Sky News 9.8.95, Guardian 10.8.95)*

WILTSHIRE

A big black cat was seen in the Woodford Valley on 29th August. Francesca Marner of Netton saw the animal walk into her garden just after 9 am. She said: 'It was about 20 yards away from me... I noticed it had large green eyes and an enormous tail. It was black, jet black, and smooth coated. It was taller than a normal cat, more like a dog.' *(Salisbury Journal 31.8.95)*

BUCKINGHAMSHIRE

A mini-catflap ran throughout July and August in the Buckingham/Winslow area. The Buckingham & Winslow Advertiser appealed for sightings of the 'Beast of Horwood', opened a 'Beastline', offered a #100 reward for photos and gave away badges inscribed 'I have seen the Beast'.

Most reports concerned a black, Labrador-sized cat seen by drivers and cyclists on roads between Great and Little Horwood, Winslow, Buckingham and Swanbourne. The animal had been seen sporadically in the area for at least two years.

Witness Ted Reeves, a gamekeeper for 24 years, said the animal is definitely not a dog or fox: 'It's a member of the cat family.' Milkman Mervyn Jenner has seen the animal twice, and believes he has also heard it: 'I've heard the most God-awful noises... It was a horrendous guttural noise and it sounded like it was killing something.'

John Dagg heard similar noises whilst camping near Little Horwood in April. 'It was a low guttural growling noise, about 20-25 feet from the tent. And I think there were two of them because about 40 feet away there was another similar noise with a hiss in it.' *(Buckingham and Winslow Advertiser 7.7.95, 14.7.95, 21.7.95, 28.7.95, 11.8.95)*

HIGHLAND, SCOTLAND

A black cat, longer and taller than a Labrador, ran out of woodland onto the Inverness - Craig Dunain road on 22nd June. Witness Carol MacFadyen braked hard and watched the animal bound across the road 15 feet ahead. She and her teenage daughter and friend jumped out of the car and chased after it, but, she said, 'it was gone in a flash'. A second sighting occurred in the same area 3 days later.

Animals & Men

THE JOURNAL OF THE CENTRE FOR FORTEAN ZOOLOGY

Issue Seven

A large cat-like animal was seen by a driver at the Doll, Brora, on 22nd June. The witness described it as the height of a large dog, with a long body and long, curving tail which trailed along the ground. It was dark grey-black with a small head, flattened snout and small ears. *(Aberdeen Press & Journal 27.6.95)*

TAYSIDE, SCOTLAND

A public warning was issued by Fife police on 26th June, advising people not to approach a giant wild cat seen in thick woodlands near Kelty. *(Aberdeen Press & Journal 27.6.95)*

GRAMPIAN, SCOTLAND

Lorry driver Norman Russell was startled by a huge black cat which bounded across the Kintore to Dunecht road, near Leylodge, on 14th August. He said: 'It was an enormous beast about 6 feet long and two and a half feet tall . . . It leapt over the twenty-foot wide road in just 3 steps. *(Aberdeen Press & Journal 15.8.95)*

ITALY

A puma and a panther are reported to be roaming the Umbria region, 200 km north of Rome. Sheep, calves and chickens have been killed in the area. *(Die Bild 17.8.95)*

DENMARK

Danish police were hunting a 'lion-like' cat on the island of Fyn in May. The animal, described as 28-33 inches in length (obviously a miniature lion), was originally seen in a field near Odense and further reports were received from various locations on the eastern side of the island. *(Die Welt 25.5.95)*

ESCAPES

Two lions and a lioness escaped from a safari park at Warragamba on the outskirts of Sydney, Australia, on 7th August. The lioness knocked down a garden fence and attacked a collie. The dog survived, but the lioness was shot dead by an animal handler. The two other lions roamed the suburbs for about two hours before being lured back to their cages. *(Daily Telegraph 8.8.95)*

Fifteen escaped lions were tracked down and shot by law enforcement officers in Idaho. The lions came from the Ligertown Game Farm, a ramshackle private zoo consisting of sheds and makeshift cages fenced in with chicken wire, near the tourist town of Lava Hot Springs. The zoo was home to nearly 50 lions, tigers and cross-bred ligers.

Up to 50 gunmen from the Sheriff's Department and other agencies were drafted in to hunt for the big cats. Some were shot right beside the compound, others fled into rugged, heavily-wooded terrain before being killed. Ligertown owners Robert Fieber and Dotti Martin were attacked by one of the escaping animals and needed hospital treatment for minor injuries. Humane Society officials were called in to care for the remaining animals. *(Daily Mail 23.9.95)*

Hundreds of visitors fled a safari park in Co. Antrim on 2nd August when 3 chimpanzees broke free and

Animals & Men   Issue Seven

started wrecking cars. One smashed the window of a cafe where twenty people had taken refuge. The three chimps escaped from a concrete compound at the Causeway Safari Park, Devock, near Ballymoney. *(Aberdeen ? Evening Express 3.8.95)*

I THOUGHT I SAW A ...

Police caught a wallaby at Brentwood, Essex, after it was spotted hopping alongside the M25. It is believed to have escaped from a private zoo. *(Guardian 10.8.95)*

An animal seen chasing sheep on a South Molton, Devon, farm was believed by observers to be a wolverine. It was last seen heading towards Combesland. *(Independent 2.9.95)*

A man in Rochester, Kent, who thought he saw a bird in the window box of his flat 70 feet above ground, looked again and realised it was a four-foot-long iguana. *(Aberdeen Press & Journal 4.8.95)*

CROCS RUN AMOK

A fisherman in Belgium, angling for pike, was astonished to find his catch was a 3-foot crocodile. He hit it with a piece of wood. *(Die Bild 2.6.95)*

Fishermen reporting an alligator in Kissena Park Lake, New York City, were proved justified when Richard Wills, formerly of San Diego Zoo, captured it bare-handed. The 3-foot male alligator was caught on 26th July at the small lake in the borough of Queens. Parks Commissioner Henry Stern said: 'We believe this is an escaped pet'. *(Minneapolis Star & Tribune 28.7.95, Mankato Free Press 28.7.95)*

Heavily armed hunters and police patrolled ditches and canals in Numansdorp, near Rotterdam, after a reptile owner reported his caiman missing. The Dutch daily 'De Telegraaf' warned readers 'The meat-eating reptile comes straight from the jungle and ferociously attacks humans without mercy'. The scare came to an abrupt end when the pet owner returned home and found the caiman hiding in a cupboard. *(Westfalenpost 23.8.95)*

KILLER FROGS

Killer Frog Fever swept London when the 'Evening Standard' ran a campaign against North American Bullfrogs. The frogs, which are on sale in petshops, and also arriving as spawn stuck to garden-centre plants, are said to be breeding in ponds in Clapham. They can reach a length of 8 inches and could cause serious damage to British pond life, eating newts and common frogs, as well as clearing a pond of tadpoles and insect life.

An early suggestion by the 'Standard' that kittens form part of the Bullfrog's diet (rapidly inflated to 'cats' in London offices), was later downgraded to hamsters. The Department of the Environment warned that allowing the frogs to escape into the wild is an offence carrying an unlimited fine under the Wildlife and Countryside Act. *(London Evening Standard 26.7.95, 4.8.95, 8.8.95, 10.8.95)*

Animals & Men — Issue Seven

BREEDING TERRAPINS

East Sussex Wildlife Rescue have launched a survey to discover whether terrapins are breeding in Britain. Of particular concern is the Red Eared Terrapin (*Trachemys scripta elegans*) which is imported in large numbers. Dr Tony Gent of English Nature stated: *'Viable eggs have been produced in Britain, so the potential is there. Most counties probably have a pond with one or two in it. One Cardiff pond has several hundred.'* (*Daily Telegraph 14.8.95*)

SPIDERS CLOSE SCHOOL

Bembridge Primary School on the Isle of Wight was closed down on 5th October while public health officials attempted to destroy a colony of poisonous spiders. The decision was taken after a bite from one of the spiders developed into a six-inch black bruise on classroom assistant Helen Blake's shoulder. The spiders, *Steatoda noblis*, are members of the Black Widow family and come from Madeira and the Canary Islands. They were first recorded in Britain in 1870, arriving in shipments of fruit, and attained breeding status in the 1960s in Hampshire and Dorset. They are now well established in the South of England. Experts warned that the fumigation attempt is unlikely to succeed and Steatoda noblis - nicknamed the Bembridge Black - will continue to roam the school classrooms.(*Daily Mail 5.10.95*)

A two and a half inch long Rhinocerous Beetle, thought to be the first ever in Britain, was found on a banana boat at Newhaven harbour. The mahogany-coloured beetle from the Ivory Coast, West Africa, is being cared for at the Living World natural history exhibition at Seven Sisters Countyr Park, near Seaford, East Sussex.(*Daily Mail 25.7.95, Eastbourne Gazette 2.8.95*)

FISHY STORIES

A foot-long piranha was caught by 13-year-old Andy Richardson in a pond near his home at Hoyland, South Yorkshire. (*Guardian 10.8.95*)

Piranhas are living in the Menango River between Verona and Lake Garda, Italy. Pet shop owner Stefano Poledri saw the fish near the village of Casaleone, then met an angler who had caught one. A biologist confirmed that it was a piranha. The Mayor of Casaleone has warned swimmers to stay out of the water. 'Experts have advised me that these fish feel stressed living in cold water, and are even more vicious than normal ones', he said. (*Die Welt 29.6.95, Daily Mail 30.6.95*)

An unusual fish caught by angler Brian Coughill's dog Sheeba in the Kessock Firth, Inverness, turned out to be a rare Angler Fish. The only one seen in the area previously was washed up dead on the shore. (*Aberdeen ? Evening Express 3.8.95*)

A 'fish from Hell' on display in a shop window at Swanland, near Hull, has been identified by Theresa Redding of the University of Hull as a rarely-seen Sail-finned Rough Shark. The shark, which lives at depths of more than 800 feet, was dredged up by Scottish fishermen and bought in Hull market by fishmonger Glad Hartley's son. The university plans to preserve the shark as an exhibit. (*Daily Mail 6.10.95*)

Fish were dissolved by hydrochloric acid in the River Cuckmere following a leak from a storage tank at Chemaide, in Hailsham, East Sussex. (*Daily Telegraph 18.7.95*)

animals & men

THE JOURNAL OF THE CENTRE FOR FORTEAN ZOOLOGY

Animals & Men — Issue Seven

GIANT TURTLE

A giant turtle sparked a sea rescue alert at Kingswear, Devon. Brixham Lifeboat, a Royal Navy helicopter, and coastguards searched the coast following a report of an upturned dinghy drifting towards rocks at the mouth of the River Dart. When the helicopter swooped down, the crew realised the object was a turtle. There have been several reports of an 8-foot hump-backed turtle off the South Devon coast. (*The Vivarium*)

PLAGUE OF MICE

British summertime plagues of biting ladybirds, thrips, saw-fly larvae, and aggressive Mediterranean median wasps, pale into insignificance in comparison with the estimated 1 billion mice devastating grain crops in Queensland. The mouse plague is the worst ever seen, stretching 220 miles from Toowoomba to Roma and Dalby, and affecting 750,000 acres of farmland. State cabinet approval has been given to bomb the mice with strychnine. (*Aberdeen Press & Journal 15.8.95*)

RARE REMAINS

Police and customs officers uncovered a huge collection of remains of some of the world's most endangered animals in a raid on the home of a taxidermist. A 40-year-old Dutchman was arrested in the raid at Newtown, Powys, on 15th August. Every room in the house was filled with animals, many still in freezers waiting to be cured.

Investigators found the skull of a Monkey-Eating Phillipine Eagle, the skin of a Komodo Dragon and the skin and head of a Red Panda. Stuffed chimpanzees, frozen black jaguar cubs, tiger skins and hundreds of bird specimens were among the remains. Crawford Allen, an investigator with Traffic, the WWF's wildlife trade monitoring programme, said: 'The final list will read like a roll-call of endangered species'. (*Aberdeen Press & Journal 16.8.95, 17.8.95*)

Newsfile Correspondents:

Tom Anderson, Karl Shuker, Wolfgang Schmidt, Richard Muirhead, COUDi, Phil Bennett, Sally Parsons, Keith Williams.

Lest We Forget

This issue of 'Animals & Men' is dedicated to the memory of Jerry Garcia and Bert the Capybara both of whom who have died within the past three months. What a long strange trip its been!

A Caseful of Cougars.
by Jonathan Downes

The events of the long hot summer of 1995 have proved one thing at least. The ongoing saga of 'The Beast of Bodmin' is not simply a zoological problem. It is a genuine sociological phenomenon, it is a political football, it has real folkloric and cultural implications, and somewhere at the bottom of it, I strongly suspect there are a few 'real' (whatever that means) cats, (probably pumas), who are as confused by the whole affair as the rest of us.

I was fairly pivotally involved in the events of this July and August and I could not let the October issue of 'Animals & Men' pass by without making some comment on them.

Tony 'Doc' Shiels is a good friend of mine. I spent some of the summer with him drinking red wine, gazing at the sky, & and trying to unravel some of the strands of the ongoing mystery that has become part of, what in A&M6 he described as 'The Case'. It is, I think interesting how some of the same strands are evident in the 'Bodmin Skull' affair, as were exhibited in the 1976 'Owlman of Mawnan' flap. I would suggest that before reading any further, the interested would be surrealchemist refer, briefly at least to Tony's article 'The Case ... for Owlperson' in A&M6.

The skull at the centre of the mystery. Although it has been shown to be a fake, its exact provenance is still unknown.

(NOTE: My attempts at a surrealchemical approach to this problem, do not effect my attitudes to cryptozoology as a whole. As a fortean zoologist, I feel that different investigations warrant different approaches, and this 'case' presents so many bizarre aspects that a surrealchemical approach is well nigh obligatory).

GRIM SUMMER, (G.S).

The weather in Britain this summer has on occasion been the hottest on record. Many people, including ex-colonial types who usually thrive in hot weather, suffered unduly. It was very reminiscent of the summer of 1976, which in Cornwall, at least produced UFO reports, bizarre animal mutilations, Sea Serpent Reports, Lights in the sky, Strange 'crackling' noises, and not the least the 'Owlman of Mawnan'. 'Doc' described the weather both then and now as 'unhealthily' hot. He said that the heat was 'unwholesome and destructive' and many people would have agreed with him. There was a plethora of inner city riots, and the newspapers were full of urban violence, rapes and child murders. It was not a summer to remember with any degree of pleasure.

Animals & Men — Issue Seven

Late one night I was driving back to Exeter from Taunton with a transit van load of musician friends when we saw the strange lights in the sky. The horizon was lit up by what seemed to be explosions but which were totally silent. Fun and Games were afoot.

GENUINELY STUPID? (G.S)

Despite the quotes attributed to me in several local papers, I never said that the MAFF report into *'The Beast of Bodmin'* was "Rubbish". I merely expressed disappointment with its findings. I have always had the gravest reservations about all the video and photographic evidence of Big Cats from Bodmin Moor, and I am quite in agreement with the main conclusions of the report which were essentially that the video and photographic evidence presented together with the sheep kills that they examined did not constitute proof that there were big cats living on the moor. This is, as any solicitor will tell you, completely different to stating, as is commonly believed, that there are 'categorically no big cats on the moor!'.

> **Report on Beast slammed**
> JOHN DOWNS, a specialist in the research of mystery animals, yesterday described as "rubbish" the controversial Government report which could find no evidence of a large beast on Bodmin Moor. Mr Downs, who is studying reports of similar beasts all over Britain.

Being seen in certain quarters as somewhat of a pundit in matters crypto, not to mention zoological, I was approached by a number of newspapers and a couple of radio stations for my views on the MAFF report. It was my appearance on one of the radio stations which lead on to the next chapter in the story.

GEMINI SOUNDWAVES (G.S)

I have a wonderful ongoing relationship with Gemini Radio in Exeter, and in particularly with one of their star D.J's, Steve Browning. It was no great surprise when one evening he telephoned me to ask me to appear on his show. I spoke for about fifteen minutes, live on air, on the subject of mystery big cats in the South West and mentioned that what *'we really need is a specimen!'*.

Half an hour later someone, identifying himself only by his Christian name, which he asked not to be divulged telephoned the radio station and claimed that three animals, including a pregnant female had been shot. He gave no further details, and as at the time I was elsewhere I knew nothing about it until the next morning.

GETTING SILLY (G.S)

My family keeps very late hours and consequently I am a late riser. I was awoken at about 8.30 AM by a telephone call from Steve Browning. He told me about his mystery caller from the day before and almost immediately put me on air. I appealed for the mystery caller to phone me back. I promised on air that I would respect his confidentiality and that, if he could get me the carcass of one of these cats, there was every chance that we could clear up a large part of the mystery. Later that day I repeated the same appeal for the 'Western Morning News' and on both occasions I took the unprecedented step of publicising my telephone number.

I had two telephone calls. One from an undoubtedly sincere, possibly mad, and somewhat annoying

Animals & Men

Issue Seven

woman who claimed that the animals were sent by God as a manifestation of His angels, and that by encouraging people to desecrate the corpse of an angel I was committing an unthinkable blasphemy. I thanked her for her advice and a few minutes later I received a call from someone who was obviously so drunk that he had difficulty in stringing words together. He burbled and swore at me for about a minute and then hung up.

A couple of days later, however, after another appeal on the 'Steve Browning Show', I received another telephone call, and this one appeared, on the surface at least, to be the genuine article.

For many years there have been persistent rumours of a government and military cover up regarding the big cats seen on Exmoor and Bodmin. I have tended to disregard these reports as merely paranoid conspiracy theorising. After all there is no real reason why such a cover up would take place. An introduced population of big cats can hardly compromise national security. This telephone call, for the first time, gives a reason why such a cover up might have taken place.

I am taking a totally neutral position as regards this report. The caller seemed plausible enough, although very paranoid. He also claimed that he had been involved with the scandal that took place when the alleged relationship between the Princess of Wales and Major James Hewitt, became public knowledge. Major Hewitt certainly lives in Devon, but I do wish to treat this whole episode with a healthy degree of scepticism until I receive some more evidence one way or another.

GOVERNMENT SCANDAL (G.S)

My informant claims that when the Royal Marines made their well publicised, and apparently fruitless hunt for the Beast of Exmoor in the mid 1980's, that he was a sergeant in charge of one of the small reconnaissance parties. He also claims that the marines were also searching for the beast in another unspecified location in the South West. He further claims that the search for 'the beast' was not the primary aim of the exercise, but that security implications forbade him to tell me what the Marines were REALLY doing there.

His main claim, however is that three animals WERE shot at unspecified locations, and that at least one was shot on private ground by a party who were not only trespassing but had not been given permission to carry fire arms. He claimed that a relatively junior officer had panicked and that the cover up had been perpetuated further up the chain of command in order to 'save face'.

My personal thoughts are that this is real life not 'the X Files' and that while 'the truth is out there', it is probably far more prosaic. I did, however tell him that I would be very interested to receive a corpse, or even the skull of one of these animals.

GRUESOME SKULL (G.S).

True to form, three days later, after another late night I was woken up by another telephone call. This time it was my good friend and fellow researcher Mrs Joan Amos, a UFOlogist from Tavistock. She told me that a skull had just been found on Bodmin Moor.

It appeared that the original owner of the skull had been a young female big cat, and initial reports were that it was either a leopard or a puma. Although 'Doc' and others had told me that 'there are no such

things as coincidences', I immediately thought that the whole affair was too good to be true. For the world to believe that only a fortnight after the apparently damning (in reality no such thing), MAFF report, a genuine beast would allow herself to be conveniently decapitated in the vicinity of one of the areas best known beauty spots was asking one to suspend disbelief to a ridiculous extent.

The telephone was red hot (figuratively) for the next three days. I told one close friend that I was sure that the skull had come from a mounted specimen and joked that I wondered which of the interested parties in the North Cornwall area had an old leopard skin rug in their loft!

This was after all the third such skull to be found in the south west. The first one from Dartmoor in 1988 was found by two schoolboys. Earlier in 1995 one of the schoolboys, now grown up, admitted to my wife that whilst the skull had been found where they claimed at Lustleigh, it had been wrapped in a plastic bag. This effectively makes a nonsense of all the wild claims that have been made for this piece of evidence.

The second skull, was probably from a tiger skin rug, and I felt that this one probably had a similar provenance. When Doug Richardson from London Zoo announced that the skull was from a recently dead animal, and still had particles of flesh adhering to it, my conceptions of reality were overturned completely, and I decided to drive into Cornwall myself, and to go and see the doctor.

GETTING SERIOUS, (G.S).

Bodmin itself had a very weird atmosphere.

One of the pubs in the high street had several little huddles of serious looking men all discussing 'the beast'. There was a persistent rumour that the army had been called in to track the animal, and the usual paranoid nonsense about creatures escaping from government genetic research laboratories was being aired. From what the drinkers were saying you would have been prepared to believe that Dr Mengele had just been made the head of "the good ol' Min of Ag and Fish", and that somehow the whole thing was all their fault.

On the way out of Bodmin towards Falmouth we passed two army trucks full of soldiers in full battle dress. They had camouflage make up on their cheeks and carried guns. I don't know what, if anything their presence signifies, and I suspect that they were perfectly innocent 'Territorials' out on an excercise.

The outside wall of a public lavatory in a car park in Bodmin Town Centre had the spray-painted graffiti :"HOW LONG BEFORE A CHILD IS KILLED?" , and the graffiti on the bridge which spanned the dual carriageway was even simpler: "MAFF IS MURDER". Feelings were running high.

Two days with 'Doc' restored my sanity. We discussed cabbages and kings, drank some wine, and did a live phone in to Gemini Radio from the public bar of 'The Seven Stars' in Falmouth.

As we were driving home Doug Richardson announced that he was seeking backers for another investigation into the Bodmin creatures. Several magazine and newspaper reports said that he intended to kill the animal. I strongly believe that if there is an animal, its danger to humans is minimal and that its danger to livestock has been greatly exaggerated. For several days some colleagues and I started plans for an expedition of our own.

GUILTY SOLDIER, (G.S).

My anonymous informant telephoned back and said that the discovery of the skull was a direct result of my appeal on the radio and in the newspapers. I had appealed for a skull and some acquaintances of his had delivered. When I made the appeal I was expecting to have to collect a gruesome parcel wrapped in a bin bag from the car park of some Cornish country pub. His acquaintances, he said, decided to be more flamboyant about it!

The inference was, ALTHOUGH HE DID NOT SAY THIS, that the skull was of one of the creatures shot in the mid 1980's. The truth was somewhat different, although I still think that my appeal for a skull had been instrumental in the events which lead to its discovery.

GOOD SCAM? (G.S).

A few days later Doug Richardson announced that he had found the egg cases of a tropical insect inside the cranium and that the apparently fresh flesh was a result of the dried tissue left inside a skull when a corpse is prepared for a skin rug being reconstituted when the skull was soaked in river water.

The matter was over—for the time being. The only person that I felt sorry for was young Barney Lanyon-Jones, the schoolboy who had found it originally. He looked so disappointed that it was obvious that he, at least had not been responsible for the hoax. For hoax it undoubtedly was.

One swallow does not make a summer, and three hoaxes do not disprove a mystery cat. Something is there, and the whole truth is stranger than it might seem. As we approach the season of mists and mellow fruitfulness 'the case' is still very much open and the loplot thickens!

On Collecting a Cryptid

by Grover S. Krantz

There is considerable controversy over whether a specimen should be collected for the purpose of demonstrating its existence. By 'collected', I mean obtaining one of the animals, or substantial parts of it by any means whatever -- this might involve live capture or, far more likely, producing a dead body. Some people argue that this is the only rational approach towards that end, while others passionately oppose such killing as unnecessary and destructive. Feelings run high on both sides of this issue, especially in America where the cryptid in question is the Sasquatch (bigfoot). Rather than confining these remarks to just that particular case, it is important to deal with the broader question relating to unknown species in general. What emerges is a clear distinction between various kinds of cryptids -- for some of them a specimen would constitute a major step in resolving the problem, while in others this action would accomplish nothing.

Issue Seven

When the International Society of Cryptozoology was founded in 1982, the original statement was that our interest was focussed on reported animals of unexpected size or morphology, or occurring in unexpected times or places. Thus we have four logically separable categories to consider. For each of these we might now consider the effects of taking a specimen, and the recovery of at least part of its skeleton. (Animals without skeletons are not dealt with here).

Unexpected Size:

The bones will demonstrate that at least one specimen existed that was an unusually large (or small) specimen of a known type. Whether there are others, and if a new species is warranted, probably cannot be ascertained by that single specimen. (The individual's adult or juvenile status would be easy for a zoologist to ascertain.) Producing the remains of an animal of this category would be of considerable interest, but would not be likely to settle a cryptozoological issue. The pygmy elephant is an example of this kind.

Unexpected Morphology:

The bones will demonstrate that the supposed new species exists in the present time. (In most cases, unusual morphology of a new kind is easily distinguished from individual variation within a known species.) Clear proof of its location might be lacking, but if the bones correspond with the morphology described by local people, there should be little argument. The North American sasquatch is an example of this category.

Unexpected Time:

The Bones will demonstrate that a species known from the fossil record occurs today. The only application of this test is to determine whether a supposedly extinct animal still lives. An obvious example of this category would be a wooly mammoth; a more recent example would be the passenger pigeon. The latter runs the risk of being challenged because the bones might actually have been collected before the supposed extinction. There is often little to distinguish modern bones from those collected 50 years ago.

Unexpected Place:

The bones will demonstrate nothing in this case. Here we are dealing with a known species, specimens of which are available from other places where its existence is unquestioned. The burden of proof is on the collector to show where the specimen was actually taken – in a disputed case this will be almost impossible. The eastern puma (mountain lion) is an example of this category.

Of these four categories, the second and fourth may now be examined in more detail, first using the American examples. These two categories represent the extremes of usefulness versus futility of collecting a specimen, whilst the others occupy intermediate positions. The sasquatch well illustrates 'unexpected morphology' and the eastern puma well illustrates 'unexpected place'. While only two other examples are mentioned below, the reader can easily fit many more cryptids into this scheme.

Producing the remains of a sasquatch in North America could well prove the existence of that species. The sceptical authorities will accept nothing less than the body, or a significant piece of it, as definitive evidence. Producing that specimen, however, will not conclusively prove that it occurs wild within the

United States and/or Canada. Some critics might argue that it could have been obtained in Siberia or China, for example and brought to America for display. This would not be a serious problem for at least two reasons.

First, simply proving the creature's existence at any location is the biggest point that has been located by the sceptics, and that point would have been won. Second, the mass of reports of creatures closely matching this description in America is so great that few people would seriously dispute the claimed location in general, though the exact spot might be disputed. In addition, the actual circumstances of the acquisition would probably be too impressive to conceal, especially if it is the whole body, and the act of bringing it from a distant location would be equally difficult to conceal.

Producing the remains of a puma, claimed to have been shot in Virginia, would be summarily dismissed by most authorities. The sceptics would immediately say that it had most likely come from some other location where the existence of the puma is not questioned. The burden of proof would be on the collector to show where it was taken. Reports of the eastern puma are not nearly as impressive as those of the sasquatch – there would be little support from local accounts simply because it is not a new animal. The actual circumstances of acquiring such a small animal would not be easily demonstrable, especially if it is just the skull, and the act of bringing it in from a not-so-distant location could have been easily concealed.

In the United Kingdom we have two comparable examples of these same second and fourth categories. The Loch Ness Monster is a case of 'unexpected morphology'; the retrieval of a specimen would almost certainly demonstrate its existence, as well as show just what kind of a creature it is.

Whether such a specimen was actually from Loch Ness is less important than proving the reality of an animal of this type (whatever that might be). Also, the long history of sightings at that location would strongly support the claim of where it was taken. Finally, its presumably large size would make it difficult for anyone to argue that it was brought in from some distant source. Accordingly, it can be argued that efforts should be made to retrieve such a specimen by any and all possible means – perhaps harpooning by (hopefully) unemployed whalers.

The beast of Exmoor is a case of 'unexpected place'; the retrieval of a specimen would not demonstrate the existence of this feline species, simply because that was generally not an issue of disagreement. The history of sightings might support the claim of where it was taken, but not strongly; there are far better accounts of large black cats from elsewhere. Also, parts of black leopards, or melanistic pumas may be small enough to bring into the country without great difficulty. Finally, the possibility exists that such an animal had recently escaped from captivity. Accordingly, it can be argued that no effort should be made to kill or even capture a specimen of this type.

There are many other aspects to the problem of whether and how to collect cryptozoological specimens. Perhaps the readership's reaction to this article will determine if and what I might address in another article.

The author and the editor welcome comments on this article for inclusion in the letters page of a future issue.

CRYPTOCETOLOGY:
Introducing a new branch of Cryptozoology

(Part one of a seven part series in which Darren Naish explores the world of mystery whales)

How mysterious are whales? It depends on how much you know about them! The more you know, the greater the number of enigmatic whales you will learn about. This might be a bit of a strange idea to begin with - animal groups well established in the dogmas of zoology aren't immediate candidates for prominence in the annals of cryptozoology. Sea serpents and almas, (maybe batsquatches and mothmen) come to mind, yes, but whales?

On the 16th September 1994 I opened a book by travelling naturalist Sir Peter Scott [1]. There, on page 254, were his illustrations of a species of dolphin that he saw in the Magellan Straits in 1968. I didn't recognise them as being members of any known species and, after consulting the literature, had to consider the possibility that here was a 'new' species of dolphin, lying undiscovered in a book printed in 1983. This was an exciting concept that really got me enthused, and I began researching in earnest. The find was, as it turned out, somewhat of an ice-berg tip. Within a very short time available literature was revealing a veritable wealth of whale species which had been seen, sometimes even photographed, but were as yet unknown from specimens. Heuvelmans recognised eight species [2] on this basis, but more seemed to be present. The more I looked, the more I found, and what started as a project involving a single illustration in a single book metamorphosed into a number of interrelated topic areas, quite extensive amongst cetology (the study of whales) in their coverage.

Was this news? I think that it would depend on who you asked. Whales are marine, mysterious and elusive; for as long as cetology has been a science, the cetologists have been hinting at what I call 'habitat-induced elusiveness'. Whales are merely proving the bias there is against the discovery of marine forms, for, if you spend a greater proportion of your life beneath the surface of the waves, mankind has not yet gotten much of a chance to get to know you. Of course, not only is this proven by as-yet-undiscovered species, modern species that have remained unknown (or practically so), until very recently endorse it also. Case studies for this are well known and in some cases becoming more so; such as the coelacanth, megamouth, even certain whale species themselves [3]. Good old-fashioned elusive species proving more diversity amongst living forms than we'd anticipated, aren't, however, the entire story. These fascinating animals will be covered in article four, whereas Scott's mystery Dolphin will be covered in article two. This topic is large enough to be considered as a subject in its own right. I have coined the name CRYPTOCETOLOGY, merging the study of whales with the principles that we have learned (or 'have yet to learn') from cryptozoology. This first article is mainly a primer to familiarise you with names and ideas which will be introduced in successive articles. To begin with, therefore, a basic introduction to the diversity amongst whales, and the evolution which has lead to this diversity is in order. I hope that you find it as interesting as I do.

The Evolution of Whales and the cryptocetological aspects therein.

The great whales and their smaller cousins form a mammalian group that we call the Cetacia, or, in common parlance just Whales. Awe inspiring, beautiful, colourful and often damn weird, these amazing creatures have adapted themselves to a realm so different from our own that they function in ways that we are still struggling to understand. Whales are a diverse group of animals and, when we consider the extinct species as well as the living ones become even more so.

The present opinion is that the Cetacea are monophyletic, which means that they all share the same single ancestor. (There have been dissentions [4] [5]). This single ancestor, one of the mesonychids [6]. (omnivorous wolf-like ungulates), was an amphibious, fish eating mammal that took to an aquatic lifestyle during the early Eocene, about 50 Million years ago. On acquiring characters that we now use to define 'whale' [7], these animals therefore became the first whales. They are called protocetids and, while very different from the fully aquatic whales that would be their eventual descendants, did enjoy success in the seas and estuaries of the world. A protocetid, as the recently discovered *Ambulocetus natans* [7], has shown, would have looked something like a long snouted sea-lion (figure one). While protocetids were ancestral to later whales, they may well have been a more explicit cryptozoological link! (I will keep you in suspense until article three). (There are I have to say, other theories on the origin of whales, some of which directly challenge the evidence presented here. These will be discussed in a future article).

Fig. 1. *Ambulocetus natans*, a 49 million year old protocetid whale from the Upper Kuldana formation in Pakistan. Note the presence of fur and the abscence of tail flukes.

On becoming more specialised, and generally better adapted to a marine existance, protocetids became basilosaurids. These whales are best known for *Basilosaurus*, a 20 metre-or-more long form from the late Eocene. It and its relatives, long known as zeuglodonts also turn out to have more than their fair share of cryptozoological importance and thus also get fuller discussion in article three. Both protocetids and zeuglodonts (and a few other poorly known Eocene families) are lumped together as 'archaeocetes' - basically whales that lack the specialisations used to identify the two later whale groups whose respective histories begin in the Oligocene (see fig 2).

The Rise of Modern Whales.

All post-archaeocete whales are separated into those with teeth - the *Odontoceti* - and those with baleen (whalebone) instead of teeth - *Mysticeti*. Both groups arose from within the *Archaeoceti*, independently, some have maintained [8], [9], [10], but there is now at least some molecular evidence suggesting that

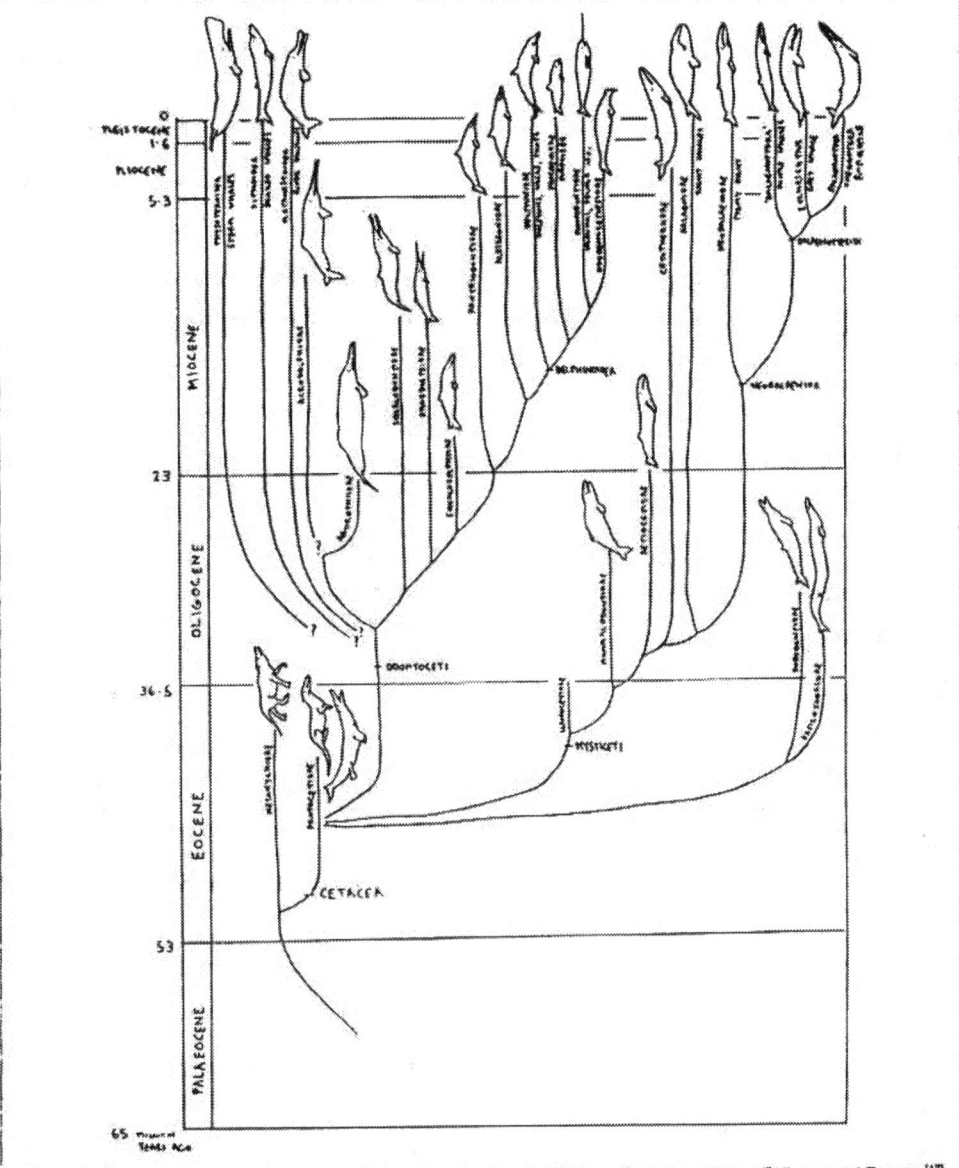

Figure 2. A phylogeny of cetaceans based on currently recognised ideas. Based mostly on Folkens and Barnes [12] with additional material from [10] and [14]. The llanocetids are too poorly known for a restoration, the two figures for the Protocetidae represent the morphological variation known in that family. No figures are to scale.

mysticetes share an ancestor with odontocetes. The first toothed whales, relatives of forms like Squalodon (fig 3), appeared early in the Oligocene[11], about 37 million years ago as shown in fig 2, and by about 30 million years ago had given rise to four lineages. Those leading to sperm whales (*physeteroids*), beaked whales (*ziphoids*), river dolphins (*platanistoids*) and typical dolphins, (*delphinoids*). During the Miocene (23-5.3 million years ago), the basic dolphin design, exemplified by the *delphinoids*, was successfully adapted to life in polar regions, rivers, and both deep water and shallow marine areas. Three families of the *Delphinoidea* survive today and, as illustrated in fig. 4 encompass the greatest variation amongst living whales.

Fig 3. A generalised squalodontid (c.f *Prosqualodon*). This family was most abundant from the Oligocene to early Miocene times, and were amongst the earliest and most primitive of odontocete whales. After Folkens[12].

Delphinoids range in size from the 36 kilo mass and 1.35 metre length of the smallest to the 8 tonnes and 9.75 metres of the biggest. Some, arguably the most exciting of all whales, are active and ferocious predators of other whales. At least one, the Orca (*Orcinus orca*), is a co-operating pack hunter. Nearly all members of the delphinoid clan have a dorsal fin - one enigmatic species may even have two [15], and one, the fabled Narwhal (*Monodon monoceros*) of the high arctic, has a 'horn' (really an incisor tooth). A recently discovered relative of the narwhal from the Pliocene of Peru, (*Odobenocetops* [13]), was a cetacean mimic of walruses. It even had tusks.

The evolution of a sophisticated sonar system has allowed whales, delphinoids among them to exploit environments where other senses, like sight, were not usable. A number of lineages seem to have independently invaded muddy rivers, and are today represented by eight species of river dwelling dolphin. Five of these species are the superficially similar, poorly sighted *platanistoids* (see figs 2 and 4). For a long time they were thought to represent a single, specialised lineage, but it now seems that some, at least evolved independantly of the others. Their marine ancestors are known from early in the Miocene and possibly invaded river systems because they were a habitat largely unexploited by large, aquatic vertebrates at the time. Mainly due to this newer habitat, though their elusive behaviour certainly helps, the living examples of this group are very poorly known and continue to tantalise us with an abundance of mystery forms, some only just revealing themselves to the eyes of man. These will be dealt with in article five.

The Oligocene period seems to have been the time of greatest divergence amongst whales [11]. The other extant groups evolved at this time also. DNA evidence presented by Milinkovitch and colleagues in 1993 [17] suggested that mysticetes diverged from sperm whales about twelve millionyears ago, during the mid-late Miocene. However, a number of fossils, both of early mysticetes and of sperm whales are known from the early Oligocene (35 million years ago)[11][18], casting doubt upon this hypothesis. A new and more thorough genetic analysis published in 1994 demonstrated that not only are mysticetes monophyletic, they are far removed from sperm whales who seem to have evolved from other odontocetes early on in odontocete history.[14] (see fig 2). Though they have now been effectively challenged Milinkovitch and

Figure 4. Some of the diversity amongst the delphinoid superfamily with one representative *platanistoid* (river dolphin). a) Orca, a *'globocephalid'*. b) Narwhal, representing one subfamily of the *Monodontidae*; c) Snubfin *(Orcaella brevirostris)*, probably a monodontid also; d) Hourglass Dolphin *(Lagenorhynchus cruciger)*; e) Northern Rightwhale Dolphin *(Lissodelphis borealis)*); f) Pygmy orca *(Feresa attenuata)*, another *'globocephalid'*; g) New Zealand Dolphin *(Cephalorhynchus hectori)*; h) Spinner *(Stenella longirostris)*; i) Ganges dolphin *(Platanista gangetica)*, a platanistid river dolphin; j) Spectacled Porpoise *(Australophocaena dioptrica)* of Phocoenidae; k) Roughtooth *(Steno bredanensis)*. Common names adapted from [16].

-23-

colleagues' DNA findings were really something of a surprise, as mysticetes were always thought to have been derived from early Oligocene archaeocetes. (*Mammalodon*, fig 5, seems like a good 'missing link', though it was actually something of a 'living fossil' of its time [19].). Sperm whales were long thought to have been allied to the beaked whales, or ziphoids, but this link is now fairly unanimously severed.

Figure 5. *Mammalodon colliveri*, a late Oligocene whale from Victoria, Australia. It is intermediate between archaeocetes and mysticetes[20].

The three (known!) species of sperm whale are probably best regarded as two separate families (21). *Kogiids*, the pygmy sperm whales, extend back as far as the late Miocene and may be descendants of the *physeterids*, today represented only by the Great Sperm Whale (*Physeter macrocephalus*). The earliest known physeterids are from the early Miocene (contradicting, incidentally, the conclusions of Milinkovitch and colleagues) [14] [18]. The sperm whales acquired numerous unique features during their evolution and together these features make *Physeter* the weirdest mammal that has ever existed (in my opinion of course). Feeding as it does on giant squid, *Physeter* is probably more linked to cryptozoology than any other known whale. The final article in this series will cover *Physeter* and all of the associations it has with the cryptic world, whereas the article before will feature *Physeter*'s pygmy cousins together with the other species that have only been discovered in relatively recent times.

To many cryptozoologists, the animals that immediately spring to mind when whales are mentioned are the *ziphoids* - the beaked whales. This group is known from the mid Miocene onwards. They share asymmetrical skulls and 21 pairs of chromosomes (as opposed to 22) with the *physeteroids*, but it now seems that the two groups are no more related to each other than they are to other *odontocetes*. An alternative suggestion is that ziphoids are the descendants of an early Miocene family called the *Squalodelphidae* (see fig.2). Modern *ziphoids* are relatively conservative, mostly deepwater forms, (though they did evolve freshwater forms in the past) that range from 4 to 12.8 metres - like some other cetacean groupgs they have a tendancy towards toothlessness. The 19 or so species are the most poorly known of all large mammals with several known only from bones. Others, known only from beached corpses, also have yet to be seen alive. One species may play a part in the story of a reptilian sea monster [22] [23], and still others form part of my fourth article, that on whales reported from sightings but as yet unknown from any specimens.

Diversification of the Mysticetes.

Mysticetes, the baleen whales, were extremely successful in the Oligocene, Miocene and lower Pliocene, and although today represented by four families (some say three), are less successful in terms of species numbers than they were. Small *mysticetes*, called *cetotheres*, comprised at least sixty species of moderate

Figure. 6. Some of the variation amongst the bigger whales, representing five of their seven families; a) Humpback (*Megaptera noveangliae*) and b) Fin whale (*Balaenoptera physalus*) - representing both traditional rorqual subfamilies; c) Great sperm whale - sole living member of *physeteridae*; d) Pygmy right whale - only living neobalaenid; e) Skew beaked whale (*Mesoplodon hectori*) and f) Northern bottlenose whale (*Hyperoodon ampullatus*), both of *Ziphiidae*, finally; g) Right whale (*Balaena glacialis*) represents *Balaenidae*. Common names adapted from [10].

Animals & Men — Issue Seven

sized whales [24] during this time of greatest success. Those that lived in the Pliocene were eaten by the 13 metre long giant shark *Carcharadon megalodon* (but that's another story!). Mysticetes today are mostly enormous filter feeders that sieve plankton and other small fare. To confuse matters, the unusual, and very mysterious Pygmy Right Whale *(Caperea marginata)* is only about five metres long, which is smaller than the biggest of the delphinoids we saw earlier. The Pygmy Right Whale has almost successfully eluded science since its official recognition as a species in 1846. More about this in article six.

Pygmy right aside, baleen whales come in three definite groups. The strangely ugly Grey whale *(Eschrichtius robustus)*, once thought to be a direct descendant of the cetotheres, is typically regarded as occupying a family of its own. However, it may in fact be a recently evolved, very specialised rorqual (read on). The bulky, slow moving *balaenidae* or right whales - the whales hunted so extensively in the past - form the second family. They seem to have been the first group of living mysticetes to have appeared, and did so probably in the mid Oligocene [11]. Following balaenids, the group I call the Neobalaenida evolved, with the pygmy right wales appearing first. Finally, with the earliest known fossil species coming from the mid Miocene, there are the balaenopterids or rorquals, the real giants with lengths up to 31m and masses of 200 tonnes for the very biggest-the Blue Whale *(Balaenoptera musculus)*, biggest animal of all time. (Please note that some recently revealed sauropod dinosaurs may eventually win the 'largest vertebrate ever' title [25] [26]). Rorquals are either sleek and streamlined (at least five species) or stout and bulky (the Humpback being the only member of that second group).(See fig. 6). Rorquals have traditionally been segregated into two sub-families on that basis [24]. Some new genetic evidence, however suggests that the rorqual family tree is in need of revision. As the issues here are coupled with interpretation of variation amongst some of the rorqual species, this area will get fuller discussion in article five.

There isn't exactly boggling diversity amongst the giants, unlike the smaller whales but perhaps surprisingly these whales are confusing in terms of variation amongst them: EXACTLY how many species are there? Which ones are definitely species? When we are that confused about such conspicuous and well known species as the Humpback and the Blue Whale then there is definite scope for an investigation into 'hidden' forms.

Cetacean systematics.

This brings me onto what is called systematics - a subject that does not just apply to the great mysticetes but to all of the smaller whales too. Within practically all species of whale there does seem to be at least some variation between populations. In the past, practically every one of these varieties was named as a separate species, so the modern count of seventy six species is in fact a very 'slimmed down' up to datecount. Whether or not a certain variety of a certain species is different enough from others of the species to be considered a species in its own right is a very contentious subject - for that reason exactly how many species there are depends on who you ask. Article five will be on this subject - it has a bearing on cryptozoology because there may be 'new' species out there currently unrecognised, maybe thought of as part of as part of another species due to lack of significant research and the right comparisons. The confusion that this issue and the others like it cause when we begin to look at whales in detail is considerable.

Hopefully, you may get to understand this in my next article; "The Page 254 Story".

Animals & Men — Issue Seven

References and Notes.

1. SCOTT, P. 1983. *Travel Diaries of a Naturalist* 1. Collins (London). See also my article, 'The page 254 Story', in the next issue of 'Animals & Men'.
2. HEUVELMANS, B. 1986. Annotated checklist of Animals with which Cryptozoology is concerned. Cryptozoology 5: 1-26.
3. NAISH, D.W. Unpublished. "Got It!". Scheduled for A&M 12.
4. LOWENSTEIN, J.M. 1985. *Marine mammal evolution: the molecular evidence*. Abstract, Proceedings of 6th Biennial Conference on the Biology of Marine Mammals. 22-26 November 1985, Vancouver. Lowenstein believes that Pakicetus, and presumably other archaeocetes too, radiated independently of other whales.
5. BERTA, A. 1994. *What is a whale?* Science 263: 180-1. Berta questions the assumption that Ambulocetus is a true cetacean, and points out that it might be a very close relative that evolved cetacean-like characteristics convergently.
6. PROTHERO, D.R., MANNING, E.M. and FISCHER, M. 1988. The phylogeny of the ungulates. In BENTON, M.J (ed.) The Phylogeny and Classification of the Tetrapods, Vol. Two: Mammals. Clarendon Press (Oxford), pp. 201-34.
7. THEWISSEN, J.G.M., HUSSAIN, S.T. and ARIF, M. 1994. *Fossil evidence for the origin of Aquatic Locomotion in Archaeocete Whales*. Science 263: 210-12.
8. KLEINENBERG, S.E. 1958. *The origin of the Cetacea*. Doklady Akad. Nauk. SSSR 122: 950-2.
9. YABLOKOV, A.V. 1964. *Convergence of parallelism in the evolution of cetaceans*. Palaentol. Zh. 1: 97-106.
10. A similar view is maintained in (16).
11. FORDYCE, R.E. 1980. *Whale evolution and Oligocene southern ocean environments*. Palaeog., Palaeoclim., Palaeoecol. 31: 319-36.
12. MAY, J (ed.) 1990. *The Greenpeace book of Dolphins*. Random Century (London).
13. de MUIZON, C. 1993. *Walrus like feeding adaptation in a new cetacean from the Pliocene of Peru*. Nature 365: 745-8.
14. ARNASON, U. and GULLBERG, A. 1994. *Relationship of baleen whales established by cytochrome b gene sequence comparison*. Nature 367: 726-8.
15. NAISH, D.W. Unpublished. "S.B.U.F.S" - scheduled for A&M10.
16. WATSON, L. 1988. *Whales of the World*. Hutchinson (London).
17. MILINKOVITCH, M.C., ORTI, G. and MEYER, A. 1993. *Revised phylogeny of whales suggested by ribosomal DNA sequence*. Nature 361: 346-8.
18. NOVACEC, M. 1993. *Genes tell a new whale tale*. Nature 361: 298-9.
19. FORDYCE, R.E. 1992. Evolution. In HARRISON, R. and BRYDEN, M.M (eds.) Whales, Dolphins and Porpoises. Blitz (Enderby, Leicester), pp. 14-23.
20. Mammalodon is traditionally restored with throat pleats, obviously to illustrate its mysticete affinities. However, throat pleats are unique to those mysticetes which gulp in vast quantities of water, and thus need expanding throats. Mammalodon could not have fed in this way, and thus would not have needed throat pleats.
21. BARNES, L.G., DOMNING, D. and RAY, C. 1985. *Status of studies on fossil marine mammals*. Marine Mammal Science 1: 15-53.
22. SHUKER, K.P.N. 1986. *The Unknown*, September 1986: 49-53 and October 1986: 31-6.
23. SHUKER, K.P.N., 1993. *Gambo - the bestkind beast of Bungalow Beach*. Fortean Times 67: 35-7.
24. EVANS, P.G.H. 1993. *The natural history of Whales and Dolphins*. Academic Press (London).
25. PAUL, G.S. 1994a. *Is Garden Park home to the world's largest known land animal?* Tracks in Time (Garden Park Palaeontology Society) vol. 4 No. 5.
26. PAUL, G.S. 1994b. *Big Sauropods - really, really big sauropods*. The Dinosaur Report Fall 1994: 12-13.

*****

STRANGENESS IN SCOTLAND
By Mark Fraser
(Excerpts edited from a much longer letter)

... During 1994 myself and family experienced numerous odd incidents while living in different parts of Scotland, including unusual animal sightings in the Highlands, strange, rather dangerous behaviour of cows, a UFO sighting, Poltergeist activity in the cottage where we lived, and a strange animal in Glenshee, (which after reading the article by C.H.Keeling (A&M6), on the Nandi Bear reminded me of that particular night). We also saw a phantom wolf of which we were to hear tales from local residents later.

Since then I have become fascinated by the reports of strange/alien animals and have written to many letters pages in Scottish newspapers asking people for their accounts concerning unusual sightings etc. The majority are of hauntings or one-off sightings of ghosts. I have received two sightings of 'big cats'. One from the 1970's and the other which occurred in late 1993 in the grounds of Dean Castle in Kilmarnock, not half a mile from my house. Also the reports of a Bigfoot type creature in Aberdeenshire, Falkirk, and Dundonald in Ayrshire. Unfortunately the majority of witnesses wish to remain anonymous. I will respect these wishes. It is now my aim and intention to gather and collect as many alien animal sightings from Scotland as I can. I find the subject very interesting.

I would like to tell you of my two sightings. My wife was present on both occasions, although she never saw the wolf. I must admit, I question my sanity sometimes.

While driving along the B9014 through the village of Drummoir in Banffshire, heading in the direction of Dufftown, I saw what at first I thought was a large dog jumping onto the boot of a car which was parked on the road outside the last house in the village when you are heading towards Dufftown. Then, as we approached alongside I was positive that what I was looking at was a wolf. As I watched, it disappeared in front of my very eyes.

My wife did not see it at all and it was some time later when we reached Dufftown that I told her of what I had seen. The 'wolf' had large red eyes...I am sure that I heard its howls once, a few days afterwards. Opposite the cottage that we then lived in sits Rosarie Forest, along the A9 between the town of Keith and the village of Mulben, Banffshire. I decided to do a little exploring inside the forest and as I put my first foot inside onto the soft, mossy grass I heard the most terrible blood curdling howls, (two in all). I left that forest with every goose pimple and every hair on my body standing to attention. I thought that my heart would explode with the rapidity of its beating. I do not know why the howling instilled so much terror in me, but they did, although they could have been just the howls of a dog. I have never once set foot in that forest again except for firewood and then I have been accompanied. I often looked out of our cottage windows at the deep, dark, large, forest which was no more than two bus lengths away from our door, and I often wished that it would go away, but it was in fact us, that was to move, for various reasons, after only three months in the cottage.

It was not until several weeks later, when talking to a couple of new friends in Keith that we learned that the area is supposedly haunted by a phantom wolf. No mention of my experience was made by me before hand and their information was offered voluntarily. The wolf has been blamed for several dead and mutilated cattle in the area, and I am told, that amongst locals the wolf's existence is well known Anyone who can get them to make a statement and then not retract it later deserves a bloody medal!

The second time that I saw a strange 'something on legs' was while driving, again with my wife, through the glorious scenery of Glenshee along the A93. It was midnight and we never saw much of the scenery around us. (This was around August 1994 and was approximately three weeks after I saw the 'wolf'). The sight of a fully antlered stag standing in the headlights is not something to be forgotten or the herds of deer running away from the roadside as you approach in the car is a wonderful sight. At what point along the A93 I do not know. I only know that there were a lot of German campers around in their motor homes. Apart from the deer and the rabbits these were the only signs of life around. While driving, and I remember that it was whilst we were driving south, and uphill, something strange ran out from the left hand side of the road and disappeared into the blackness on our right.

"The Spot in Drummuir where I saw the wolf"
Pic. Copyright Mark Fraser.

It first put me in mind of a cross between a kangaroo and a hyena. Its hind legs were larger than its front ones as it ran by on all four legs. Like the 'wolf' in Drummuir it had red, glowing eyes. I know that it sounds silly, but I got the feeling that it was laughing at us as it crossed our path and turned to look at us as it disappeared amongst the heather and the blackness of the night. Maybe that's why I thought that it was hyena like.

I will say, that the drawing in A&M6 of the 'Nandi Bear' put me in mind of someone who had seen the same thing that my wife and I encountered amidst the wilds of Glenshee. Although its hind legs were higher the animal stood no more than two or two and a half feet in height and maybe three feet in length. Remember, however, it was night time, and very dark and my estimation of lengths is not so hot at the best of times! The rest of the journey to my home town of Hull in Yorkshire was uneventful.

As mentioned, 1994 was a strange year for us. It is certainly a year that we don't want to experience again. Why it was so we really do not have any idea. It seems to have taken six or seven months to get over it, after bad luck and maybe depression on both our parts which we attribute still to the cottage and the whole area in which we stayed. It was a strange oppressing place although the beauty in some areas is breathtaking. We do hope that it is an end to it all.

*****

Editors Note:

This sighting of a Zooform Phenomenon which appears on the face of it to be a cryptid known only from some far distant land is not unique:

At 3.30 AM on the 7th April 1974 Joan Gilbert saw a strange creature at Branksome in Dorset. I have never been sure whether this sighting should be filed with the 'mystery cats', 'mystery dogs', or even, conceivably 'mystery kangaroos', because the beast Joan Gilbert saw, she identified as a Thylacine. The Thylacine, as every cryptozoologist knows, in historic times at least, has only been known from the Australian island of Tasmania, where apart from the fact that it occupies pride of place on the Tasmanian coat of arms, it has been presumed to have been extinct since the 1930's. Her description was uncanny:

"It had stripes, a long thin tail, and seemed to be all grey, though it might have had some yellow on it. It was thin and definitely not a fox". She later identified the animal as a Thylacine from a picture in an illustrated book!

('*Alien Animals*' by J & C Bord 1980).

The implications of these sightings are enormous, but as a true fortean I try not to draw conclusions (especially when I can't think of any) and so for the moment at least, the matter rests.

*****

A BIBLIOGRAPHY OF CRYPTOZOOLOGICAL AND ZOOMYTHOLOGICAL BOOKS
by Dr Karl P.N.Shuker and Stephen Shipp

PART TWO

MAN-BEASTS
ALLEN, Benedict, *Hunting the Gugu: In Search of the Lost Ape-Men of Sumatra* (Macmillan: London, 1989).
ARMEN, Jean-Claude, *Gazelle-Boy* (The Bodley Head: London, 1974).
BAUMANN, Elwood D., *Bigfoot: America's Abominable Snowman* (Franklin Watts: New York, 1975).
BERNHEIMER, Richard, *Wild Men in the Middle Ages* (Harvard University Press: Cambridge [Mass.], 1952).
BERRY, Rick, *Bigfoot on the East Coast* (Privately published: Stuart's Draft, 1993).
BORD, Janet & BORD, Colin, *The Bigfoot Casebook* (Granada: London, 1982).
BORD, Janet & BORD, Colin, *The Evidence For Bigfoot and Other Man-Beasts* (Aquarian Press: Wellingborough, 1984).
BYRNE, Peter, *The Search For Bigfoot: Monster, Myth or Man?* (Acropolis: Washington D.C., 1975).
CANTAGALLI, Renzo, *Sasquatch Enigma Anthropologica* (SugarCo: Milan, 1975).
CLARKE, Sallie A., *The Lake Worth Monster* (Privately published: Fort Worth, 1969).

COLEMAN, Loren, *Tom Slick and the Search For the Yeti* (Faber & Faber: London, 1989).
CREMO, Michael and THOMPSON, Richard, *Forbidden Archeology: The Hidden History of the Human Race* (Govardhan Hill Publishing: Badger, 1994).
GORDON, David G., *Field Guide to the Sasquatch* (Sasquatch Books: Seattle, 1992).
GRAFFIGNA, Carlo, *L'Enigme du Yéti* (Julliard: Paris, 1964).
GRAY, Affleck, *The Big Grey Man of Ben MacDhui* (Impulse: Aberdeen, 1970; 2nd edit., Lochar Publishing: Bankhead, 1989).
GREEN, John, *On the Track of the Sasquatch* (Cheam: Agassiz, 1968).
GREEN, John, *Year of the Sasquatch* (Cheam: Agassiz, 1970).
GREEN, John, *The Sasquatch File* (Cheam: Agassiz, 1973).
GREEN, John, *Sasquatch: The Apes Among Us* (Hancock House: Seattle, 1978).
GREEN, John, *On the Track of the Sasquatch: Encounters With Bigfoot From California to Canada* (2 vols) (Cheam: Harrison Hot Springs, 1980).
GRUMLEY, Michael, *There are Giants in the Earth* (Doubleday: Garden City, 1974; U.K. edit., Sidgwick & Jackson: London, 1975).
GUENETTE, Robert & GUENETTE, Frances, *Bigfoot: The Mysterious Monster* (Sun Classic: Los Angeles, 1975).
HALL, Mark A., *The Yeti, Bigfoot and True Giants* (M.A.H.P.: Minneapolis, 1994).
HALPIN, Marjorie M. & AMES, Michael M. (Eds.), *Manlike Monsters on Trial: Early Records and Modern Evidence* (University of British Columbia: Vancouver, 1980).
HEUVELMANS, Bernard, *Les Bêtes Humaines d'Afrique* (Plon: Paris, 1980).
HEUVELMANS, Bernard & PORCHNEV, Boris F., *L'Homme de Néanderthal est Toujours Vivant* (Plon: Paris, 1974).
HUNTER, Don & DAHINDEN, Rene, *Sasquatch* (McClelland & Stewart: Toronto, 1973).
HUSBAND, Timothy, *The Wild Man: Medieval Myth and Symbolism* (Metropolitan Museum of Art: New York, 1972).
HUTCHISON, Robert A., *In the Tracks of the Yeti* (Macdonald: London, 1989).
IZZARD, Ralph, *The Abominable Snowman Adventure* [U.S.A. title: *Abominable Snowman*] (Hodder & Stoughton: London, 1955).
JOHNSON, Paul G. & JEFFERS, Joan L., *The Pennsylvania Bigfoot* (Privately published: Pittsburgh, 1986).
JOYNER, Graham C., *The Hairy Man of South Eastern Australia* (Privately published: Kingston, 1977).
KEATING, Don, *The Sasquatch Triangle* (Privately published: Newcomerstown, 1987).
KEATING, Don, *The Eastern Ohio Sasquatch* (Privately published: Newcomerstown, 1989).
KNERR, Michael E., *Sasquatch: Monster of the Northwest Woods* (Belmont Tower: New York, 1977).
KRANTZ, Grover S., *Big Footprints* (Johnson Books: Boulder, 1992).
LALL, Kesar, *Lore and Legend of the Yeti* (Pilgrims' Book House: Thamel, 1988).
LANE, Harlan, *The Wild Boy of Aveyron* (George Allen & Unwin: London, 1977).
MACLEAN, Charles, *The Wolf Children: Fact or Fantasy?* (Allen Lane: London, 1977).
MALSON, Lucien, *Les Enfants Sauvages* (Union Générale d'Editions: Paris, 1964).
MALSON, Lucien, *Wolf Children and the Wild Boy of Aveyron* (NLB: London, 1972).
MARKOTIC, Vladimir & KRANTZ, Grover S. (Eds.), *The Sasquatch and Other Unknown Hominoids* (Western Publishers: Calgary, 1984).
MORRIS, Tom, *California's Bigfoot/Sasquatch* (Bigfoot Investigations: Pleasant Hill, 1994).
NAPIER, John, *Bigfoot: The Yeti and Sasquatch in Myth and Reality* (Jonathan Cape: London, 1972).
NORMAN, Eric, *The Abominable Snowmen* (Award: New York, 1969).
NORVILL, Roy, *Giants: The Vanished Race of Mighty Men* (Aquarian Press: Wellingborough, 1979).

Animals & Men

Issue Seven

PATTERSON, Roger. *Do Abominable Snowmen of America Really Exist?* (Franklin Press: Yakima, 1966).
PATTERSON, Roger. *Bigfoot* (Northwest Research Association: Yakima, 1968).
PEREZ, Danny. *Big Footnotes* (Perez Publishing: Norwalk, 1988).
PILICHIS, Dennis (Ed.), *Bigfoot: Tales of Unexplained Creatures* (Page Research Library: Rome [Ohio], 1978).
PLACE, Marian T., *On the Track of Bigfoot* (Dodd, Mead: New York, 1974).
PLACE, Marian T., *Bigfoot All Over the Country* (Dodd, Mead: New York, 1978).
PORCHNEV, Boris F., *Sovremennoe Sostoyanie Voprosa o Relikhtovykh Hominoidakh* (VINITI: Moscow, 1963).
PORCHNEV, Boris, et al., *Snomannens Gata* (Fram: Gottenburg, 1986).
QUAST, Mike, *The Sasquatch in Minnesota* (Privately published: Fargo, 1990).
RATSCH, Christian & PROBST, Heinz J. (Eds.), *Namaste Yeti - Sei Gegrusst, Wilder Mann!* (Knaur: Munich, 1985).
ROUMEGUERE-EBERHARDT, Jacqueline, *Dossier X: Les Hominides Non Identifiés des Forêts d'Afrique* (Robert Laffont: Paris, 1990).
SANDERSON, Ivan T., *Abominable Snowmen: Legend Come To Life* (Chilton: Philadelphia, 1961).
SHACKLEY, Myra, *Wildmen: Yeti, Sasquatch and the Neanderthal Enigma* [American title: *Still Living?*] (Thames & Hudson: London, 1983).
SLATE, Barbara A. & BERRY, Alan, *Bigfoot* (Bantam: New York, 1976).
SMITH, Warren, *Strange Abominable Snowmen* (Popular Library: New York, 1970).
SMITH, Warren, *The Secret Origins of Bigfoot* (Zebra/Kensington: New York, 1977).
SOULE, Gardner, *Trail of the Abominable Snowman* (G.P. Putnam's Sons: New York, 1966).
SPRAGUE, Roderick & KRANTZ, Grover S. (Eds.), *The Scientist Looks at the Sasquatch* (University Press of Idaho: Moscow [Idaho], 1977).
SPRAGUE, Roderick & KRANTZ, Grover S. (Eds.), *The Scientist Looks at the Sasquatch II* (University Press of Idaho: Moscow [Idaho], 1979).
STEENBURG, Thomas N., *The Sasquatch in Alberta* (Western Publishers: Calgary, 1990).
STEENBURG, Thomas N., *Sasquatch: Bigfoot - The Continuing Mystery* (Hancock House: Blaine, 1993).
STONOR, Charles, *The Sherpa and the Snowman* (Hollis & Carter: London, 1955).
TCHERNINE, Odette, *The Snowman and Company* (Robert Hale: London, 1961).
TCHERNINE, Odette, *The Yeti* (Neville Spearman: London, 1970).
TCHERNINE, Odette, *In Pursuit of the Abominable Snowman* (Taplinger: New York, 1971).
TERRY, James, *Sculptured Anthropoid Ape Heads Down In or Near the Valley of the John Day River, a Tributary of the Columbia* (J.J. Little: New York, 1891).
WASSON, Barbara, *Sasquatch Apparitions: A Critique on the Pacific Northwest Hominoids* (Privately published: Bend, 1979).
WYLIE, Kenneth, *Bigfoot: A Personal Inquiry Into a Phenomenon* (Viking: New York, 1980).
YUAN ZHENXIN & HUANG WANPO, *Wild Man: China's Yeti* [Fortean Times Occasional Paper No. 1] (Fortean Times: London, 1981).
ZINGG, Robert M. & SINGH, J.A.L., *Wolf-Children and Feral Man* (Harper: New York, 1939).

FLYING MYSTERY BEASTS

ARMSTRONG, Perry A., *The Piasa, or The Devil Among the Indians* (E.B. Fletcher: Morris, 1887).

Animals & Men — Issue Seven

BARLOY, Jean-Jacques & CIVET, Pierre, *Fabuleux Oiseaux de la Préhistoire à Nos Jours* (Robert Laffont: Paris, 1980).
COLLINS, Andrew, *The Brentford Griffin: The Truth Behind the Tales* (Earthquest: Wickford, 1985).
CONSTABLE, Trevor J., *Sky Creatures* (Pocket Books: New York, 1978).
HALL, Mark A., *Thunderbirds! The Living Legend of Giant Birds* (M.A.H.P.: Bloomington, 1988; rev. 1994).
KEEL, John, *The Mothman Prophecies* [U.K. title: *Visitors From Space*] (Saturday Review: New York, 1975).
McCLOY, James & MILLER, Ray, *The Jersey Devil* (Middle Atlantic: Wallingford, 1976).
SANDERSON, Ivan T., *Investigating the Unexplained: A Compendium of Disquieting Mysteries of the Natural World* (Prentice-Hall: Englewood Cliffs, 1972).
STAP, Don, *Parrot Without a Name: The Search For the Last Unknown Birds of the Earth* (Alfred A. Knopf: New York, 1990).

WATER MONSTERS

ANON., *An Essay on the Credibility of the Existence of the Kraken, Sea Serpent, and Other Sea Monsters* (W. Tegg: London, 1849).
AKINS, William, *The Loch Ness Monster* (Signet: New York, 1977).
BARLOY, Jean-Jacques, *Serpents de Mer et Monstres Aquatiques* (Famot/François Beauval: Paris, 1978).
BAUER, Henry H., *The Enigma of Loch Ness: Making Sense of a Mystery* (University of Illinois Press: Urbana, 1986).
BAUMANN, Elwood D., *The Loch Ness Monster* (Franklin Watts: New York, 1972).
BERTON, Jean, *Les Monstres du Loch Ness et d'Ailleurs* (France-Empire: Paris, 1977).
BINNS, Ronald, *The Loch Ness Mystery Solved* (Open Books: Shepton Mallet, 1983).
BRADLEY, Michael, *More Than a Myth: The Search For the Monster of Muskrat Lake* (Hounslow Press: Willowdale, 1989).
BRIGHT, Michael, *There are Giants in the Sea* (Robson: London, 1989).
BURTON, Maurice, *The Elusive Monster: An Analysis of the Evidence From Loch Ness* (Rupert Hart-Davis: London, 1961).
CAMPBELL, Elizabeth M. & SOLOMON, David, *The Search For Morag* (Tom Stacey: London, 1972).
CAMPBELL, Steuart, *The Loch Ness Monster: The Evidence* (Aquarian: Wellingborough, 1986; rev. edit., Aberdeen University Press: London, 1991).
CORNELL, James, *The Monster of Loch Ness* (Scholastic Book Services: New York, 1977).
COSTELLO, Peter, *In Search of Lake Monsters* (Garnstone Press: London, 1974).
DINSDALE, Tim, *Loch Ness Monster* (Routledge & Kegan Paul: London, 1961; 4th edit., 1982).
DINSDALE, Tim, *The Leviathans* (Routledge & Kegan Paul: London, 1966; rev. edit., Futura: London, 1976).
DINSDALE, Tim, *Monster Hunt* (Acropolis: Washington D.C., 1972).
DINSDALE, Tim, *The Story of the Loch Ness Monster* (Allan Wingate: London, 1973).
DINSDALE, Tim, *Project Water Horse: The True Story of the Monster Quest at Loch Ness* (Routledge & Kegan Paul: London, 1975).
ELLIS, Richard, *Monsters of the Sea* (Alfred A. Knopf: New York, 1994; U.K. edit., Robert Hale: London, 1995).
GAAL, Arlene, *Beneath the Depths: The True Story of Ogopogo, Okanagan Lake Monster* (Valley Review: [no place of publication details], 1976).

Animals & Men — Issue Seven

GAAL, Arlene, *Ogopogo: the True Story of the Okanagan Lake Million Dollar Monster* (Hancock House: Surrey [British Columbia], 1986).

GIBSON, John A. & HEPPELL, David (Eds.), *Proceedings of the Symposium on the Loch Ness Monster: "The Search For Nessie in the 1980s"* (Scottish Natural History Library: Foremount House, 1988).

GOULD, Rupert T., *The Case For the Sea-Serpent* (Phillip Allen: London, 1930).

GOULD, Rupert T., *The Loch Ness Monster and Others* (Geoffrey Bles: London, 1934).

GRIMSHAW, Roger & LESTER, Paul, *The Meaning of the Loch Ness Monster* (Birmingham University: Birmingham, 1976).

HANSEN, Kim M., *Mysteriet om Nessie - Søslangen i Loch Ness* (Gyldendal: Copenhagen, 1988).

HASTAIN, Ronald & WITCHELL, Nicholas, *Loch Ness and the Monster: A Handbook For Tourists* (J. Arthur Dixon: Inverness, 1971).

HEUVELMANS, Bernard, *Dans le Sillage des Monstres Marins: Le Kraken et le Poulpe Colossal* (Plon: Paris, 1958).

HEUVELMANS, Bernard, *Le Grand Serpent-de-Mer* (Plon: Paris, 1965; rev. 1975).

HEUVELMANS, Bernard, *In the Wake of the Sea-Serpents* (Rupert Hart-Davis: London, 1968).

HOLIDAY, F.W., *The Great Orm of Loch Ness: A Practical Inquiry Into the Nature and Habits of Water-Monsters* (Faber & Faber: London, 1968).

HOLIDAY, F.W., *The Dragon and the Disc* (Sidgwick & Jackson: London, 1973).

HUTCHINS, J., *Discovering Mermaids and Sea Monsters* (Shire: Tring, 1968).

IZZARD, Ralph, *The Hunt For the Buru* (Hodder & Stoughton: London, 1951).

JAMES, David, *Loch Ness Investigation* (Loch Ness Phenomena Investigation Bureau: London, 1968).

KLEIN, Martin, et al., *Underwater Search at Loch Ness* [Monograph No. 1] (Academy of Applied Science: Belmont, 1972).

LANGE, P. Werner, *Seeungeheuer: Fabeln und Fakten* (Edition Leipzig: Leipzig, 1979).

LEE, Henry, *Sea Monsters Unmasked* (William Clowes: London, 1883).

LESTER, Paul, *The Great Sea-Serpent Controversy: A Cultural Study* (Privately published: Birmingham 1984).

McEWAN, Graham, *Sea Serpents, Sailors and Sceptics* (Routledge & Kegan Paul: London, 1978).

MACKAL, Roy P., *The Monsters of Loch Ness* (Macdonald and Janes: London, 1976).

MACKAL, Roy P., *A Living Dinosaur? In Search of Mokele-Mbembe* (Brill: Leiden, 1987).

McLEOD, James R., *Mysterious Lake Pend Oreille and Its "Monster": Fact and Folklore* (North Idaho College: Coeur d'Alene, 1987).

MARKS, William, *I Saw Ogopogo!* (Privately published: Peachland, 1971).

MAWNAN-PELLER, A., *Morgawr: The Monster of Falmouth Bay* (Morgawr Productions: Falmouth, 1976).

MEREDITH, Dennis L., *The Search at Loch Ness: The Expedition of the New York Times and the Academy of Applied Science* (Quadrangle: New York, 1977).

MEURGER, Michel & GAGNON, Claude, *Monstres des Lacs du Québec: Mythes et Troublantes Réalités* (Stanke: Montreal, 1982).

MEURGER, Michel & GAGNON, Claude, *Lake Monster Traditions. A Cross-Cultural Analysis* (Fortean Tomes: London, 1988).

MOON, Mary, *Ogopogo: The Okanagan Mystery* (J.J. Douglas: Vancouver, 1977).

NOLANE, Richard A., *Monstres des Lacs et des Océans* (Dossiers Vaugirard: Paris, 1993).

NUGENT, Rory, *Drums Along the Congo: On the Trail of Mokele-Mbembe, the Last Living Dinosaur* (Houghton Mifflin: New York, 1993).

Animals & Men — Issue Seven

OLSSON, Peter, *Storsjöodjuret, Framställning af Fakta och Utredning* (Jamtland postens Bocktrykeri: Östersund, 1899).
OUDEMANS, Antoon C., *The Great Sea-Serpent: An Historical and Critical Treatise* (Brill: Leiden, 1892).
OWEN, William, *Loch Ness Revealing Its Monsters* (Jarrold: Norwich, 1976).
PERERA, Vicor, *The Loch Ness Monster Watchers* (Capra Press: Santa Barbara, 1974).
REINSTEDT, Randall A., *Shipwrecks and Sea Monsters of California's Central Coast* (Ghost Town: Carmel, 1975).
REINSTEDT, Randall A., *Mysterious Sea Monsters of California's Central Coast* (Ghost Town: Carmel, 1979).
SEARLE, Frank, *Nessie: Seven Years in Search of the Monster* (Coronet: London, 1976).
SEARLE, Frank, *Around Loch Ness: A Handbook For Nessie Hunters* (Privately published: [no place of publication details], 1977).
SNYDER, Gerald S., *Is There a Loch Ness Monster? The Search For a Legend* (Julian Messner: New York, 1977).
STREICHER, Sonnfried, *Fabelwesen des Meeres* (Hinstorff Verlag: Rostock, 1984).
SWEENEY, James B., *A Pictorial History of Sea Monsters and Other Dangerous Marine Life* (Nelson-Crown: New York, 1972).
SWEENEY, James B., *Sea Monsters: A Collection of Eyewitness Accounts* (David McKay: New York, 1977).
THOMAS, Lars, *Mysteriet om Havuhyrerne* (Gyldendal: Copenhagen, 1992).
VIBE, Palle, *Gaden I Loch Ness* (Rhodos: Copenhagen, 1970).
WASEDADAIGAKU TANKENBU, *Maboroshi no Kaiju Mubenbe o Oe* [re mokele-mbembe] (PHP Kenkyujo: Tokyo, 1989).
WHYTE, Constance, *More Than a Legend: the Story of the Loch Ness Monster* (Hamish Hamilton: London, 1957; rev. 1961).
WIGNELL, Edel (Ed.), *A Boggle of Bunyips* (Hodder & Stoughton: Sydney, 1981).
WITCHELL, Nicholas, *The Loch Ness Story* (Terence Dalton: Lavenham, 1974; 3rd edit., Corgi Books: London, 1989).
WITCHELL, Nicholas, *Loch Ness and the Monster* (J. Arthur Dixon: Newport, 1975).
ZARZYNSKI, Joseph W., *Champ: Beyond the Legend* (Bannister: Port Henry, 1984; rev. edit., M-Z Information: Wilton, 1988).

On Special Offer from
THE CRYPTO SHOP

"In Search of Prehistoric Survivors" by Dr Karl P.N. Shuker
rrp 17.99 ONLY £16.00 (plus 50p p&p)
This can be personally autographed at no extra cost.
Telephone for details

"On the Track of Unknown Animals" by Dr Bernard Heuvelmans
rrp 25.00 ONLY £23.00 (plus 50p p&p)

animals & men

THE JOURNAL OF THE CENTRE FOR FORTEAN ZOOLOGY

Animals & Men — Issue Seven

LETTERS TO THE EDITOR

BIRD BRAINED

Life is strange. The famous astronomer Sir Fred Hoyle declared the old bird Archaeopteryx to be a manufactured hoax designed to fit the theory of evolution a few years ago. He based his argumentation on the fossil's surface structure, not satisfied with the feathers. If we shuffle the letters in Archaeopteryx a bit we get a sentence:

"*Try a crepe hoax*" or "*Creepy hoax art*". Another possibility is "*Try a hoax, creep!*"

Greetings

Eric Sorensen, Copenhagen.

TO WIT TO WOO

Dear Jonathan,

My main reason for writing is to comment on "Gavin's" account of an encounter with the Cornish Owlman. He did mention our identification of this creature as an owl, as suggested in our book 'Modern Mysteries of Britain', but only in passing, and I would like to expand on it if I may. I have been interested in the owlman ever since he was first reported in the 1970's, and I have been to the woods where he was seen in the company of Doc Shiels who was instrumental in publicising the sightings. I was uncertain what to make of the reports for some time, but tended like most people, to accept them as genuine, in view of all the other activity in the Falmouth bay area at the time (Morgawr and UFO sightings). More recently, however, now that some doubt has been cast on certain of the Falmouth events (see Mark Chorvinsky's painstaking research as published in his 'Strange' magazine), I am much more inclined to believe that the sightings have a much more prosaic explanation. It was my own sighting in Hafren Forest (Powys), a few years ago which clarified my thinking on Owlman, as here described in 'Modern Mysteries of Britain':

"*I was sitting in a car when my attention was caught by a disturbance in the trees across a stream. I saw a large bird, definitely an owl, rise up vertically, facing me with its whole face and body visible, its legs and feet hanging down. It rose straight up above the trees and flapped off, in broad daylight*".

This very closely resembles what the witnesses of Owlman have described - indeed the very name 'Owlman' suggests that the creature was owl-like. The creature's size is the problem - 'Gavin' says that it was "definitely a great deal bigger than any owl". But I suspect that anyone taken by surprise when an owl rises up close by them, would think the creature bigger than it really was, and with its legs and feet hanging down, and wings lifted, these would add to its apparent size and bulk. There's no doubt that owls are frightening to encounter in an eerie wood at night, and they do tend to be alarmed and fly off if people approach them. So despite "Gavin's" protestation that the creature was definitely not an owl, I have my suspicions that that's exactly what it was.

Keep up the good work,
Best wishes,

Janet Bord,
The Fortean Picture Library,
Clwyd.

> OPINIONS EXPRESSED IN THESE LETTERS ARE NOT NECESSARILY THOSE OF THE MAGAZINE OR OF THE CENTRE FOR FORTEAN ZOOLOGY. LETTERS MAY BE EDITED FOR INCLUSION.

THE BEAR FACTS

I'd like to comment on C.H.Keeling's article about the Nandi Bear in A&M6. He explicitly implies that chalicotheres were carnivorous. This is totally incorrect. Chalicotheres were certainly herbivores, like their closest relatives the brontotheres and horses. There does remain some argument about how they used their strong fore limbs and hooked claws. Did they dig up roots and tubers for a living, or were they semi-bipedal browsers that pulled branches down towards their mouths? The massiveness of the hips, arguing that a semi-bipedal stance was behaviourally important, endorse the latter interpretation. Like the living horses, rhinos and tapirs, chalicotheres were caecal fermenters.

De Sarre in 'The Mysterious Hominoids of Africa' (A&M6) refers to 'Australopithecus ramidus. It is now known that ramidus lacked derived characteristics of Australopithecus and thus deserves its own genus. Thus it is now Aldipithecus ramidus.

All the best 'till next time.

Darren Naish,
Southampton.

NEPALESE HUMPED ELEPHANTS

As a cryptozoologist since the early 1950's (before a lot of the present day crop were born, or even thought of), I am anxious that the whole field of investigation should be taken seriously. However, a chain is only as strong as its weakest link - and those amongst us that we could well do without are those who compulsively grab at straws, no matter how short and flimsy, in their apparently insatiable desire to create new species or resurrect extremely old ones. Scanty or fragmentary evidence - as often as not just in the eye of the beholder - is all too often the 'basis' of much heralded investigation that turns out to be the pursuit of wild examples of Anser anser - which does cryptozoology no good at all. A superb example of this is the attempt to see two perfectly ordinary bull Asiatic Elephants (Elephas maximus) as specimens of the extinct Stegodon. (A&M6 pp.11-12).

The two, admittedly, not particularly clear), photographs show typical large bulls of the forma typica without a vestige of evidence to suggest that they are anything else. The 'domes' on the forehead are so characteristic that in Indian folklore they are known as 'domes of wisdom', while the 'bridge' that gives the area of the front of the head a decidedly convex appearance, is again, the norm: this was very marked on a large bull exhibited for many years in the Leningrad Zoological Gardens, and I observed a similar excrescence on another animal in the Jardin des Plantes, Paris, in the 1960's. It would appear to be a natural sign of ageing, common in bulls and sometimes in cows.

The size of Raja Gaj and Kuncha is nothing to get excited about either, as although Nepal is just about the northernmost limit of the range of the Asiatic Elephant it does seem to grow to a particularly large size there. Just look at the mounted, (unfortunately tuskless) specimen in the British Museum (Natural History), in South Kensington: this is, or was Jung Pershad who lived at the London Zoological Garden from 1876 until 1897 - and came from that part of the world.

Animals & Men — Issue Seven

Hares of this nature, no matter how excitedly and enthusiastically they may be put up, have no place in serious cryptozoology - in fact I'm reminded of something that an old Peakland farmer once said to me, getting on for half a century ago: "Tha sees, lad, most folk see what they want to see...."

Well....?

Clinton Keeling.
Guildford.

ON THE BONNIE BONNIE BANKS....

Dear Sir,

With reference to Nick Morgan's letter (A&M5) in which he states that Loch Lomond "has not sustained any tradition of monster sightings". I wonder if he is aware of some fairly recent claims of sightings and one from the early eighteenth century.

1. Alexander Graham, writing in 1724 stated that where the river of Enrick falls into the Loch, that locals sometimes see the 'Hippopotam or Waterhorse' (Holiday 1968; Costello 1974).

2. On the 22nd of September 1964, a married couple observed a long humped back moving up the Loch. (Dinsdale 1966; Costello 1974).

3. Summer 1964, Sandy Watt and Bob Wilson from their train on a stretch of track above the Loch observed a huge object bigger than a long boat and moving fast 'like a torpedo' across the water. (Dinsdale 1966; Costello 1974).

4. Easter 1980, at around 8.00 a.m. The Maltmans and their daughter from approximately two hundred yards observed a patch of water which seemed to boil. A head appeared and a long neck approximately five feet long and behind this a long curved shape. They viewed this for around thirty seconds before they fled from the scene. (Nessletter 112).

I have visited Loch Lomond on a number of occasions, and I would have thought that if there is a resident population of unknown animals in there that there would have been far more sightings, especially considering the amount of leisure pursuits and sporting activity on the Loch. (Perhaps this activity has made the animals even more elusive, or driven them to recent extinction?)

These sighting reports remain and do seem to have been made by reliable witnesses. Perhaps the solution is abnormal sized individuals of known animals of the Loch. Eels for example?

I would be interested to hear other readers views.

Yours faithfully,

M.Playfair.
Leicestershire.

Book Reviews.

On the Track of Unknown Animals by Bernard Heuvelmans (Kegan Paul £25.00 676pp)

Forty years ago this book first propounded the theory and methodology of Cryptozoology. Above all else it is this book which earned Heuvelmans the well deserved title of 'The Father of Cryptozoology'. It has been out of print for many years but at last it is now available again.

This is a book that should be on the shelves of every cryptozoologist, whatever their degree of involvement, and is as enjoyable a read for me now as it was when I first read it twenty years ago.

It covers many of the main icons of terrestrial cryptozoology like the yeti and the orang pendek, but also covers such half forgotten cryptids as the agogwe and the spotted lion. There are notable omissions, such as Bigfoot, the yeren and the thylacine, but it has to be remembered that this book was first written over forty years ago, when the political, and even the geographical map of the world was far different to how it is today.

This is a reprint and not a new edition. There is a new introduction and many new illustrations, but the text remains the same as the first UK edition published by Rupert Hart Davis in 1958. It is still, however an essential part of your library, and if you have not already done so, I strongly urge you to buy it.

In Search of Prehistoric Survivors by Dr Karl P.N.Shuker (Blandford 192pp £17.99)

This is quite simply the most important Cryptozoological book to have been published in English since the above book first saw the light forty years ago. It is nothing less than a detailed description of dozens of possible, and probable, 'prehistoric survivors', which may still exist in the less well trodden parts of the globe.

Books on general cryptoinvestigative theory (as opposed to books about a specific cryptid or group of cryptids), tend to fall into one of two categories. One group drifts towards other areas of fortean investigation by including zooform phenomena and other less tangible occurrences within the scope of their studies. These, whilst within the remit of this magazine, are not the subject of cryptozoology, and have no place in a work of this kind.

The other main type of cryptozoology book sticks to strict zoological criteria, but indulges, self-indulgently in wishful thinking and presents a series of flimsy argument to suggest that hardly any creature actually becomes extinct.

Thankfully, like Heuvelmans before him, Karl Shuker has avoided either path, and has produced a logical, meticulously researched, but massively entertaining book on general cryptozoology which should act as a benchmark for the next forty years.

Animals & Men

THE JOURNAL OF THE CENTRE FOR FORTEAN ZOOLOGY

Issue Seven

Dragons - a Natural-History by Dr Karl P.N.Shuker. (Aurum £12.95).

We always knew that Karl Shuker was a meticulous and erudite scholar. This book proves that he is a superbly entertaining story teller. This book is a must for those with an interest in all things draconian. Shuker writes in a witty and entertaining style, which I have a sneaking suspicion will lead him to becoming the first cryptozoologist presenter of 'Jackanory'. I haven't even mentioned the lavish and quite stunning illustrations which make this probably the most attractive book on any fortean subject I have seen in a long time. (I, however know which 'Whitesnake' LP Dr Karl had in mind when he suggested the layout for the section about the Lindorm).

It covers a wide range of dragon stories and folklore from across theworld but also has a smattering of cryptozoological theorising to provide possible explanations for some of them.

This is the perfect Christmas gift for anyone with even the most vague interest in zoomythology of any description. If Shuker carries on at this rate, with two such excellent books which will, after all appeal to such diverse audiences then he will put the rest of us who write about such things out of business.

In common with much of the rest of the cryptozoological world, we at 'Animals & Men' are fascinated to know what he is going to write next!

Reading the Vampire by Ken Gelder (Routledge pb 160pp)

An excellent addition to the vampirologists library. This erudite little book examines the cultural and literary perspectives of vampirism, from a sober, unsensational, but entertaining viewpoint. It examines vampirism as an adjunct to pan european anti semitism and deep rooted homophobia, as well as in terms of a deep rooted mistrust of Romanians across much of Magyar Europe.

Although, unlike much of my library on the subject, it avoids discussing 'real' vampirism, and ignores contemporary accounts in favour of learned literary and socio-political analysis this is a fine book and one which I have no hesitation in reccommending.

It should however be read in conjunction with Underwood or Summers (but maybe not Sean Manchester) in order to provide a holistic overview of the subject.

(P.S For those of you who may wonder, I think that Sean Manchester and David Farrant's books are both highly entertaining and well written, but are too irrevocably entangled with the cult of the personality to be more than a highly personal insight into one specific outbreak of vampirism).

All the books reviewed this issue are available at a discount from The Crypto Shop.

Crypto rock is a rare and wondrous creation in its own right sharing with the elusive creatures that we all seek those attributes of fascination......... oh hell, let's cut the pretentious drivel. On more cut from the mighty album we all know as

"Now That's what I Call Crypto!"

by Neil Nixon

Richard Scott with Rex Crasswell: 'Slug Talk'.

The crypto world includes animals of rare and mutated forms as much as rare animals per se. Hell, of course it does, and for what its worth I think that Gef the Talking Mongoose got a seriously severe press, he certainly had me convinced. Anyway, animals don't come any more mutated than on this seminal slice of sonorial weirdness. The album itself is an elongated trawl through sounds and textures of varied forms that occasionally touches upon some recognisable musical form. One of the more left-field excursions is the opening track 'Slug Talk'. By my reckoning these slugs have been tunneling right under the pile at Sellafield and imbibing the trickling radio-active juices to such an extent that they've mutated into something from a splatterpunk horror novel. Either that or Scott and Casswell are a couple of pale skinned techno fiends who won't even know that there was a heatwave in 1995 because they were too busy playing with their keyboards, samplers and tape equipment.

Whatever, we have here less than two minutes of gurgling, slurping, droning and humming that takes a sharp turn into sampled electronic piano around half way through. These are slugs with something to say about their subterranean sojourns and a curious reflective quality to their thinking given their relatively low position in the ranking of animal intelligence. If you want to hear the bizarre slug sounds I'd suggest going to Sellafield and tunneling under the pile yourself. You've probably got more chance of meeting a slug down there than you have a chance of turning up a copy of the CD 'The Magnificence of Stereo' which contains this track. For the record (heh heh geddit?), the album came out in 1992 on the Sruti Box label, and rejoices in the catalogue number CD 01. I use the term 'catalogue number' a bit loosely here since this album doesn't appear in official lists of the record industry like the 'Music Master' CD catalogue. Your best bet, if you're that bothered, would be trying the small ads in the more out to lunch music mags. And if you are 'that bothered' then you'll already know which mags I mean!

****

Material printed in this magazine, (and there is no significance to this notice appearing on this page-it merely happened to be the only spare space in the magazine), is the opinion of the author and not necessarily that of the editorial team, or of The Centre for Fortean Zoology. Every effort has been made to ensure that no copyright restrictions have been infringed and that no defamatory statements are published within these pages.

PERIODICAL REVIEWS

We welcome an exchange of periodicals with magazines of mutual interest although because we now exchange with so many magazines we have been forced, much against our fortean methodology, to categorise them.

CRYPTOZOOLOGY AND ZOOMYTHOLOGY

DRAGON CHRONICLE, The dragon trust, PO Box 3369, London SW6 6JN. A fascinating collection of all things draconian which now appears four times a year. Now A4 and Glossy..how do they DO it?

THE BRITISH COLUMBIA CRYPTOZOOLOGY CLUB NEWSLETTER, 3773 West 18th Avenue, Vancouver, British Columbia, Canada. V65 1B3. Excellent and well put together, and they are now on the Internet as well!

CREATURE RESEARCH JOURNAL, Paul Johnson, 721 Old Greensburg Pike, North Versailles, PA 15137-1111 USA. A fascinating periodical about the correlation between mystery animals and UFO reports.

CRYPTOZOOLOGIA, Association Belge d'Etude et de Protection des Animaux Rares, Square des Latins 49/4, 1050 Bruxelles, Belgium. A French language magazine published by the Belgian society for Cryptozoology.

FRINGE SCIENCE

NEXUS 55 Queens Rd, E. Grinstead, West Sussex RH19 1BG. Intelligent look at the fringes of science. Well put together. Very impressive.

FORTEAN

TEMS NEWS, 115 Hollybush Lane, Hampton, Middlesex, TW12 2QY. An entertaining collection of odds and sods and generally weird stuff. A magazine I always enjoy reading. Reccomended.

DEAD OF NIGHT, 156 Bolton Road East, Newferry, Wirral, Merseyside, L62 4RY. An amusing and intelligently put together Fortean magazine. The latest issue includes the trippiest peice on the occult aspects of Loch Ness that I have read in a long time.

ENIGMAS, 41 The Braes, Tullibody, Clackmannanshire, Scotland, FK10 2TT A Fine 'mysteries' magazine with a UFO bias. An article by me on animal mutilation will be appearing eventually!

THIRD STONE PO BOX 258, Cheltenham, Glocs,GL53 0HR. The magazine of the Gloucester Earth Mysteries group. A wonderful, witty and stylish look at earth mysteries in general and Gloucestershire ones in particular.

EARTHLY DELIGHTS, PO Box 2, Lostwithiel, Cornwall, PL22 0YY. A wonderful mixture of anarchic silliness and oddball synchronicity. Magazines like this make my day.

Animals & Men — Issue Seven

ZOOLOGY/NATURAL HISTORY

SOUTH WEST HERPETOLOGICAL SOCIETY NEWSLETTER, Frank Gibbons, Acanthus, 59 St Marychurch Rd, Torquay, Devon. Entertaining and informative newsletter from a thriving organisation. Contains some quasi fortean oddments.

PORTSMOUTH REPTILE AND AMPHIBIAN SOCIETY NEWSLETTER M Jones, 7 Hazelmere Rd, Southsea, Hants. Another thriving regional organisation whose publications ooze with authoritativeness and professionalism.

MILTON KEYNES HERPETOLOGICAL SOCIETY 15 Esk Way, Bletchley, Milton Keynes. Excellent A5 magazine containing handy hints, informative articles and news of what appears to be an exciting organisation.

MAINLY ABOUT ANIMALS, 13 Pound Place, Shalford, Guildford, Surrey GU4 8HH. Veteran Zoologist Clinton Keeling edits this wonbderful A5 magazine which is, as the title says, mainly about animals. This is a genre of magazine that I and many others feared was lost forever and it comes with your editor's highest reccomendation.

WILD EQUID SOCIETY, 5 Percy Rd., London E16 4RB. An intelligent and well written journal about all the wild animals of the horse tribe. Well worth investigating.

ANIMAL KEEPER, PO Box 1, Gillingham, Dorset SP8 5NE. As the name implies this is a magazine aimed at, and written by those who keep exotic wild animals. Glossy, but erudite. An excellent publication.

ASSOCIATION OF PRIVATE ANIMAL KEEPERS, 8 Yewlands Walk, Ifield, Crawleigh, W. Sussex RH11 0QE. Britain needs organisations like this to safeguard hobbyists from draconian and often unnecessary legislation.

YOUNG HERPETOLOGISTS CLUB c/o Zoological Society of London, Regents Park, London NW1 4RY. Excellent organisation for the young reptile buff.

NATIONAL TERRAPIN PROJECT, 151 South Rd., Hailsham, East Sussex, BN27 3NT. These are the people who keep a register of out of place Chelonians found in the UK. Invaluable.

ESSEX REPTILES AND AMPHIBIANS SOCIETY, 6 Chestnut Way, Tiptree, Colchester, Essex, CO5 0NX. Another excellent and lively regional reptile society. Contains much invaluable information.

We also exchange with 'The Cereaologist', Bipedia, Nessletter, Promises and Disappointments, Touchstone, Annals 2, The Reptilian, Kingsbridge Natural History Society, South West Tarantula Society, 'The Bigfoot Record', and 'Track Record but we have not received anything from them during the past three months!

animals&men
THE JOURNAL OF THE CENTRE FOR FORTEAN ZOOLOGY

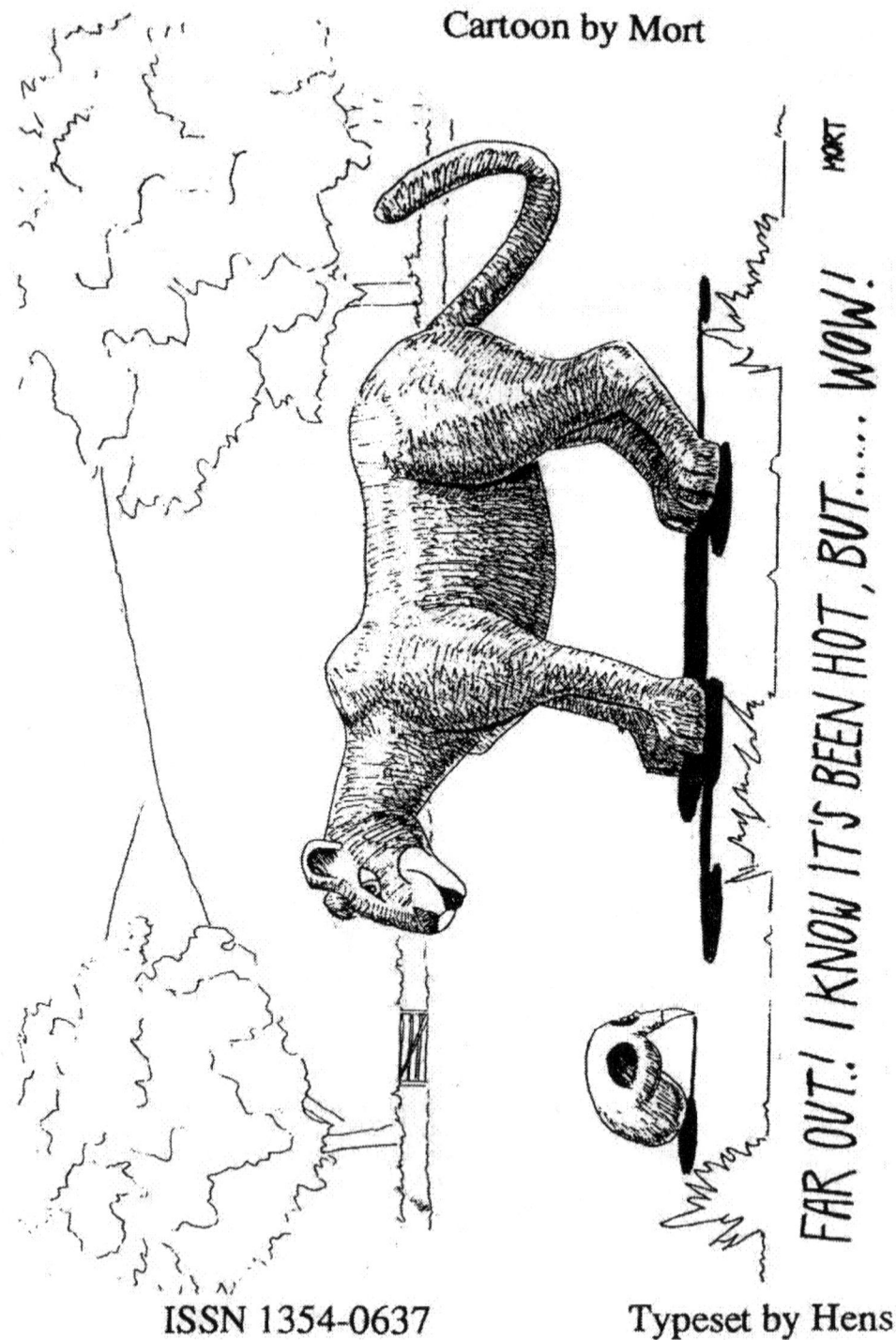

Cartoon by Mort

ISSUE 8
OCTOBER 1995

animals&men

THE JOURNAL OF THE CENTRE FOR FORTEAN ZOOLOGY

This issue saw the writing debut of Clinton Keeling, and perhaps more importantly of Chris Moiser - a zoologist from Plymouth who was eventually to become one of the major members of the CFZ Board of consultants. It saw the end of the initial phase of the *magazine* - the last articles we had inherited from SCAN were used up and we were now standing firmly on our own two feet

animals&men
THE JOURNAL OF THE CENTRE FOR FORTEAN ZOOLOGY

Animals & Men
The Journal of the Centre for Fortean Zoology

The Quagga Project ... Green Cats and Dogs
The Burden of Proof ... Man Beast in Malaya
New Species in Devonshire.
Issue Eight   £1.75

animals&men

THE JOURNAL OF THE CENTRE FOR FORTEAN ZOOLOGY

Animals & Men — Issue Eight

This issue of 'Animals & Men' was put together by the following zoological malcontents.

Jonathan Downes: Editor
Jan Williams: Newsfile Editor
Alison Downes: Administratrix supreme
Lisa Peach: Artist
Mort: Cartoons (but does he exist?)
Graham Inglis: Saviour of the Road Crew

CONSULTANTS

Dr Bernard Heuvelmans
(Honorary Consulting Editor)
Dr Karl P.N.Shuker
(Cryptozoological Consultant)
C.H.Keeling
(Zoological Consultant)
Tony 'Doc' Shiels
(Surrealchemist in Residence)

REGIONAL REPRESENTATIVES

West Midlands: Dr Karl Shuker
Mexico: Dr Lara Palmeros
Spain: Alberto Lopez Acha
Germany: Wolfgang Schmidt & Hermann Reichenbach
France: Francois de Sarre
Wiltshire: Richard Muirhead
Scotland: Tom Anderson
Kent: Neil Arnold
Sussex: Sally Parsons
Hampshire: Darren Naish
Lancashire: Stuart Leadbetter
Belgium: ABEPAR
Norfolk: Justin Boote
Leicestershire: A000laistair Curzon
Cumbria: Brian Goodwin
Home Counties: Philip Kiberd
S.Wales/Salop: Jon Matthias
Denmark: Lars Thomas
Sweden: Eric Sorenson
Eire: The Wizard of the western world.

CONTENTS

P 3. Editorial
P.4. Newsfile
P 12. 'The Quagga Project' by Chris Moiser
15. 'A Malayan Man Beast' by C.H.Keeling
p.17 A Bibliography of Cryptozoological and Zoomythological books..part 3. by Dr Karl Shuker and Stephen Shipp.
p.22. 'Mort wrote this but he can't prove it'
p.23. 'Cryptocetology-the Page 254 Story' by Darren Naish
p.30. 'New and rediscovered species in Devonshire' by David Bolton
p.33 'The story of a green dog' by Richard Muirhead
p.34. 'A Green Kitten' by Eric Sorensen.
p.35. 'The A-Z of Cryptozoology' part 6 by Jan Williams.
p.37. Letters to the Editor by M.Grayson, T.Anderson,, J.Love, J.Heath-Stubbs, 'Hampshire Hog', and 'A.Sasquatch Esq'.
p.40 Book Reviews
p.42. Periodical Reviews
p.44 Cartoon

**'ANIMALS & MEN',
THE CENTRE FOR FORTEAN ZOOLOGY,
15 HOLNE COURT,
EXWICK, EXETER.
EX4 2NA**

01392 424811

DISCLAIMER

The Views published in articles and letters in this magazine are not necesarily those of the publisher or editorial team, who although they have taken all lengths not to print anything defamatory or which infringes anyone's copyright take no responsibility for any such statement which is inadvertantly included.

THE GREAT DAYS OF ZOOLOGY ARE NOT DONE

Dear Friends,

Another year, another issue. Thank you very much for your support during 1995. Thank you also to everyone who wrote to us and sent us cards at Christmas. Its heartwarming to realise how many of you have become real friends over the past two years.

This year looks as if it is going to be a particularly exciting one. We have a number of new and on-going projects that will be bearing fruit over the next twelve months. The sales of the 1996 Yearbook have been spectacularly successful and we have high hopes for the books we are intending to publish this year. My book on 'The Smaller Mystery Carnivores of the Westcountry' is due in the Spring and I have another book on The Owlman of Mawnan in preparation. Richard Muirhead and I are working on a book tentatively called 'The Mystery Animals of Hong-Kong', and we are hoping to print an edition of 'Doc' Shiels' "The Cantrip Codex" sometime in 1996. We are also involved in the production of several television projects and a movie-length video which covers fortean goings-on in Cornwall, together with music and elements of surrealism.

We are going to be out and about this year, and once again we should like to appeal for help. We now have a hard-working and successful network of regional representatives, but we now want something more! We are looking for people who can help us in two ways. Firstly by coming along to events in their area with us, (for example, County Shows, Zoologica, Unconvention and Animal Fairs), and help us out on the stall. We cannot pay anyone but we usually buy them lunch and always ensure that they get in free to whatever event we are attending. We are mounting exhibitions at various events around the country this year and would be grateful for an extra pair of hands or so at several of them.

Secondly, during our travels to places of fortean interest we usually sleep in the van, but if anyone, especially in parts of Scotland, the Midlands or the Home Counties can ever offer us a bed for the night during our travels they would make two travelling cryptozoologists (and sometimes Graham the Roadie) very happy.

Finally, in a world where a whole new Phylum of animal life can be discovered living on the upper lip of a Norwegian lobster, (Jan says that she will never eat scampi again, whereas Alison and I are even more thankful that we are vegetarians), then it proves that as we enter the third millenium after Christ, there are many mysteries left to solve. As Goethe said: "In her abnormalities, Nature reveals her secrets", a maxim which, if I believed in such things, and I don't know whether I do or not, should possibly become the motto of all the earnest seekers after truth at the Centre for Fortean Zoology.

Jan '96

-3-

NEWSFILE

ALL THE ZOOLOGICAL NEWS THATS FIT TO PRINT COMPILED BY JAN WILLIAMS AND HER MERRY BAND

Lake Monsters.

Lake Van Monster.

Reports of a 'dinosaur-like' monster in the saline waters of Lake Van in Eastern Turkey have inspired a government-funded investigation. The search follows a reported sighting by the provincial deputy governor, Bestami Alkan. He said 'It was black and had triangular spikes on its back. It looked like a dinosaur'. Nadir Kartal, head of the parliamentary commission which is conducting the search, added 'its head is black and hairy, and it had horns' Orhan Erman, a biology professor at Ataturk University, Erzurum, was sceptical. He said 'it is not possible for a creature of the size claimed by witnesses to live in a closed lake like Van'. (Daily Telegraph 2.11.95; Westfalenpost 2.11.95).

Eastern Turkey showing Lake Van

BURRUM BEAST.

A witness reported a sighting of the Burrum Beast, near Childers, Queensland, Australia in September. The Burrum Beast, a long necked lake monster, has been seen in the area, 40 kilometres south of Bundaberg, since the beginning of the century. (Brisbane Sunday Mail 1.10.1995).

TEGGIE ON FILM?

A recent story on the Internet claimed that C.P.Bureau, a Reading-based closed-circuit film company, may have succeeded in filming 'Teggie', the legendary monster of Lake Bala in North Wales.

According to a story in the Reading Evening Post (9.11.1995), the company were hired by a Japanese TV crew, which has detected a large object moving about in the depths of the lake by sonar soundings. C.P Bureau mounted thirteen cameras in boats, eight around the shore and five in a mobile control room. One of the pictures obtained seems to show a humped creature moving across the lake's surface, leaving a trail in its wake hundreds of yards long. Another shows what appears to be a long neck and head breaking from

the surface of the lake with a hump just behind.

Unfortunately there is only one thing wrong with the story. It is completely untrue! We spoke to Mr Meredith at C.P Bureau, who told us that the story in the Reading newspaper had been written by a local journalist as a spoof. Whoever transferred it to the Internet, removed the 'jokey' aspects of the story, and presented it as pure fact.

C.P Bureau did film an object on Lake Bala but it proved to be inanimate. Mr Meredith remarked wryly that he wished they had managed to film a 'real' monster because the publicity for his company would have been overwhelming!

HORSES

ANCIENT EQUINES

A joint French and British expedition led by ethnologist Michel Peissel, has discovered a small population of horses which resemble those of European cave paintings. They were found in a remote mountain valley, not shown on maps, in the isolated Riwoche area of north-eastern Tibet. 'When we saw the first of these animals', Peissel said, 'we thought it was a mutation of sorts, but then we discovered a second and third specimen, finally an entire herd - two dozen pony-sized, short-maned, beige-coloured horses with angular heads'. The dark line of hair along the back and the black lower legs were also similar to cave paintings of horses thought to be long extinct.

According to expedition member Ignasi Casas, an animal biologist at the Horse Research Centre in Newmarket, the Riwoche horses cannot leave the protective valley, since the high mountain passes they would have to cross supply no grass for food. A blood sample taken from one of the herd is currently being analysed in a British laboratory. (*New York Times 12.11.1995; Der Spiegel, # 49, 4.12.1995*).

ZORSE RACING

American horse breeder Diane Richards is hoping 'White Cloud', a zebra-horse hybrid will have a great future in racing. Born to a registered mare, via artificial insemination with a zebra, the foal - called a zorse - has the speed of a race horse and the stamina of a zebra. Miss Richards, who keeps zebras at her ranch near Big Bear Lake in California's San Bernadino mountains, has persevered with the artificial insemination programme despite problems. Previous experiments have produced hybrids which are often vicious and defy domestication. (*Daily Mail 12.1.1996*).

PONY POWER

Five Konik ponies have been imported from Poland to help save fenland near Diss, Norfolk. Suffolk Wildlife Trust hopes that the ponies and their offspring will graze on sedge scrub and reeds which are choking Redgrave and Lopham Fen. The fenland has been drained by a borehole supplying local villages allowing sedge and reeds to take over from the natural vegetation. The borehole is to be moved under a three million pound restoration scheme, allowing water levels to return to normal, but the scrubland needs to be cleared. British ponies were not considered hardy enough to graze on the marshy ground, but Trust

Director Derek Moore says the Koniks are *'very hardy and will eat anything'*. (*Daily Mail 13.11.1995*).

MYSTERY MARSUPIALS

QUEENSLAND THYLACINE.

Roy Swaby from Woodgate, near Bundaberg, Queensland, reported an animal he believed to be a thylacine, which had chased a terrified kangaroo into the path of his car. He said, 'This incredible sandy coloured striped animal leapt out from the side of the road a full fifteen feet, and into the glare of my 100 watt halogen spots and four headlights. It stopped on the road, turned to look at me and fell back on its huge hindquarters, its large green-yellow eyes glowing in the light, and then it opened its jaws and snarled at me. I have never seen anything like it. The white teeth were large, and the jaws like a crocodile, like a mantrap. It took two steps and then suddenly crouched and sprang again, 15 - 20 feet, this time into the scrub. I was 20 metres away from it and my lights lit up the road and the creature like it was daylight. I could even see whiskers'.

Mr Swaby returned to the spot the following day and photographed paw prints measuring 12cm by 10cm. He said the animal was 4-5 feet long with a 2-3 foot tail, and looked as if someone had cut a dingo and a kangaroo in half and joined them together. The stripes started halfway down its back, and was sleek and healthy looking. (*Brisbane Sunday Mail 27.8.1995*).

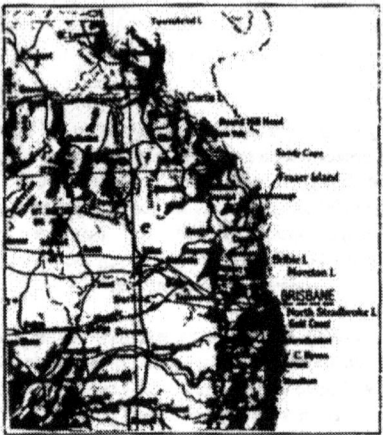

Bundburg, Queensland, the site for two items in this Newsfile

WALLABIES ON THE WANE

Wildlife experts believe only two wallabies may be left in the Roaches area of the Staffordshire Peak District, and the Peak Park officials are urging sightseers to stay away from the animals. (*Daily Mail 26.12.1995*).

Five Bennet's Wallabies escaped from a private menagerie at Swythamley Hall near Leek in 1939, and established a colony in heather moorland and thick scrub north-west of Leek and in woodlands near Hoo Moor in neighbouring Derbyshire. The population has fluctuated over the years, dropping dramatically after the exceptionally hard winters of 1947, 1962 and 1978, and increasing to 30-50 animals in milder conditions.

The colony has been reported as close to extinction in previous years, but to date has always managed to bound back. A yak which also escaped from Swythamley in 1939 survived on the moors until 1951.

MYSTERY CATS

Cornwall.

A big cat was reported at Trevenning Farm, Fowey in October. David Byrne saw the animal whilst he was driving at night, and described it as black, long and slender. *(Cornish Guardian 5.10.1995)*

(THE David Byrne? '....*and you may ask yourself how did that Alien Big Cat get in the headlights of your great big automobile?*' Rock and Roll Ed.)

North Yorkshire.

Ken Harrison of Hovingham, near Malton, saw a large white cat in woods near his farm on the 14th November. The animal was about the size of a fox, had a 'leopard shaped head', a long tail, and may have had grey markings. *(Scarborough Evening News 16.11.1995)*.

Buckinghamshire.

A big cat was seen in the Page Hill area of Buckingham on the 22nd November. A resident of Cheyne Close saw the animal from her window at about 5 a.m and described it as a '*big cat with pointed ears. It definitely was not a dog or a fox, you could tell by the way it moved*'. *(Brackley and Towcester Advertiser 1.12.1995)*. The report follows a number of sightings in the rural area around Buckingham and Winslow (see '*Animals & Men*' #7), but is the first from the town itself.

Cambridgeshire.

The Fen Tiger is stalking again. A cat described as '*waist-high and bigger than a Great Dane*' was seen by student Andrew Fry in October, and a week later prints were found in a newly cultivated field at Comberton, near Cambridge, by landowner Brian Hague. the large prints were examined by university zoologist Dr. Keith Eltringham, who said that they were not caused by any native wild animal. *'I cannot be absolutely certain, but they are almost certainly those of a large cat*', he said. *'Looking at the size of the prints and the gaps between them, it was obviously a big animal. The only other thing it could possibly be is a very large dog, but the prints are not the right shape*'. (Local newspaper, unreferenced). A labrador sized black-cat, with a white patch on its chest, was seen by several residents of Comberton during a two week period in September 1993.

Leicestershire.

A big cat was reported close to a residential estate in Leicester in March 1995. Diane Russell spotted the cat in the Blackbird Road area of the city at 11.30 p.m. She described it as having a small head, and a long body and tail. Police in Leicestershire have received other reports from rural areas. *(Leicestershire Mercury 8.3.95)*.

Animals & Men — Issue Eight

Dyfed, Wales.

More than a hundred farmers gathered at a public meeting in Pontrhydfenigaid, near Tregaron, on the 16th December to discuss livestock deaths in the area. Ex-zookeeper, Quentin Rose, formerly an employee of Howlett's Zoo in Kent, claimed that either a puma or a leopard was responsible for the deaths of more than 20 sheep. The farmers want to employ Mr Rose to track down the animal and will ask the Welsh Office for official support. (BBC Wales Ceefax 17.12.1995).

Highland, Scotland.

Prints believed to be those of a big cat were found by Stuart and Tina Grant, near their home in remote Strathglass, near Beauly. They made a plaster cast of one of the prints, which measured 12 cm by 8 cm. (Aberdeen Evening Express 20.11.1995).

OTHER MAMMALS

GOATSUCKER ATE TEDDY BEAR

A 'mysterious blood-sucking beast' known as 'Chupacabras' or 'Goat-Sucker', is causing uproar in Puerto Rico. Police state the animal is responsible for the deaths of dozens of goats, cats, dogs, turkeys and rabbits, and even horses and cows. It is said to rip out the organs of its animal victims. In November attacks were being reported daily on news radio, and in the newspaper El Vocero. A witness from the city of Canovanas described the animal as about four feet tall, and resembling a monkey with no tail. The beast was said to have attacked thirty five times in the city during the autumn months, despite being hunted by a posse led by the mayor every Sunday.

In Caguas the beast was said to have entered a house through a bedroom window, destroyed a teddy bear, and left *'a puddle of slime and a piece of rancid white meat on the windowsill'*. The householder described the Chupacabras as having huge red eyes and hairy arms. (No description of the Teddy Bear was available). In an early morning raid on a junkyard in the same city, five sheep, four geese and a turkey were reportedly killed. A vet from the Agriculture department investigated and concluded that the animals had died from natural causes, and that none had bled to death. Local sceptics claimed that wild monkeys had attacked the livestock.

There were similar unexplained animal deaths on the island in 1975, when goats, ducks, geese and rabbits were killed in the vicinity of Moca. UFO sightings were also reported in the area. (See *'Modern Mysteries of the World'* by J & C Bord). (Aberdeen Press and Journal 21.11.1995).

WILD ROCKER

Police in Suffolk are probing claims that a wild animal terrorised travellers by rocking their caravan. (ITV Teletext 25.12.1995)

Animals & Men — Issue Eight

DINOSAURS

DINOSAUR DEATH THEORY ON TEST

The voyage of the Joides Resolution may explain the extinction of the dinosaurs. A team on board the research ship, run by the Joint Oceanographic Institute's Deep Earth Sampling programme, will drill into the seabed at the Chicxulub crater off the Mexico coast, hoping to find evidence of a giant meteorite which lead to mass extinction of life-forms. Recent images from the space-shuttle identified concentric circles 180km - 300km in diameter at the site.

The theory to be tested by the team of thirty five scientists is that a giant meteorite plunged through the atmosphere 65 million years ago, and impacted with such force that debris was thrown into the upper atmosphere causing total darkness for fifty years. This killed off plants, causing many animals to starve, and extraterrestrial material polluted sea and land creating further destruction.

The team will take core samples from the sediment and seabed at the bottom of the crater. The critical level is the K-T line between the end of the Cretaceous period and the start of the Tertiary - the point in time when dinosaurs became extinct. If the theory is correct, this layer should show high levels of Iridium gases, extraterrestrial amino acids, and other debris.

Chandra Wickramasinghe, who, together with Sir Fred Hoyle, first put forward the meteorite theory in 1976, said *'The events of sixty five million years ago, we believe, involved the break-up of a large comet as it swerved past Jupiter. Large pieces collided with Earth and caused the extinction of dinosaurs and 75% of all living species'*. *(Sunday Times 24.12.1995)*.

DINOSAUR DISCOVERIES

The fossil of an Oviraptor killed in a sandstorm whilst hatching eggs, has been discovered in Mongolia. According to Mark Norrell, of the American Museum of Natural History in New York, whose team discovered the 75 million year old fossil, the find 'changes the way we look at dinosaurs'. It suggests that dinosaurs protected and reared their young in a bird-like way, rather than leaving eggs to hatch by themselves. Robin Cocks, Keeper of Palaeontology at the Natural History Museum in London, said *"We've always suspected this happened, but we've never seen it. We know about the eggs and we've seen dinosaurs close to them, but we've never seen the two together before. It's very exciting"* *(Independent 2.12.1995)*.

A new species of pterodactyl, discovered by British scientists, has been named *Arthurdactylus conandoylei*, in celebration of Conan Doyle's classic novel 'The Lost World'.

The fossil, which has a wing-span of six metres, was identified by Dr. David Martill of Portsmouth University, and Dino Frey of the State Natural History Museum, in Karlsruhe, Germany. Dr. Martill said that the site where it was found, at Shapada Do Araripe in north-eastern Brazil, resembled Conan Doyle's mythical lost world. *(The Times 19.8.1995)*.

Animals & Men — Issue Eight

ESCAPES.

Two chimpanzees caused chaos when they escaped from Southport Zoo on Christmas Eve. One fled to a pitch and putt course, where she was cornered and shot with a tranquilizer gun. She lurched into a cafe causing customers to abandon their afternoon teas, and swung on to the roof, before the drug finally took effect. The other, a male, headed for the pier and created havoc amongst a group of pensioners on a day trip. A 73 year old woman was treated for cuts, bruises and shock after she fended off the chimp which was trying to steal her handbag. Zoo owner Douglas Petrie, keepers and police, including marksmen from the Tactical Aid Unit, chased the chimp to the end of the pier where it trapped three people inside a building. Officers used loud-hailers to warn them to stay inside. Concerned that the animal might climb down to the beach and head back into town, Mr Petrie reluctantly agreed it should be shot. Police said the escape was the subject of further enquiries. *(ITV Teletext, BBC Ceefax 25.12.1995, Daily Mail 26.12.1995).*

More than 300 crocodiles which escaped when flood waters inundated farms near Bangkok, Thailand, are being hunted down by a speedboat task force armed with assault rifles, stun guns and nets. Some of the crocodiles are reported to be more than thirteen feet long. Local fishermen have been hauling up crocodiles in their nets, and two have been bitten. A bounty of £75 has been placed on each croc, and tourists have been warned to swim only in hotel pools. *(The Times 28.9.1995).*

MISCELLANEOUS

TRANS-SEXUAL FISH.

A species of fish has been discovered off the coast of Japan that can change sex at will, altering the structure of its genitalia and brain to match the social occasion. *(Independent 24.11.1995).*

GIANT LOBSTER

Divers clearing a sea-bed rubbish mound near a disused section of the naval base at Portland, Dorset caught a giant lobster. The 15lb lobster, christened 'Neptune' is five times normal size. It has been transferred to the Sea Life centre at Weymouth until the clearance work is completed. *(Daily Mail 8.1.1996)*

MULTI-STOREY SNAKE

A three-foot long black Taiwanese Beauty was found slithering along the sixth floor of the West Park multi-storey car park in Southampton, in October. Two white 'snake eggs' found in the car park turned out to be peppermints. *(Southampton Daily Echo 12.10.1995).*

Animals & Men — Issue Eight

A ZOO IN HIS LUGGAGE

Airport security staff in Cairo, Egypt, discovered a mini-zoo in a Russian passenger's suitcase. The case contained two live crocodiles, two baby foxes, 17 chameleons, 5 gerbils and 28 lizards. *(Daily Star 2.10.1995)*.

STRANGE SMELL IN SALISBURY

Police officers digging near a Salisbury footpath, after complaints from residents of an awful smell in the area, unearthed a shallow grave. It contained the body of a large lizard, three feet, six inches long. The lizard was disposed of by environmental health officers. *(Salisbury Journal 17.8.1995)*.

INVEST IN PESTS

Shares in Fumakilla surged on the Tokyo stock market, following news that poisonous Australian Red Backed Spiders have been sighted several times in Osaka, Japan. *(Independent 29.11.1995)*.

TAKE MY LLAMA

Argentinian animal breeder Leopoldo Canari wants to exchange his six-legged llama for a television set. He would prefer to make the deal with a scientist, as he thinks that the animal may help advance science, and requires a battery operated TV set as there is no electricity supply to his home in the Andean Mountains. Form an orderly queue please... *(Die Welt 30.11.1995)*.

Newsfile Correspondents:

Tom Anderson, Sally Parsons, Mr and Mrs J Love, Richard Muirhead, COUDi, Ian Sherred, Wolfgang Schmidt, Keith Williams.

HAVE YOU ANY SURPLUS BOOKS, MAGAZINES OR VIDEO TAPES FEATURING CRYPTOZOOLOGICAL, ZOOLOGICAL OR FORTEAN MATERIAL? WE BUY AND SELL SUCH THINGS AND ARE ALWAYS INTERESTED IN BUYING, OR EXCHANGING YOUR SURPLUS.

TELEPHONE OR WRITE

The Quagga Project.

by Chris Moiser.

The Quagga (*Equus quagga quagga*) was a type of zebra. It lacked stripes at its rear end and the background colour to its stripes was brown. It is thought to have become extinct on the 12th of August 1883 when the last individual in captivity died. The last wild Quagga had almost certainly died before 1870. Their demise was most probably as a result of being hunted for meat, and as a source of leather for grain bags.

These animals had initially been common, and possibly because their stripes were less spectacular than those of other zebras, no serious attempts were made to breed them in European zoos. Certainly there were Quaggas in Europe. In Great Britain they were exhibited in several zoological collections and some were in private hands.

They seemed to domesticate very easily and in the 1820's a gentleman called Sherrif Parkin was regularly drawn through Hyde Park in a carriage pulled by a pair that were trained to harness. Unfortunately, by the time that the increasing rarity of the animals was discovered the European Zoos were down to a few elderly mares. South African game conservation laws came too late as well, and at that time would have been difficult, if not impossible, to enforce anyway.

Zebra classification is, even now, somewhat confused, and the taxonomic position of the Quagga was, until recently, extremely uncertain. Some of the confusion existing because one eminent taxonomist suggested that the Quagga was more closely related to the horse than the zebras.

The position of the Quagga's classification was effectively resolved during the 1980s as a result of a series of coincidental happenings.

An American researcher had contacted Reinhold Rau, the chief taxidermist at the South African Museum in Cape Town, to see if he could obtain some zebra tissue samples for DNA and protein analysis. Mr. Rau, probably the most knowledgeable man in the world on matters relating to the Quagga, unbeknownst to the American had some dried muscle and blood from the Quagga. He had obtained these when he remounted the South African museum Quagga foal in 1969.

This material was of great interest to the Americans, and they were subsequently able to extract DNA from it. The DNA was in small fragments, but these were big enough to be compared with DNA from modern, extant zebras. These comparisons showed the Zebra and Quagga DNA to be very similar. The similarity was so great that it is now thought that the Quagga was almost certainly a subspecies of the Common or Plains Zebra.

From the geographical viewpoint this would make sense as the Quagga lived, as far as we know, in the Karoo and the Orange Free State in South Africa, i.e. on the edge of the normal range of the Plains Zebra.

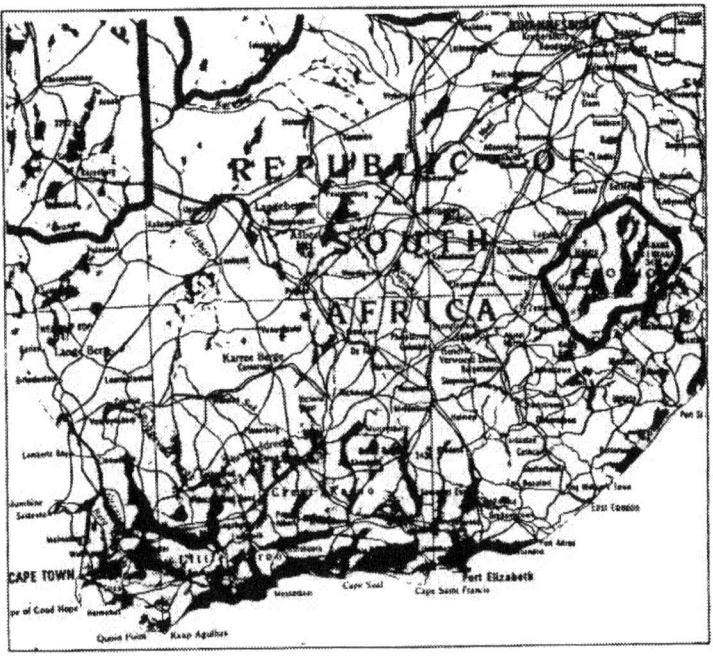

South Africa showing the Orange Free State and the Karoo

If the Quagga was only a subspecies of the Plains Zebra then the genes that made the animal a Quagga may still exist, hidden, in other Plains Zebra. If this is so it should be possible to re-create the Quagga by appropriate selective breeding.

Interestingly, if the Quagga was a subspecies of the Plains Zebra then it's Latin name should be changed accordingly. As the Quagga was described BEFORE the Plains Zebra, under the rules of Zoological Nomenclature, the Quagga's name has priority and the Plains Zebra loses the name *Equus burchelli* to become Equus quagga followed by the subspecies name; i.e. The Quagga would be *Equus quagga quagga*, and Chapman's Zebra would be *Equus quagga antiquorum*, etc. Thus another degree of confusion is added to Zebra classification.

The Quagga project came into being in the mid 1980's, and when sufficient funds had been collected the initial breeding stock was brought together in 1987/8. To start the project Plains Zebra were brought from Etosha National park and from Zululand. These animals were selected on the basis of their lack of stripes on the rear end, and their brown background colour.

Animals & Men — Issue Eight

Originally the animals were kept at Vrolijkheid, near Robertson; but they were subsequently moved to four separate sites in the Cape Town Area, where they now reside. The project is effectively in its early days, but it is progressing quite well. There are now some zebra foals that are of the second generation born into the project. Some of these foals have an appearance slightly closer to that of the Quagga than their parents; others remain more zebra like. The zebra like foals are being removed from the programme and the Quagga like foals are kept for breeding.

According to most estimates it will be something like ten to twenty-five generations before a truly Quagga like animal will be produced. It is possible that it may occur sooner; it may never occur!

Whether or not it is morally or biologically correct to try to recreate an extinct organism is debatable. Even if it was generally inappropriate to do so, the Quagga project must be as close to being acceptable as it is possible to be when the circumstances of the extinction are considered. The Quagga only went extinct, as far as we know, as a result of hunting by man. They did not die out as a result of habitat destruction, indeed some of their original habitat is still available, apparently unaltered; and would be suitable for re-introductions if Quagga were to become available again.

To replace the Quagga in some of the areas in which they originally roamed, would, on a world wide scale, be a tiny act that is unlikely to produce any ecologically negative effects. In the intellectual sense it would perhaps herald the start, in a small way at least, of an almost 'post-conservation' world, where many of the threatened species have at least had their numbers stabilised in captivity and effort is being committed to reintroductions where possible, and, where feasible, to trying to recreate other recently extinct types.

Although none of the four sites where the project zebra are kept is open to the public it is possible to view them on one site without leaving Cape Town. This is the Groot Schuur estate which is between the city and the airport. Here there is a herd of about fifteen zebra in a very large paddock together with several Bontebok and a larger herd of Black Wildebeest. Whilst it is not possible to enter the paddock it is possible to walk along the side of much of it. Cars may be parked at the Cecil Rhodes monument car park, where there is a display board giving details of the Quagga project. Behind the monument there is also a tea room which serves excellent gooseberry cheese-cake and is on the way to view the zebra.

Dr. David Barnaby and Chris Moiser visited South Africa in the summer of 1995 to view the Quagga project in progress. David Barnaby hopes to publish a book on the Quagga in 1996.

*****

EDITORIAL COMMENT: The probable re-birth of the Quagga is an exciting prospect for zoologists worldwide, but the concept of re-constituting species, whether, as in this case by selective breeding, or by use of genetic technology as in the case of the Japanese Crested Ibis is potentially revolutionary. There are persistent rumours that zoologists in the United States are carrying out experiments whereby DNA from a frozen mammoth from the Siberian permafrost has been 'injected' into a fertilised ovum from an Asiatic Elephant, with the intention of attempting to 're-constitute' the Wooly Mammoth. Whatever the truth of this rumour it seems certain that zoologists across the science will have to adjust to some revolutionary new concepts over the next century.

A MALAYAN MYSTERY MAN-BEAST
by
Clinton Keeling.

The following was told to me in March 1961, and I believe it to be perfectly true. As an introduction, I am a professional zoologist and ex-zoological garden curator who is primarily concerned with the educational side of his work, and wild animal husbandry; I've written a total of thirty-three animal books and, since the age of nine, have kept no less than seven hundred and thirty-five animal species.

In January 1961 I went to stay in the village of Kirkby Misperton in North Yorkshire as resident director at the zoological park being built there: however, I soon (correctly), detected the way it was going, and left there with no regrets at the end of the following March. In retrospect my decision to pull out was a wise one, as the place, now known as Flamingoland, has had a chequered career, to say the very least.....

During my time there I was befriended by a local family, and spent many evenings in their hospitable home. The man - perhaps I'd better not give his name, but his initials were T.B - sometimes did casual work for me, and I got to know him quite well. His whole life was bound up in the surrounding Vale of Pickering, and he had few interests outside his family, although he had served in Malaya during the Emergency in the mid 1950's, during which he had often gone out on anti-terrorist patrols. In short, he was a simple, but by no means stupid, man who I never found out to be a liar. If this latter comment sounds somewhat strange it's because I've been let down and lied to so often that long ago I arrived at the unfortunate stage whereby I trust hardly anyone, but I never found T.B out to be a liar. Note that well, as its highly relevant to this article.

Like so many Yorkshiremen T.B had an excessively soft, almost effeminate, accent and spoke in a dozy sort of way (just as a certain well-known broadcaster on gardening does), with the result that my attention sometimes wandered from what he was saying, but on this occasion I soon found myself listening intently to him. One evening he asked:

"Are tha goin' ter 'ave any Moonkeys ovvert roard?"

"Yes, definitely, as I'm particularly interested in Apes and Monkeys".

"Wooncc when Ah were in Malaya Ah nearly shot a great big Moonkey".

"Oh, yes?"

"Ar, Ah were on patrol and Ah saw what Ah thought were a bandit in t' grass, so Ah cocked me goon an' were just goin' ter shoot when it turned away an' Ah saw it were a great big Moonkey".

"Just how big?"

"About as big as him" - and he pointed to his eleven year-old son.

Now, the biggest Monkey in Malaya, by far, is the pig-tailed Macaque (*Macacus nemestrinus*), but even a

-15-

large male would have been nothing like the size of that hefty lad, so I pricked up my ears a little more intelligently.

"*What colour was it?*"

"*Like that*", and he pointed to a mid-brown cushion.

At that stage I was not even half-convinced, so I thought I'd catch him out.

"Oh yes, I know the species you mean; I cannot remember its name offhand, but it's got a long tail".

"No, definitely not, it 'addent got a tail at all, that I do remember" - he spoke with quite uncharacteristic verve for a Yorkshireman.

"I think you are mistaken there T".

"Naw, Ah tell thee it 'addent got one. Ah ought ter knaw because it'd just turned it's back on me, and Ah were surprised because Ah allus thought all Moonkeys 'ad tails".

Nothing I could say would induce him to alter his description of the creature, which of course fits no known Primate native to the Malayan mainland, but he was a most unimaginative person, who had nothing whatsoever to gain by spinning me a yarn, so since then I have often wondered what it was I am certain that he really did see.

Offhand it might be argued that it was a fair to middling description of a large female Orang Utan, but of course this species is restricted to Sumatra and Borneo, so what other explanation could there be?

For many years I was convinced he'd seen an example of the strange, if not semi-mythical, Orang Pendek ("Little Man"), but here I'm the first to admit that, again, we are talking about something that seems to be confined to Sumatra. It has been only fairly recently that I've recalled some strange events in Perak, in the early 1950's, when several reports and sightings were made of a number of Ape-like or Man-like creatures that struck such terror into some rubber-tappers who saw them that a police escort had to be provided before they agreed to return to work.

I think this was the area where T.B performed his military duties - and certainly the time of day is about right - so could this strange beast have been one of these - whatever they were, as they appeared in various places so suddenly and disappeared so completely that they were never, to my knowledge, given a name?

We'll probably never know, but one thing I'm certain of is that T.B., who now lives in retirement in Pickering, was telling the absolute truth.

******

Animals & Men   Issue Eight

A BIBLIOGRAPHY OF CRYPTOZOOLOGICAL AND ZOOMYTHOLOGICAL BOOKS
(Part Three) ZOOMYTHOLOGY

by Dr Karl P.N.Shuker and Stephen Shipp.

GENERAL ZOOMYTHOLOGY

ASHTON, John (1890), *Curious Creatures in Zoology* (John C. Nimmo: London, 1890).
BARBER, Dulan, *The Horrific World of Monsters* (Marshall Cavendish: London, 1974).
BARBER, Richard & RICHES, Anne, *A Dictionary of Fabulous Beasts* (Macmillan: London, 1971).
BARRETT, Charles, *The Bunyip and Other Mythical Monsters and Legends* (Mail Newspapers: Melbourne, 1946).
BEISNER, Monika & LURIE, Alison, *Fabulous Beasts* (Jonathan Cape: London, 1981).
BORGES, Jorge L. & GUERRERO, Margarita, *The Book of Imaginary Beings* (Jonathan Cape: London, 1970; rev. edit., Penguin: Harmondsworth, 1974).
BRIGGS, Katharine, *A Dictionary of Fairies* [U.S.A. title: *The Encyclopedia of Fairies*] (Allen Lane: London, 1976).
BYRNE, M. St Clare (Ed.), *The Elizabethan Zoo* (Frederick Etchells & Hugh MacDonald: London, 1926).
CLAIR, Colin, *Unnatural History: An Illustrated Bestiary* (Abelard-Schuman: London, 1967).
CLARK, Anne, *Beasts and Bawdy* (J.M. Dent: London, 1975).
CLEBERT, Jean-Paul, *Bestiaire Fabuleux* (Albin Michel: Paris, 1971).
COFFIN, Tristram P. (Consultant), *The Enchanted World: Magical Beasts* (Time-Life: Amsterdam, 1985).
COOPER, J.C., *Symbolic and Mythological Animals* (Aquarian Press: London, 1992).
COSTELLO, Peter, *The Magic Zoo: The Natural History of Fabulous Animals* (Sphere Books: London, 1979).
COX, Molly & ATTENBOROUGH, David, *David Attenborough's Fabulous Animals* (BBC: London, 1975).
DANCE, S. Peter, *Animal Fakes and Frauds* (Sampson Low: Maidenhead, 1976).
EPSTEIN, Perle, *Monsters: Their Histories, Homes, and Habits* (Doubleday: Garden City, 1973).
GESNER, Conrad, *Historiae Animalium* (4 vols) (Christoph Froschauer: Zurich, 1551, 1554, 1555, 1558).
GUBERNATIS, Angelo de, *Zoological Mythology: or, The Legends of Animals* (2 vols) (Trübner: London, 1872).
HAMEL, Frank, *Human Animals* (William Rider & Son: London, 1915).
HARGREAVES, Joyce, *Hargreaves New Illustrated Bestiary* (Gothic Image: (Glastonbury, 1990).
HEADON, Deidre, *Mythical Beasts* (Hutchinson: London, 1981).
HORTUS SANITATIS, *Quatuor Libris haec quae Subsequuntur Complectens* (Argentorati, 1536).
HUDSON, Noel, *An Early English Version of Hortus Sanitatis: A Recent Bibliographical Discovery by Noel Hudson* (Bernard Quaritch: London, 1954).
HULME, F. Edward, *Natural History Lore and Legend* (Bernard Quaritch: London, 1895).
IZZI, Massimo, *I Mostri e l'Immaginario* (Manilo Basia: Rome, 1982).

Animals & Men — Issue Eight

IZZI, Massimo, *Il Dizionario Illustrato dei Mostri* (Gremese Editore: Rome, 1989).
LEHNER, Ernst & LEHNER, Johanna, *A Fantastic Bestiary* (Tudor: New York, 1969).
LLOYD-JONES, H., *Mythical Beasts* (Duckworths: London, 1980).
LUM, Peter, *Fabulous Beasts* (Thames & Hudson: London, 1952).
McGOWEN, Tom, *Hamlyn Book of Legendary Creatures* (Hamlyn: London, 1982).
MILLER, Carey, *A Dictionary of Monsters and Mysterious Beasts* (Piccolo: London, 1974).
PAGE, Michael and INGPEN, Robert, *Encyclopaedia of Things That Never Were* (Lansdowne Press/Dragon's World: Limpsfield, 1985).
POVAH, Frank, *You Kids Count Your Shadows* (Privately published: Wollar, 1990).
ROBINSON, Margaret W., *Fictitious Beasts: A Bibliography* (The Library Association: London, 1961).
SMITH, Malcolm (Ed.), *Mythical and Fabulous Creatures* (Greenwood: Westport, 1987).
SOUTH, Malcolm (Ed.), *Topsell's Histories of Beasts* (Nelson-Hall: Chicago, 1981).
TOPSELL, Edward, *The Historie of Foure-Footed Beastes* (William Iaggard: London, 1607).
VINYCOMB, John, *Fictitious and Symbolic Creatures in Art* (Chapman & Hall: London, 1906).
WATKINS, M.G., *Gleanings From the Natural History of the Ancients* (Elliot Stock: London, 1885).
WHARTON, Violet, *Dragons and Fabulous Beasts* (Pavilion: London, 1994).
WHITE, T.H., *The Book of Beasts* (Jonathan Cape: London, 1954).
WYMAN, Walker D., *Mythical Creatures of the U.S.A. and Canada* (University of Wisconsin-River Falls: River Falls, 1978).

DRAGONS

ALDROVANDI, Ulisse, *Serpentum et Draconum Historiae Libri Duo* (Bononiae, 1640).
ALLEN, Judy & GRIFFITHS, Jeanne, *The Book of the Dragon* (Orbis: London, 1979).
BINYON, Laurence, *The Flight of the Dragon* (John Murray: London, 1911).
BOLSCHE, Wilhelm, *Drachen: Sagen und Naturwissenschaft* (Franckh'sche Verlagshandlung: Stuttgart, 1929).
BOSE, Hampden C. du, *The Dragon, Image and Demon* (Presbyterian Committee of Publications: Richmond, 1899).
CAMPBELL, John F., *The Celtic Dragon Myth* (John Grant: Edinburgh, 1911).
CARTER, Frederick, *The Dragon of the Alchemists* (E. Matthews: London, 1926).
COFFIN, Tristram P. (Consultant), *The Enchanted World: Dragons* (Time-Life: Amsterdam, 1984).
DICKINSON, Peter, *The Flight of Dragons* (Pierrot Publishing: London, 1979).
DIMMICK, Adrian N., *Worme Worlde: The Dragon Trivia Source Book* (The Dragon Trust: London, 1994).
DUMONT, Leon, *La Tarasque* (Abbeville, 1949).
DUMONT, Louis, *La Tarasque* (Paris: 1951).
ELLIOT-SMITH, Grafton, *The Evolution of the Dragon* (University Press: Manchester, 1919).
FOX, David, *Saint George: The Saint With Three Faces* (Kensal: Shooter's Lodge, 1983).
GOULD, Charles [SMITH, Malcolm (Ed.)], *The Dragon* (Wildwood House: London, 1977).
GREEN, Roger L. (Ed.), *A Cavalcade of Dragons* (H.Z. Walck: New York, 1970).
HARGREAVES, Joyce, *The Dragon Hunter's Handbook* (Granada: London, 1983).
HAYES, L. Newton, *The Chinese Dragon* (Commercial Press: Shanghai, 1922).
HOGARTH, Peter & CLERY, Val, *Dragons* (Allen Lane: London, 1979).
HOKE, Helen (Ed.), *Dragons, Dragons, Dragons* (Franklin Watts: New York, 1972).
HOLMAN, Felice & VALEN, Nanine, *The Drac: French Tales of Dragons and Demons* (Charles Scribner's Sons: New York, 1975).

Animals & Men — Issue Eight

HOULT, Janet, *Dragons: Their History and Symbolism* (Gothic Image: Glastonbury, 1987).
HUXLEY, Francis, *The Dragon: Nature of Spirit, Spirit of Nature* (Thames & Hudson: London, 1979).
INGERSOLL, Ernest, *Dragons and Dragon Lore* (Payson & Clarke: New York, 1928).
JOHNSGARD, Paul & JOHNSGARD, Karin, *Dragons and Unicorns: A Natural History* (St. Martin's Press: New York, 1982).
NEWMAN, Paul, *The Hill of the Dragon: An Enquiry Into the Nature of Dragon Legends* (Rowman & Littlefield: Ottowa, 1980).
PHILLIPS, Henry, *Basilisks and Cockatrices* (E. Stern: Philadelphia, 1882).
RUDD, Elizabeth (Ed.), *Dragons* (W.H. Allen: London, 1980).
SALVERTE, Eusèbe B. de, *Des Dragons et des Serpents Monstrueux qui Figurent dans un Grand Nombre de Récits Fabuleux ou Historiques* (Rignoux: Paris, 1826).
SANDERS, Tao Tao Liu, *Dragons, Gods and Spirits From Chinese Mythology* (Schocken Books: New York, 1983).
SCREETON, Paul, *The Lambton Worm and Other Northumbrian Dragon Legends* (Zodiac House: Fulham, 1978).
SHUKER, Karl P.N., *Dragons – a Natural History* (Simon & Schuster: London, 1995).
SIMPSON, Jacqueline, *British Dragons* (B.T. Batsford: London, 1980).
TOPSELL, Edward, *The Historie of Serpents* (William Iaggard: London, 1608).
TRUBSHAW, Bob, *Dragon Slaying Myths Ancient and Modern* (Heart of Albion Press: Wymeswold, 1993).
VISSER, Marinus de, *The Dragon in China and Japan* (Johannes Müller: Amsterdam, 1858).
WHITLOCK, Ralph, *Here Be Dragons* (George Allen & Unwin: London, 1983).

OTHER SPECIFIC MYTHOLOGICAL ANIMALS

BARING-GOULD, Sabine, *The Book of Werewolves* (Smith, Elder: London, 1865).
BEER, Rüdiger R., *Unicorn: Myth and Reality* (James J. Kery: London, 1977).
BENWELL, Gwen & WAUGH, Arthur, *Sea-Enchantress: The Tale of the Mermaid and Her Kin* (Hutchinson: London, 1961).
BISI, Anna M., *Il Grifone* (Universita di Roma: Rome, 1965).
BOURAS, Laskarina, *The Griffin Through the Ages* (Midland Bank: Athens, 1983).
BROWN, Robert, *The Unicorn: A Mythological Investigation* (Longmans, Green: London, 1881).
BURTON, Maurice, *Phoenix Re-born* (Hutchinson: London, 1959).
COPPER, Basil, *The Werewolf in Legend, Fact and Art* (St. Martins: New York, 1977).
DOUGLAS, Adam, *The Beast Within: A History of the Werewolf* (Chapmans: London, 1992).
EISLER, R., *Man Into Wolf* (Spring: London, 1950).
GRIFFITHS, Jeanne (Ed.), *Unicorns* (W.H. Allen: London, 1981)

HATHAWAY, B., *The Unicorn* (Penguin: Harmondsworth, 1982).
NIGG, Joe, *The Book of Gryphons* (Apple-wood: Cambridge [Mass.], 1982).
NIGG, Joe, *A Guide to the Imaginary Birds of the World* (Apple-wood: Cambridge, 1984).
O'DONNELL, Elliott, *Werwolves* (Methuen: London, 1912).
OTTEN, Charlotte (Ed.), *A Lycanthropy Reader: Werewolves in Western Culture* (Dorse Press: New York, 1986).
PHILPOTTS, Beatrice, *Mermaids* (Ballantine: New York, 1980).
POLLARD, John, *Wolves and Werewolves* (Robet Hale: London, 1964).
SHEPARD, Odell, *The Lore of the Unicorn* (George Allen & Unwin: London, 1930).
SUMMERS, Montague, *The Werewolf* (Kegan Paul, Trench, Trübner: London, 1933).
WOODWARD, Ian, *The Werewolf Delusion* (Paddington: London, 1979).

Animals & Men

Issue Eight

BIOLOGICAL CURIOSITIES AND CONTROVERSIES - A BRIEF SELECTION OF WORKS

ANON., *The Rites and Mysteries Connected With the Origin, Rise, and Development of Serpent Worship* (Reprinted by Tutor Press: Toronto, 1980).
ARMSTRONG, Edward A., *The Folklore of Birds* (Collins: London, 1958).
AYMAR, Brandt, *Treasury of Snake Lore* (Greenberg: New York, 1956).
BAKER, Robin (Ed.), *The Mystery of Migration* (Macdonald Futura: London, 1980).
BARBUK, Bernard, *Famous and Fabulous Dogs* (Peter Lowe/Eurobook: London, 1973).
BARDENS, Dennis, *Psychic Animals: An Investigation of Their Secret Powers* (Robert Hale: London, 1987).
BARLOY, Jean-Jacques, *Man and Animal* (Gordon & Cremonesi: London, 1978).
BARLOY, Jean-Jacques, *Merveilles et Mystères du Monde Animal* (2 vols) (François Beauval: Paris, 1979).
BARTHOLIN, Thomas, *De Luce Animalium* (3 vols) [Luminous animals] (Amsterdam, 1647).
BAYLESS, Raymond, *Animal Ghosts* (University Books: New York, 1970).
BERMAN, Lucy, *Famous and Fabulous Horses* (Peter Lowe/Eurobook: Wallingford, 1972).
BERMAN, Lucy, *Famous and Fabulous Cats* (Peter Lowe/Eurobook: Wallingford, 1973).
BOLTON, Brett L., *The Secret Powers of Plants* (Abacus: London, 1975).
BOUDET, Jacques, *Man and Beast: A Visual History* (The Bodley Head: London, 1964).
BOULENGER, E.G., *Animal Mysteries* (Duckworth: London, 1927).
BRAIDER, Donald, *The Life, History and Magic of the Horse* (Grosset & Dunlap: New York, 1973).
BROWN, Beth, *E.S.P. With Plants and Animals* (Simon & Schuster: New York, 1971).
BUCKLAND, Frank T., *Curiosities of Natural History* (Series 1-3) (Richard Bentley: London, 1858-1888).
BURTON, Maurice, *Curiosities of Animal Life* (Ward Lock: London, 1952).
BURTON, Maurice, *Animal Legends* (Frederick Muller: London, 1955).
BURTON, Maurice, *More Animal Legends* (Frederick Muller: London, 1959).
BURTON, Maurice, *Just Like an Animal* (J.M. Dent: London, 1978).
CANDLAND, Douglas K., *Feral Children and Clever Animals* (Oxford University Press: New York, 1993).
CLAUSEN, Lucy W., *Insect Fact and Folklore* (Macmillan: New York, 1954).
COCHRANE, Amanda & CALLEN, Karena, *Dolphins and Their Power to Heal* (Bloomsbury: London, 1992).
COLYER, Penrose, *Famous and Fabulous Animals* (Peter Lowe/Eurobook: Wallingford, 1973).
COOKE, M.C., *Freaks and Marvels of Plant Life* (Society For Promoting Christian Knowledge: London, 1880s).
CORLISS, William R., *Strange Life* (Sourcebook Project: Glen Arm, 1975).
CORLISS, William R., *Incredible Life: A Handbook of Biological Mysteries* (Sourcebook Project: Glen Arm, 1981).
CORLISS, William R., *Science Frontiers: Some Anomalies and Curiosities of Nature* (The Sourcebook Project: Glen Arm, 1994).
DALE-GREEN, Patricia, *The Cult of the Cat* (Rupert Hart-Davis: London, 1965).
DALE-GREEN, Patricia, *Dog* (Rupert Hart-Davis: London, 1966).
DIXON, Douglas, *After Man: A Zoology of the Future* (Granada: London, 1981).
DOBBS, Horace, *Dance to a Dolphin's Song* (Jonathan Cape: London, 1990).
DOBBS, Horace, *Journey Into Dolphin Dreamtime* (Jonathan Cape: London, 1992).
EMBODEN, William A., *Bizarre Plants - Magical, Monstrous, Mythical* (Studio Vista: London, 1974).
GOSSE, Philip H., *The Romance of Natural History* (James Nisbet: London, 1860).

Animals & Men
Issue Eight

GOSSE, Philip H., *The Romance of Natural History, Second Series* (Nisbet: London, 1862).
GOULD, Stephen J., *The Panda's Thumb* (W.W. Norton: New York, 1980).
GOULD, Stephen J., *Hen's Teeth and Horse's Toes* (W.W. Norton: New York, 1983).
GOULD, Stephen J., *The Flamingo's Smile* (W.W. Norton: New York, 1985).
GOULD, Stephen J., *Bully For Brontosaurus* (Hutchinson Radius: London, 1991).
GRAY, Annie, *Mammalian Hybrids: A Check-List With Bibliography* (Commonwealth Agricultural Bureaux: Farnham Royal, 1954; 2nd Edit., 1972).
GRAY, Annie, *Bird Hybrids* (Commonwealth Agricultural Bureaux: Farnham Royal, 1958).
GREENE, David, *Incredible Cats: The Secret Powers of Your Pet* (Methuen London: London, 1984).
HAINING, Peter, *The Man Who Was Frankenstein* [re Crosse's acari] (Frederick Muller: London, 1979).
HÖHN, Reinhardt, *Curiosities of the Plant Kingdom* (Cassell: London, 1980).
HOPLEY, C.C., *Snakes: Curiosities and Wonders of Serpent Life* (Griffiths & Farran: London, 1882).
HOWEY, M. Oldfield, *The Horse in Magic and Myth* (William Rider: London, 1923).
INGERSOLL, Ernest, *Birds in Legend, Fable and Folklore* (Longmans, Green: London, 1923).
KERVILLE, H.G. de, *Les Animaux et les Vegetaux Lumineux* (Paris, 1890).
KILPATRICK, Cathy, *Mysteries of Nature* (Aldus: London, 1979).
KOESTLER, Arthur, *The Case of the Midwife Toad* (Hutchinson: London, 1971).
LANE, Frank W., *Animal Parade* (Jarrolds: London, 1939; 4th edit., 1955).
LANE, Frank W., *Animal Wonderland* (Country Life: London, 1948; rev. edit., Oliver & Boyd: London, 1962).
LEHANE, Brendan, *The Power of Plants* (John Murray/McGraw-Hill: London, 1977).
LOYD, Lewis R.W., *Bird Facts and Fallacies* (Hutchinson: London, 1927).
MERY, Fernand, *The Life, History and Magic of the Cat* (Paul Hamlyn: London, 1967).
MÉRY, Fernand, *The Life, History and Magic of the Dog* (Grosset & Dunlap: New York, 1970).
MICHELL, John & RICKARD, Robert J.M., *Living Wonders: Mysteries and Curiosities of the Animal World* (Thames & Hudson: London, 1982).
MORGAN, Elaine, *The Aquatic Ape* (Souvenir Press: London, 1982).
'MORUS' [LEWINSOHN, Richard], *Animals, Men and Myths* (Victor Gollancz: London, 1954).
MORRIS, Ramona & MORRIS, Desmond, *Men and Snakes* (Hutchinson: London, 1965).
MUNDKUR, B., *The Cult of the Serpent* (State University of New York: New York, 1983).
NEWALL, Venetia, *Discovering the Folklore of Birds and Beasts* (Shire: Tring, 1971).
O'DONNELL, Elliott, *Animal Ghosts* (William Rider: London, 1913).
OLIVER, James A., *Snakes in Fact and Fiction* (Macmillan: New York, 1958).
PARKER, Eric, *Oddities of Natural History* (Seeley, Service: London, 1943).
RETALLACK, Dorothy, *The Sound of Music and Plants* (De Vorss: Santa Monica, 1973).
ROWDON, Maurice, *The Talking Dogs* (Macmillan London: London, 1978).
ROWLAND, Beryl, *Animals With Human Faces: A Guide to Animal Symbolism* (George Allen & Unwin: London, 1974).
SAUNDERS, Nicholas J., *The Cult of the Cat* (Thames & Hudson: London, 1991).
SAUNDERS, Nicholas J., *Animal Spirits* (Macmillan/Duncan Baird: London, 1995).
SCHUL, Bill, *The Psychic Power of Animals* (Fawcett: Greenwich [Conn.], 1977).

...Continued on page 30

MORT SAYS HE WROTE THIS BUT WE CAN'T PROVE IT!

by Mort (or so we are lead to believe)

Proof. What is it about proof that sends people into such a frenzy? Their constant search for it, and the consequences when it is obtained to their satisfaction never cease to amaze. proof cannot be had...allow me to demonstrate.

In recent issues of 'Animals & Men' much has been made of the unreliability of eye-witness evidence. Why? Surely this is a case of stating the obvious. Why stop at eyewitness evidence? Surely almost all evidence is unreliable.

If I was to state that I had seen our esteemed editor on TV you either believe me or you don't. I could produce a photograph of the screen, but lets face it, it could be an elaborate hoax. I could go the whole hog and provide you with a video of the programme together with a video of me watching it, but the cynics amongst you could, no doubt, provide a fiendishly complicated explanation as to how I could have faked it.

What the whole thing boils down to is this. The only person who knows whether I saw Jon on the TV is me. As it happens I did (nice hat Jon). Obviously all the above applies to unknown animals.

Having dealt with the witness side of it - bring on a corpse! If a corpse was found, what has actually been proved? Say, for example, the body of a marine elephant was washed up on the shores of Loch Ness. The papers would all go mad with the story and the identity of the Loch Ness Monster would have been proved for them, and for the vast majority of their readers .... but has it? All that has been proved, if we are to accept that nobody fabricated the elephants adaptations and then dumped it, is that a marine elephant died in Loch Ness.

Reading this back, it makes me sound like a Fortean. I'm not. When it comes to my area of cryptozoology, (lake monsters, sea serpents and dinosaur survivals), I'm a believer. what I'm trying to say is that we shouldn't become tied down by trying to accomplish the impossible. Unless, in the case of Loch Ness, for example, we can follow every single 'monster' with a camera and eyewitnesses, twenty-four hours a day for some time, nothing is proved.

None of the above is saying that you shouldn't filter evidence. I, for example, don't regard any of Frank Searles' photographs as useful, but I can't prove that they don't show the Loch Ness Monster. The only person who knows for certain is Frank!

In the end, however, it basically comes down to belief. You either do or you don't. Life is a lot more interesting WITH these creatures around, so stop trying to prove it and have a little faith!

Cryptocetology: The Page 254 Story.
Part Two in a series of articles on Mystery Whales by Darren Naish.

(Having given a general introduction to cryptocetology in a previous issue of Animals & Men [1], I here concentrate on a single event. It could serve as a case study giving a wider view of diversity among the Cetacea while also demonstrating their prominence in modern cryptozoology, hopefully expanding the notions I propounded in my first article. certainly, there can be no turning back.....)

This is the story of Scott's mystery dolphin: an animal I found in a book. Before going on any further, I must introduce the man to whom we owe this mystery. Sir Peter Scott.

Sir Peter was born in 1909, the son of the famed Antarctic explorer, and early on developed an interest in natural history [2]. Fortunately gifted with an artistic ability, he became increasingly skilled at painting and drawing animal subjects. By 1933 he was exhibiting his work. Scott's passion was birds and, judging from his paintings and later conservation work, waterfowl were especially close to his heart. Scott was, however, a student of all Nature and in the course of his life became closely involved with probably every group of living organisms. In 1946, after war-time service, he founded the Slimbridge Wildfowl and Wetlands Trust (then just the Wildfowl Trust), and later expanded it to incorporate six centres in England and one in Scotland. Scott's conservation work is also marked by his role as co-founder of the Worldwide Fund for Nature (then the World Wildlife Fund) in 1961. He was responsible for designing their Panda logo [3], [4]. Sir Peter was also influential in a great many other conservational bodies. He travelled all over the world, starting officially in 1956, and in 1983 and 1985 published his travel diaries [5], [6]. These provide a stunning visual record of the places and the living things he saw around the world (it is one of these living things that we are interested in).

He created hundreds of stunning wildlife paintings, even providing illustrations for a Brooke Bond picture card series.(3).

(Editors Note: For readers outside the UK, I should explain that Brook Bond are a company who sell packaged tea and tea bags, and for many years they have given away collectors cards, similar to Bubblegum Cards, as an incentive for potential purchasers of their products. Many of these sets featured animals and plants, and were avidly collected by young naturalists during the 1960's and 1970's. Some of these sets of cards are now very collectible).

A special point of interest to Cryptozoologists is that Sir Peter was a firm believer in the Loch Ness Monster [7]. He made several graphic versions of what he believed the Loch Ness Monster looked like [8], and, in 1975, teamed up with Robert Rhines to name it *Nessiteras rhombopteryx* [9]. (Incidentally, also on a cryptozoological note, he believed that a large chameleon he kept at Slimbridge, informally referred to as 'The Oldeani Monster', represented a new species for which he suggested the name *Chamaeleo oldeanii* [5],). Scott achieved more than probably any other conservationist in history, and anyone who gains any enjoyment from the natural world should hold the greatest reverence for him. Sadly in 1990, the year after his 80th birthday, he died.

Animals & Men — Issue Eight

Less than two years ago, I began a private 'study' of whales and dolphins, basically to familiarise myself with their appearances in preparation for possible field sightings. Obtaining the available literature, and paying particular attention to how well illustrations matched available photographs, I learned morphologies, colours, markings and the respective names of the seventy six (or so) species.

Scott's renditions of things natural are works of great panache and accuracy. I adore his crisp, colourful style. As he painted creatures from the field as accurately as I can imagine, I chose a couple of books he wrote and illustrated so that I could examine his renditions of cetaceans, plus, in any case, I like looking at his paintings. Two books I found were the two volumes of *'Travel Diaries of a Naturalist'*. [5] [6].

In these volumes Scott records and illustrates a number of cetaceans he encountered on his voyages, and there, on page 254, was an illustration featuring a dolphin species completely unrecognisable to me - because, I hasten to add, the species was not one officially recognised! This animal then, is the subject of this article and it is my purpose here to attempt to identify it satisfactorily. Before we can begin to consider other possibilities, let us see what Scott himself had to say about it.

Fig. 1. The two dolphin species seen by Peter Scott in the Magellan Straits: the mysterious 'white bellied dolphin' (above) and the Piebald Dolphin. In the original painting, a second 'white belly' is illustrated behind the first and five more Piebalds can be seen further away still. Adult Piebalds measure between 1.3 and 1.7 metres: by comparing the two species in the painting we can see that the two 'white bellies' are not much bigger. (Illustration by the author after Scott [5].).

Scott's caption to the illustration reads:

'Two unidentified dolphins, possibly the White-bellied, (Cephalorhynchus albiventris), riding the Navarino's stern wave'.

Seen on the fourth of February 1968, they were actually amongst a largeool of Piebald dolphins (*C. commersoni*) [10], - one of these being the other individual pictured in Fig.1 - and, whilst the Piebalds got quite some description in the narrative, the only mention of the 'mystery' dolphins in the text is '...at one stage two of a different kind came in - rather brownish with white belly only'.

PROCESSES OF ELIMINATION.

Before saying anything else about the 'mystery' dolphins ('M' from now on), I think that we must first consider the identity that Scott himself forwarded; that of the 'White-bellied dolphin'.

THE WHITE BELLIED DOLPHIN.

I ran into serious research problems at this point. Exactly what a 'white-bellied' dolphin is turned out to be quite a problem - this name had been used for at least five completely different dolphin species (amongst whom white bellies are common!). However, Scott narrowed down the particular type of 'white belly' he was talking about by assigning it the scientific name of *Cephalorhynchus albiventris*.

This name, created by either Perez Canto or Rudolph Philippi between 1893 and 1896 [11], though, at the time, they thought that the animal belonged to the porpoise genus *Phocaena*), has since been sunk into that of the Chilean dolphin (*C. eutropia*), a species first named by Gray in 1846. Therefore, this species is the one that Scott thought he was dealing with. But, with only this cryptic illustration to bear him out, could he have been right in the identification?

'M' AS CHILEAN DOLPHIN.

Fig. Two is an illustration of the Chilean Dolphin. As is uniform throughout the four Cephalorhynchus species, its head is quite blunt and the beak is not sharply demarcated from the forehead. The dorsal fin ..."*is very low, backward leaning and with a blunt apex*" [11]. It is a small dolphin, averaging 1.2 m and 45 kg, described as pure black (but with three white patches beneath the throat, behind the flippers and around the anus); confusingly, however, in 1972, Japanese cetologist Masharu Nishiwaki described it as 'generally grey'.

This description of colour is not consistent with other texts - indeed - some authors have elected to call it the 'Black Dolphin'! Anyhow, virtually nothing is known about this species. Except, of course, that it is found around the Chilean coast and, as far as is known, nowhere else.

Fig. 2. The Chilean Dolphin *(Cephalorhynchus eutropia)*. This depiction is probably less than 90% accurate; all the illustrations I have seen feature markedly different animals! Furthermore, no good photos have yet been published. Picture by the author based on Ritchie [11], Camm [12], and Camm [13].

Given the known details of the Chilean dolphin ('C' from now on), I am not convinced that 'M' represents the same animal. Scott described, (and painted), 'M' as 'rather brownish'. 'C' is pure black. Whilst this may seem somewhat niggling, Scott recorded, (and painted), the black markings on the accompanying piebalds as simply 'black', yet 'C' and the piebalds are the same kind of black, and I would argue that the shade of blackness in the markings of the two cannot be distinguished in the field. Possibly, therefore, Scott was recording the definite hue of 'M', therefore proving it different from 'C'. Scott also gave 'M' white lower jaws, which do not occur in 'C', and an unbroken, white underside extending from the lower jaw to beneath the tailstock, which again does not occur in 'C'. Two other features, but this time of morphology rather than pigmentation, are not consistent with an identity of 'C' for 'M'.

First is the shape of the head which, in Scott's painting isnot comparable with that of any *Cephalorhynchus*, being long-beaked, fairly low and with a high degree of demarcation between beak and forehead. Scott illustrates the head of the Piebald Dolphin quite correctly and, if 'M' were really depicting 'C', then we would expect it to have almost exactly the same shape of head as do Scott's Piebalds. As it does not, my doubts are raised.

The second morphological feature is the dorsal fin. We have already seen how, in 'C' this is a low-lying, backward-pointing structure with a blunt apex, (described in ref. 13 as 'rounded'). 'M', however, has a moderately high, somewhat pointed dorsal fin that does not really compare to the previously given description.

THE BOTTLENOSE DOLPHIN.

The Bottlenose *(Tursiops truncatus)*, was the only species (without other immediate non-qualifying features), that compared at all well with these morphological features. However, it can be eliminated as a candidate because, as far as I know, there have been no bottlenoses reported with bright, white undersides. (Actually, bottlenoses with white undersides are known, but the white grades up into the darker body colour - it is not sharply demarcated from it as in 'M'). Likewise, though the dorsal fin of 'M' resembles the tall, pointed fin of a bottlenose more than it does that of 'C', it is not really that much like a bottlenose fin, which always has a sickle-like curve. Also, the average length of a bottlenose is about 3m, which is more than twice the average length of 'M' (its length is suggested by comparison with the Piebalds in the illustration - they are abut 1.5 metres long and 'M' appears only slightly larger). Bottlenoses, I believe, can therefore definitely be eliminated as possible candidates for 'M'.

WAS SCOTT TOTALLY ACCURATE?

Up till now, I have been assuming one aspect without question and that is the degree of accuracy of Scott's painting. Clearly, 'M' does not match any known dolphin species in either morphology or pigmentation and this, in view of Scott's super-accurate renditions elsewhere, lean towards the conclusion that he saw and painted a dolphin species as yet unknown to science.

However, the paintings Scott is so famous for being meticulously detailed and accurate with are those of birds, the animals he had the closest ties with in his work. Having praised Scott's attention to detail and accuracy it seems that Scott might not have been as accurate with cetaceans as he was with birds. Could analysis of his illustrations provide any answers to the enigma?

ASSESSING ACCURACY OF CETACEANS IN ILLUSTRATIONS.

Cetaceans have never been illustrated well, mostly because they are creatures almost permanently submerged. Many are extremely rare and/or poorly known, and many famous illustrations are based entirely on dead, faded specimens. For these reasons, cetaceans as illustrated are, generally, dreadfully inaccurate. It is only with recent advances in underwater photography that the true life appearances of many species have become, or are becoming known. It is clear nowadays, for example, that rorquals are sleek and streamlined. Prior to the 1970's, however, this was not really acknowledged and rorquals were illustrated as heavy throated, chunky creatures. Scott, who illustrated during this period, therefore made the same forgivable errors as any other artist depicting a cetacean. Other errors are unique to the individual, and, as does anyone, Scott made these too. In all, I found 35 graphic renditions of cetaceans made by Scott between the years 1956 and 1968, depicting 23 different species ('M' not being included incidentally), and, in an attempt to assess the likelihood of 'M' being an inaccurate painting, classified all renditions in terms of their accuracy.

'Accuracy' is a very relative concept but was here determined on two simple factors: depiction of gross morphology (shape of body and extremities) and of pigmentation (distribution of colour on body, and colours used in depiction). Where either was deemed lifelike, it was rated "1", where not it was rated "0". 'True' life appearance of species concerned was based on comparison of various photos of species in life, with as little reference to other artists renditions as possible. For reasons of space, the table that resulted is not reproduced here, but what did the results indicate?

RESULTS OF ACCURACY 'ASSESSMENT'.

Of the twenty-three species illustrated by Scott (therefore eliciting forty-six separate accuracy assessments), only six of the assessments deserved a "0": none of the species illustrated were deemed inaccurate in both morphology AND pigmentation. Also, only two of the six inaccuracies were deemed 'major' (discussed below in 'What to conclude?'). By my criteria, therefore, Scott was practically 87% accurate in his cetacean renditions: a most illustrious achievement.

WHAT TO CONCLUDE?

However, in that this assessment provides overall judgement, it might be misleading in what it tells us about the validity of 'M'. Particularly telling in this regard are Scott's renditions of Hourglass dolphins (*Lagenorhynchus cruciger*) (see Fig. 3). These illustrations scored "1" on pigmentation, but "0" on morphology as can be seen by the more accurate Hourglass dolphin depicted below Scott's rendition. In this instance Scott was quite inaccurate. Despite his OVERALL excellence in the illustrations, Scott did make notable errors. The validity of 'M', must therefore, remain suspect.

Fig. 3. 3a. An Hourglass dolphin (*Lagenorhynchus cruciger*) as painted by Scott in 1968. Compare this with 3b, an accurate rendition of the same species. (3a from [5], 3b after a photograph in [12]. Pictures by the author).

Other authors appear to have reached this conclusion and subsequently considered 'M' to represent inaccurately depicted Chilean dolphins (though no-one, to my knowledge, has considered the problem posed by 'M' in the depth presented here). For example, Jean-Pierre Sylvestre [14], in his entry on 'C', includes what sounds suspiciously like Scott's sighting. Others have remarked on recorded instances of Chilean and Piebald dolphins seen together, and I wonder if they were considering Scott's sighting when they wrote these remarks.

I am in two minds about this whole issue, given the dual nature of the evidence presented in this article. Ultimately, the only way of resolving the issue would be to interview those present with Sir Peter at the time of the sighting, sadly an option not available to me due to financial and time restraints. Until then, we are left with an open-ended mystery and a possible new species of the dolphin family left in limbo.

REFERENCES AND NOTES.

1. NAISH, D.W. *An Introduction to Cryptocetology* ('Animals & Men' # 7, October 1995).
2. SCOTT, Sir P. 1986. *Observations of Wildlife.* Phaidon (Oxford).
3. SCOTT, Sir P. (Undated) *Wildlife in Danger.* Brooke Bond Picture Cards.
4. ALLEN, R. 1989. *The Man with the window.* ('BBC Wildlife' 7 (9) 582-5.
5. SCOTT, Sir P. 1983. *Travel Diaries of a Naturalist I.* Collins (London).
6. SCOTT, Sir P. 1985. *Travel Diaries of a Naturalist II.* Collins (London).
7. ANON. 1982. *The Unfortunate Anagram.* In CALKINS, C.C. (project editor) *Mysteries of the Unexplained.* The Readers Digest Assoc. p.67.
8. Sir Peter created a fine painting of Nessie, presently on display at Torosay Castle on the Isle of Mull, home of David Guthrie-James. A reproduction can be seen on the back cover of RICKARD, R.J.M. *Unexplained Mysteries of the World!* Brook Bond Oxo Ltd. Other Scott 'Nessies' can be seen in refs [2] and [9].
9. SCOTT, Sir P. and RHINES, R. (1975). *Naming the Loch Ness Monster.* ('Nature' 258: 466-468).
10. Common names used here follow those of ref [11].
11. WATSON, L. (1988). *Whales of the World.* (London, Hutchinson).
12. MAY, J (ed) 1990. *The Greenpeace book of Dolphins.* Century (London).
13. CARWARDINE, M. 1995. *Eyewitness Handbooks: Whales, Dolphins and Porpoises.* Dorling-Kindersley (London).
14. SYLVESTRE, J-P. 1993. *Dolphins and Porpoises: A Worldwide Guide.* Sterling (New York).

animals&men

THE JOURNAL OF THE CENTRE FOR FORTEAN ZOOLOGY

Animals & Men

Issue Eight

COMPLETE BIBLIOGRAPHY...Continued from page 21

SHARP, Harold, *Animals in the Spirit World* (Spiritualist Association of Great Britain: London, 1966).
SHUKER, Karl P.N. (Consultant), *Secrets of the Natural World* (Reader's Digest: Pleasantville, 1993).
SKINNER, Bob, *Toad in the Hole: Source Material on the Entombed Toad Phenomenon* [Fortean Times Occasional Paper No. 2] (Fortean Times: London, 1986).
STEIGER, Brad & STEIGER, Sherry H., *Strange Powers of Pets* (Headline: London, 1993).
STORER, Doug, *Amazing But True Animals* (Gold Medal: Greenwich [Conn.], 1963).
THOMPSON, C.J.S., *The Mystic Mandrake* (Rider: London, 1934).

TOMPKINS, Peter & BIRD, Christopher, *The Secret Life of Plants* (Harper & Row: New York, 1973; rev. edit., Allen Lane: London, 1974).
TRIBUTSCH, Helmut, *When the Snakes Awake: Animals and Earthquake Prediction* (Massachusetts Institute of Technology: Cambridge [Mass.], 1982).
WATSON, Lyall, *Earthworks* (Hodder & Stoughton: London, 1986).
WHITMAN, John, *The Psychic Power of Plants* (Star: London, 1975).
WOOD, Gerald L., *The Guinness Book of Animal Facts and Feats* (Guinness Superlatives: Enfield: 1972; 3rd edit., 1982).
WOOTTON, Anthony, *Animal Folklore, Myths and Legend* (Blandford: Poole, 1986).
WYLDER, Joseph, *Psychic Pets: The Secret World of Animals* (J.M Dent: London, 1980).

* * * * * * * * * * * *

New and Rediscovered species in Devonshire

by David Bolton

On the trails of snails

Perhaps you have already sensed an undercurrent of excitement going the country rounds, thro' woods, across fields and moor, communicating down the super-highways of hedgerows. The clamouring of rook parliaments have been in extra session whilst the larks have been exalting the news from on high. Murmurings of starlings sussurate with gossip. Something has happened. Not more Royal scandal, nor a pop-star's peccadillo, but events of a completely different magnitude. Now the truth behind the rumours can finally be told. Its official. The secret of 10,000 years can at last be revealed - Spermodea lamellata is alive and well and residing in North Devon!!

'What', I can imagine you saying, 'is *Spermodea lamellata* when its about, in Devon or anywhere else?' and 'Why all the excitement?'.

Well, it's a small snail and it has never before been found alive in the south-west peninsula. The plated or plaited snail is about 2mm high and the same broad. Shaped a little like a straw bee skep, its shell bears an ornamentation of raised ribs or lamallae that makes it immediately distinctive and imparts a beautiful iridescent sheen, alas, only appreciated with the aid of magnifying lens or microscope.

Geoff Musker, a volunteer working with Museum staff on a survey of the land and freshwater mollusca of Devon, had the good fortune to find a few of these delightful snails whilst sorting samples of leaf-litter and vegetation debris collected from the edge of Exmoor. *Spermodea lamellata* has been recorded from Devon before, but only as fossils from the limestone caves of South-Devon. These Flandrian fossils probably lived in a cooler climate than today's, as the effects of the previous glaciation were wearing off. Essentially a species of northern Britain, with a few relict outposts in the Weald, they normally live in ancient woodland. The relatively recent upsurge of interest in detailed recording of the distributions of our flora and fauna has resulted in several recent finds across the other side of the Bristol Channel. This led to Dr. Michael Kerney, recorder for the National Mollusc recording Scheme, to suggest that we might yet find it surviving in Devon.

Happily we can report this to be the case.

If you can take just a bit more excitement, we can report another mollusc find which in its way is equally intriguing and perhaps a telling reflection on the dedication of Victorian naturalists. On the 23rd of September 1994, A fresh-water snail, *Gyraulus laevis*, the Smooth Ram's-horn Snail, was re-discovered in Devon after a gap of 144 years. Molluscs were a popular group for Victorian collectors though the large and showy marine species were frequently preferred since they were more aesthetically pleasing to the untutored eye. There was a thriving interest in all forms of natural history and the building of collections was an important part of this phase. For completeness sake many collectors swapped or exchanged specimens and even bought them. It was thus that on the 21st November 1884, J.W.Taylor, THE Victorian mollusc expert authenticated the record in Canon A.M.Norman's collection of *Planorbis glaber* (the old name for *G.laevis* - from Totnes, collected by Miss Bolton in 1850. So, it was purely fortuitous, that with Geoff, I visited the old leat which comes off the River Dart at Totnes. Eight years ago I had noticed the presence of the Curled Pond-weed *Potamogeton crispus*, which I have now come to associate with relatively rich frsh-water mollusc communities.

Armed with a sampling net, I found that the channel, previously dominated by this pond weed, is now choked with the Canadian Pond-Weed, *Elodea canadensis* and Beautiful Water Starwort, *Callitriche cf hamulata*. The associated mollusc fauna was not exceptional save in the presence of a large Pea-mussel, *Pisidium amnicum*, which until that day, had previously been found only in the lower Exe and Clyst catchments. Whatever these finds contribute towards our understanding of our national faunal distributions, it clearly demonstrates the diversity of wildlife to be found in Devon. It also shows the tremendous contributions made by past workers, and the value of voucher specimens in old collections, and hints at the undiscovered potential for even the most basic natural science research.

Barber's many linked chain.

With the Schengen agreement, allowing citizens of a number of European countries free movement across national borders, but a few days in operation, we can report upon a hitherto unrecognised invasion of our island nation by residents of the Haute Maritime area of France, remarkable for their exaggerated reputation for possessing a thousand legs apiece. Apparently uninvited, but possibly assisted by UK residents holidaying abroad, these diminutive immigrants have somehow evaded customs controls and phytosanitation to establish a transit camp in a pleasant corner of Plymouth's Central Park. A rapid breeding cycle has resulted in a strong presence and the new residents are now spreading to new areas of the city.

Although the setting of the new population centre is within pleasant park-land, the conditions in which the new residents are surviving are far from salubrious, indeed they border upon our own concepts of festering, beridden by fungi and bacteria. But, although they must seek their shelter under stones, bricks, or even jettisoned plastic bags and the typical rubbish of western civilisations, they appear to be healthy and prolific. We should give them a warm welcome as they are assisting the local residents to recycle both natural plant products but also the deposits of various pets.

Who are these newcomers? The recording team at the Royal Albert Memorial Museum (RAMM) in Exeter, have just received news of their positive identification from Dick Jones of the British Myriapod Group, as *Polydesmus barberii*, a millipede. They are new members of a growing band of immigrant species to the South-West, joining plants and animals from around the world. Each newcomer must find a niche in which it can successfully compete, against natives or other introductions, according to its preferences. *Polydesmus barberii* finds itself in competition with the likes of the Pale Worm-slug, *Boetgerilla pallens*, first recorded in the south-west in 1981 and of eastern European descent; Puny Toltecium snails, purportedly from the Mediterranean via new-Zealand, first south-west records made in 1989, but undoubtedly resident for some time before that date. Also from New-Zealand and resident for many generations, *Talitroides dorrieni*, the Woodhopper. *P.barberri* may well feel at home with the Girdled Snail, *Hygromia cinctella* from central and southern France, well established and spreading rapidly after 44 years residence, and its close relative, the Hedge Snail, *Hygromia limbata*, established since 1917. But how much foreignness does the garden snail impart, after perhaps 2,000 years, unless you eat it with garlic butter.

These are just a few of the thousands of recognised alien species which have made the successful transition from continental to island dwellers. There are potentially thousands of others which have received assisted passage, some to fail the test of survival through lack of a suitable niche, or an inclement climate, some to become the scourge of agriculture like the Keeled slug, *Miles sowerbyi*, bane of the potato growers, or the New-Zealand Flatworm, whose impact upon the fertility of the soil through its reportedly prodigious appetite for earthworms, we can at this stage only conjecture. Time alone will tell, but it is only by regular observation and monitoring that we can hope to keep apace with a rapidly developing, cosmopolitan flora and fauna.

*****

EDITORIAL NOTE: These two articles were originally commissioned for inclusion in the 1996 Yearbook. A combination of events, especially lack of time, lack of space and computer error, meant that it was not included and had to be held over to this issue. Our apologies to David Bolton, of the Royal Albert Memorial Museum, in Exeter (Natural History Section) for the delay.

A GREEN PIECE.

In the weeks immediately preceding the Christmas Holiday I received a number of startling submissions and pieces of information. It all started when just after nine one morning the telephone rang. I picked up the receiver to be greeted with the dulcet tones of an old cryptozoological pal.."*This is Eric from Denmark here...have you heard about the green cat?*". Of course, I hadn't. I don't take a daily paper, and my news input comes from the Teletext and from letters and 'phone calls from colleagues and friends across the globe. Eric promised me an article and a few days later it arrived together with the most extraordinary photograph of an unbearably cute, olive green kitten with the most verdantly green underparts I have ever seen on any animal, except possibly a Chinese Bamboo Snake. As we print in black and white I decided to regretfully forego the privilege of paying an exorbitant sum of money for the rights to print the picture, and therefore I ask you just to accept my word that the animal was totally extraordinary in appearance.

I mentioned this fantastic felid to Karl Shuker, who bowled me over by saying that he, in fact, had a file on anomalous green creatures, and mentioned a 1979 paper by R.A.LEWIN and P.T.ROBINSON (Nature 278 (March 29): 445-447). This discussed the peculiar greening of polar bears in several zoos across the world. These were eventually found to be due to an unlikely algae infestation.

A few days later, Richard Muirhead came to visit. He too had a tale to tell. This time it was a dog, and once again, in the words of a reasonably well known Manchester Beat Combo called 'New Order', *"Everything's gone Green!"* Richard sent me a story as well, and it seems logical to present them here, together,,

A TRUE STORY OF A GREEN DOG

by Richard Muirhead.

In January 1987 I, your roving Wiltshire correspondent saw a green dog! Yes, I was sober! No, I was not hallucinating.!

Fortunately I was living close to where the dog was born, so I was able to see for myself that yes, indeed, a peppermint-green coloured puppy had been born sometime around the 24th January 1987. I took a photograph of the dog, indoors, but it didn't come out! Now, doesn't that sound familiar?

The dog was one of a litter of nine puppies born to a three year old Labrador x Collie bitch. Four of them were black, four of them golden, and the ninth light green. Judging from the appearance of the green dog in the photograph printed in the local newspaper the dog itself looked rather feeble and forlorn but I would not necessarily suggest that its feebleness and unusual colour were necessarily related. Unfortunately this photograph, which appeared in the Middleseborough Evening Gazette on January 29th 1987, was in black and white!

The owner of this dog, Joyce Morris said *"we are not sure which dog fathered the pups, but I am certain that it wasn't green!"*. This is certainly a comforting thought for residents of Middlesborough, because by now, nine years would presumably be overwhelmed with green dogs!

Officialdom, in the form of a vet put the greenness down to 'Utera verdi' in the mother's womb. This is a thick, dark green substance which can, apparently stain things it touches. Why, however was only one puppy affected? If 'Utera Verdi' exists why do we hardly ever hear of light, or even dark green dogs? Unless, of course 'Utera Verdi' is particularly rare.

The official source said that the stain would wear off as the dog grew up. This, I find more plausible. I have not, however been able to follow this story up more recently.

Two final thoughts:

Why are there so few naturally green mammals?

and

Is it merely a coincidence that the Chernobyl disaster took place only nine months before the peppermint pub was born?

REFERENCE,

1. Middlesborough Evening Gazette. January 29th 1987.

A GREEN KITTEN
by ERIC SORENSEN

A Zoological sensation just could be on its way from Denmark, as a green (yes) kitten was found on a hayloft. Experts are puzzled as the cat's fur and claws are as green as a copper roof.

Her owner, Pia Bischoff, for many years a breeder of Persian Cats, was wildly surprised and is now talking care of the green wonder, naturally called Miss Greeny, watching its development. The kitten's mother was a tail-less Manx Cat, that had previously only given birth to one (tailed) kitten.

Knud Steensborg, a veterinarian from Bruband has declared the cat totally healthy. Hair samples are currently being investigated. If Miss Greeny keeps her colour, Pia Bischoff will be exhibiting it around the country hoping to start a new breed.

This raises many questions. Jyllandsposten, the newspaper which carried the story, is a serious publication, and has not fabricated this story for a laugh. The cat has even been on television. It has been theorised that it suffers from copper poisoning, but it looks too healthy! The only green mammal that I know of is the sloth, which in the wild has green algae in its fur, but after all we have green reptiles and birds, why shouldn't a green cat evolve? Or is it, perhaps a regression or an atavism? Time will tell.

EDITORS NOTE: The story broke in England in the Daily Mail a week or so later. they speculated that the kitten might have been suffering from an unspecified metabolic disorder, but as Eric says, it looks too healthy for that....

THE A-Z OF CRYPTOZOOLOGY
Part 6

by Jan Williams.

(The latest installment of the series in which our intrepid Newsfile Editor attempts the Herculean task of listing all the animals of interest to cryptozoologist in alphabetical order. C is for Catfish - (snigger) Ed.)

CHIPEKWE

Beast of Lake Bangwelu, Zambia. Quoting native reports in 1933, J.E.Hughes described the Chipekwe as having a smooth, dark, body and a single horn fixed like that of a rhinoceros.

CHUCHUNAA

Name used in Yakut language for remnant hominids of north-eastern Siberia.

COCKATRICE

Creature which in the Middle Ages was believed to be a four legged cock with a crown, thorny pinions and a tail which ended in a hook. When the church at Renwick in Cumbria was demolished in 1733, a 'cockatrice' flew out from the foundations and attacked the workmen. It was destroyed with the branch of a rowan tree, but a huge, black, bird-like creature was still being reported flying around Renwick in the 1960's. In the 15th century a 'cockatrice' was sometimes served at banquets. The dish was prepared by cutting a capon and a suckling pig in half, and sewing the front part of the chicken onto the back part of the pig.

COJE YA MENIA

Water Lion of eastern Angola. Hippo-killing, semi aquatic beast, with large canine teeth or tusks. Tracks resemble those of an elephant, but contain the impression of toes.

COROMANDEL MAN.

Man-Beast reported from Coromandel peninsula, east of Auckland, North Island, New Zealand.

CU SITH

Scottish Highland fairy dog. Described as the size of a two year old heifer, sometimes white, but usually green, with tails flat and plaited, or curled over their backs. Legend states they always bay three times - loudly enough to be heard by sailors out at sea. One is supposed to haunt the B9008 in Glenlivet forest, Banffshire.

DAEDELUS SEA SERPENT

Captain Peter M'Quhae gave a detailed account of a 60 foot serpent witnessed by the crew of HMS Daedelus in 1848. The creature had a diameter of 15-16 inches, and was dark brown in colour with yellowish white about the throat. It had no fins, but *something like the mane of a horse, or rather a bunch of seaweed washed about its back*.

DARD

Folkloric creature of Austria. A four-legged serpent with the head of a cat, and a mane along its spine.

DI-DI

Wildman of Venezuela and Guyana. Described as short, thick-set, and powerful with reddish-brown fur, and said to live in pairs. (EDITORS NOTE: It has also been suggested that this animal and Ameranthropoides loysii (q.v) are one and the same).

DINGONEK

Aquatic beast of Kenya. Said to be 14-15 feet long, with scale-covered body, and long, broad, tail. Other characteristics include leopard-like spots, and two long fangs in the upper jaw.

DOGLA

Indian native name for large cat which they believe is a hybrid between tiger and leopard.

DOVER DEMON

Four-foot tall entity with huge head and thin, monkey-like body, seen in Dover, Massachusetts, U.S.A in 1977. It had large, shiny orange eyes, long toes and fingers, and a rough, hairless, peach-coloured skin.

DZU-TEH

Huge ape-man of Tibet and northern China. Taller and bulkier than a human, with dark shaggy coat, flat head, and long, powerful arms. Footprints show two pads on the first toe, which points away from the others.

LETTERS PAGE

POSSIBLY THE BEST PIECE OF ADVICE THE EDITOR EVER RECEIVED FROM HIS FATHER! THANX DAD!

WHALE OF A TIME.

(The 'CFZ Yearbook 1996' includes a fascinating article about the Scottish Whaling Industry, that we commissioned from our Scottish Correspondent. With typical bad synchronicity, he sent us a letter containing a few more horrifying facts a few weeks after we had gone to press...)

Dear Jonathan,

Just a few jottings from Smith's book, a lot of which has a local slant, dialect folk songs, etc.

* Rorquals, which included Humpbacks, Finbacks, Blues and Sei Whales, the latter too fast to take until the advent of the Bomb Harpoon by the 'saintly' Svend Foyn were named from the Norwegian 'Royrkval' meaning 'Whale with pleats', referring to its body ridges.

* The aforementioned Scandinavian also devised the Inflation Lance, through which air was pumped to raise the corpse to the surface. The whalers thought it acceptable to cut the whale's eardrum and keep it on the sideboard to 'listen to the sea', as we would a sea shell. However, they thought it barbaric when the Innuit would stand over the body of a whale and catch the diving Fulmars by biting off their heads. Whalemeat tasted like horse-flesh, you hung it 'till it turned black when the oil drips out. Then it was ready. Yum Yum!

* The crew was paid 1s 3d per ton, Fin Whales worked out at one ton per foot.

* Captured Polar Bears were sold to zoos at £35 each and in 1913 Salvesens shipped 800 penguins to London and Edinburgh Zoos.

* 'Moby Dick' was apparently based on 'Mocha Dick', an immense Bull Sperm which attacked a whale boat off Chile in 1810.

* I'll spare you the recipes involving blubber.

Fins ain't what they orca be,

Tom Anderson.
Aberdeen.

Animals & Men — Issue Eight

THE CASE'... Growing Slowly.

A paper tiger for all case working cryptozoologists to consider. In peaceful West Wellow, a pensioner and her dachshund are set upon by a giant American Cob Chicken (a fighting Kentuckian, perhaps?). Hot wings? certainly, which might put us in mind of Icarus the Bird man and his dad, Stephen Daedelus. In the New Forest, Pony Trekkers and ramblers are terrorised by a rogue pig near Minstead. Funnily enough with its lycanthropic trusty servant pub sign, William Rufus is mixed up in this too. Pinky, and Purkess, the carter who carried poor William to Winchester. If you fancy a spot of twitching in Southampton, you could do worse than Peartree Green, where a pair of picnicking parakeets have been observed.

Cheers,

Hampshire Hog.

CHEMOSIT CAPERS

Dear Mr Downes,

.... I enjoyed the article by Clinton Keeling on the Nandi Bear, in A&M6, especially as this is a cryptid one tends to hear little about these days. I would like to suggest a possible identity for the 'young half and half', that was apparently on display in Halifax in the 1730s.

It is described as having a head like a Hyena, and the hind parts of a 'Frieseland Bear'. Mr Keeling suggests that a Polar Bear is meant by this, but I wonder if some form of the widespread Brown Bear is the species actually referred to? If so, it may be that the 'half and half' was a specimen of the Brown Hyena.

In the eighteenth Century, the most familiar species of Hyena would have been the Striped Hyena, which has a wide range over the northern half of Africa, the Near-East and India. No doubt, many examples of Striped Hyena entered European menageries. The brown Hyena is a much rarer beast, from Southern Africa, and was not officially described by science until 1820. Perhaps if a Brown Hyena came into the hands of a menagerie owner, he might well have described it as having the head of a (striped) hyena, and the body of a (brown) bear, due to the rough, long-haired, brown coat of this species.

The 'Indian Prairie Fiends', in Mander's Menagerie, with their hippo's head and tiger's claws, etc., are much harder to explain. Maybe these were real Nandi Bears: If so, it is a great pity that they do not seem to have come to the attention of any naturalist of the time.

Keep on Crypto-ing,

Yours,

Mike Grayson.

MAWNAN HAS BROKEN.

Dear Sir,

May I suggest that the creature seen by 'Gavin' in the article in A&M6 was almost certainly an Eagle Owl (Bubo bubo). This bird is found in continental Europe but has been found in Britain occasionally. It is about 26 inches in length, so that the five feet given by the observer is wrong. It is difficult to be accurate at night with measurements. It is characteristic of owls in general to perch with two toes pointing forward and with the outer toe reversed.

Yours sincerely,

John Heath Stubbs.

ALL YOU NEED IS LOVE.

I've heard of a blind cave salamander and a flying frog, but does evolution ever go wrong? Will they find a new kind of Namibian Amphibian, a blind cave frog perhaps, which uses sonar? Is there a bat in Acre? If so what will they call it? An acre-bat of course, and will they find the bod of Beastman Moor, wherever they may be?

John Love,
Scotland.

A Tribute to Eric Sorensen.

Caddy was swimming in the sea
In the early morning mist
He did his very best to make
His coils writhe and Twist
And this was off, as technically
He just did not exist.

The Sasquatch and his hairy wife
were walking in the distance
Discussing Zoomorphically
The meaning of Existence
"T'would be a shame, should we be real,
to go extinct by mischance".

"The time has come", the Sasquatch said,
"To talk of many things,
of Tatzelwurms and Giant Sloths,
Bunyips and Otter Kings,
and Zeuglodons and Nandi Bears,
and whether snakes have wings".

"Publicity, as Vu-Quang shows,
is what we chiefly need
I'll write to 'Animals & Men'
then people will take heed.
And we and others of our kind
may safely live and breed".

So, Mr Downes, I'm begging you,
continue to inspire
those students of Zoology
who knowledge would acquire.
I remain, Sir,
Your's respectfully,
A. Sasquatch, Esquire.

> **EDITOR'S NOTE**
>
> "This wonderful slice of relict hominid verse appeared mysteriously on my doorstep on Christmas Eve and although I have my suspicions I have absolutely no idea of the identity of the author

BOOK REVIEWS

'*Latin Names Explained - a guide to the scientific classification of Reptiles, Birds and Mammals*' by A.F.Gootch (Blandford £20.00 713pp hb).

By admitting the following statement I am quite possibly showing my self up do be a dull pedant who should, in the current idiom, 'Get a Life', but it has been years since I received such an enthralling book.

The title explains it all, What you see is what you get, and what you get is an exhaustive work covering the nomenclature of the Animal Kingdom in more depth than I have ever seen elsewhere. It also, and this is possibly its greatest strength, at least as far as pure entertainment value is concerned, explains the meanings of the latin names of thousands of individual species.

Some are prosaic, some self-explanatory, and some so poetically bizarre that they invoke a whole new sub-science of Fortean Zoology. My life has never been the same since discovering that *Caloprymnus campestris* (The Desert Rat Kangaroo) means, almost exactly "*Creature with the beautiful rear end that lives in the desert*", or that Ospreys were named after a legendary king of Athens.

'*Fortean Studies Volume Two*' Edited by Steve Moore. (John Brown Publications £19.99 320pp)

Steve Moore has once again done an excellent job, and here, presents another miscellany of Fortean goodies, which would otherwise be completely unavailable. All this for less than the price of that rather nasty 'new' Beatles CD. You can't complain can you?

There are thirteen articles, four of which have direct relevance to the readers of this magazine, but all of which are both fascinating and massively entertaining to anyone with an enquiring mind.

Bob Rickard has completed an exhaustive analysis of the collected Fish-Fall papers of American Ichthyologist E.W.Gudger (1866-1956) which not only presents the available data in a concise and usable manner but suggests several new avenues of investigation into one of the most fascinating Fortean Zoological mysteries. (My only sadness being that if his name had been E.W.Gudeon the 'forteanness' would have been even greater.

Karl Shuker has presented an excellent paper listing all the living and dead specimens of alien cat species found to date in the United Kingdom. Several of these are very ill-known and there was at least two specimens, a puma found in Barnstaple during the late 1970's and a leopard cub found in Manchester in 1975 which were completely unknown to me. Shuker's article also includes several unfamiliar photographs and is the most important piece to be written on the subject of ABC's in Britain for many years.

Michel Meurger has produced another hatchet job on conventional cryptozoological ethics and attitudes with his comprehensive analysis of Scandinavian lake monster stories. I never know quite what I feel about Michel Meurger's writings. There is no doubt that he is a fine academic and a incisive investigator, but there is also no doubt that he manages to raise the hackles of much of the cryptozoological

establishment, and although I do not consider myself to be a traditional cryptozoologist at all, I find him difficult to say the least.

Michel Raynal and Gary Mangiacopra have produced a stunning compendium of all that is known about 'out of place' Coelecanth sightings, which includes the recent speculation about fishes from the Gulf of Mexico, and also includes photographs of the scale specimens found in Biloxi, Mississippi.

Less relevant to the Fortean Zoologist but equally interesting are a fascinating article on UFOs and the media by 'Animals & Men' contributor Neil Nixon, a review of Nazi Archaeology by Ulrich Magin and a wonderful dissection of the *Russians with snow on their boots* ' legends from the first world war, (which incidentally I heard from my grandmother when I was a small child). An essential book. Roll on Volume Three.

'*On the Track of Unknown Animals*' by Bernard Heuvelmans (Kegan Paul £25 677pp)

We reviewed this in the last issue of 'Animals & Men' but on consideration it appears that our review contained some inaccuracies which may have detracted from the overall impression we hoped to give. Firstly, and most importantly this is a reprint of the revised edition from the early sixties, which means that it contains considerably more information than does the better known first English Language edition of 1958. Secondly this new version contains a brand new thirteen page introduction by the author who describes the progress of the science of Cryptozoology over the forty years since he first wrote the book. He also lists new species that have been discovered over the last four decades and whets our collective appetite for the advent of Heuvelmans' complete Cryptozoological works which are being published in English for the first time over the next few years.

The addition of many new and unfamiliar pictures missing from the first UK edition (as I don't own the original second edition I don't know whether they are new with this volume or were first published in 1962), also make this an essential purchase. It is after all not only the book which first promulgated the science of cryptozoology, but it is the most important book ever written on the subject of Unknown Animals.

'*Mysterious Australia*' by Rex Gilroy (Nexus pb 288pp £10.99)

Rex Gilroy has done for Antipodean forteana what Loren Coleman did for transatlantic forteana with his classic 'Mysterious America'. Written in a similar style this book chronicles fortean events 'down under' in a witty but concise style. Like Coleman before him, much of the contents of this book is broadly cryptozoological. It covers the Blue Mountain 'panthers', the riddle of thylacine survival, river monsters, the yowie and much more. The chapter on the giant monitor lizards which have been reported from so much of the island continent is especially interesting, but it is hard to single out one single chapter when the whole book is of such an excellent standard.

Much of the material in this book is totally new to me, and I have no hesitation in reccomending this book to you. Gilroy has researched most of these cryptids in person, and is a painstaking investigator. This is an essential purchase and should be on the book shelves of every fortean with even the most passing interest in the subject. I cannot reccomend this book highly enough.

Animals & Men — Issue Eight

PERIODICAL REVIEWS

We welcome an exchange of periodicals with magazines of mutual interest although because we now exchange with so many magazines we have been forced, much against our fortean methodology, to categorise them.

CRYPTOZOOLOGY AND ZOOMYTHOLOGY

DRAGON CHRONICLE, The dragon trust, PO Box 3369, London SW6 6JN. A quarterly magazine about all things draconian. The new issue features a fascinating article about sky dragons and celestial serpents. Also Celtic Dragon Myths, British Dragon legends and more.

THE BRITISH COLUMBIA CRYPTOZOOLOGY CLUB NEWSLETTER, 3773 West 18th Avenue, Vancouver, British Columbia, Canada. V65 1B3. Excellent and well put together, and they are now on the Internet as well! Latest issue features Loch Ness, the monster of Lake Tanganika and much more

CRYPTOZOOLOGIA, Association Belge d'Etude et de Protection des Animaux Rares, Square des Latins 49/4, 1050 Bruxelles. Belgium. A French language magazine published by the Belgian society for Cryptozoology.

FRINGE SCIENCE

NEXUS 55 Queens Rd, E. Grinstead, West Sussex RH19 1BG. Intelligent look at the fringes of science. Well put together. Very impressive. The latest issue features a peculiar article on sugar substitutes and their possible toxicity and much more..

FORTEAN

TEMS NEWS, 115 Hollybush Lane, Hampton, Middlesex, TW12 2QY. An entertaining collection of odds and sods and generally weird stuff. A magazine I always enjoy reading. Reccomended.

DEAD OF NIGHT, 156 Bolton Road East, Newferry, Wirral, Merseyside, L62 4RY. An amusing and intelligently put together Fortean magazine. The latest issue includes a wonderful piece on Afro-Carribean magic in contemporary Britain by Roy Kerridge. My favourite Fortean Magazine!

THIRD STONE PO BOX 258, Cheltenham, Glocs,GL53 0HR. The magazine of the Gloucester Earth Mysteries group. A wonderful, witty and stylish look at earth mysteries in general and Gloucestershire ones in particular.

ANNALS 2, Gerry Lovell, 4G Preston Manor, Wick Hollow, Glastonbury, Somerset BA6 8JQ. UK. Wonderful and witty A4 fortean magazine. #26 features the best resume of the Roswell autopsy video that I have yet read, plus a fascinating piece on the US Airforce's experiments with anti-gravity, plus much more.

FOAFTALE NEWS, MUN Folklore & Language Archive, Memorial University of Newfoundland, St. John's, Newfoundland, A1B 3XB Canada. Scholarly magazine about folklore, and the mechanics of how it becomes assimilated into societies. Highly reccomended.

Animals & Men — Issue Eight

ZOOLOGY/NATURAL HISTORY

SOUTH WEST HERPETOLOGICAL SOCIETY NEWSLETTER, Frank Gibbons, Acanthus, 59 St Marychurch Rd, Torquay, Devon. Entertaining and informative newsletter from a thriving organisation. Contains some quasi fortean oddments. The latest issue (#206) features an interesting piece on the reptiles of the Galapagos Islands.

BIPEDIA, Francois de Sarre, C.E.R.B.I, 6 Avenue George V, 06000 Nice, France. Issue twelve of this scholarly magazine is now available. Written partly in French, partly in English, it explores the obscure, but fascinating theory of Initial Bipedalism, and its allied disciplines.

PORTSMOUTH REPTILE AND AMPHIBIAN SOCIETY NEWSLETTER M Jones, 7 Hazelmere Rd, Southsea, Hants. Another thriving regional organisation whose publications ooze with authorativeness and professionalism.

MILTON KEYNES HERPETOLOGICAL SOCIETY 15 Esk Way, Bletchley, Milton Keynes. Excellent A5 magazine containing handy hints, informative articles and news of what appears to be an exciting organisation. The latest issue has a particularly interesting article about the biodiversity of monitor lizards. I reccomend this magazine highly!

MAINLY ABOUT ANIMALS, 13 Pound Place, Shalford, Guildford, Surrey GU4 8HH, Veteran Zoologist Clinton Keeling edits this wonbderful A5 magazine which is, as the title says, mainly about animals. This is a genre of magazine that I and many others feared was lost forever and it comes with your -ditor's highest reccomendation.

ESSEX REPTILES AND AMPHIBIANS SOCIETY. 6 Chestnut Way, Tiptree, Colchester, Essex, CO5 ONX. Another excellent and lively regional reptile society. Contains much invaluable information, and the latest issue contains a quasi fortean snippet about a man biting the head off a rattlesnake.

We also exchange with 'The Cereaologist', The Creature Research Journal, Enigmas, Earthly Delights, The Wild Equid Society, Animal Keeper, Association of Private Animal Keepers, The Young Herpetologists Club, National Terrapin Project, Nessletter, Promises and Disappointments, Touchstone, Annals 2, The Reptilian, Kingsbridge Natural History Society, South West Tarantula Society, and 'Track Record but we have not received anything from them during the past three months!

UNFORTUNATELY, BECAUSE OF PRESSURES OF SPACE.
AND BECAUSEWE CANNOT AFFORD TO INCREASE THE
NUMBER OF PAGES IN THE MAGAZINE WITHOUT INCREASING
THE COST, 'NERVOUS TWITCH', 'HELP' AND 'NOW THAT'S WHAT I CALL
CRYPTO' HAVE BEEN HELD OVER UNTIL THE NEXT ISSUE. THE NEXT ISSUE
WILL BE PUBLISHED IN APRIL AND WILL BE POSTED OUT
IMMEDIATELY AFTER THE F.T UNCONVENTION 1996.
COME AND SEE US THERE!

animals&men

THE JOURNAL OF THE CENTRE FOR FORTEAN ZOOLOGY

ISSN 1354-0637
TYPESET IN THE FARMYARD
Give me peace on earth, and a chicken suit, and a star to sail her by

Cartoon by Mort

ISSUE 9

APRIL 1996

THE JOURNAL OF THE CENTRE FOR FORTEAN ZOOLOGY

I was particularly proud of this issue. It contained, what I feet even now to be a major piece of crypto-fortean investigation into the tigers of Hong Kong.

It was also the first issue to be written and designed especially for sale at the annual Unconvention in London. Although we had attended the previous two years this was the first time that we had both an exhibition and that I was speaking on the main stage. We believed at this stage that nothing could possibly go wrong.

animals&men
THE JOURNAL OF THE CENTRE FOR FORTEAN ZOOLOGY

Animals & Men
The Journal of the Centre for Fortean Zoology

A Tiger in Hong Kong; The Congo Peacock; The Horseman of Lincolnshire; BHM phenomena in Scotland.

Issue Nine   £1.75

animals&men

THE JOURNAL OF THE CENTRE FOR FORTEAN ZOOLOGY

Animals & Men

Issue Nine

This issue of 'Animals & Men' was put together by the following animals and men.

Jonathan Downes: Editor
Jan Williams: Newsfile Editor
Alison Downes: Administratrix supreme
Mark North: Artist
Graham Inglis/Dave Penna: We are the Road Crew

CONSULTANTS

Dr Bernard Heuvelmans
(Honorary Consulting Editor)
Dr Karl P.N.Shuker
(Cryptozoological Consultant)
C.H.Keeling
(Zoological Consultant)
Tony 'Doc' Shiels
(Surrealchemist in Residence)

REGIONAL REPRESENTATIVES
U.K

Scotland: Tom Anderson
Surrey: Nck Smith
West Midlands: Dr Karl Shuker
Wiltshire: Richard Muirhead
Kent: Neil Arnold
Sussex: Sally Parsons
Hampshire: Darren Naish
Lancashire: Stuart Leadbetter
Norfolk: Justin Boote
Leicestershire: Alaistair Curzon
Cumbria: Brian Goodwin
Home Counties: Philip Kiberd
S.Wales/Salop: Jon Matthias

EUROPE

Switzerland: Sunila Sen-Gupta
Spain: Alberto Lopez Acha
Germany: Wolfgang Schmidt
& Hermann Reichenbach
France: Francois de Sarre
Denmark: Lars Thomas
Sweden: Eric Sorenson
Eire: The Wizard of the western world

OUTSIDE EUROPE

Mexico: Dr R.A Lara Palmeros
Canada: Ben Roesch
New Zealand: Steve Matthewman

DISCLAIMER

The Views published in articles and letters in this magazine are not necessarily those of the publisher or editorial team, who although they have taken all lengths not to print anything defamatory or which infringes anyone's copyright take no responsibility for any such statement which is inadvertantly included.

CONTENTS

P 3. Editorial
P 4. Newsfile
p. 13. 'Bigfoot' in Scotland?
p 16. Cryptocetology Part 3
p 24. The Horse-man of Lincolnshire
p 25. The Congo Peacock
p 29. Now thats what I call Crypto
p 30. Bert the Capybara
p 32. A Tiger in Hong Kong
p 36. Odd Ornithology
p 37. Obituary - Martin 'Mort' Brown.
p 38 HELP
p 38. Bigfoot Reports
p 38. Green Kitten Update
p 39. Letters
p 41 Loch Ness Society
p 41. Future Plans for the CFZ
p 42. Book Reviews
p 43. Periodical Reviews
p.44 Cartoon

Contributors to this issue:
Dr Bernard Heuvelmans; Richard Muirhead; Mark Fraser; Darren Naish; Tom Anderson; Neil Nixon; Chris Moiser; Bill Green; Eric Sorenson; Stephen Shipp; 'Gavin'; Francois de Sarre; Martin Mannetje.

SUBSCRIPTIONS

For a Four Issue Subscription
£7.00 UK
£8.00 EEC
£10.00 US,CANADA, OZ, NZ
(Surface Mail)
£12.00 US,CANADA, OZ, NZ *(Air Mail)*
£14.00 Rest of World *(Air Mail)*

'ANIMALS & MEN',

THE CENTRE FOR FORTEAN ZOOLOGY,
15 HOLNE COURT,
EXWICK, EXETER.
EX4 2NA

01392 424811

Animals & Men — Issue Nine

THE GREAT DAYS OF ZOOLOGY ARE NOT DONE

Dear Friends and Colleagues,

Welcome to another issue of 'Animals & Men'. This issue will be available in time for UNCONVENTION 1996 and will in effect mark our third anniversary. So far we have managed to meet most of our objectives, but there is far more to achieve.

With the one notable exception; the sad death of our cartoonist Mort, in February, this is a very auspicious year. We have several interesting projects in the pipeline, and those of you who bought this years yearbook will be pleased to know that we have already collected over half the articles for the 1997 volume, and I am typing this in the first week of March.

Issue ten will be available some time in July, and both the 1997 Yearbook and Issue 11 will be published in October. We are currently negotiating with a Manchester based publishing firm about my Owlman book, 'The Owlman and Others' which will either be available in July or October, depending on whether they publish it or we do. My new book, 'The Smaller Mystery Carnivores of the South-West', with a forward by Karl Shuker, is now available through the editorial address.

It is peculiar that whereas practically without exception we have received nothing but help, encouragement and good wishes from the folk in the fortean world, in the world of natural history the story has been very different. We have some very good friends and colleagues within the world of orthodox zoology, and within the worlds of exotic pet keeping, but have been 'snubbed' by practically all the natural history societies and discussion groups we have approached.

Indeed in a 'mail out' of this magazine to forty seven Natural History Societies, we received two answers. One from the ex-secretary of one society to say that the organisation in question had closed down, and the other, a rude note, saying that 'we shouldn't expect' his members to be interested in 'a subject like ours'.

This is sad, because in a world where the pursuit of zoological truth is increasingly the domain of the enthusiastic amateur, people working on the 'fringe' of the natural sciences should work together, not against each other. After all, at the

After all, at the risk of appearing pretentious, we are all in the business of trying to increase the sum total of human knowledge. Sadly we have also had an unhelpful response from some of the major institutions. Whilst the smaller zoos and museums we have talked to have been interested in our work, and have helped us a lot, and whilst all the Scottish Museums, have been equally helpful, several major English Museums and Zoos have been unhelpful, rude and hostile towards us and our aims. Maybe Charles Fort was the 'arch-enemy' of science after all? I don't think so..

Finally, we are planning to go 'on line' with an Internet web Site within the next 12 months. However if any reader is able to let us have some space on the web so we can start earlier we would be extremely grateful.

Keep on the track...

Jonathan D

animals&men

THE JOURNAL OF THE CENTRE FOR FORTEAN ZOOLOGY

Animals & Men   Issue Nine

NEWSFILE

Compiled and Edited by Jan Williams
(that was a DREADFUL joke about the Lada)
and her Merry Band of correspondents.

NEW SPECIES

IT'S LIFE JIM, (BUT NOT AS WE KNOW IT).

Explorations in Romania have revealed an alien environment, an ecosystem surviving without light or oxygen. The Movile Cave system near Mangalia, west of the Black Sea, was first discovered ten years ago by building workers. Scientists from the Speleological Institute in Bucharest carried out a preliminary survey, but research was halted whilst Romanian dictator Nicolai Ceausescu was in power. Biologist Serban Sarbu of the University of Cincinnati has now been able to return to the cave and continue explorations. Forty-seven previously unknown species have so far been found in the cave system, living in an atmosphere of Hydrogen Sulphide that would poison most life on earth.

The species include earthworms, roundworms, pseudo-scorpions, spiders, mites, pill-bugs, centipedes, beetles, primitive insects and bacteria. All are blind and pale yellow in colour.

The caves are believed to have been isolated for five million years, and the creatures scuttle for cover when they detect a change in oxygen levels.

Dr. Sarbu says: *"In the absence of sunlight, the microbes at the bottom of the food chain have turned to using hydrogen sulphide to live. Their energy comes not from the sun but from chemicals seeping from the rocks".*

The Movile Cave is a freshwater environment, but similar life forms have been found in deep sea vents, where hydrogen sulphide seeps up from magmatic hot springs. (Daily Mail 15.2.96; Express 15.2.96).

Editorial Comment: "Stuck inside of Movile with the Memphis Blues again!"

COUNTY BOUNDARIES.

A Leeds University team led by Dr. John Altringham has discovered that Pipistrelle Bats in Yorkshire and those in Lancashire form two distinct species. The possibility was first suggested three years ago by Dr. Gareth Jones of Bristol University, who found the bats were squeaking at different frequencies.

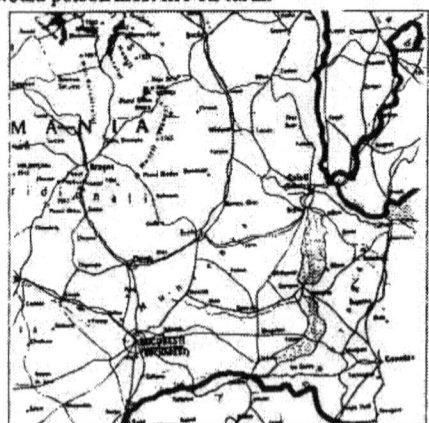

ROMANIA

Animals & Men

Issue Nine

The majority of Lancashire Pipistrelles squeak at 55kHz as opposed to the 45kHz of Yorkshire bats. Females are only attracted to the pulses of their own kind, so bats of the two counties never mate. Yorkshire bats have darker faces and longer, more pointed snouts, whilst Lancashire bats are leaner and better at flying. *(Daily Mail 6.3.96)*

EDITOR'S NOTE: The taxonomy of the British Pipistrelles seems to be in a state of flux at the moment. See Tom Anderson's letter 'North of the Border' in this issue's letters page!

CAMBODIAN CURIOSITIES

Researchers in Cambodia and Vietnam believe they have found evidence of a previously unknown cow-like mammal which, if confirmed, would be the second discovery of a new bovine species this decade in Indochina.

Horns, previously believed to belong to an immature female kouprey or "jungle cow" are now thought to have come from another species of mammal entirely, according to articles in scientific journals.

Comparison of horns discovered over the past two years with similar horns found in the 1920s and classified as those of a young female kouprey has shown that the horns are from a full-grown animal, according to an article in the latest edition of the quaterly publication *Mammalia*, the magazine of the French Museum of Natural History.

In addition, the horns are ringed and turn in on themselves and up at their tips, something kouprey's horns do not do, according to the article's author, zoologist Maurizio Dioli. Dioli is not the only researcher to make these observations.

Two german zoologists, Wolfgang Peter and Alfred Feiler, came to the same conclusion last year after finding similar horns near the Cambodian border in the southern Vietnamese province of Dak Lak and wildlife experts at the British Museum of Natural History have seconded the theory.

"This means, there is another large-bodied animal unknown to the scientific community present in Vietnam and Cambodia", Dioli said in a recent interview.

Unknown to the scientific community, the possible new species has apparently been present in the remote northeastern Cambodian provinces of Rattankiri and Mondulkiri for centuries.

Villagers have called the extremely shy, rarely-seen mammal *"Kthing Voar"* or *"Khting Sipu"* according to Dioli and Cambodians who have heard of it. The word *"Kthing"* has no English translation but refers to a horned animal about the size of a rhinoceros or hippopotamus.

"Voar" means *"vine"* indicating that the animal is herbivorous but *"sipoh"* means *"eats snakes"*. Folklore has it that the Khting eats snakes which struggle and bite its horns, giving them rings. The snake legend also explains why so few Khting horns, though prized for alleged medicinal value, have been found in good condition, as local villagers believe the horns to be covered with venom and burn them before handling them.

Dioli believes the Khting-Voar may exist in larger numbers in Cambodia:

"Since Vietnam has 72 million people, there is a much greater chance for an animal to survive in Cambodia".

Because of their isolation from much of the world community since 1975, Vietnam, Cambodia and Laos have become treasure troves for wildlife researchers as the countries have opened up. A large but unknown number of rare, endangered and possibly undiscovered species of primates, reptiles, amphibians, birds and mammals including big cats live in Indochina.

"To answer- 'how many?' correctly you have to say "unknown" because no one has done any kind of complete inventory", Dioli said. *(MRL/BSM News Agency via Christophe Bealieu)*

LOOKING FOR A GOOD TIME BIG BOY?

It is a monster by any scientific definition, it has survived undetected for 80 million years and it rules the roost in its habitat, the murky depths of the Pacific ocean of Australia's east coast.

It is a sludge-dwelling scavenging giant sea louse, rather like the common-or-garden woodlouse or

Animals & Men — Issue Nine

slater, but many times larger and dubbed *"Big Boy"* by the scientists who recently discovered it. They have also given it the more scientific name of *Bathynomus*.

"Big Boy", which grows to 30 cm. is likely to be ferocious to those smaller creatures that inhabit the deep a kilometre down, claimed crustacean expert Jim Lowry of the Australian Museum.

"We don't know yet whether they are predators, but we know they are scavengers and voracious eaters who will try to eat anything alive or dead", he said. *"One of them even bit my hand"*.

Two other similar, but smaller species, *"Wide Boy"* and *"Mono Brow"* that also survive by feeding on dead creatures that fall to the bottom have also been discovered.

"We have found more than 200 species of marine invertebrates, more than 120 of which are unknown and Bathynomus was just one of them", Lowry told AFP. *"Some of the others were totally unknown and others were previously undescribed."*

More than 100 new species of ostracods, pea-sized shrimp-like creatures, have also been discovered. *"Big boy"* is a real giant", Lowry added. *"They seem to rule the whole situation down there. Not even the fish get into the depths where we found these creatures"*. (AFP News Agency via Christophe Bealieu)

NEW TARSIER?

In January 1996, a joint American/Indonesian scientific expedition announced the discovery of what appears to be a new species of Tarsier, one of the world's tiniest primates, on an island off the Sulawesi Archipelago. According to Myron Shekelle of Washington University the animal is a little larger than the Spectral Tarsier, with greyer, lighter fur and a golden-brown streak on its back. It also has whitish hairs around the mouth and a larger nose. It has been theorised that it may be a hybrid between a Spectral Tarsier and *T.syrichta* a related species from the Phillipines.

The animal has been named *T.sangirensis*, but we must await the results of DNA testing to find whether it is indeed a new species. (BS/ML News Agency via Christophe Bealieu)

NEW SPECIES OF PHILIPPINE CLOUD RAT

A mammal species previously unknown to science, a nocturnal, squirrel-like rodent, has been discovered in the Philippines. Named the Panay Cloudrunner, *(Crateromys heaneyi)*, it is the fourth known species of cloud rat, a little known family of tree living rodents endemic to the Philippines. Two of the species, are, according to the New York Times, known only from single specimens, but the first species to be discovered, the Bushy Tailed Cloud Rat, known since 1895 is relatively common in the mountainous areas of northern Luzon. (New York Times 20.2.96).

NEW RAT IN HONG KONG

Experts have discovered what they think may be a new species of rat described as 'quite cute' by Michael Lau a senior researcher. The team stumbled on the distinctive, small, white pawed rodent, with a distinctive white underbelly on several outlying islands in February 1996. Fifteen specimens were caught in traps baited with peanut butter.

Although it is not yet sure whether this is a new species, a new sub species, or merely a new record from Hong Kong, it is not the first time that peanut butter has helped add to our knowledge of the biodiversity of the territory. In 1990, the first Hong Kong specimen of the Javan Mongoose *(Herpestes javanicus)* was caught in a trap similarly baited, in Mai Po marshes.

THE CENTRE FOR FORTEAN ZOOLOGY HONG KONG PROJECT

The sharp eyed among you will have noticed several references to Hong Kong scattered across this issue of Animals & Men.

Hong Kong is ecologically so important, and has been the site for so many peculiar animal discoveries over the last few years, that in the opinion of the Centre for Fortean Zoology, it is as important as Vu Quang, and far more easily accessible.

We are starting a new project to map, in great depth, the fortean zoology of Hong Kong, both throughout history, now and into the future. Next year it reverts to Chinese rule, and whilst it seems that some of the scare stories in the British Press may not be justified, it is bound to be a significant change, and these changes will reflect themselves within the infrastructure of the environment.

We realise that because of the nature of our discipline, some less liberal scientists tend to ignore us, and even be actively obstructive. We would merely say, that as forteans we are in the business of gathering data, and not necessarily in the business of drawing conclusions from it. Which ever way you look at our activities, we are compiling a data resource which is available to all. That, unfortunately, is something that one cannot say about all the organisations involved in the study of the more established branches of the natural sciences. Unlike them we receive no state funding, but unlike them it is in our remit to assist anyone who approaches us with their research, and not just those of whom we approve.

We have already made some excellent contacts in Hong Kong, most notably with the editors of the journal *Porcupine!* which is published by the Department of Ecology and Biodiversity at the University of Hong Kong, and we hope that the fruits of this project will be many, varied and fulfilling!

BACK WHERE THEY BELONG.

BEAVERS

Scottish Natural Heritage is conducting a study to investigate the viability of reintroducing beavers to northern Scotland. The U.K.Government is required to investigate the possible reintroduction of species such as the beaver, the lynx and the wolf under the EU Habitats Directive. A team from SNH will visit a site in Brittany where a beaver reintroduction is proving successful and will then evaluate suitable sites in Scotland. *(Aberdeen Press & Journal 15.2.96)*

EDITOR'S NOTE: Tom Anderson, our Scottish representative has written a four part paper which is scheduled either four A&M10/11 or, more probably for the 1997 Yearbook (due out in October 1996).

BURBOT

No-one knows why the Burbot vanished from British rivers. In the sixteenth century the fish were so common that they were used as pig food, but they became increasingly rare during this century and the last burbot was recorded in the River Cam in 1970. One hundred and fifty burbot imported from Moravia are being kept at Nottingham University, but scientists want to know why the fish became extinct before releasing them into rivers. Dr. Jim Reader, a lecturer in life science, is studying various theories including over-fishing, disease, changes in habitat, and a rise in water temperatures due to industrial pollution. *(Daily Mail 8.3.96)*.

LAKE AND SEA MONSTERS

SOUTH AFRICAN NESSIE

Bob Teeney, Publicity Spokesman for Howick, in Kwa-Zulu-Natal province, South Africa, claims that he will soon reveal shocking evidence of a local water monster. Mr Teeney says he first spotted the 20 metre long creature in October 1995 at a waterfall near the town. "We will unveil evidence proving the existence of the Howick Monster that will shock people ... it will prove beyond a doubt these things exist". *(Southampton Daily Echo 21.1.96)*.

TEGGIE TALES

In the wake of the revelations surrounding the supposed photographs and/or film taken of 'Teggie' the monster of Lake Bala in North Wales, a Welsh newspaper published a dubious photograph of what someone, at least, claims is the elusive lake monster. We doubt it!

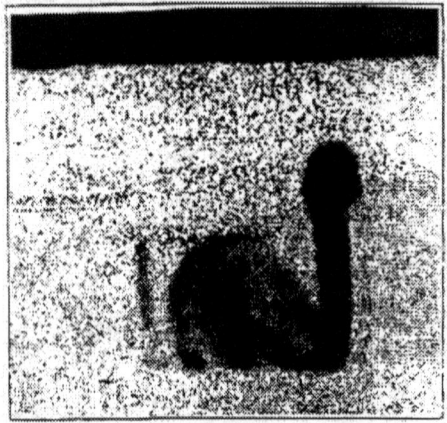

MOKELE MBEMBE ON FILM?

There are rumours flying about the wonderful world of cryptozoology that a Japanese film crew have succeeded in filming the legendary 'dinosaur' of the Congo. The descriptions do not, however appear to tally with those usually accepted for Mokele Mbembe, but until we SEE a copy of the film we will not comment further.

We have been told, but it has not been confirmed, that the film was taken by the same team who filmed the Lake Dakataua creature a couple of years ago, and who were responsible for the Lake Bala fiasco reported in A&M8.

The Welsh newspaper story which published the photo purporting to be 'Teggie' (above) included the following paragraphs:

The Japanese programme, called 'The Presenter' has already made three similar programmes. In North America they searched for the monster Champ on Lake Champlain, but didn't get anything on film.

In New Guinea they were looking for a monster called Migo, and they had pictures of a large animal there. In the Congo, in Africa, they have footage from the air of something very large moving through the water".

Unfortunately neither of these stories can be referenced as my clipping, which includes a nice colour picture of a Japanese film crew getting into a mini submarine, had no details of were or when it appeared.

On a related topic, our Japanese correspondent Mr Takabayashi has sent us a couple of video tapes taken on earlier expeditions to the Congo. We are having them translated into PAL format, and will report on them further next issue.

(On a similar subject: There is a rumour that the Debbie Martyr expedition to Sumatra has managed to photograph, or even film the elusive Orang Pendek. We cannot confirm this, and have not seen any film or photographs!)

G.S in N.Z

A Giant Squid (*Architeuthis dux*) was caught by marine scientists aboard a research ship, 600 miles east of New Zealand. The female squid, 26 feet long, and nearly a ton in weight, was found 1400 feet underwater, near the Chatham Islands. The squid did not survive long aboard ship, and was stored in a walk-in freezer until it could be transported to Wellington. (*Aberdeen Press and Journal 1.2.96; Daily Mail 2.2.96; Aberdeen Evening Express 31.1.96*).

STRANDINGS.

Six male sperm whales stranded at Cruden Bay, near Peterhead, Grampian died despite rescue efforts. The whales were each around 30 feet long and weighed 20 tons. Vet Laurence Brain of Grampian Wildlife Rehabilitation Trust said one of the whales appeared badly damaged. "It's possible that it was ill and came in too close. The rest of the pod would have followed, becoming beached as the tide turned".

Animals & Men

Issue Nine

samples of skin and stomach contents were taken by marine Biologist Bob Reid, Stranding Officer for the Department of Agriculture and Fisheries. Tests on these will reveal pollutant levels and where the whales had been travelling. According to the press rewports, although not according to our man on the spot, Tooth size showed the whales were all young males, about 20-25 years old, and initial results of genetic testing suggested that they were from different family lines. *(Aberdeen Press & Journal 29.1.96, 30.1.96, 31.1.96; Aberdeen Evening Express 1.2.96, 2.2.96, 3.2.96).*

(See NEWSFILE EXTRA report by Tom Anderson..opposite)

Two weeks earlier, Mr Reid carried out a post-mortem on a Blue Shark, which was washed up on East Beach in the Moray Firth. Blue Sharks are rare in British waters. An increasing number of tropical turtles have also recently been found off the coast of Scotland. *(Aberdeen Press & Journal 11.1.96)*

Eleven dolphin carcasses were washed ashore in the Gerrans Bay area, near Portscatho, Cornwall, in the second week of January. Dr Nick Treganza of Cornwall Wildlife Trust said, *"These are healthy animals that are dying. We do not think pollution is the problem. It has probably been caused by trawlers fishing in mid-Channel".* *(Daily Mail 10.1.96).*

The decomposing bodies of more than 100 dolphins were found on a three-mile stretch of beach in Mauretania, north-west Africa. Newspapers blamed dragnets from trawlers fishing for sharks, but government scientists say a virus may be the cause. *(Daily Mail 10.1.96)*

Two seals normally restricted to arctic and sub-arctic waters arrived in Britain last Autumn. A Harp Seal was found in marshes at Holy Island, Northumbria, in September. The six-foot male was transported to the RSPCA Wildlife Rescue Unit in Norfolk. In October, a Hooded Seal was discovered at Treyarnon Cove, near Padstow, Cornwall. The exhausted animal was taken to the Cornish Seal Sanctuary at Gweek. *(Teletext 15.9.95; Daily Mail 18.10.95).*

A Moonfish or Opah was washed up at Water Sound, South Ronaldsay, Orkney, in October 1995. The rarely-seen fish may reach five feet in length, but this specimen was about half that size. In July a thirteen foot long Ocean Sunfish was reported off the Isle of Wight. *(Aberdeen Press and Journal 11.10.95; The Sun 22.7.95).*

NEWSFILE EXTRA
WHALE STRANDINGS IN SCOTLAND.
by Tom Anderson.

On Sunday January 28th, six sperm whales beached themselves at Cruden Bay, north of Aberdeen.

The four males and two females were around ten metres long and weighed upwards of 20 tonnes each. One was badly injured, and the thinking was that rough seas took it to the coast, followed by the pod, and a combination of white water and loyalty was their undoing. Coastguards were in attendance overnight to deter souvenir hunters (lower jaw? flukes?), from unwelcome intrusion. Marine Biologists took samples to determine cause of death and the local populace was assured that under a Scots law of the 17th Century, whales, classed as a royal fish, were the responsibility of the Receiver of Wreck and the Department of Transport is liable for their removal and disposal. As they migrate northwards off the west coast this stranding is quite rare, the last major incident being eleven Sperms off Orkney in December 1994.

Monday January 29th: Scottish Natural Heritage is concerned interment would damage valuable dune structures. B.P. is worried as they have two pipelines in the vicinity.

Tuesday January 30th: Environmental Health authorities turn down £4000 from an animal feed company on health grounds. Tracked diggers are to tow the whales to 15' deep, 30' long pits above the high water mark for burial.

Wednesday January 31st: Burial suspended following collapse of the first pit following interment and covering with quick-lime when water undermined it. Even worse, nine holes of the adjacent golf course had to be closed due to the prevailing odour. Stories emerging from the villagers relate strange noises emanating from the beach on the night of the stranding.

Thursday February 1st: Excavators again thwarted as pits fill with water. Thinking now revised and alternatives of burning, towing out to see and dumping and selling to feed companies re-considered.

Friday February 2nd: Local farmer offers land for mass grave. All official bodies breathe sigh of relief as rumours

of expose by Esther Rantzen rife in the area. All deceased, (including the first one buried and exhumed) deposited in clay soil, which prevents leakage, doused in quicklime and covered in 15' of topsoil. Sorted.

CONTINUED OVER

Animals & Men

Issue Nine

OUT OF PLACE

EASY MISTAKE TO MAKE

Poisonous *Steatoda noblis* spiders which forced the closure of Bembridge Primary School on the Isle of Wight (See A&M7), have been unmasked. The spiders are a non-poisonous English relative *Steatoda grossa*, common in coastal areas of the South West. According to spider expert Ian Burgess of Cambridge University, "The only difference between the two 'spiders is in the genitalia so it is obviously difficult to spot". *(Southampton Daily Echo 8.2.96).*

RACCOON ON THE RUN

Police in Hampshire appealed for sightings of strange animals, after a raccoon escaped from Hansard Pet Centre at Awbridge, near Romsey on 11th February. The two-foot long male raccoon was spotted in Wellow and Awbridge. *(Southampton Daily Echo 12.2.96, 16.2.96).*

EDITOR'S NOTE: Several people, including Simon Baker of MAFF suggested that the North American Raccoon and the European Wild Boar would become the next two exotic species to become acclaimatised in Britain. Whereas his predictions about the wild boar seem to have been 'spot on' (see forthcoming 'special' in A&M), the raccoon has singularly failed to become established. They are now found in several European countries, but there is no real evidence to suggest that they will follow suit in Britain. they were not included in the first Dangerous Wild Animals Act in 1976, and, together with the Coati, were only included on an amendment a few years later. Zoologist Chris Moiser has suggested to us that, they will not become established because, there simply were not that many of them being kept. They were never 'high status' exotic pets, like Pumas and Ocelots, and they were always relatively cheap. His suggestion for the next animal species to become established in Britain? The Chipmunk!

NEWSFILE EXTRA

... Reading this over I detect a levity which was not intended. The picture content makes this unforgiveable. Even by local press standards they convey a sense of awe and a loss of dignity which is almost embarrassing.

The final humiliation of being dragged by machine to the lime pit was more than I was willing to witness. The contractor being an acquaintance, access was not a problem. I never used my camera. Nor do I exult in road-kills. I'm not queasy by nature; when I was a teenager I had to pull a pitchfork out of someone's abdomen as no-one else would, most were throwing up around me.

I think it's the size that does it. You feel in the presence of a superior being, which, I happen to think, they are, in the things that are important...

BEWARE OF THE BANANAS

("Cos you know they're gonna get you ... yeah." Eh? Ed)

A four inch long centipede found in a box of bananas at Chard, Somerset, was identified by Jon Flynn of Cannington College, Cricket St. Thomas, as a Scolopendra. The Scolopendra has venomous fangs at both ends. Its bite can cause a human limb to swell to twice its size, and in extreme cases can even kill. *(Daily Mail 8.3.96).*

EDITOR'S NOTE: We will provide a year's free subscription to the first person who telephones us (or comes up to us at 'The Unconvention' with the source of my cryptic comment under the above sub-heading. By the way, no-one got the answer to my last silly quiz, but in answer to the four people who wrote asking the answer, the line 'Baal in silence dines on Vulture Soup' comes from the title song of a musical play, called *Baal*, written sometime previous to WW2 by German Playwrite Berthold Brecht. If anyone can get me a copy of the 1981 video or record featuring David Bowie, I will be eternally grateful!

Animals & Men — Issue Nine

FROG FEVER SPREADS

Following the killer Bullfrog scare, concern is now being expressed over French Frogs said to be invading the south of England and eating their British cousins. Jim Foster of the conservation charity Herpetofauna described the situation as 'very worrying. They seem to be adapting to our habitat and spreading'. As with American Bullfrogs, the invasion is being blamed on breeders who imported Marsh Frogs, Edible Frogs and Pool Frogs into Britain for sale at garden centres and pet shops.

I don't know about Pool Frogs (Rana lessonae), but Marsh Frogs (Rana ridibunda) were introduced to Romney Marsh, Kent in 1935 and were well established by the 1950's. Edible Frogs (Rana esculenta) were released in several areas prior to 1960, most notably in the fens around Stoke Ferry, Norfolk in 1837. By the 1950's they were naturalised in Norfolk and Suffolk, and also in Surrey and around London, and were known as 'Dutch Nightingales'. After 160 years residence, it's hardly surprising if "they seem to be adapting to our habitat". (Daily Mail 18.1.96).

MORE FLAMING PETS

Lothian firefighters dashed to the rescue when 14 gerbils were trapped in Gaby Dareau's blazing bedroom at Howgate near Edinburgh. The gerbils had stopped breathing, but the resourceful crew produced oxygen masks and managed to bring them all round. A heartwarming story - well it was for the gerbils....

MYSTERY CATS

Essex.

Sheep and a goat were attacked at Chelmsford, and at Abberton near Colchester, in January. Essex Police blamed the attacks on a four foot long black cat seen around Great Wigborough, six miles south of Colchester, and said it "may be a mountain lion". On 31st January, 17 six-inch wide pawprints showing razor-sharp claws were found at Cooper's Beach Caravan Park in East Mersea. PC Michael Aitcheson said "This is the first concrete evidence that there is some sort of big cat out there". (Daily Mail 22.1.96, 1.2.96; Sunday Times 21.1.96).

Hertfordshire.

Something attacked Madelaine Dinsmore's Range Rover on 23rd January. The car was parked on her front drive, on the outskirts of Brookmans Park, a commuter village just north of Potter's Bar. "It had gone bananas", said Mrs Dinsmore. "There were bits of rubber all over the drive. The rubber part of the front bumper, which is very tough, had been chewed and shredded. There were large, muddy pawmarks high up on the car and deep scratches on the paintwork, so that you could see the metal underneath. The bull bars had teeth marks in". The brake pipes had also been chewed through, and there was brake fluid all over the drive.

Anne Suter, environmental health animal welfare technician for Welwyn and Hatfield Council videoed the damage and took plaster casts of large pawprints found on the drive. She said "No dog would have the strength to do this. My theory is that we are dealing with a large cat, possibly a puma". Ten months previously, there were reports of a large cat seen on the local golf course, described as "like a black labrador with a three foot tail". The evidence was examined by Doug Richardson, Assistant Curator of Mammals at London Zoo. His conclusion was that the damage and the prints were "in all probability caused by a large domestic dog".

So, was it a crazed Rottweiler, protesting against bull bars? Or are those who believe mystery cats are an alien life form right after all? Has an attention-seeking superior intelligence finally worked out that eating Home Counties Range Rovers is a better bet than Cornish Sheep? Take me to your Lada. Or perhaps not. (Daily Telegraph 24.1.96; Daily Mail 25.1.96).

Animals & Men — Issue Nine

Cambridgeshire.

Motorist Karl Robinson nearly collided with the Fen Tiger, near Willingham in February. He said "I've lived in the country all my life and I've never seen anything like this thing. It just stopped in the road and watched me - I had to swerve to miss it". He described it as a tan-coloured cat, larger than a greyhound and with a long, thick tail, similar to a dog's.

Norfolk.

A huge black cat seen close to a railway bridge, near Attleborough, waited patiently while the witness drove to the police station and returned with P.C Peter Walmsley from the local force. The cat was described as six feet long and the height of a man's waist. No prints were found despite a search of the area. (*Eastern Daily Press 6.3.96*).

Warwickshire.

A large sandy-coloured cat was seen in a field close to the main Birmingham to Stratford-upon-Avon railway line, just south of Wooton Wawen, on 25th January. The witness identified the animal as a puma from photographs, and said it appeared to be stalking sheep in the field.

Grampian, Scotland.

Traps are being set by two landowners in the neighbouring Garioch and Gordon regions, north of Banchory, following numerous reports of a large, black animal in and around the Midmar and Bennachie Forests. Ric Wharton of Midmar Castle, near Echt, decided to try and trap the beast after finding 4-inch wide prints on his land. Photographs of the prints were examined by Hans Kruuk, of the Institute of Terrestrial Ecology, who said: "*They are certainly the prints of a large dog*".

Christopher Burgess-Lumsden of Pitcaple Castle, believes a panther-like predator was responsible for killing three of his lambs. He has set a live trap in an attempt to catch the "*big animal, black, but with brindle marks, and a large, bushy tail*" which he saw in January. Joanna Davidson, of Braeside Equestrian Centre, has been warning riders to avoid Durno Forest, which borders Bennachie Forest, after a similar animal was seen eating a carcase on a woodland track. She believes that the animal could be a feral dog - a black Rottweiler puppy was lost in the area several years ago. She said "*it would be between four and five years old, and a massive beast. Its tail had not been docked, so it could pass for a different kind of animal altogether*. and the continuing reports have varied between a big cat and a big dog". (*Aberdeen Press and Journal 6.11.95, 9.1.96, 24.1.96*).

Co. Tyrone, Northern Ireland.

A lynx was shot by a R.U.C marksman near the village of Fintona on the 18th February. The shooting followed days of reports of a 'young lion' in the area. The lynx, which was wearing a collar, was believed to have escaped from a private collection. The incident has increased demands for legislation in the province, which is not covered by the Dangerous Wild Animals Act of 1976. At present, there is no requirement for a license to keep a wild animal in private premises, and as shown on recent BBC Television "Watchdog" programmes, large cats are still being kept in makeshift cages in back gardens. (*Daily Telegraph 16.2.96; Aberdeen Press and Journal 19.2.96*).

The night previous to the killing of the lynx, (which according to some reports was a caracal), another mystery cat was shot a few miles away. This was described as 'a wildcat', and was apparently 'tabby, but twice the size of a domestic cat'.

This is particularly interesting because, there are not, officially any wild cats in Ireland. In Dr Karl Shuker's book '*Mystery Cats of the World*', and again in the Editor's forthcoming book '*The Smaller Mystery Carnivores of the Westcountry*', evidence by Scharff and others suggesting that not only have wildcats survived in parts of Ireland until recently, if not the present day, but that they appear to be *F.lybica* rather than *F.silvestris*, is discussed. This corpse would, therefore have been a potentially invaluable piece of Cryptozoological evidence. Alison Downes contacted the R.U.C. She was told that the corpses were to be stuffed for the R.U.C Museum. We were promised photographs but at the time of writing, six weeks after the event, it seems unlikely that they will arrive. Alison 'phoned again a few weeks later, to be told that the corpses were still waiting for autopsy, and that contrary to the previous report they will probably be destroyed. We have made tentative efforts to purchase the wildcat corpse for the CFZ, but it seems highly unlikely that we shall succeed.

Newsfile Correspondents.

Tom Anderson, Neil Arnold, Penny Keenan, Christophe Beaulieu, Phil Bennett, Mr and Mrs J Love, Ian Sherred, Heather Thurgar, Raymond Trew, COUDi, Associated French Press, Richard Muirhead, Herman Reichenbach.

Strangeness in Scotland II
by
Mark Fraser.

BHM Phenomena.

In my last letter I mentioned sightings of Bigfoot type 'creatures' in Falkirk. I was contacted via the telephone by a chap from Falkind in Fife who told me of his sighting of two of these 'creatures'. He would not give me his name or a contact address and did not write to me as promised. He describes the creatures as being four foot in height, very agile - being able to jump from a standing position to a height of ten feet or more into the branches of trees. He claims to have seen this. He also claims that several people in the area have seen the same things, and that the area 'from way back' was said to be the haunt of strange creatures. I cannot add any more to this report unless I hear from him again.

Dundonald Hill in Ayrshire, is said to have a similar phenomenon to that reported at Ben McDhui. These 'big man' reports seem to be 'ghostly' rather than a flesh and blood animal.

Derek R, who does not wish his true name known), was out walking with two friends (identified only as Ben and Andrew), in the woods near their home at Torphins, about twenty miles from Aberdeen. Through the forest there is a wide track, about the width of a three laned motorway. As they reached the end of the trail, Ben saw a dark figure of what he took to be a man, run from the trees on the right, a couple of hundred yards in front of him. It disappeared into the trees on the left. Ben was left with a feeling of foreboding. Andrew and Derek did not see the figure, and were busy telling Ben that he had been imagining things, when they too were shocked rigid at seeing a face that they described as 'human, but not human', pop out of the trees behind Ben's back on the right. It darted away just as quickly as it had come when Andrew threw a large stone at it.

A few weeks later, all three friends were to have another sighting of the creature as they were driving along the road into Torphins, about two miles from the site of their first encounter.

Suddenly, from the side of the road bounded out a great, muscular, hairy figure. It started to run behindthe car. At one point it caught up with them and started to run along side the car. It did not seem 'out of breath' as it reached speeds of between thirty-five and forty-five miles per hour. Derek described the man like 'creature' as being very strong and muscular. It had red eyes and a body covered with hair. He also said that the creature seemed to be 'more curious than anything'. After about five minutes the 'thing' stopped in the middle of the road, leaving the three friends, somewhat frightened to carry on with their journey into Torphins alone.

-13-

Animals & Men

Issue Nine

According to Derek, a female friend of his, living in a secluded cottage has twice seen a dark, hairy figure standing in the forest watching her cottage, before slinking away into the undergrowth. Derek drew me a sketch, which has not reproduced well, so the picture on the previous page is a copy,-done by my nine year old nephew!

Editor's note: Whilst the possibility of pockets of relict hominoids living in Scotland is so remote as to be dirisible, it cannot be denied that BHM phenomena have been seen across the British Isles. I refer the interested reader to my article in the December 1996 issue of Fortean Times, in which I discussed several such cases from South-Western England. I believe that these BHM sightings, like so many other anomalous phenomena are part of a much wider pattern of activity, which has little or nothing to do with conventional zoology. This is not to dismiss these occurences however. They are important, either as a genuine paranormal phenomenon or as a sociopathological one and deserve serious study!

Alien Big Cats.

Lee Conelly, (15), came running into his parents bedroom one morning saying that there was a strange animal in the field opposite. He lived with his parents on farm land between Dairy and Kilwinning in Ayrshire, and was quite used to the sights and sounds of the country along with its animals. As his parents jumped up to look, whatever was there had gone. Lee then became a little bashful, and reluctant to describe what he had seen, especially because now there was no proof. He did say, however, that the animal was jet black, and larger than any dog he had ever seen. He said it was cat like, perhaps like a panther. Lee's father told me that his son is a remarkably level headed lad for his age and certainly not given to flights of fancy. If he says he saw something unusual, then his father has no reservations at all about believing him.

Editor's note: At the risk of appearing cynical, I have to point out that in my experience the father of EVERY teenege witness of an anomalous phenomenon claims that his offspring is 'unusually level headed for their age'.

I have not come across a parent yet who will admit to researchers that their child is a hormone driven idiot, fixated with 'Take That', who would not recognise a panther if you shot it and put it in front of them on a chafing dish with an orange in its mouth! However, there is no evidence to suggest that young Master Donelly is other than what his father claims!

Duncan and Alex Binning use the Dean Park Country Estate pretty often for walking their dogs. Late one evening in February 1994, the two dogs began acting nervously.

The largest and oldest dog had spent all its life on working farms, it had been used to going out late on dark, winter's nights and was not easily frightened. They walked on a few more more paces and they heard the sound of snapping twigs coming from the trees that lined the drive way on which they were walking, heading in the direction of the car park on the edge of Dean Rd in Kilmarnock.

The couple then became a little nervous as they had never seen their dogs react in such a manner before. The younger of the two dogs was by this time walking, nervously, in between the legs of its owners. As they reached the car park, Duncan then looked over his shoulder and in the darkness behind him he saw two, yellow, cat-like eyes which belonged to a large, black animal, standing much taller than the dogs, about forty feet away. Becoming more than a little afraid at the presence of the unknown creature the couple leashed the dogs and left the area rapidly.

Duncan tells me that the creature was definitely cat-like. He has said that maybe it was a wildcat, but he has never heard of one that size before, and certainly not one that could make dogs react in such obvious terror.

He drew this sketch of the animal they had seen.

A few days later whilst out walking the dogs, but this time in the area of the walled garden near Assloss Cottage which is a part of the Dean Castle Country Estate, the dogs again began acting strangely. Then, both Duncan and Alex heard the sound of purring, like that of a domestic cat but much louder.

This time, remembering what they had seen a few evenings before, they left quickly, and did not bother to look over their shoulders. Duncan also mentions that in all the years they had been using the Dean Castle estates, it has only been on these two occasions that they had experienced anything like that. The dogs, when in the grounds both before and after the two incidents have been fine and have displayed no odd behaviour at all.

Another resident of the area close by the castle, who does not wish his name to be known at all told me of the strange behaviour of his dog in the early part of 1994. He cannot remember which month.

For years he, and his faithful hound have walked the estate without incident, except for the time when his dog flatly refused to enter the grounds each evening for about a week. No amount of coaxing would entice the yelping, quivering animal into the estate. Then, one evening, after sniffing the air, the animal entered without any problem at all. The dog's owner is puzzled and has no clue to the reasons for his pet's behaviour.

*****

These stories were given to me in good faith. I have made no judgement but have passed them on as they were given.

Editor's Note: Mark Fraser is the editor of the 'Haunted Scotland' newsletter. He can be contacted at

Haunted Scotland
35, South Dean Rd.,
Kilmarnock,
Ayrshire.
Scotland.
KA3 7RD
Scotland.

ALWAYS WANTED

BOOKS ON MYSTERY ANIMALS, FOLKLORE, NATURAL AND UN-NATURAL HISTORY.
CASH PAID
WRITE TO EDITORIAL ADDRESS

Animals & Men   Issue Nine

Ancient Whales, Sea Serpents and Nessies Part One: Pros and Cons.

(Part three in our series on Cryptocetology)

By Darren Naish

This is the third article in a series on Cryptocetology and, as you may have gathered from the title, represents a blend of discussion on sea 'serpents', lake 'monsters' and, of course whales. Novices among you may be wondering what the connection is. Well, for some time now, an explicit link has been postulated between these cryptids and the fossil whales that I introduced in article 1. [1], the basilosaurid archaeocetes, generally known to cryptozoologists as 'zeuglodonts'. This is because, for most of zoological history, zeuglodonts have been reconstructed as wriggling, serpentine beasts that would fit descriptions of certain aquatic cryptids rather well - presuming, of course, that they had not died out over 30 Million years ago! In this article I hope to review all of the problems - anatomical, philosophical, and palaeontological - that beset notions of zeuglodont survival.

Modern whales are all of pretty much the same plan: torpedo shaped with body and tail streamlined but not elongated to the extreme. The basilosaurid 'zeuglodonts', however, apparently had enormously elongated bodies and tails resulting in a serpentine form. (Fig 1a). Unlike modern whales, zeuglodonts could still move their flippers at the elbow [2], their tiny hindlimbs still externally visible and mobile [3], and, unlike the majority of modern whales, they had a definite neck and could obviously move the head around. Zeuglodonts certainly had tail flukes (as shown by special vertebrae at the end of the tail), but differed from living whales in that the main body of each vertebra (the centrum) was elongate while the processes atop centra were not (see Fig. 2). The vertebrae were not, therefore, firmly 'locked' together. This is important: it has traditionally been regarded as meaning that the entirety of the tail and most of the body would have been of extraordinary flexibility. Authors favouring this interpretation have postulated that, during swimming, several vertical 'waves' would have passed along the hind part of the body at a time. The famous 19th Century American palaeontologist Edward Cope even suggested that, because their bodies were so long, zeuglodonts may have been able to lift their forequarters out of the water when they needed to see above the surface [4], effectively pulling the thorax into a position perpendicular to the back and tail. In modern whales, raising the head above water is called spy-hopping, they accomplish it by 'standing' vertically in the water. (Fig 1b).

Zeuglodonts appeared early in the history of whales - toward the end of the Eocene (about 45 m.y.a), and were descended from an earlier family called the Protocetidae (sometimes informally called 'pro-zeuglodonts' or 'pre-zeuglodonts'). Unlike zeuglodonts, protocetids were small (up to 3.5 m) and almost certainly were capable of movement on land, albeit rather clumsy movement (some people believe that even the giant zeuglodonts were still capable of terrestrial locomotion) [2] [5] [6]. Two recently discovered protocetid species, *Ambulocetus natans* [7] and *Rodhocetus kasrani* [8], both from the early Eocene of Pakistan, were somewhat more like their wolf-like 'mesonychid' ancestors than later whales (see fig 3.). Even so, known protocetids present somewhat different morphologies showing that different forms were adapted to different environments. *Ambulocetus*, for example, had four well developed limbs, distinct digits with small hooves, and, almost certainly, a furry pelage (lost in later whales) and a tail lacking flukes [7]. It must have lived in the same way as do sealions: a capable swimmer but one tied to rocky shorelines and shelving beaches. Most protocetids seem to have been denizens of warm, epicontinental seas [9], and not of tropical rivers as initially suggested [10]. Seemingly, they first took to piscivory around estuaries and river mouths, and on evolving a less land-dependent lifestyle, spread from their area of origin (the modern Middle East, or thereabouts) to most of the Eocene world's shallow seas. [11]. *Rodhocetus*, however was a deepwater protocetid that spent most of its time off the shallow continental shelf. Unlike *Ambulocetus*, it had a powerful, heavy tail (more like that of a modern whale) that would certainly have born flukes [8].

-16-

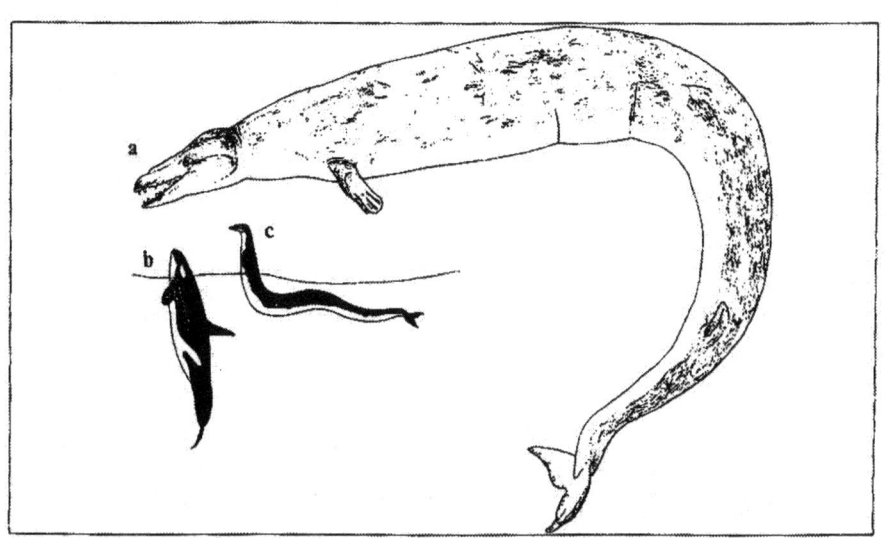

Figure One. 1a: A traditional restoration of *Basilosaurus isis*, the best known species of all ancient whales: a 16m long zeuglodont named by H. Beadnell in 1904 from the late mid Eocene (Bartonian - 42-40 million years ago) of Egypt. Note the serpentine morphology and the tiny hindlimbs. 1b: 'Spy-hopping' posture as adopted by a modern cetacean, the Orca (*Orcinus orca*). The long axis of the body becomes vertical in order that the head be raised above water. 1c: Imaginary 'spy-hopping' posture adopted by Basilosaurus. The long axis remains horizontal, the entirety of the thorax is raised out of the water.

Rodhocetus proves that not all protocetids were restricted to coastal shallows as was previously assumed, and modified themselves to suit very different habitats. As I write, evidence continues to come in of new protocetids and protocetid relatives (most notably the bizarre remingtoncetids [12] that endorse this interpretation - these early whales were more diverse than we could ever have imagined, both morphologically and ecologically).

Despite this recent influx of pro-zeuglodont information, zeuglodonts remain the most famous and most studied of all archaeocetes (literally, 'ancient whales'). They fall into two groups that some people believe should be treated as separate families and others believe should be treated as subfamilies of the same family. The zeuglodonts that we have already seen - the huge, supposedly serpentine ones - are different habitats.

Despite this recent influx of pro-zeuglodont information, zeuglodonts remain the most famous and most studied of all archaeocetes (literally, 'ancient whales'). They fall into two groups that some people believe should be treated as separate families and others believe should be treated as subfamilies of the same family. The zeuglodonts that we have already seen - the huge, supposedly serpentine ones - are the basilosaurines, the group with which we are mostly concerned. The other zeuglodonts are the dorudontines: not as elongate as basilosaurs, and not as large either, reaching a maximum of 7 metres. Looking more like modern whales than basilosaurs, dorudonts had a proportionally larger head and a shorter backbone (see fig 4). In fact, restored with a dorsal fin, they look little different from modern dolphins, and some cetologists think that this group is ancestral to all later whales [5] [14]. Remember all this, because we shall be returning to it later.

Basilosaurus and the sea-serpent.

Not long after its discovery by James Harlan in

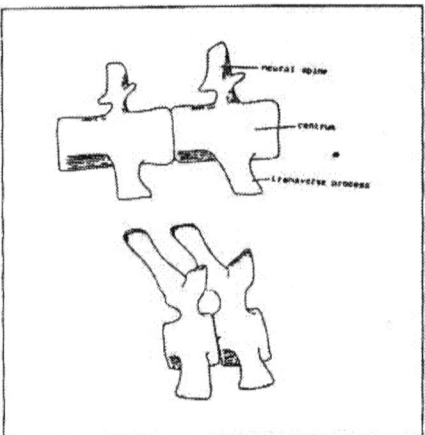

Figure Two: Lumbar vertebrae of Basilosaurus compared with those of a modern day balaenopterid baleen whale. In the basilosaur, the processes of the vertebrae do not contact one another and each centrum is very elongate.

1832, comments were made on how Basilosaurus resembled some 'mythical sea serpent', a comparison that you can find in even the most modern texts. It seems that the extraordinary appearance of this prehistoric creature invokes some act of recognition in people: there is imagery of sea serpents firmly impressed in the human mind (they are 'beast icons', see [17]). This is an issue that cannot be discussed here, but it relates to zeuglodonts because the comparisons between them and sea serpents have been so unequivocal. It has even been used to financial advantage: in 1845 Dr Albert Koch strung together bones from at least two basilosaur skeletons to make one and then exhibited it as a 'genuine' sea serpent skeleton.

Naming it *Hydragos sillimanii*, he exhibited it in New York and then various European cities, reaping profit. Koch's creation was eventually exposed as a fraud but was merely re-named *Hydrachos harlani* and put back on the road [18] [19].

Figure Three: Morphological variation amongst the protocetids, the most primitive of all whales. 3a) *Ambulocetus natans*, a 3m long species from the 49 million year old Pakistani Kuldani Formation. 3b) *Rodhocetus kasrani*, a deepwater form more like later whales than Ambulocetus (13). In life, around 3m long. A little younger than Ambulocetus at 46 million years old, its fossils are from Pakistan's Lower Domanada Formation. 3a restored from Fig. 2b in 7, 3b from 1a in 8 (and see 13).

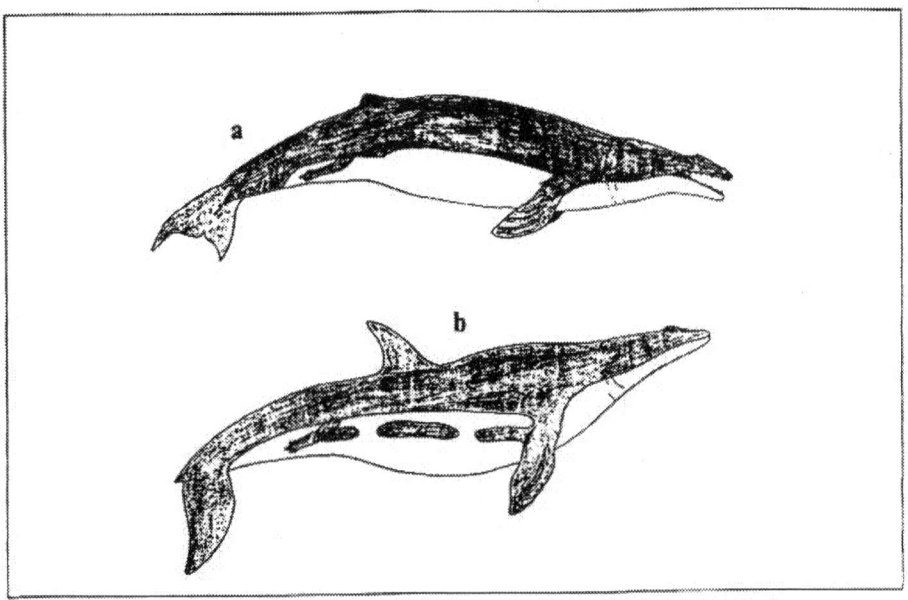

Figure Four. 4a) A typical dorudontine zeuglodont, *Zygorhiza kochii*, from the late Eocene Atlantic coast of N.America. In life, about 6m long. 4b) A different restoration of Zygorhiza, in which there is a tall dorsal fin. Dorsal fins certainly existed in a number of extinct whales, but are hypothetical in restorations. 4a after Folkens in (15), 4b after Bakker in (16).

So, if a couple of strung together basilosaur skeletons can be taken by people to be a genuine sea-serpent, how might they respond to seeing a live one?

Sea serpents as basilosaurids.

It is not surprising, then, that over the years a number of writers have proposed zeuglodonts as candidates for certain types of sea serpent. Even respected cetologists speculate on the possibility of their survival [20]. Amongst cryptozoologists Bernard Heuvelmans, obviously, has been most influential. He has suggested that sea-serpents described as having a line of humps along the back are actually modified zeuglodonts that swim by wriggling vertically. In theory, these animals, though lacking long necks, would be capable of lifting the front of their body out of the water, exactly as we saw proposed for the basilosaurids earlier on, and might be responsible for sightings of 'rearing', long bodied sea-serpents [21] [22]. A great many other aquatic cryptids too, have been seen as 'surviving zeuglodonts': so many have, in fact, that they will be reviewed in the second part of this article. [23] Protocetids, too, have received much attention in the cryptozoological literature, so more about them next time (see [23]). But for it to be seriously considered that sea-serpents are descendants of any archaeocete, several obstacles need to be overcome. In the rest of this article I consider the pros and cons for and against zeuglodont survival, and attempt to form conclusions.

First, and most obvious, is the fact that zeuglodonts disappear from the fossil record at the end of the

Animals & Men   Issue Nine

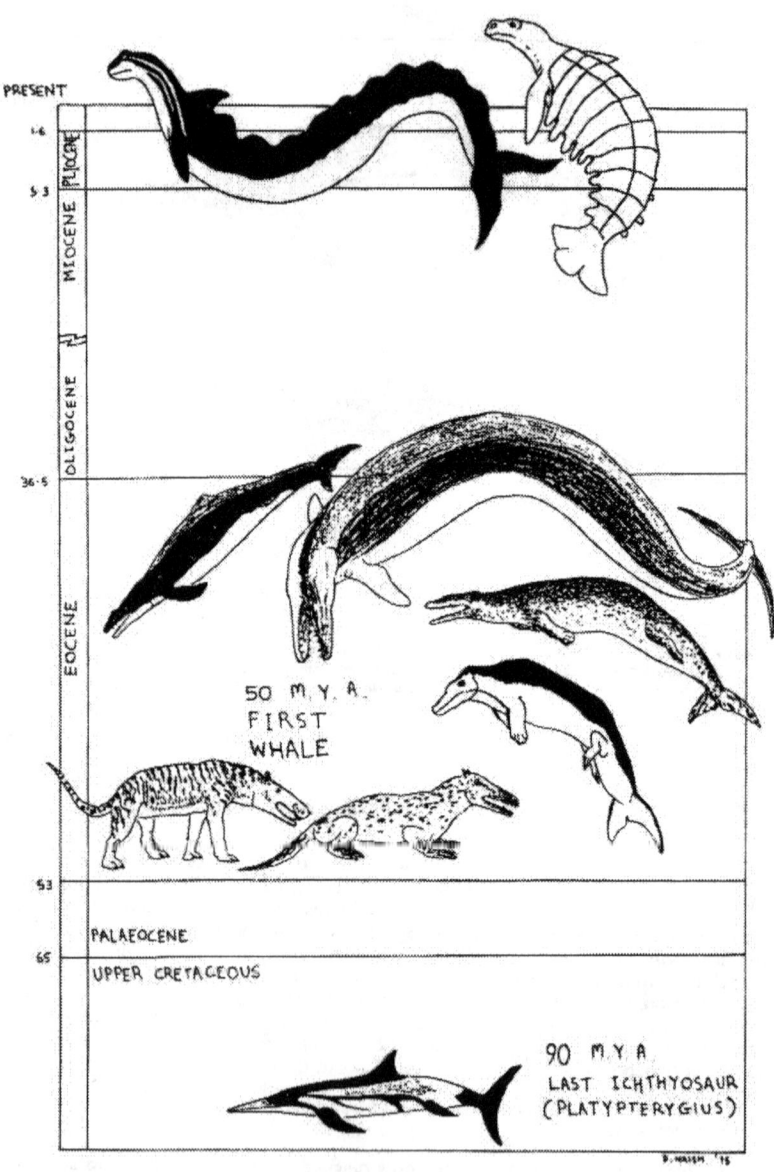

Figure Five: We have traced the evolution of archaeocete whales through the early Cenozoic. Protocetids appear in the early Eocene, become more whale-like, and give rise to giant basilosaurs and dolphin-like dorudonts by the late Eocene - are these the ancestors of modern 'sea-serpents'?

m.y.a). To argue that these animals have actually survived to the present, we must account for at least 36 million years of missing fossils.

The Fossil Problem.

This is a familiar problem in cryptozoology: an extinct form seems to best fit the description of a modern cryptic one. At various times during the past, most large, extinct vertebrates have been 'theorised' back to life (see [24]). So need the same old pleas be summoned to argue for the survival of supposedly long-gone zeuglodonts? We would cite the patchiness of the fossil record and point out both the coelecanth and the okapi. But what else can be said? While we are prone to rely on negative evidence with fossils (i.e. if a group disappears from the record, surely it has gone extinct), we must constantly be reminded of the famous words of palaeontologist Leon Bertin: *'In palaeontology negative by evidence means nothing'*.

The zeuglodonts we have seen were, unlike their earliest relatives, fully marine creatures well capable of exploring oceanic realms well away from land. If one zeuglodont lineage evolved a 'deep ocean' lifestyle - amplifying this pelagic trend - then their chances of becoming fossils would be much smaller than that of the mostly coastal whales whose fossils we have recorded in some abundance. Other truly oceanic whales, most notably the true dolphins (family Delphinidae), have very poor fossil records [25]. So we could consider the possibility that zeuglodonts were changing ecological roles to avoid competing with 'modern' whales. By the mid Oligocene, modern whales - both toothed and baleen - had appeared and, as their fossils show, were becoming important in marine environments where zeuglodonts were previously dominant [26]. Also, and supposedly more importantly, while zeuglodonts might have been becoming rarer in the Northern Hemisphere by latest Eocene times (the Priabonian stage), they remained at moderate diversity deep in the south, as shown by the possible presence of three or more forms in New Zealand of this time. [27]. This, in theory, reduces the possibility of any of their fossils being found because the Southern Hemisphere is less yeilding than the Northern. This is a separate argument.

The 'Elusive Southerners' Theory.

While it is known that late Eocene zeuglodonts swam over what is now Antarctica, we have no Antarctic zeuglodonts younger than that. So is Antarctica hiding zeuglodont fossils younger than the late Eocene age? It's usually argued that, covered as it is by an enormous ice cap, Antarctica is unyielding in fossils. This would make the unrecorded presence of post-Eocene zeuglodonts there a fair possibility. But, Marine Plain in Antarctica has now yielded vertebrate fossils from the late Eocene onward, including numerous extinct whales [28]. As yet, no definite post-Eocene zeuglodonts. Does this argue against their existence as fossils there? Or are we still relying on absence of evidence for a conclusion? We could certainly argue that the reason zeuglodonts drop out of the fossil record of Antarctica was that they could not adapt to the extreme cold (Antarctica became truly glaciated in the Oligocene). But this does not explain their extinction elsewhere. One of the ten biggest mass extinctions in the history of life, and the biggest of all in the Cenozoic era, occurred at the close of the Eocene - this was probably a major factor in the eventual extinction of these whales. Or was it? Other whales made it through (and, furthermore, gave rise to gigantic descendants as soon as the early Oligocene. [29]). Whales are also the only big mammals to have made it through the Pleistocene mass extinction (about 0.01 m.y.a) without experiencing the decimation of taxonomic variety that other mammals underwent [30]. This shows that whales are 'durable' mammals, at least at the family level. The possibility of zeuglodont survival could therefore be quite high. But to verify this, a post-Eocene zeuglodont is needed. Are there any?

For some time it seemed that the very youngest of known fossil zeuglodonts was Kekenodon onamata, from the mid Oligocene of New Zealand [31]. It is particularly notable in combining both the 'elusive Southern Hemisphere fauna' theory and the 'ecological niche not usually fossilised' theory - it is not only from New Zealand, but follows a '7 million year plus' hiatus in the record of fossil zeuglodonts. Here might be evidence that not only were the last zeuglodonts animals of the Southern Hemisphere, they were also becoming less 'available' candidates for fossilisation. Opinions have changed much on the relationship of this species to other whales: early interpretations were that it was a possible 'last archaeocete', but others expressed doubts [32]. In 1989, Mitchell decided that Kekenodon was, after all, a late surviving archaeocete and created a monotypic family for it [33]. But by 1992, the work of Fordyce [29], changed opinions again - now it seemed that Kekenodon was an early toothed mysticete. So much for Kekenodon then. Indeed, a recent review states that 'supposed (post-Eocene) archaeocetes are either misidentified or are too incomplete to place conclusively' [34].

One final argument remains and, like the lack of fossil evidence, it argues against zeuglodont survival. This argument begins with the very fact that first led zeuglodonts to be even considered as sea-serpent candidates. This is their 'serpentiformity' for, as we saw earlier, the best known members of this group - the giant basilosaurines - have long been restored as sinuous serpentine animals. In fact, ever since the skeleton of *Basilosaurus cetoides* from Alabama was first reconstructed in the 1830's, this is thought to have been the case. But suppose they weren't serpentine after all. If this were so then the notions of surviving zeuglodonts would have to be dispelled. Earlier in this article, we saw how the dorudonts were definitely not serpentine, but proportioned more like modern whales (see fig. 4). If dorudonts were really close relatives of basilosaurs, could the two really have been that different in morphology?

In 1984 [35], Barnes re-assessed the skeletal material of Basilosaurus and, concluding that the animal was NOT serpentine but, in fact, more like what a giant dorudont might look like, submitted a brand new reconstruction. As we can see from fig.6, Barnes' Basilosaurus would not be thought of as a 'sea serpent' if seen in the flesh and, if this reconstruction is accurate, then we are wasting our time even considering the survival of zeuglodonts!

Other, more recent analyses have also shown that Basilosaurus was not a serpentine animal. The centra of its vertebrae were wide and bulky with very little space in between them - in fact they did not have any adaptations to allow greater flexibility. The serpentiformity of Basilosaurus is an illusion - it is caused by allometric increase in the length of the centra, rather than an increase in the number of vertebrae [36]. Some modern whales, while being of similar length to Basilosaurus, actually have more vertebrae. Ironically, therefore, basilosaurs increased their length at the expense of flexibility, the very opposite of traditional interpretations! So they could not 'wriggle' vertically. Technically, the jury is still out over whether they could have survived beyond the Eocene, let alone to within recent times, but there is no fossil evidence that they did. So, do descendants of Basilosaurus still cruise the oceans? It is up to you to make your own decision, but, as will be seen in part two of this article, others have already made theirs...

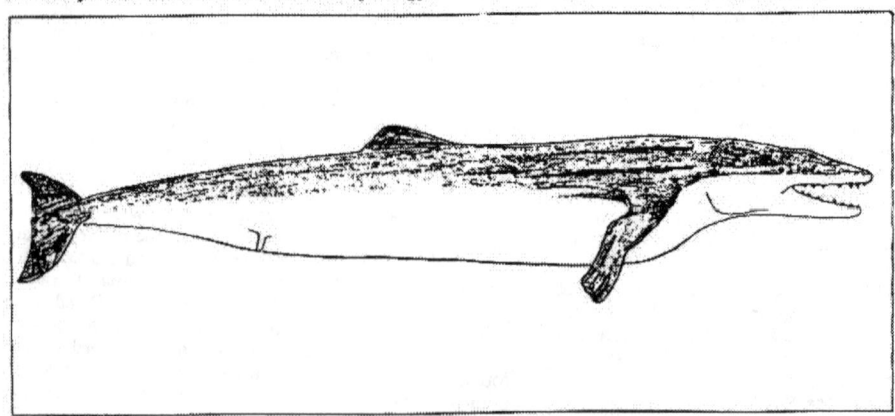

Figure Six: Basilosaurus in its more dorudont-like guise.
After Barnes 1984 (35).

References and Notes.

1. NAISH, D.W. 'Cryptocetology - Introducing a new branch of Cryptozoology' (A&M #7)
2. ANON, 1992. 'Basilosaurus (Zeuglodon), an ancestral whale. in HARRISON, R & BRYDEN, M.M. 'Whales, Dolphins and Porpoises'. Blitz Editions (Enderby, Leicestershire), p.17.
3. GINGERICH P.D., SMITH, B.H. and SIMONS, E.L. 1990. 'Hindlimbs of Eocene Basilosaurus: evidence of feet in whales'. Science 249; 154-7.
4. COPE, E.D., quoted in HEUVELMANS, B, 'In the Wake of the Sea Serpents' (1968). Rupert Hart-Davis (London).
5. FORDYCE, R.E. 1980 'Whale Evolution and Oligocene southern ocean environments'. Palaeogeog., Palaeoclim., Palaeoecol. 31: 319-336.
6. WATSON, L. 1988. 'Whales of the World'. Hutchinson (London).
7. THEWISSEN, J.G.M., HUSSAIN, S.T. and ARIF, M. 1994. 'Fossil evidence for the origin of aquatic locomotion in archaeocete whales'. Science 263: 210-12.
8. GINGERICH, P.D., RAZA, S.M., ARIF, M., ANWAR, M., and ZHOU, X. 1994. 'New whale from the Eocene of Pakistan and the origin of cetacean swimming'. Nature 368: 844-7.
9. GINGERICH, P.D., WELLS, N.A., RUSSELL, D.E. and IBRAHIM SHAH, S.M. 1983 'Origin of whales in epicontinental remnant seas: new evidence from the early Eocene of Pakistan'. Science 220: 403-6.
10. KELLOG, A.R. 1936. 'A review of the Archaeoceti'. Carnegie Inst. Washington Publ. 482: 1-366.
11. Their fossils are known from mid Eocene rocks in west Africa and Texas, as well as those of southern Asia.
12. J.Head pers. comm. 1995.
13. As fossils of this type go, Rodhocetus is surprisingly complete. However, forelimbs remain unknown and, of the hind limbs, only a femur is known. Thus what you see in this restoration is speculative. Also, whether such an animal would have a furry pelt as illustrated is debatable. Given that Rodhocetus was not far removed from Terrestrial, certainly furry ancestors, I decided on a furry pelt being a fair possibility. This implies that the animal was still in the habit of returning to land, unlike the zeuglodonts, which, like the extant whales, I restore as lacking integument.
14. FORDYCE, R.E. 1992. 'Evolution'. In HARRISON, R & BRYDEN, M.M. 'Whales, Dolphins and Porpoises' Blitz Editions (Enderby, Leicestershire), p.14-23.
15. MAY, J. (ed) 1990. 'The Greenpeace book of Dolphins'. Random Century (London).
16. BAKKER, R. 1988. 'The Dinosaur Heresies'. (Penguin (London).
17. CONSIDINE, B. and NAISH, D.W. In preparation, 'Monsters: A cross-cultural comparison' (working title) to be published in Strange Magazine.
18. MICHELL, J. and RICKARD, R.J.M. 1982. 'Living Wonders'. Thames and Hudson (London).
19. SLIJPER, E.J. 1962. 'Whales'. Hutchinson (London).
20. BONNER, N. 1989. 'Whales of the World'. Blandford (London). '(Archaeocetes) would fit very well the usual description of sea serpents or lake monsters, so perhaps the indefatigable searchers of Loch Ness will yet provide us with an archaeocete' - p.23
21. McEWAN, G.J. 1978 'Sea Serpents, Sailors and Sceptics'. Routledge & Kegan Paul (London).
22. HEUVELMANS, B. 1986. 'Annotated Checklist of apparently unknown animals with which cryptozoology is concerned'. Cryptozoology 5: 1-26.
23. NAISH, D.W. 'Ancient Whales, Sea Serpents and Nessies part 2'. Unpublished. Scheduled for A&M #10.
24. SHUKER, K.P.N., 'In Search of Prehistoric Survivors - do giant 'extinct' creatures still exist?' (Unpublished at time of writing). Blandford (London) 1995
25. BARNES, L.G. 1984. 'Whales, Dolphins and Porpoises: Origin and Evolution of the Cetacea'. In BROADHEAD, T.W. (ed.) 'Mammals notes for a short course organised by P.D.Gingerich and C.E.Badgely (Uni. of Tennessee Dept. of Geol. Sciences in Geology). pp 139-54.
26. Interestingly, however, Fordyce (in 5) writes: 'archaeocetes apparently persisted in the southwest Pacific, where they co-existed with potential competitors, the odontocetes'. At the time, however, Fordyce considered Kekenodon and others to be archaeocetes.
27. FORDYCE, R.E. 1985. 'Late Eocene archaeocete whale (Archaeoceti: Dorudontinae) from Waiho, South Canterbury, New Zealand'. New Zealand Journal of Geology and Geophysics 28: 351-7.
28. SELBY, J. 1990. 'Antarctica: The changing Ice Cap'. Geology Today 6 (3):83.
29. FORDYCE, R.E. 1992. 'Cetacean Evolution and Eocene/Oligocene Environments', in PROTHERO, D. and BERGGREN, W. (eds) 'Eocene and Oligocene Climatic and Biotic Evolution', Princeton Uni Press (Princeton, NJ), pp. 368-381.
30. MARTIN, P.S & KLEIN, R.G. 1989. 'Quaternary Extinctions - A Prehistoric Revolution'. Uni of Arizona Press (Tucson).
31. The New Zealand Strata to which Kekenodon belongs is believed by some to be of Lower Miocene age (about 22 m.y.a). If, therefore, Kekenodon is an archaeocete (see (32),) it is the first post Oligocene one of which we know.32. In (25), Barnes questioned the affinities of supposed archaeocetes 'Even though it has been considered such, Kekenodon .... is not a proven archaeocete ... and Platyosphys is known only by vertebrae of Oligocene age from Russia' - p. 146.
33. MITCHELL, E.D. 1989. 'A new cetacean from the Late Eocene La Meseta Formation, Seymour Island, Antarctic Peninsula'. Can. Jour. Fish. Aquat, Sci. 46: 2219-35.
34. FORDYCE, R.E. and BARNES, L.G. 1994. 'The evolutionary history of whales and dolphins'. Annu. Rev. Earth Planet. Sci. 22:419-55.
35. BARNES, L.G. 1984. 'Search for the first whale: retracing the ancestry of cetaceans'. Oceans 17 (2): 20-34.
36. J.Head pers. comm. 1995.

The Horse-Man of Lincolnshire:
A hitherto unrecorded Zooform Phenomenon.
by Alison Downes.

Dr. Karl P.N. Shuker recently appeared on the Good Morning show, (ITV Weekday mornings), and was one of the featured panellists for a viewers 'phone in' on the subject of mystery animals. Well over a thousand people telephoned in. Most of the eyewitness accounts were of 'big cats' or lake monsters, but a few were far more unusual. One was from a lady who claimed that her husband had undergone a very unusual experience.

I contacted the gentleman to get the true facts of the case. This is the gist of what he told me.

"It was very late one night, a few couple of years ago. I used to work on an oil rig platform in the North Sea and I was coming home on leave. I'm not naturally given to flights of fancy so I'm fairly sure of what I saw.

I was driving down the back road from Great Yarmouth to Lincoln. It was very dark and quite rural in that area - lots of fields and trees around. As I drove down the road I noticed a shape in the fields at the right hand side. I thought it was probably a horse or a deer, as it seemed to be the right size and shape. But, as I got closer it moved nearer towards the road and I got the shock of my life - it had the body and legs of a horse but a man's face!

It was very scary and unpleasant. I didn't hang around, but put my foot down hard on the accelerator and 'got the hell' out of there! I had the sensation that it was following me down the road. I didn't look back - I was terrified.

When I got home I told my wife and friends about it, but most people just laughed at me and said I was mad, or imagining things. As you can imagine, I didn't want to be a laughing stock so I kept quite about it after that, but I am convinced about what I saw. I know it seems impossible, but I DID see it and it wasn't just a horse or a deer.

I've never heard of anyone else seeing anything like it around this area, but I would be interested if anybody knows anything about it, or any legends about similar creatures".

I looked into the situation, and found that this bears an uncanny resemblance to 'The Horse-man of County Louth', as described in 'Mystery Animals of Britain and Ireland' by Graham McEwan. (Hale, London 1986). This apparition was seen near Drogheda, County Louth, Eire in 1966, and appeared as "A huge horse with a man's face and horrible bulging eyes".

The Lincolnshire witness, Mr K., whose identity we have decided to keep confidential for the moment, had never heard of the irish story, and apart from a mild interest in ghosts (which, of course, many people have), has little interest in the paranormal. He appears to be a reliable and objective witness. I found him a credible and sensible person who seemed slightly embarrassed by it all.

For this reason, I consider the story to be an interesting one, and would certainly not dismiss it. If anyone has any similar reports, please feel free to contact us at the Editorial Address.

The Mystery of the Zebra-Striped feather.

by

Dr Bernard Heuvelmans

In 1901 it was finally realised that the presumed zebra, called okapi by the pygmies of the great equatorial forest of Africa, was in reality a sort of ancestral giraffe with a short neck. At that point, several expeditions were organised with the aim of capturing one of these survivors from the past. The one arranged by the American Museum of Natural History was led by Herbert Lang, who in turn was assisted by a very promising young ornithologist, James P. Chapin.

Despite its assiduous and continuing peregrinations through the Belgian Congo, the present day Zaire, the expedition carried on from 1909 to 1915, and in spite of the support of more than 38,000 natives, the Yankee team did not succeed in bringing back alive even the slightest shadow of an okapi. The young one which it had succeeded in capturing had perished after a few days, owing to an insufficient supply of condensed milk. However, this expedition did bring back a piece of evidence which was going to lead to another striking zoological discovery, this time in the world of birds.

In 1913, on the occasion of a festival in the village of Avakubi, in the forest of the Ituri, the habitat of the okapi, Chapin was much interested in the costumes of the dancers, and in particular their head-dresses of feathers, as these, in general were decorated with a variety of feathers collected from the local birds. From one of these pieces of headgear the zoologist collected a feather which did not appear familiar to him. It was reddish, with regular black, zebra-like stripes, and in 1915 he brought it back to the United States in a bundle of a variety of different feathers.

The zebra-striped feather posed a problem which was to prove even more difficult to resolve than that of the similarly zebra striped hide of the impossible 'forest ass' first reported by Stanley. One could even be lead to think that, in this dark and mysterious region, all mysteries had a zebra-like aspect.

The world of birds is indeed infinitely diversified. Moreover, the feathers worn by this limitless variety of birds are even more diversified, for there can sometimes be even very different types of feather on one and the same bird. But, let us be reassured: Chapin, in his efforts to identify the original owner of the famous black-striped feather, was not going to be obliged to review the feathers of the some 8500 species of birds then known. In fact, the feathers had certain characteristics which in any event were going to limit the scope of the research needed. To begin with, the mysterious zebra-striped feather bore a resemblance to the secondary remiges - i.e., the feathers that make up the second row on the wing - of certain coucals, birds which are related to the cuckoos but which are much larger than the latter. Because of the robustness and curvature of the stem, it also resembled the feather of a gallinacean, but it was still of too considerable a size to have come from a guinea-fowl or a francolin and, besides, its colouration was entirely different. Chapin long considered the possibility of some domestic hybrid between guinea-fowl and chicken, but his research in this direction lead to nothing. Could it be that this feather came from a still unknown species of African Gallinacean? This idea seemed to him to be so nonsensical that he ended up dropping his investigation.

A quarter of a century later, an unexpected stroke of good luck was going to reveal to him how ill founded was his disbelief. In July 1936, he went to the Museum of the Belgian Congo, in Tervuren, not far from Brussels, in order to work on the second volume of his book 'Birds of the Belgian Congo'. His friend, Dr. Henri Schouteden (1881-1972), at that time director of this museum, had given him complete freedom to study all of the collections which had been accumulated there on the fauna of this immense Belgian colony, and which were of an incomparable richness.

As it turned out, on one day early in the month of August, a torrential summer rain meant that Chapin was obliged to enter the museum through a service door at the side, in order not to be soaked to the skin. And there, passing through a hallway that was being used for temporary storage, our ornithologist stumbled upon a whole series of stuffed fowl which were about to be burned in a stove, either because they were completely moth-eaten or because they were of no scientific interest whatever. Among them, perched on a packing case, Chapin came across a pair of birds which caught his attention immediately, as there was nothing at all african about them. One had blackish plumage with an iridescent sheen of violet and green, and the other - no doubt the female of the same species - was of a duller, more or less reddish colour overall. And, the big reddish feathers of its wings were marked with black zebra stripes!

This brought abruptly back to Chapin's mind a memory which had long lain buried: yes, indeed, these feathers were very much like the one, whose owner he had so long sought .... A glance at the label attached to one claw revealed this brief note: 'Pavo cristatus, young imported'.

This was clearly an error. The male had powerful spurs and thus had to be an adult. Moreover, Pavo cristatus is the scientific name of the ordinary blue peacock, a native of India, and with which the bird in question could not really be confused, even though it did bear a slight family resemblance. But, a peacock in the Congo? No such thing had ever been seen.

Imported? Imported from where? Without further ado Chapin rushed to Dr. Schouteden, to put the question to him. He was told that the two specimens in question came from a collection of at least sixty naturalised birds, which had been assembled by the Copagnie du Kasai, an important trading company operating in the southwest of the Congo, and which had made a gift of this collection to the Tevuren museum in 1913. As the lot included some representatives of a few barnyard species, the person charged with identifying the specimens had doubtless concluded that the two birds which vaguely resembled peacocks even though not having their magnificent tail-feathers or brilliant colours, must have been Indian peacocks imported into the Congo for ornamental reasons.

What were they really? They could have been hybrids of peacocks and other domestic birds, since it was known that such cross-breeding had been acheived. Chapin did not think so however, as the offspring so obtained did not at all resemble the fowl in question. This being said, if they really were of an unknown species, how the devil to verify it, as he had no idea where to begin looking for them.

A first valuable clue came to Chapin in circumstances no less unusual than the circumstances surrounding the discovery of the feather of Akabuki.

Several days after the unexpected encounter with the two stuffed birds destined for the bonfire, on 12 August, the ornithologist had been invited to lunch in Brussels by one of his old friends, Monsieur de Mathelin de Papigny, an engineer in the Kilo gold mines whom he had met in the Congo in 1911. In the course of the meal - as was the custom - they spoke about gastronomy, and the engineer mentioned in passing a delicious bird which he had tasted at a dinner in 1930 at his gold mine in Angumu. The bird had been shot by a native hunter in the dense forest nearby. Monsieur de Mathelin had never succeeded in learning the identity of this feathered game, but he did not doubt at all that Chapin, the great specialist on Avian fauna of the Congo, could finally shed some light on the matter.

When his host began to describe the bird, the American ornithologist nearly choked and, by his own admission, was thereafter totally unaware of whatever it was that he continued to chew on mechanically for the rest of the meal. For, the description of the animal corresponded exactly to the male of the couple of specimens which he had stumbled across in the storage hallway of the museum of the Belgian Congo! But it did differ in one minor detail: Monsieur de Mathelin claimed that his bird had a 'white badger brush' on the top of its head, in front of the little black crest that was quite visible on the naturalised bird. However this latter bird had, at this point on its head, only a few short, white silky hairs, and Chapin felt that his luncheon partner might be exaggerating the importance of this ornament just a bit.

However that may have been, the account of the engineer seemed to indicate that this mysterious bird lived in the region of Angumu, from which a specimen could very well have managed to reach the village of Avakubi, located scarcely 160 km to the north.

By way of checking, and for a comparison, Chapin had sent to the museum in New York, one of the secondary remiges of the stuffed female bird, so that it could be compared with the feather that he had collected from the head-dress of a Congolese dancer: these two feathers proved to be almost identical! In short the feather from Avakubi, the game bird of Angumu, and the naturalised birds from the Compagnie du Kasai appeared to belong to one and the same species, which apparently frequented the northeast and the centre of the Belgian Congo. The pieces of the puzzle were beginning to come together.

On the basis of the stuffed specimens, James P.Chapin then undertook to describe the new bird under the name of *Afropavo congensis*, in other words 'the African peacock of the Congo'. The anatomical examination, and in particular the discovery of the little bony tubercule on the wing, which characterised the family of the Phasianidae, disclosed clearly that the unknown creature was indeed a relative of the peacocks and the pheasants, and definitely was not some other African guinea-fowl.

This description appeared first, in English, in the *Revue de zoologie et de botanique africaines* in November 1936. It was then translated at once into French and published in the *Bulletin de Cercle zoologique conglaise*, which was widely

This description appeared first, in English, in the *Revue de zoologie et de botanique africaines* in November 1936. It was then translated at once into French and published in the *Bulletin de Cercle zoologique conglaise*, which was widely circulated among Belgian colonists interested in natural history. The article was then reproduced in a very condensed form in a Brussels daily newspaper. In this form in amounted effectively to a 'Notice of Missing Person', and it subsequently produced the desired result.

Little by little, a whole series of people began to write in, to report that they had seen or even shot birds of this sort in the Congo: some in the region of the Lower Uele, i.e., quite in the northern part of the state, and another, the Reverend Thomas H.Wilson, at Inkongo, in the Kasai, in the very heart of the country. All of this, of course, was rather vague, and perhaps even a little embroidered and, in any case, quite unverifiable over the immediate future.

Finally, a police officer of the Congo, M.R.Geldof, claimed to have naturalised the Congolese peacock which he had shot in 1930 at a distance of 180 km to the south of Stanleyville (today Kisangani), and had given it to his sister, who lived at Eecloo, in Belgium. This time a verification was possible. Dr. Schouteden immediately sent his taxidermist, Rene Opdenbosch, to call on this lady and to

ascertain that she did in fact have in her possession a good specimen of the Congolese peacock.

Here, in any event was a point which established that the range of distribution of the bird was fairly extensive. Then, of course, more had to be learned, and, in particular, a specimen had to be collected in the field. But in those days, one did not travel as easily, nor as rapidly, as is the case today. Moreover, Chapin, being attached to a scientific institution, had a major project to complete, little time to devote to other matters, and, furthermore, no fortune at all to throw about. Nevertheless, the game was worth the candle. Thus, a well defined plan began to take form in his mind.

First of all, he had to train several natives to prepare in the field the skins of any specimens which could be obtained. Chapin had also been assured by Monsieur de Mathelin that, at Angumu, he would receive all necessary assistance from Dr. Pierre Dyleff, the physician of the mining company. The best would be to have assigned to him, as his assistant, a Congolese taxidermist by the name of Musoba, whom the American ornithologist had trained himself in 1926, and whom at that time was working in the Albert national park.

On top of this, Chapin had been warmly congratulated for his unexpected success by the authorities of the Museum of New York, from which he had obtained a special leave of two months. And then, from several American benefactors living in Europe, he was able to procure the funds necessary for this undertaking. Then, Professor Victor van Straelen, curator of the national parks of the Belgian Congo, proved to be more than pleased to send the taxidermist Musoba to Angumu. Thus, all was ready for the decisive stroke.

On 23rd May 1937, a very encouraging report reached Chapin. Dr. Dyleff had shot a first specimen of Afropavo, a female, which Musoba had then prepared with his habitual skill. On 17th June the ornithologist had an even greater surprise: The Reverend Wilson had obtained another individual, this time a male, which he had naturalised and which he wrote was being despatched to Chapin. Again, he had shot the specimen in the region of Inkongo, which earlier had appeared to be so unlikely, given its distance from Angumu: 750 kilometres!

On the photo which the missionary had attached to his letter, it could be seen that the male of the Congolese peacock did indeed have on the top of its head a true 'badger-brush' of fine white hairs. Monsieur de Mathelin de Papigny had in no way exaggerated: rather it was the specimen of Tevuren which had been dreadfully 'moth eaten'.

Finally, on the 25th May, Chapin - already sure of not returning empty handed - left Brussels in a trimotor aeroplane of Sabena, which was to take him, in four and a half days, to the aerodrome of Stanleyville. Waiting for him there was a letter from Dr. Dyleff, who informed him that four duly prepared specimens of the Congolese peacock were awaiting him in Angumu, as well as a 'stretched' skin provided by a Russian friend. Moreover, a Veterinary in Stanleyville itself, Dr. Els, was quite anxious to show Chapin two other specimens which, for their part, had been conserved by means of injections of formol: they had been killed the preceding month by Monsieur Phillipe de Braconier near the Ayena River, some hundred km to the east of Stanleyville. In short, the news of the 'discovery' of the Congolese peacock had spread like wildfire among all of those who were already familiar with it, and who in some cases had known about it for quite a long time.

Chapin went first to Angumu, where he made the acquaintance of Dr. Dyleff as well as of the new black taxidermist Nkotiba, who had been trained in the meantime by the veteran Musoba. A whole company of trackers, hunters and trappers had been assembled. Twelve days of frenetic searching, however, did not enable Chapin to see a single Congolese peacock. Thus, he took the decision to follow Dr. Dyleff, on the 13th of July, to Ayena, to the Braconiers, where an excellent hunter of the region, Anyasi, was placed at his disposal. Three days later, in company with this latter, the scientific godfather of the Congolese peacock finally had the opportunity to see one of his godchildren, a male. He at first had a glimpse of it in a thicket, whereupon Anyassi had fired his arm at it, but had missed. The magnificent bird rose in a single bound, flapping its wings majestically. Immediately afterward, another peacock also flew up nearby.

It was only on the 18th that Anyassi succeeded in killing a first specimen under the very eyes of Chapin, who collected it while it was still quivering, and was then able to dissect it with all of the care and skill to be expected. Moreover, it was to be the only one that he was ever to see shot. He, himself, never succeeded in shooting one, as he always trembled so with emotion.

Once back in Angumu, Chapin found there a new specimen that had been obtained during his brief absence and which had been prepared by Nkotiba. When he finally left Africa on 27th August, the specimens of Congolese peacocks which had been collected for him here and there numbered about ten. He had scarcely left when Dr. Dyleff obtained yet another one, bringing the total number of specimens known, including the types, to fourteen.

Thus, it emerged little by little that the Congolese peacock, one isolated feather of which had excited so much interest for some 25 years, but which in spite of it all had succeeded in preserving its incognito until 1936, did indeed have a limited range. Nevertheless, this range was as extensive as the whole of Great Britain; a territory in the form of a pear, with the stem at Lusambo, in the Kasai, and the base on the Lindi river, which flows into the principal arm of the Congo River, a little downstream from Stanleyville. Moreover, the bird appeared to be rather common and had always been well known to the native peoples. The Bakumu of the region of Angumu, called it *itundu*, and the Wabali of Ayena ngowe, in imitation, it would seem, of one of its cries. Even certain colonists knew it, that is, at least those who risked venturing into the forest.

Moreover, subsequent research was going to uncover the identity of the one, who in the last century, had assembled for the Compagnie du Kasai the collection of birds among which figured the type specimens of Afropavo congensis. This turned out to be the Botanist and Entomologist from Luxembourg Edouard Luja, whose name is carried today by many species of plants and insects. His Congolese collection had even been exhibited in 1910 by the Compagnie du Kasai at the Brussels Exposition where, it must be said, not a single visitor had noticed in it a couple of birds which were entirely unknown to science. It is true that when a distinguished Belgian ornithologist, Alphonse Dubois (1839-?1910) had been charged with identifying the pieces of the collection before it was given to the Museum of Tevuren, this expert was so convinced that peacocks could not exist in Africa that he took this couple for a pair of common peacocks which had come from elsewhere - which is almost unthinkable, and so he had catalogued them as such. '*Pavo cristatus, young, imported*'.

Yet once again, conventional knowledge had well and truly blinded a specialist, and a great discovery had been set back by several decades, and, if the badly labelled birds had been destroyed, as was about to be done, we would perhaps be unaware, even today that a species of peacock is strutting proudly about in the dark forests in the heart of Zaire!

The Editor would like to thank Dr. Heuvelmans for this article which is previously unpublished, in French or English,, and is therefore an exclusive for 'Animals & Men'.

NOW THAT'S WHAT I CALL CRYPTO
by NEIL NIXON

Rare, elusive, the stuff of legend. Once encountered, forever pondered. No, not the water horse of New France. We're talking music here. Specifically, the tracks that make up the legendary album. '*Now that's what I call Crypto*'. This edition brings you....

"Bo Meets the Monster"

Starting with a pick on string guitar grind that would be impressive from any of the current crop of ace indie haircuts this basic blues soon settles down into the classic skeletal beat until the great man himself starts to intone another improbably adventure.

Waking up to find the Purple People Eater sitting in his old apple tree Diddley takes to the sky in his own plane and on the way to see his 'Baby' notices '*All those funny people from another land*'. Having got to his 'baby's' house Diddley has to leave again right away. It doesn't make a lot of sense but it does give his 'baby' the chance to break down and beg '*Bo Diddley, Bo Diddley, don't leave me in this house*'. Advising the hysterical chick to '*lock all the windows and bolt all the doors*', Diddley rambles in classic fashion. This is musical rambling with a burst of scratchy riffing and a rough edged short solo, before heading for the skies and arriving back home at which point he discovers that the Purple People Eater has 'had' his 'baby' and gone. Scratch riff/rapid fade.

We're talking cheapo production, continuity errors which make your average Charles Berlitz book look like the Encyclopaedia Britannica and a story that has more events than logic. Yup, its 1961, the teen market and the musical equivalent of those tacky films '*The Giant Gila Monster*', '*Plan 9 from Outer Space*', etc. If you're the picky type who can't understand how Diddley's baby from her own place to his faster than Diddley's plane, give this one a wide berth. If you're up for a bit of tack with attitude from a guy whose riff history makes ZZ Top look like Mozart then buy up the whole Diddley catalogue now!!! On the way you'll find this obscure gem nestled three quarters of the way through '*Chess Masters Volume 2*'. From the crypto point of view this is an interesting diversion. For starters its an insight into late fifties/early sixties values and monster archetypes. The Purple People Eater is, well, whatever you want him, her or it to be. Anything from an escaped circus geek to some bizarre biological offshoot that would give Mulder and Scully an adventure to remember. Short on genuine crypto substance maybe, but this is a crypto adventure to match any other committed to vinyl!

The Life and Times of Bert Palmer 1989-1995
by Chris Moiser.
(Photographs by the author).

Although born in Paignton, Devon, Bert spent most of his life in Cornwall. He had left 'home' as the capybara equivalent of a teenager, to be one of the main exhibits at Joy and John Palmer's Porfell Animal Land, near Lanreath, in late 1989. Little is known of his early days at Porfell, except that he had a spacious enclosure with a stream running through it. This domestic, but mundane life did not last though.

The gales of January 1990 were some of the most severe to hit the South West in living memory. Nationally thirty seven people were killed and a considerable amount of damage was done to property. Bert's back wall, was one of the unreported casualties of this storm. Whether Bert was frightened by the storm, or whether he just fancied exploring Cornwall we will never know, but he left home and disappeared for three weeks. At the end of this time he was reported to be at Shill-a-mill lakes, a man-made fishery, two miles away. This establishment was originally constructed with the angler in mind, but serendipitously was also ideal capybara habitat.

Bert spent seventeen months living here. It was an almost idyllic type of existence, no-one really bothered him, the food was excellent, and there were lots of good hiding places. The only thing that was lacking was female (capybara) company. Knowlege of Bert's presence became local knowledge, and many local anglers who considered themselves to be good field naturalists looked on a sighting of Bert as a good omen. Sadly though, Bert's absence from Porfell was causing Joy and John major headaches. Initial attempts to catch him had proved unsuccessful, and the local authority was taking more than a passing interest.

Under English law, Capybaras are listed as being 'dangerous', and the local authority are therefore permitted to do just about whatever they like to control or capture ones that venture abroad unlawfully.

-30-

Bert, being the gentleman rodent that he was, decided not to be dangerous. In fact, the only thing that he proved dangerous to during seventeen months of freedom was a bucket full of groundbait that had, rather carelessly, been left under a caravan overnight. The owner of the groundbait had immediately forgiven him this peccadillo.

A point was reached, though, where the local authority issued an ultimatum; either Bert was recaptured quickly or they would use a marksman to kill him. At this stage the media started to take a greater interest and Bert became national, and then international news. Many letters of support came in, including one from a South American country where they still eat capybara! The local authority, sensing trouble, backed down a little and gave the Palmers some time to reconvene the 'capture committee'. Bert carried on regardless.

One saturday afternoon a group of us met at the fishery, we had borrowed and scrounged nets and other pieces of equipment, knowing that this might be our last chance. After what might loosely be described as a hectic three hours, Bert was back in captivity. Both capybara and human honour was intact and there were no serious injuries on either side.

Once back in captivity Bert was no longer a national media figure although the local newspaper did do a piece on him, together with rather a nice photograph. He was kept off show for a few months to try and get him used to human company again, at the same time a large enclosure was built. Female company seemed a good idea too, so Bertha was acquired from Twycross. Although an arranged marriage, it worked, they became inseparable companions and over the following years several babies were born. Sadly Bertha died, in labour, earlier in 1995,. It would be almost unacceptably anthropomorphic to say that Bert never got over losing her; perhaps it is just better to say that capybaras are almost all very social rodents.

Bert died suddenly, but peacefully on 30th August 1995, leaving several surviving offspring. Bert was, perhaps, the epitome of a liberated (in every sense of the word), 20th century rodent. He had an inauspicious start in life, he found fame as a young adult, and returned to normality and family life after stardom. He will be sadly missed by all who knew him. I'm glad to be one of many humans in that list.

THE STANLEY TIGER
by Jonathan Downes and Richard Muirhead.

Our current project is a book with the working title of 'The Mystery Animals of Hong Kong'. Numerous people have asked, one or other of us, why we are writing this book, when it is perfectly obvious that a territory the size of Hong Kong can't have any mystery animals? This could not be further from the truth. Hong Kong, is a collection of small islands and peninsular mainland in the estuary of the Pearl River in South China, and being on the cusp between the Northern Eurasian and Tropical Asian regions provides a unique habitat for a bizarre mix of wildlife.

There are indeed, genuine cryptids to be discovered, and these are discussed more fully in the pages of our book, but the truth of the matter is that there are so many anomalies between the diferent accounts of the fauna of the territory, and so many truths, half-truths and downright lies have been printed about it that nearly all of the wildlife of Hong Kong is a mystery.

In this article we present one particular story with some facets to it which are of interest to the fortean zoologist. It concerns the (now almost extinct) South China race of the Tiger, *Panthera tigris amoyensis*, and the man who was, perhaps one of the greatest naturalists to work in Hong Kong: Dr. Geoffrey Herklots.

In 1951, Dr. Herklots published a book called 'The Hong Kong Countryside'. This was the natural history bible to the authors when they were growing up in Hong Kong. Large portions of the book was written whilst he was interned by the Japanese in Stanley Internment Camp between 1941 and 1945.

There is no doubt at all that tigers were regular visitors tto Hong Kong during the first half of the century. One particular visit, however is rather more problematical. Herklots seemed unsure of what had actually happened: [1]

"During our internment at Stanley a remarkable story filtered into the camp that there was a tiger at large on Hong-Kong Island. Later it was reported to be on Stanley Peninsula. The guards got excited and it was risky walking about in the evening for an excited guard might fire at a prisoner mistaking him for a tiger! Soon pug marks were seen at the camp: I examined some myself but was by no means convinced. Then the

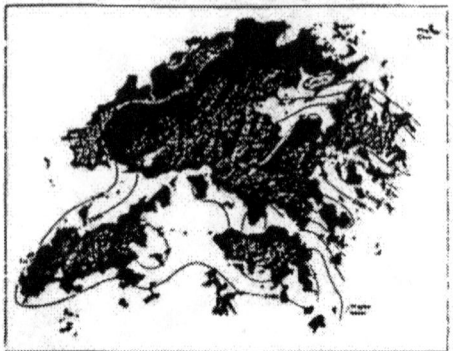

The Colony of Hong Kong

Stanley Peninsula
on Hong Kong Island

story was spread that the tiger had been shot and finally there came into camp a Chinese or Japanese paper containing a photograph of the dead tiger. This photograph I saw. People said that it was a menagerie animal that had got loose; a likely story! It is strange how loth people are to believe that tigers do visit the Colony and occasionally swim the harbour and visit the island".

We are loth to appear judgemental, but it appears from the above passage that Herklots himself was not fully impressed with the truth of this episode. There are, however several other pieces of supportive evidence, and it seems almost certain, to paraphrase 'Alice' that 'someone killed something' and that the 'something' was a large Tiger. The exact provenance of this tiger is less certain. 'Thagorus' (1979) wrote [2].

"During the war, a tiger was shot by a party of Japanese Militiamen near Stanley in May 1942. A Mr E.W.Bradbury, who was once a butcher with the Dairy Farm Company, was brought from the Stanley Internment camp to skin the animal, the meat from which subsequently provided a feast for members of the Hong Kong race club. The animal was three feet high, six feet long, weighed 240lbs and had a nineteen inch tail. The skin of the tiger was stuffed and mounted in the hall of Government House, from which it was subsequently transferred to Japan in 1944.

One theory about its presence on the island was that it had escaped from a menagerie during the Japanese invasion; another and more likely theory was that it had swum over from the mainland".

Although there are discrepancies between the two stories we shall avoid discussing them for the moment. Let us examine the supportive evidence for the claims. There is no doubt that a tiger is capable of swimming from the mainland to the island of Hong Kong, (or Lantau as well, as the 1915 beast is supposed to have done). As Guggisberg wrote in 1975: [3].

" (Tigers) can easily swim four or five miles"

Guggisberg also provides useful evidence to support the claims by Herklots and others that the regular visits by tigers to Hong Kong were a perfectly natural piece of behaviour on the part of an animal with a relatively large territorial range:

"The extent of a tiger's range varies considerably according to habitat and availability of prey. Corbett knew a tigress which for four and a half s years roamed over an area of 3885 square kilometres.

Kaplanov, who made a study of the Sikhote-Alin tigers and travelled hundreds of kilometres on skis following their tracks, found ten or twelve individuals within a region of 30,000 kilometres"...

A third account of the 1942 Stanley Tiger, whilst initially appearing to be valuable and exciting evidence in favour of the event actually casts some important doubts on its veracity. In 'Captive Years', their study of Hong Kong under Japanese occupation Birch and Cole (1982), describe conditions in Stanley Internment Camp, (now Stanley Prison). They quote a newspaper story from 'The Hong Kong News', an English language newspaper published by the occupying Japanese: [3]

"Fierce Tiger shot in Stanley Woods!

Successful Hong-Kong police hunt in early morning.

Although for some years past, rumours had circulated that there were tigers roaming the Hong Kong hills, it was only yesterday morning that such was shown to be fact and the feat of shooting the first tiger on the island was accomplished by Nipponese gendarmes and Indian and Chinese police at the back of Stanley village. Early yesterday morning the lowing of wild beasts was heard by many residents in Stanley village and gendarmes and police and military set off fully armed to search the hills. The search party consisting of Nipponese gendarmes and Indian and Chinese policemen was headed by Lt. Colonel Hirabayashi. The party was divided into smaller groups and a net was spread around the woods. After going over the ground for some considerable time, one group of searchers came across the tigers lair. They immediately opened fire but despite all efforts and the use of big wire netting the beast succeeded in evading the hunters. Not discouraged by the failure of the first attempt, the Nipponese police continued their search and a bigger cordon was thrown around the whole area.

Apparently alarmed by the noise the tiger rushed about the forest for some time when it was again encountered by the police party. The police opened fire, and shots from an Indian policeman this time found their mark, causing the tiger to halt. The Indian fired three shots, hitting the tiger in the head, left shoulder and lungs".

This is, presumably the newspaper article to which

Herklots refers, although of course, Herklots refers to a 'Chinese or Japanese' publication, inferring that the article might have been in Chinese or Japanese writing. This article, was of course, in English. Birch and Cole's book also includes a photograph of the dead beast, credited to 'Lady May Ride', (see below right), which is captioned:

"The famous Stanley Tiger which was shot by the guards in 1942. This appears to be the only unofficial photograph taken by an inmate at Stanley". (6)

The first thing that has to be ascertained is the identity of Lady May Ride. The only 'Ride', referred to in the text was Colonel Ride, the leader of the British Army Aid Group, the organisation which helped British Servicemen and other internees escape. Whether or not 'Lady May', is/was the wife of the gallant Colonel, it is unclear whether she is the copyright owner or if she indeed was the photographer.

If this is the photograph from the Japanese newspaper, referred to by Herklots, why was it taken by an internee, whoever he or she was? Collaborating with the enemy to the extent of becoming an unofficial press photographer for a newspaper full of propaganda, which was published by the occupying would have been considered almost treasonable? If this isn't the photograph, then it means that there is /was at least one other photograph purporting to be of the Stanley Tiger in existence! Despite the claims that this is an 'unofficial' photograph, it is obviously posed and well composed. The stringency of Japanese security arrangements, especially earlier on in the War, is clearly documented over again in this book. Violence, torture and even executions were relatively commonplace for what the Japanese considered to be infringements of security. If, indeed it was taken by an internee and not by a Japanese Press Photographer, then the evidence suggests that it was done so with the connivance, tacit, or overt of the Japanese Military.

The head of the creature is being supported by a man who appears to be an Indian, presumably the policeman that shot it. If the man in the picture is a guard/policeman, as seems probable, he was certainly aware that he was being photographed. He is even smiling for the camera! It seems almost impossible that the Japanese Security Forces could not have been aware of the photograph.

Two, seeming anomalies can be cleared up immediately. The guards/policemen are referred to as Indians and Formosans. Formosa (TAIWAN), was at the time a Japanese Colony. And although as Oliver Lindsay wrote: (7)

"The Japanese put great pressure on the Indians to turn traitor against Britain. the vast majority remained loyal",

This implies that some, including, presumably, the Indian man who is seen clutching the head of the Stanley Tiger, did not.

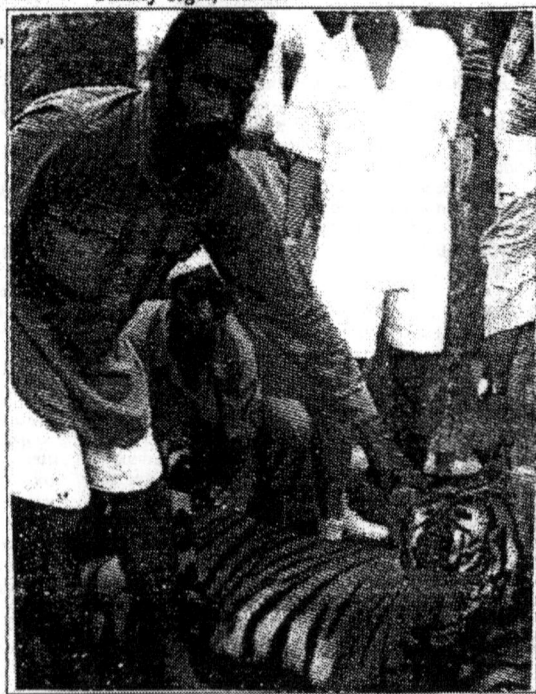

Editor's Note: If this picture is genuine it was taken in 1942 and is therefore, now, out of copyright

Lindsay continues: [8]

"The guards were later Formosan (Taiwanese) and were pettily officious and quick to take offence".

There is, however, another paradox. There may have been three thousand internees but it seems almost impossible that Herklots, who was after all Hong Kong's leading naturalist and the editor of the Hong Kong Naturalist magazine, and a minor celebrity in his own right, would not have known about the tiger incident from more than hearsay and rumours. Dr Herklots was important enough to be put in charge of revitalising the post war fishing industry for the region, in a successful attempt to restore food stocks as quickly as possible. Welsh (1993), gives more details of this affair and implies that Herklots, whom he describes, [9] as a *'Biologist just released from Stanley Internment Camp'* was a person of considerable importance. Even if he had not been taken to view the carcass in person, it seems certain that the photographer, who did see the carcass would have spoken to Herklots about it!

We have examined enough evidence from Herklots to suggest that he is a reliable and indeed an expert witness. His mind may have been vague about minor details, but surely an event as important to the sum total knowledge of the fauna of Hong Kong as this would have remained fresh in his mind. As forteans, the present authors are often accused of paranoid conspiracy theorising, but in this case, something doesn't add up!

The mounted skin was taken to a place of honour in the newly restored Government House and eventually to Tokyo as a trophy of war. The occupying army were inordinately proud of their trophy! At the time the Hong Kong News reported: [10]

"A party of press-men, invited to Stanley to see the tiger yesterday morning found it weighed about 240 lbs and measured three foot high, 73 inches long with a tail of 90 inches. According to the Chinese, the appearance of a tiger is an omen of the approach of a period of prosperity".

It seems likely that the invading Japanese were determined to extract the maximum of publicity from the event by exploiting local folk beliefs. Near the end of the war when it was obvious that they would lose they were still fermenting Chinese Nationalist feelings, often through the use of cultural motifs, and sometimes by recruiting collaborators, in an attempt to ensure that at least the British would no longer be in power in Hong Kong. They, as history has proven, failed, but what seems almost certain is that forty years later when Birch and Cole were researching the incident for their book someone, either wittingly or unwittingly, was not telling the whole truth!

Herklots was not the only person to report rumours that the animal had in fact escaped from Captivity. Writing in 1978 Lindsay said firmly that *"it had escaped from a circus during the invasion"*, [11] and had therefore only been on the loose for five months. It would be interesting to know whether he had any further evidence to support this supposition and was not just sharing in the view, so scorned by Herklots, that bona fide wild tigers never actually visited Hong Kong.

One is left to speculate that the 1942 Stanley Tiger may not be a genuine example of a rare animal visiting the Colony. If it was in fact an animal brought in from somewhere else and released so that it could be killed as a potent piece of psychological warfare then the incident is something far rarer and far more interesting to the fortean and to the student of military history!

The confusion surrounding this unfortunate beast does not end here, however.

A 1955 book by V.R.Burkhardt, describes the interior of the temple of the Queen of Heaven at Stanley: [12]

" A wooden tiger, about to spring, is a notorious enemy of evil spirits, and it is reinforced by a skin of the real beast hanging on the wall, whose resistance to moths has not been commensurate with his influence over the powers of darkness. This was the gift of an individual who attributed his escape from demoniac possession to the intervention of the image".

Jules Brown and Helen Lee (1993) [13] also mention the Tin Hau Temple, giving the additional information that it was built in 1767, and is therefore comparatively ancient by Hong Kong standards. They, too mention the tiger skin, and they claim that it was the skin of an animal that 'got his at the hands of an Indian Policeman in 1942', which presumably refers to the animal discussed above. (They also point out that whereas the name 'Stanley' serves to commemorate a nineteenth century Colonial Secretary, its Chinese name Chek Chue means lair of robbers or cheats, after the pirates who used the village as a base).

It would be tempting to theorise that this skin is

Animals & Men

Issue Nine

the pelt of the Stanley Tiger, finally come to rest in a spiritual environment after its theoretical use as a weapon of psychological warfare, but it is highly unlikely, especially as it seems that Burkhardt was only stationed in the colony between 1936 and 1939, three years before the unfortunate beast met its ignominious end at the hands of an un-named Indian policeman.

Both the references cited above which claim that the tiger pelt in the temple is that of the Stanley tiger, are therefore wrong!

A final observation is that it is interesting to note that Chang T'ien Shih, the Master of Heaven, and presumably the husband of the Queen to whom the temple at Stanley is dedicated is said to ride a tiger instead of a horse as his steed as he brandishes his demon vanquishing sword.[14]

This is just one bizarre incident of many in our files. Our forthcoming book will include as many more as we can discover, and will prove not only that those who scoff at the concept of 'mystery animals' in Hong Kong, are completely wrong, but that Heuvelmans, again was right when he claimed that 'There are lost worlds everywhere'.[15]

REFERENCES

1. HERKLOTS, G.A.K, 'The Hong Kong Countryside' (Hong Kong, SCMP, 1951)
2. 'THAGORUS', 'The Hong Kong Book of Records'. (Hong Kong, SCMP 1979)
3. GUGGISBERG, C.A.W. 'Wild Cats of the World' (Newton Abbot, David & Charles, 1975) p.196
4. GUGGISBERG C.A.W. op cit. p.199
5. BIRCH, A, & COLE M, 'Captive Years - The Occupation of Hong Kong 1941-51. (Hong Kong, Heinemann Educational Books (Asia), 1982).
6. ibid
7. LINDSAY O. 'The Lasting Honour - The Fall of Hong Kong 1941' (London. Hamish-Hamilton. 1978) p.1177
8. ibid
9. WELSH, Frank 'A History of Hong Kong' (London, Harper Collins, 1993) p.433
10. BIRCH, A, & COLE M, op cit.
11. LINDSAY O, 'The Lasting Honour - The Fall of Hong Kong 1941' (London. Hamish-Hamilton. 1978)12. BURKHARDT V.R., 'Chinese Creeds and Customs Volume 2' (HK, SCMP 1955) p.99
13. BROWN J, and LEE H, 'Hong Kong and Macao - the rough guide' (Rough Guides. London 1993)
14. BURKHARDT V.R., 'Chinese Creeds and Customs Volume 1' (HK SCMP 1953) p.179
15. HEUVELMANS Dr. B. 'On the Track of Unknown Animals' (1958. London, Hart-Davis).

ODD ORNITHOLOGY by Alison Downes

The artist formerly known as the Nervous Twitcher.

In August 1995, it was reported that a new species of nightjar had been discovered in Ethiopia. Dr Roger Stafford found the wing of a dead, squashed bird on the road one night in 1990, whilst on an expedition to Nechisar Plain. It has taken five years to establish what kind of bird it was. Now, experts are keen to find a live specimen. *Daily Telegraph 15.8.95*

From Hong Kong comes news of a rare Thick Billed Pigeon *(Treon cumrosta)*. Unfortunately it was found dead after hitting a fence at full speed. Coincidentally, several years earlier another specimen was found dead at almost exactly the same spot!

The skin of the first specimen is now in the British Museum. *Porcupine! March 1996 #14.*

People on the lookout for flocks of free flying parrot likes in Britain may well see the flock of Patagonian Conures (hello Socrates!) which live over Surrey and West Sussex.

These, however, belong to bird keeper Paul Bailey of Oakland Park farm, Surrey. They escaped one day about nine years ago by chewing through the aviary wire, but returned the following night to roost. Since then they have lived free, flying around the villages and countryside by day, and returning 'home' each night. This just goes to show how easily foriegn 'exotics' can live in our countryside. *Cage and Aviary Birds March 9 1996.*

As part of our new project about rare, vagrant and out of place birds, would all readers who would like to be involved send me photocopies of their county bird reports, and any birdwatching notes from their local newspapers. We would also be interested in news of any rare or unuausal animals seen in pet shops or for sale privately. Thanks AD.

OBITUARY: MARTIN "MORT" BROWN 1969-96

I didn't know Martin very well. He was just an anonymous name on a list of subscribers until the tragic death of our previous cartoonist. He offered to become our cartoonist, sent us some funny drawings that made me laugh, and didn't want paying. All the criteria were there and we gave him the job.

He telephoned occasionally and we would have long telephone conversations about Science Fiction, rock music, magick, and, oh yes, cryptozoology. He was a lake monster buff, and furthermore one with a wicked sense of humour as shown by his article in A&M8. What we didn't know was that for many years he had suffered from a depressive illness, and that in February this year he was to take his own life. His father telephoned me to tell us the news and to say that 'Mort' had left us his entire collection of books and papers on cryptozoology. I was touched, but immensely sad. A part of my life, and moreover, one that I valued, had been taken away. JD

A few weeks before he died he sent us this letter for publication. We print it as a tribute to a very talented man:

"Regarding Grover S.Krantz's article 'On Collecting a Cryptid' and to a lesser extent my own article on proof.

I'm against collecting a specimen. I don't think that it's necessary to say "far more likely producing a dead body", only dead will do. I should imagine that its very hard to dissect something when it can still breathe, I also expect that it would be unrealistic to expect the scientists to be satisfied with one dead body. There would be too much competition and always one more thing to check. The very best scenario we could expect would be live capture and live study, but how long would it take to get things right?

The late Gerald Durrell seems to have lost a great many specimens trying to keep them alive in captivity and HE cared about animals. The problem with both these approaches is the 'Cans in the Fridge' problem: "I'll just have one more..." before you know where you are there's no beer left!

The question raised in my mind is this: If we care about Unknown Animals, should we want to prove their existence at all? Humanity's track record seems to suggest that the future for any unknown proven to exist is black in the extreme. I don't think that it would be exaggerated to suggest that in the case of a cryptid with a limited range which is easily accessable, even relatively so, discovery would very soon lead to extinction! If science didn't finish them off the chances are that the rest of us, either by accident or design, probably would.

Regards,

Mort, England".

I had known Martin for over three years when he became a customer of Midnight Books in early 1993. He mainly bought material on Cryptozoology, but showed an interest in most mysteries. I found him articulate, open minded, intelligent and of great humour in our many telephone conversations. He was someone who loved to talk on a diverse range of subjects, and we would enjoyably work our way through a whole spectrum of topics in the course of a lengthy telephone conversation.

I remember well his first 'phone call to me which lasted well over two hours! Martin was a man of Principle too. If he felt he was being wronged he wouldn't let up until justice had been done. Shortly before his death he had finally won a five year battle with TIME-LIFE over some video material he was buying from them. I admired him for that.

He did promise to visit me last year but circumstances prevented him from doing so. It would have been nice to have met him - to have put a face to the voice. He was one of those rare kindred spirits one encounters now and then. I will miss his calls greatly and it will be strange not to speak to him again.

I do hope that wherever he is now he has one or two mysteries to solve - he'll be at home then!

Stephen Shipp,
Midnight Books,
Sidmouth.

Animals & Men

Issue Nine

HELP!

In issue 4 of this magazine we printed an appeal from Newsfile Editor Jan Williams for more information about two mysterious corpses washed up on an Essex beach. We received this reply last year, we think from a correspondent in Germany or France, but it became separated from the letter, and we cannot remember who sent it in. If you recognise the piece below, please contact the Editor!

"As already mentioned, in November of 1953, nearly a hundred years (after the mysterious footprints had been found on the Devon coast) a strange creature was washed ashore on the coast of the British Canvey Islands (sic). Nobody had ever seen anything like it. The finder covered the 80cm (33 inch) large creature, which had thick, red-brown skin and a deformed head with protruding eyes with seaweed and notified the local authorities.

The local authorities did not know what to think of the creature and asked the government in London for assistance. Two famous biologists arrived in Canvey. They examined, measured, and photographed the unidentified creature and announced that it was not related to or showed any resemblance to known animals.

It probably came out of the ocean. Its extremities allowed both bowed and/or erect movements. This is all that is known, since the two scientists decided to get rid of the mystery once and forever. They had the creature burned and refused any official comment.

Their attempt to conceal details about the creature would have been more successful if it wasn't for another cadaver being found on August 11th the next year.

Reverend Joseph Overs literally stumbled over it when he went for a walk on the beach not far from where the first creature had been found. The thing was lying in a little pool left from the last tide. The priest called the police. Bobbys carried the creature on land (sic). Again experts were called. This time, the investigation was done much more thoroughly. Again, no official classification of the creature was done.

The animal (?) was nearly twice the size of its predecessor, weighed around 25 lbs, and was in a good condition. It had two large eyes, nostrils, a mouth with strong, sharp teeth, and gills. Instead of the scales which would be expected, it had pink skin, resembling the colour of a healthy pig. Just like its predecessor it stood on two short legs which ended in U shaped soles. Every other information was treated with secrecy"...

We do not wish to comment until we have identified the source of the above passage, so watch this space! Any further information would be gratefully appreciated.

Recent Bigfoot Research
from Bill Green of the N.E.Bigfoot Centre.

* Pocetello, Iowa. A woman claimed she encountered a 7-8 foot tall, brownish grey bigfoot-type creature standing in her back-yard watching her. This sighting took place three years ago this March.

* A friend of mine claimed that he found fifteen inch long footprints in the snow on South Mountain near a reservoir in Bristol, Conneticut during the winter of 1994/5.

Green Kitten Update
by Eric Sorenson.

The latest news about Miss Greeny, the Danish green cat is both good and bad. The colour has, according to an article in the Danish newspaper, 'Ekstrabladet', Feb 3rd 1996, faded almost away, meaning that sadly, the green was probably of a secondary nature. Good news for the cat, though, because it was obviously fed up with being on exhibition, photographed and being handled endlessly. It can now concentrate on cat business.

The hair sample was confirmed as being genuinely green by the laboratory, so the risk of a clever hoax must be considered to be minimal. The presence of copper was not mentioned. Strangely, things tend to pop up together, with the help of the Editor, ('Gee Thanks Eric' JD). It seems that the green dog described by Richard Muirhead (A&M8) was explained as beiung Utera Verdi - greening in its mothers womb. This sounds a very good hypothesis to me, and a good explanation for the loss of colour with subsequent hair growth.Anyway, the cat's days as a celebrity, getting attention from the BBC, Readers Digest, Associated press, and the cat fanciers' home page on the Internet, where it created a raging success, are over. The family, her owners, are not dissatisfied. They were being accused of money-making, (all they got were three bottles of wine from a museum), and were getting strange letters and telephone calls. An American doctor (?) claimed to have three patients with green hair, a German wanted the cat for a peace crusade etc...

But the cat is not green anymore. Clever Cat!

HELP!

In issue 4 of this magazine we printed an appeal from Newsfile Editor Jan Williams for more information about two mysterious corpses washed up on an Essex beach. We received this reply last year, we think from a correspondent in Germany or France, but it became separated from the letter, and we cannot remember who sent it in. If you recognise the piece below, please contact the Editor!

"As already mentioned, in November of 1953, nearly a hundred years (after the mysterious footprints had been found on the Devon coast) a strange creature was washed ashore on the coast of the British Canvey Islands (sic). Nobody had ever seen anything like it. The finder covered the 80cm (33 inch) large creature, which had thick, red-brown skin and a deformed head with protruding eyes with seaweed and notified the local authorities.

The local authorities did not know what to think of the creature and asked the government in London for assistance. Two famous biologists arrived in Canvey. They examined, measured, and photographed the unidentified creature and announced that it was not related to or showed any resemblance to known animals.

It probably came out of the ocean. Its extremities allowed both bowed and/or erect movements. This is all that is known, since the two scientists decided to get rid of the mystery once and forever. They had the creature burned and refused any official comment.

Their attempt to conceal details about the creature would have been more successful if it wasn't for another cadaver being found on August 11th the next year.

Reverend Joseph Overs literally stumbled over it when he went for a walk on the beach not far from where the first creature had been found. The thing was lying in a little pool left from the last tide. The priest called the police. Bobbys carried the creature on land (sic). Again experts were called. This time, the investigation was done much more thoroughly. Again, no official classification of the creature was done.

The animal (?) was nearly twice the size of its predecessor, weighed around 25 lbs, and was in a good condition. It had two large eyes, nostrils, a mouth with strong, sharp teeth, and gills. Instead of the scales which would be expected, it had pink skin, resembling the colour of a healthy pig. Just like its predecessor it stood on two short legs which ended in U shaped soles. Every other information was treated with secrecy"...

We do not wish to comment until we have identified the source of the above passage, so watch this space! Any further information would be gratefully appreciated.

Recent Bigfoot Research
from Bill Green of the N.E. Bigfoot Centre.

* Pocetello, Iowa. A woman claimed she encountered a 7-8 foot tall, brownish grey bigfoot-type creature standing in her back-yard watching her. This sighting took place three years ago this March.

* A friend of mine claimed that he found fifteen inch long footprints in the snow on South Mountain near a reservoir in Bristol, Conneticut during the winter of 1994/5.

Green Kitten Update
by Eric Sorenson.

The latest news about Miss Greeny, the Danish green cat is both good and bad. The colour has, according to an article in the Danish newspaper, 'Ekstrabladet', Feb 3rd 1996, faded almost away, meaning that sadly, the green was probably of a secondary nature. Good news for the cat, though, because it was obviously fed up with being on exhibition, photographed and being handled endlessly. It can now concentrate on cat business.

The hair sample was confirmed as being genuinely green by the laboratory, so the risk of a clever hoax must be considered to be minimal. The presence of copper was not mentioned. Strangely, things tend to pop up together, with the help of the Editor, ('Gee Thanks Eric' JD). It seems that the green dog described by Richard Muirhead (A&M8) was explained as beiung Utera Verdi - greening in its mothers womb. This sounds a very good hypothesis to me, and a good explanation for the loss of colour with subsequent hair growth. Anyway, the cat's days as a celebrity, getting attention from the BBC, Readers Digest, Associated press, and the cat fanciers' home page on the Internet, where it created a raging success, are over. The family, her owners, are not dissatisfied. They were being accused of money-making, (all they got were three bottles of wine from a museum), and were getting strange letters and telephone calls. An American doctor (?) claimed to have three patients with green hair, a German wanted the cat for a peace crusade etc...

But the cat is not green anymore. Clever Cat!

LETTERS TO THE EDITOR

'THE OWLMAN STRIKES BACK'

Dear Jon,

Forget about the whole thing? Are you kidding? For now I'll die fighting. The objections to the reality of 'owlman' recently brought up in your letters are hard to dismiss at all convincingly but at the same time, to my mind, they are ridiculous. We have some very big problems here. Owlman looks like a very large owl (hey, it's not called owlman for nothing guys?), I've seen it and those who object haven't. Janet Bord wrote of her suspicions that the creature, despite my protestations was an owl. The only way to ever be sure that you have seen an image as recorded in your mind is to see that image again, and, as I don't think (and hope) it likely that I will ever see the creature again, I do remain sceptical of my own conscience. Owls tend not to grow to more than four feet in height, nor would sightings of them result in the construction of exactly the same mental image, as drawn independently by witnesses including myself. That, for me, is the biggest problem. If I see an owl I draw an owl, not the same quasi-bird humanoid that teenage girls and Doc Shiels were drawing back in the late 'seventies.

John Heath-Stubbs clearly did not read my account: if he did he considers me either a liar or a pathetic observer. 'The five feet given by the observer is wrong' ?????!!! Excuse me, but trying to say that 'owlman cannot be five foot tall because eagle owls do not exceed two feet', is an absurd approach to the data, and a poor attempt to dismiss it. I have decided that to prove to myself, if no-one else, that the animal I saw was considerably bigger than an eagle owl, I need to find the actual tree in which my sighting occurred. Photos, when obtained, will be published.

John Heath-Stubbs notes it is characteristic of owls that two toes point forward while 'the outer toe' is reversed. Actually the 'inner toe' (digit 1), is reversed too. This could be the case in owlman, but the large, bulky, pincer feet (again remarked upon independently by

witnesses), don't remind me one bit of an owl's slim feet. Look at my drawings for god's sake.

'Gavin',
Somewhere.

AUSTRALOPITHECINES AHOY!

Dear Jonathan,

... regarding a communication of Darren Naish, Southampton (A&M7), about my article 'Mysterious Hominoids of Africa' ((A&M6), would you be very kind and publish this short reply:

As I submitted my manuscript to Jonathan Downes, the corrigendum to 'Australopithecus ramidus, a new species of early hominid' was not yet published (Nature Vol. 375:88, 4.May 1995). I fully agree the generic separation from Australopithecus. Effectively Ardipithecus (not 'Aldipithecus'!), lacked some specialised features known from the Australopithecus lineages, regarding is thin molar enamel, and the large canines, Ardipithecus ramidus seems to have been more closely related to Pan (chimps), as I already emphasised in my paper in A&M6.

Keep up your good work for Fortean Zoology.
Best wishes,

Francois de Sarre.

animals&men

THE JOURNAL OF THE CENTRE FOR FORTEAN ZOOLOGY

Animals & Men — Issue Nine

NORTH OF THE BORDER

Musings on Fortean Zoology from our Scottish correspondent Tom Anderson.

The institute of Terrestrial Ecology has launched an otter research project to discover the reasons behind its Scottish increase as against its southern decline. They cite roadkills as a possible source of information using DNA testing.

Re DNA. Aberdeen University claim to have found the Common Pipistrelle population to consist of two separate but closely related species. *(Did this come before, after or coincidentally with the discovery of two species of Pipistrelle in Yorkshire making different sounds? Are there in fact three species? Ed)*

Perusing an early volume of this worthy journal, I noticed an interest in the mustelidae on the behalf of the editor. Some years ago, when I worked for Marconi, we used to service the radars and the echo-sounders of the fishing fleet. In those days the west coast boats sailed round into Aberdeen to land their catch. This caused great anguish and angst among our engineers as wild mink infested these boats and led to much tucking of trousers into socks. A sort of Scottish version of the Yorkshire ferret olympics!

Yesterday, driving from Tomintoul to Braemar across moorland I was buzzed by red grouse. Half a dozen males flew straight at the car, swerving at the last second, only a metre or so away. They then settled on the road and commenced displaying to the females, using the tarmac as a 'leck'. I hadn't realised they were so aggressive. Mind you, bearing in mind the recent 'death plunge' perpetrated by a grouse on one YOUR Monarch *(REALLY, Thomas! ...Your friendly Editor who approves of the Act of Union, but then he's English)*, I'm starting to consider the possibility of role reversal on the moors. I quite like the idea of the Aristocracy being thinned out by 'death wish' grouse catching them in the plus fours when least expected. Add to that the likely future escapees from proliferating ostrich farms, and green wellies and Range Rovers could soon become a folk memory!

Yours still ducking and weaving,

Tom Anderson.
Aberdeen.

MORE IS NESS

Dear A&M,

I wonder if it is still possible to comment on something written in issue five. Mr Leadbetter commented on some of the things I wrote in reaction to his earlier article. He seems to wonder why I assemble a collection of Loch Ness reports if I can not be sure that the stories from which they come are true or fact. My answer is this: You've got to start somewhere when you want to study a thing like the case for the Loch Ness phenomena. One of the most important ingredients in this case are the sightings. The sightings come from various sources. Mr Leadbetter should know this as he stated that he considers himself familiar with the vast majority of Loch Ness sightings. He must therefore be familiar with the fact that a lot of books and other material on the Loch Ness Monster state the same sightings but not always the same data. Sometimes you have to deal with additional information on a sighting and other times you have to deal with completely different information concerning the same sighting. This is not always due to a messed up witness but very often to a messed up author who has difficulty in copying material from earlier sources, like other books. I agree with Mr Leadbetter that this makes the sightings liable to being unreliable. By putting the different versions together in one collection I hope to get a clearer view into these sightings and try to take out of this collection the data 'most likely to be reliable', in order to make analyses on various details from this data. A lot of the sightings are indeed unverifiable and could be flawed but that does not mean that they cannot be used for study.

Even recent sightings which can be verified could be flawed, so for me there is no reason not to look at the older sightings. If being verifiable, or 'may be subject to being flawed' were the main criteria in this study for me, then there would be no use to study the Loch Ness phenomena at all, but I agree with Mr Leadbetter that you have to keep these criteria in mind; and so does he when he states that sturgeon of 20 foot or more were common in the Danube and the Volga during the 19th Century. This statement looks unverifiable and could be highly flawed, or did he find a witness? I heard that people in the USSR sometimes reach a great age, but I cannot verify this, and this to might be flawed information.

Yours faithfully,
M. 't Mannetje
The Netherlands.

animals&men

THE JOURNAL OF THE CENTRE FOR FORTEAN ZOOLOGY

Animals & Men   Issue Nine

THE LOCH NESS SOCIETY

We recently received the following press release:

"Following the recent release of the Hollywood film 'Loch Ness', a new society has been formed to further investigate and conserve Loch Ness itself and the 'Nessie' mystery.

The new society aims to bring together all the thousands of people who visit and share an interest in the Loch. It intends to launch further and more up to date techniques in the search to solve the mystery of the monster. It will also involve itself in the many environmental and conservation issues around the shores of Loch Ness.

There will be an annual expedition to the Loch in the desire to re-kindle the spirit of the old Loch Ness Investigation Bureau expeditions of the 60's and 70's. In those days thousands of people from all ages and backgrounds took part in camera watches, boat surveillance and collating the many eye witness reports.

This new Society has been formed by Richard A Carter and Ian Kelloway who among many others have been interested in the Loch and its mysteries for many years. They have become aware of the lack of one organisation to which people can relate and partake in organised activity and which can update current information. It is a shame that there has been less and less promotion of Loch Ness, which attracts millions of visitors each year, and it is our intention to reverse that trend".

You can contact the Loch Ness Society at:

34 Weston Crescent, Horfield Common, Bristol BS7 8UT

FUTURE PLANS FOR THE CENTRE FOR FORTEAN ZOOLOGY

The Centre for Fortean Zoology has now been in existence for over four years, and we have been active for the last two and a half. The time has come to try and move onto a higher plane.

We have, as regular readers will know, an active and enthusiastic team of regional and national representatives. As of the first of April, Alison Downes is taking over the coordination of this team of enthusiasts and she will be actively organising several new areas of research.

Starting this summer, we shall be producing an irregular series of 'ANIMALS & MEN SUPPLEMENTS'. The first two will cover exotic pets, (their husbandry, taxonomy and potential threat to the UK Ecosystem) and Vagrant Birds (A twitcher's delight - a list of every record of an aberrant bird during the previous twelve months, together with ornithological details, maps and as much other information as we can find).

The supplement series will be edited by Alison Downes.

We are working on a number of new and reissued publications as well. The first of our 'new wave' of products is now available:

"Morgawr-the monster of Falmouth Bay"
by Anthony Mawnan-Peller.

This booklet was originally published in 1976, but with the permission of the author, we have reissued it with a new introduction by Tony 'Doc' Shiels and an explanatory essay by Jonathan Downes. It costs £1.50 (plus 25p p&p) and is available from the editorial address.

BOOK REVIEWS

'The Moron's Guide to the Paranormal'
by Jon D Inman (JD £3.99 32pp).

As an author who has worked hard on his three or four self published books, and a publisher who has worked hard for years to produce quality product at a reasonable price I find the elevation of what Frank Zappa once called 'A Tacky Little Pamphlet' into a book quite offensive. My prices are not cheap, some of the second hand books we sell are quite expensive, it all depends on what I had to pay to get hold of them. This is nothing short of exorbitant.

The contents? It is one of those immensely sad tomes; a 'funny' book which singularly fails to amuse. Its mildly amusing in parts, tedious in others and veers towards blasphemy in one particularly annoying section.

It has only two thirds of the pages of an issue of 'Animals & Men', and costs twice the price. Buy it at your peril!

'Mythical Beasts' Edited by John Cherry
(British Museum Publications 192pp £18.99).

Gloriously produced and as scholarly as one would have expected. This isn't chock full of revelations destined to take the 'crypto' world by storm, but it is a good solid primer on the subject which presents the available facts in a concise and pleasing manner.

This is not a book about cryptozoology, nor does it pretend to be. It covers historical matters to a far greater depth than I have seen before. It is probably the best book to be written on the subject of zoomythology since Peter Costello's "The Magic Zoo", and should probably be read in conjunction with it.

It is a highly pleasing book to read from an aesthetic point of view, andbeautifully laid out and designed.

The chapter on the Sphynx is particularly good, presenting, as it does a wealth of information that has not to my knowledge been gathered together in the same place before. Excellent!

'Hong Kong's Wild Places - an environmental exploration' by Edward Stokes (OUP 196pp £25.00).

This lavishly illustrated book presents many of the reasons why Hong Kong is rapidly becoming of greater interest to the fortean zoologist than most other places (except possibly New Guinea and Vu Quang). Stokes writes in a clear and happy style, and explains how although like the rest of southern China Hong Kong waspractically deforested by the time that the British arrived in 1841, but how a concerted programme of reforestation starting in about 1904 started to restore the landscape to the way it would have been three or four hundred years ago.

The next twist in the tale happened when the Japanese invaded in 1941, and over the next four years cut down much of the carefully restored forest as firewood. Stokes shows how the process started again in 1946, and how, with the exodus of people from the villages of the New Territories, the traditional feng shui woods have spread, so now areas which even when your editor knew them in the late 1960's were barren rocks and grassland, are now dense forest. What Stokes has not discussed is the way that the original fauna is returning, and some totally new beasts are arriving to populate these new forests, but that is, after all what the book currently being written by your editor and Richard Muirhead is all about, so it is probably a good thing at least as far as we are concerned!

This is an excellent book and moreover one which we reccomend wholeheartedly to anyone with even the most passing interest in the orient, its wild places, and what is probably the most fortean place on earth. Even if you just buy it for the photographs, (which are outstanding) it is, by anyone's standards, worth the money!

Animals & Men — Issue Nine

PERIODICAL REVIEWS

We now exchange with so many publications that only those magazines received those magazines who have sent us material within the previous three months will be reviewed each issue.

CRYPTOZOOLOGY AND ZOOMYTHOLOGY

THE BRITISH COLUMBIA CRYPTOZOOLOGY CLUB NEWSLETTER, 3773 West 18th Avenue, Vancouver, British Columbia, Canada. V65 1B3. Excellent and well put together, and they are now on the Internet as well! Latest issue features Loch Ness, the monster of Lake Tanganika and much more

CRYPTOZOOLOGIA, Association Belge d'Etude et de Protection des Animaux Rares, Square des Latins 49/4, 1050 Bruxelles. Belgium. A French language magazine published by the Belgian society for Cryptozoology.

BIGFOOT RECORD, Bill Green, NE Bigfoot Centre, 21 Benham St. #F, Bristol. CT 06010. USA Round up of BHM News from the N.E. USA

EXOTIC ZOOLOGY, Matthew Bille, 3405 Windjammer Drive, Colorado Springs. CO 80920. USA. Excellent newsletter on new and rediscovered species.

FORTEAN

TEMS NEWS, 115 Hollybush Lane, Hampton, Middlesex, TW12 2QY. An entertaining collection of odds and sods and generally weird stuff. A magazine I alwaysenjoy reading Reccomended.

FOAFTALE NEWS, MUN Folklore & Language Archive, Memorial University of Newfoundland, St. John's, Newfoundland, A1B 3XB Canada. Scholarly magazine about folklore, and the mechanics of how it becomes assimilated into societies. Highly reccomended.

THE ANOMALIST, available in the UK from this office. Excellent bi-annual book about anomalous phenomena, cryptozoology and general forteana. Highly reccomended.

ZOOLOGY

SOUTH WEST HERPETOLOGICAL SOCIETY, Frank Gibbons, Acanthus, 59 St Marychurch Road, Torquay, Devon. Entertaining and informative newsletter from a thriving organisation.

BIPEDIA, Francois de Sarre, CERBI, 6, Avenue George V. 06000 Nice, France. Interesting journal about the theory of Initial Bipedalism.

PORTSMOUTH REPTILE AND AMPHIBIAN SOCIETY, M.Jones, 7 Haslemere Rd., Southsea, Hants. Erudite and witty magazine from another excellent society.

MILTON KEYNES HERPETOLOGICAL SOCIETY, 15 Esk Way, Bletchley, Milton Keynes. Fascinating reptilian facts and hints on husbandry. Reccomended.

MAINLY ABOUT ANIMALS, 13 Pound Place, Shalford, Guildford, Surrey. GU4 8HH. A zoological magazine of the sort most of us feared was lost forever.

ESSEX REPTILES AND AMPHIBIANS SOCIETY, 6 Chestnut Way, Tiptree, Colchester, Essex. CO5 0NX. Insightful and well researched look at Reptiles and Amphibians.

PORCUPINE! c/o Kadoorie Agricultural Research Centre, HKU, Lam Kam Road, Yueng Long, New Territories, Hong Kong. Wonderful newsletter about rare and newly discovered species in the territory of Hong Kong. I cannot praise this magazine highly enough.

FRINGE SCIENCE

NEXUS 55 Queens Rd, E. Grinstead, West Sussex RH19 1BG. Intelligent look at the fringes of science. Well put together. Very impressive.

SCIENCE FRONTIERS, P.O.Box 107, Glen Arm, MD21057. Produced by William Corliss, of the Sourcebook Project, this is a marvellous pot pourri of fringe science information.

THE EDITORIAL TEAM APOLOGISE TO THE EDITORS OF THE MAGAZINES NOT LISTED ABOVE FOR OUR CHANGE IN POLICY, BUT SEVERE LACK OF SPACE PRECLUDES US HAVING THREE PAGES OF MAG-LISTINGS

BOOK REVIEWS

'The Moron's Guide to the Paranormal'
by Jon D Inman (JD £3.99 32pp).

As an author who has worked hard on his three or four self published books, and a publisher who has worked hard for years to produce quality product at a reasonable price I find the elevation of what Frank Zappa once called 'A Tacky Little Pamphlet' into a book quite offensive. My prices are not cheap, some of the second hand books we sell are quite expensive, it all depends on what I had to pay to get hold of them. This is nothing short of exorbitant.

The contents? It is one of those immensely sad tomes; a 'funny' book which singularly fails to amuse. Its mildly amusing in parts, tedious in others and veers towards blasphemy in one particularly annoying section.

It has only two thirds of the pages of an issue of 'Animals & Men', and costs twice the price. Buy it at your peril!

'Mythical Beasts' Edited by John Cherry
(British Museum Publications 192pp £18.99).

Gloriously produced and as scholarly as one would have expected. This isn't chock full of revelations destined to take the 'crypto' world by storm, but it is a good solid primer on the subject which presents the available facts in a concise and pleasing manner.

This is not a book about cryptozoology, nor does it pretend to be. It covers historical matters to a far greater depth than I have seen before. It is probably the best book to be written on the subject of zoomythology since Peter Costello's "The Magic Zoo", and should probably be read in conjunction with it.

It is a highly pleasing book to read from an aesthetic point of view, and beautifully laid out and designed.

The chapter on the Sphynx is particularly good, presenting, as it does a wealth of information that has not to my knowledge been gathered together in the same place before. Excellent!

'Hong Kong's Wild Places - an environmental exploration' by Edward Stokes (OUP 196pp £25.00).

This lavishly illustrated book presents many of the reasons why Hong Kong is rapidly becoming of greater interest to the fortean zoologist than most other places (except possibly New Guinea and Vu Quang). Stokes writes in a clear and happy style, and explains how although like the rest of southern China Hong Kong was practically deforested by the time that the British arrived in 1841, but how a concerted programme of re-forestation starting in about 1904 started to restore the landscape to the way it would have been three or four hundred years ago.

The next twist in the tale happened when the Japanese invaded in 1941, and over the next four years cut down much of the carefully restored forest as firewood. Stokes shows how the process started again in 1946, and how, with the exodus of people from the villages of the New Territories, the traditional feng shui woods have spread, so now areas which even when your editor knew them in the late 1960's were barren rocks and grassland, are now dense forest. What Stokes has not discussed is the way that the original fauna is returning, and some totally new beasts are arriving to populate these new forests, but that is, after all what the book currently being written by your editor and Richard Muirhead is all about, so it is probably a good thing at least as far as we are concerned!

This is an excellent book and moreover one which we reccomend wholeheartedly to anyone with even the most passing interest in the orient, its wild places, and what is probably the most fortean place on earth. Even if you just buy it for the photographs, (which are outstanding) it is, by anyone's standards, worth the money!

animals&men

THE JOURNAL OF THE CENTRE FOR FORTEAN ZOOLOGY

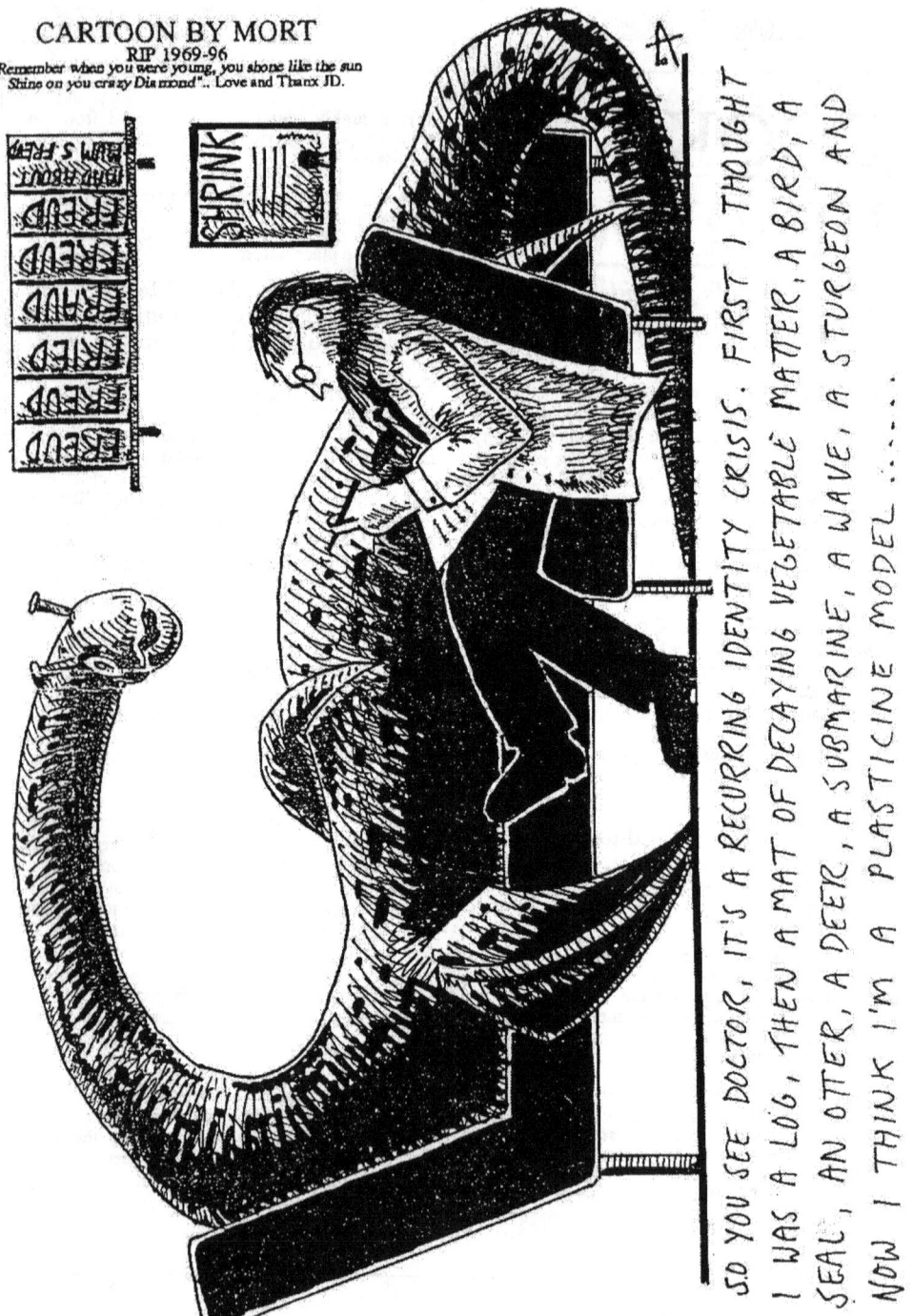

CARTOON BY MORT
RIP 1969-96
"Remember when you were young, you shone like the sun
Shine on you crazy Diamond".. Love and Thanx JD.

SO YOU SEE DOCTOR, IT'S A RECURRING IDENTITY CRISIS. FIRST I THOUGHT I WAS A LOG, THEN A MAT OF DECAYING VEGETABLE MATTER, A BIRD, A SEAL, AN OTTER, A DEER, A SUBMARINE, A WAVE, A STURGEON AND NOW I THINK I'M A PLASTICINE MODEL ......

© STP 1996 ISSN 1354-0637

ISSUE 10
JULY 1996

animals&men

THE JOURNAL OF THE CENTRE FOR FORTEAN ZOOLOGY

This issue is particularly poignant for me because it was the last issue that I worked on with my ex-wife. Between the time the issue was finished and sent off to the printers and the time that it was sent out we were separated and she was suing me for divorce. Perhaps because of my personal problems at the time I tend to overlook what a cracking issue this was! Looking again at it I am very proud of our achievements. Ten years later, as I write this, we have come a long way further....

Animals & Men

THE JOURNAL OF THE CENTRE FOR FORTEAN ZOOLOGY

The Journal of the Centre for Fortean Zoology

The Mystery Moth of Madagascar; Leopard Cats; The Lake Storsjon Monster; Mystery Whales; Wild Boar in Kent

Issue Ten   £1.75

animals&men

THE JOURNAL OF THE CENTRE FOR FORTEAN ZOOLOGY

Animals & Men

Issue Nine

The ever changing crew of the 'Animals & Men' mothership presently consists of:

Jonathan Downes: Editor
Jan Williams: Newsfile Editor
Alison Downes: Administratrix supreme
Mark North: Artist
Graham Inglis: You name it he does it

CONSULTANTS

Dr Bernard Heuvelmans
(Honorary Consulting Editor)
Dr Karl P.N.Shuker
(Cryptozoological Consultant)
C.H.Keeling
(Zoological Consultant)
Tony 'Doc' Shiels
(Surrealchemist in Residence)

REGIONAL REPRESENTATIVES
UK
Scotland: Tom Anderson
Surrey: Nck Smith
Yorkshire: Richard Freeman
Somerset: Dave McNally
West Midlands: Dr Karl Shuker
Kent: Neil Arnold
Sussex: Sally Parsons
Hampshire: Darren Naish
Lancashire: Stuart Leadbetter
Norfolk: Justin Boote
Leicestershire: Alaistair Curzon
Cumbria: Brian Goodwin
S.Wales/Salop: Jon Matthias

EUROPE
Switzerland: Sunila Sen-Gupta
Spain: Alberto Lopez Acha
Germany: Wolfgang Schmidt & Hermann Reichenbach
France: Francois de Sarre
Denmark: Lars Thomas and Eric Sorenson
Eire: The Wizard of the western world.

OUTSIDE EUROPE
Mexico: Dr R.A Lara Palmeros
Canada: Ben Roesch
New Zealand: Steve Matthewman

DISCLAIMER
The Views published in articles and letters in this magazine are not necessarily those of the publisher or editorial team, who although they have taken all lengths not to print anything defamatory or which infringes anyone's copyright take no responsibility for any such statement which is inadvertantly included.

CONTENTS
P 3. Editorial
P 4. Newsfile
p. 12. A-Z of Cryptozoology
p.12. Wolf Scare
p 13. Cryptocetology
p 22. Spotting Cats with Spots
p 24. North of the Border
p 25. The predicted moth of Madagascar
p 27. Of Moose, Men and Monsters
p 29. The Derry
p 31.The boars are back in town.
p 32. Now thats what I call crypto
p 33. West African 'Owlman'
p. 33. Letter from the Lochside
p 34 HELP
p 35 Odd Ornithology
p 36 Letters
p 40. Book Reviews
p 43. Periodical Reviews
p.44 Cartoon

Contributors to this issue:
Darren Naish, Eric Sorenson, Anita Cox, Clinton Keeling, Michel Raynal, Tom Anderson, Lars Thomas, Sunila Sen Gupta, Neil Arnold, Neil Nixon, Owen Burnham, Richard Carter, Richard Freeman, Michael Goss, Colin Mather, Marien Mannetje.

SUBSCRIPTIONS
For a Four Issue Subscription
£7.00 UK
£8.00 EEC
£10.00 US,CANADA, OZ, NZ
(Surface Mail)
£12.00 US,CANADA, OZ, NZ
(Air Mail)
£14.00 Rest of World
(Air Mail)

Payment in cash, (UK, or US currency-other currencies by arrangement), IMO, Eurocheque, cheque drawn on a UK bank. All cheques made payable to 'A&J Downes' if you please.

'Animals & Men'

THE CENTRE FOR FORTEAN ZOOLOGY,
15 Holne Court,
Exwick, Exeter.
EX4 2NA

Telephone   01392 424811
Mobile Telephone 0402 007 302
Fax   01392 496896

THE GREAT DAYS OF ZOOLOGY ARE NOT DONE

With this issue we have now reached double figures, and the Centre for Fortean Zoology is going from strength to strength. We are now in the position where we are able to do something more than just publish magazines and books.

At the Fortean Times sponsored Unconvention this year, Karl Shuker introduced me to someone who almost by accident has steered us onto the course which will hopefully define the next few years of our existence. The person Karl introduced me to was Owen Burnham, who as a schoolboy discovered the carcass of what many people believe was a sea-serpent on a beach in The Gambia. I chatted to him with interest, and was amazed when he told me that he was 'pretty sure' that he could find the spot on the beach where the carcass had been buried.

Since then events have gathered momentum, and plans are being drawn up for an expedition to The Gambia. We have a map of the beach, a little like Long John Silver's Treasure Map in 'Treasure Island' with a large 'X' marking the spot where we believe that the carcass of the Gambian Sea Serpent (good initials eh?) is buried. Within the past few weeks one of our associates went to The Gambia, and drew a detailed map of the portion of the beach where Owen remembers the creature as being buried. This map proves that whether or not the bones are still there, the building development which has taken place in the area over the past decade and a half has not affected the place where the carcass is buried.

We have got the backing of a television company, and it looks as if we are on course to investigate one of the most tantalising mysteries of contemporary cryptozoology.

We are also thinking about an expedition to search for the Tatzelwurm in Switzerland, possibly also during 1997. We will be in a position to take a limited number of people with us. Are there any readers of 'Animals & Men' who would be interested in accompanying us? If so, you would have to meet your own costs, but we are planning to make block bookings so that we can keep the costs to a minimum. The expedition would split into two groups; one group who would explore the areas in which the animal has been seen most recently and the other who plan to investigate museums, libraries and records offices, as well as interviewing eyewitnesses, with the aim of building up as complete a dossier as possible on this reclusive cryptid. This expedition is still at the earliest planning stages but we would welcome feedback from our readership, and if there are enough people interested in becoming involved to make this expedition a viable possibility then we shall definitely be going ahead!

If you are interested, give us a ring...

animals & men

THE JOURNAL OF THE CENTRE FOR FORTEAN ZOOLOGY

Animals & Men   Issue Ten

This will be Jan Williams' last Newsfile. After two and a half years of sterling service she has decided to call it a day as Newsfile Editor. She will be continuing as regional representative for Buckinghamshire, author of the A-Z of Cryptozoology, and as occasional contributor of other articles. We wish her well, and are glad that she has not gone for good, because we would miss her terribly if she were to leave us completely, because in a very real sense, none of this would have happened if it had not been for her. Thanx Jan.

NEW AND REDISCOVERED SPECIES

EVERYBODY'S GOT SOMETHING TO HIDE EXCEPT FOR ME AND MY MONKEY

Various newspapers in April reported that *"A tiny monkey weighing just seven ounces and thought to be extinct has been rediscovered in southeast China". (The Times 23.4.96).* The stories went on to report that these animals, known as 'Ink Monkeys' had been the traditional pets of Chinese scholars. They gained their name because they had been kept to prepare ink, known for the last 4,000 years in China. They were also supposed to assist the scholars by passing brushes and turning pages. Zhu Xi, the 12th Century Chinese scholar was said to have kept one as a pet.

These stories were so bizarre that our intrepid reporter Tom Anderson decided to investigate. The tale recounted below is pieced together from several pun filled letters from Tom to us...

The story was also carried by the ubiquitous Aberdeen Press and Journal, so he contacted them for more information. They said that the story had come from The Press Association, but on contacting them he was told that their agency only dealt with UK stories, and suggested that he try Reuters. In his own words:

"A very nice man in their library told me (despite the fact that I'm not a subscriber), that it emanated from the Chinese News Agency Shin Wa, and that the only details that he had was that the monkeys weighed 200 grammes each.

After various confusing (or Confucian) calls I at last reached their scientific correspondent, Mr

Animals & Men — Issue Ten

Jiang Yan.

Between his accent and mine (Tom is fairly seriously Caledonian. Ed.), *progress was not too rapid but I faxed him down a request for some more details which he said he would have in 24-48 hours"*...

Tom signed off by promising..

"I'll be gibbon you the details before much langur"...

And we awaited the next stage of the investigation with baited breath.

Three days later we received a letter from Tom, which for various reasons is unprintable, and a photocopy of the fax he had received back.

APRIL 23, 1996
TO: MR TOM ANDERSON
FAX 012244 S90576

FROM: MR JIANG YAN
XINHUA NEWS AGENCY LONODN BUREAU
FAX: 0171 722 8512
TEL: 0171 586 8271

Dear Sir:

Today I receive a fax from Beijing which contains very brief information about rediscovered ink monkeys.

I am terrible sorry for our headquarters couldn't collect more detail for your inquiry.

Sincerely Yours

Mr Jiang Yan

It is now only left to us to speculate whether the original story was made up in Beijing or London...

THE WURM TURNS

A 73 year old retired butcher from Austria was charged recently for attempted fraud. With the aid of a salami sausage and a felt pen he had been faking photographs of the legendary Tatzelwurm, and pestering tourists to buy them. His excuse? He couldn't afford to live on his pension or to feed his ferrets. He was unconditionally discharged. Scottish Evening Express 21.6.96.

ORANGE BLOSSOM SPECIAL

A new species of monkey, the sixth since 1990 has been discovered in the Brazilian rain forest. *Callithris sateret* is bright orange and the size of a squirrel. Experts claim that another five species are likely to be discovered in the same area within the next decade. *Die Welt* 22.6.96

PRIMAL PRIMATE

The fossil remains of a mouse sized creature that could be the missing link between the most ancient monkeys and higher primates has been discovered in China. *Eosimias centennicus* was discovered along the banks of the Yellow River. In life it would have weighed only 99 grammes and lived 40 million years ago. *The Times* 5.4.96.

I'M ALWAYS TOUCHED BY YOUR PRESENCE DEER.

Tibetan Red Deer, or Shou, have been rediscovered in Alpine meadows about seventy five miles east of Lhasa. George B. Schaller of the Wildlife Conservation Society and Chinese colleagues Wang Xiaoming and Liu Wulin found more than 100 of the deer in the region last October. Shou were last seen in the wild in the 1940s.

EARLY AMPHIBIANS

New fossil evidence from Australia proves that The first amphibious creatures crawled onto land more than 150,000,000 years earlier than was previously thought. Schoolboys Angus Hamley and Guy Thulborn found fossilised teeth and bones in a strata in Queensland dating to 333 million years ago. Guy's father, Dr Tony Thulborn, a zoologist at Queensland University, is leading a team carrying out further investigations at the site. He said:

"Those ancient creatures were nearly three feet high and resembled a cross between a crocodile and a salamander from Hell. They had a powerful tail, a massive head, and lots of nasty teeth". (Daily Mail 28.4.96).

SEA AND LAKE MONSTERS

(and other marine stories that don't fit in anywhere else)

MALAYSIAN DRAGON.

Several newspapers in late May reported that Malaysian Fishermen had found the carcass (some reports said skeleton) of what they thought was a 'dragon'. The cynics amongst the world of cryptozoology were convinced that it would turn

Lake Monsters

out, like so many others before it, to be the decomposing carcass of a Basking Shark. We were all wrong! It was the decomposing carcass of a Killer Whale. Aberdeen Press and Journal 28.5.96; Teletext BBC 27.5.96.; ITV Teletext 28.5.96. Dr Karl Shuker Pers. Comm.

'DOC' DOES IT AGAIN

In a letter dated 25th June 1996 Tony 'Doc' Shiels writes:

"At around ten, last night, I took a stroll down to Lough Cullaun and - sure enough - saw a single dark, low hump gliding through the water, in the Corofin direction. It didn't surprise me. It was nothing spectacular, just a dark shape about four feet long, visible for six or seven seconds. (....) It's not important - it just happened - and there were no other witnesses (as far as I know).

Some few years back, there was a rumour about a giant eel in Lough Cullaun, but almost every lake in Ireland has such 'legends'..."

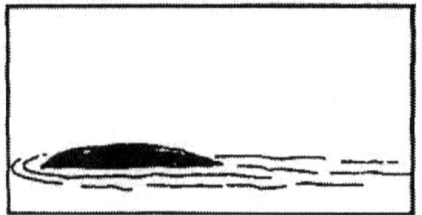

PIC BY TONY SHIELS

IDENTITY CRISIS.

The headline read: *'Whale dies'* but the story was about a 12 foot Basking Shark stranded, still alive, on a beach at Tenby in Pembrokeshire. Wildlife experts joined concerned holiday-makers in a fruitless six hour struggle to save the creature. What was the headline writer drinking when he wrote the article though? Where can the Editor of this journal get some? *Aberdeen Press & Journal 10.6.1996*

THE 'CASE' FOR G.S

Clyde Roper, from the Smithsonian Institute is in the South Pacific searching for living specimens of Architeuthis. He hopes, in November, with the aid of a mini submarine, to be the first person to see one of these giant squid alive in its natural habitat. He plans to follow squid hunting whales up to 900m beneath the sea. To date, only dead and dying specimens have been found washed up in beaches, ensnared in fishing nets and vomited up by sperm whales. *The Times 18.2.96; Die Welt 29.4.96.*

IT'S FOR YOU-OOO

Fishermen in Borneo have started to steal pay-phones for use as electronic bait in fish traps. The electricity passing through the microphones produces a high pitched sound which seemingly attracts the fish. This is somewhat reminiscent of an episode in *'Songs of Distant Earth'* by Arthur C Clarke (who I, for one much prefer outside his 'mysterious world' persona). Weird! *(Aberdeen Press and Journal 26.4.96).*

WHAT A WHOPPER!

A giant Conger Eel, nearly 10 feet long which weighed almost as much of a man was caught off the Scottish coast in February. It was, according to the newspaper report, an almost legendary fish that had been eluding trawlermen for years. *Aberdeen Press and Journal 23.2.96.*

PASSION KILLER

The strange deaths of sea-lions on the South California coast have been attributed to the 'Marauder of San Miguel Island', a rogue giant male sea-lion.

Marine biologists say that up to 200 female sea-lions have been crushed to death in the last five years by the Marauder (thought to be a hybrid of Steller's sea-lion and a smaller Californian species. The male is said to weigh about eight times more than his victims. (Daily Mail 4.6.96).

Other mysterious deaths amongst North American marine mammals took place amongst the Florida manatee population which was decimated by an unknown cause. Scientists were worried that an unknown virus might have reached epidemic proportions amongst the species, but the deaths were eventually identified as being the result of a 'red tide' algal infestation.

BHM ETC

TOO MUCH MONKEY BUSINESS

Scientists in the Brazilian jungle have discovered an almost complete skeleton of an extinct monkey (*Protopithecus brasiliensis*). Individual bones of this animal, which lived until about 10,000 years ago have been found since 1835, but this is the most complete specimen yet. In life the animal would have looked like the head of a howler monkey transplanted onto the body of a spider monkey. This is of considerable interest to those cryptozoologists interested in the notorious and controversial De-Loys' Ape. (*Ameranthropoides loysii*).

Although, recent information has suggested that those who have always believed that the classic photograph from 1920 was a hoax, were correct, the existence, within relatively recent historical times, of a large spidermonkey like primate is undeniably interesting. *Die Welt* 23.5.96; Darren Naish Pers Comm.

NEVER WHICH WAY BUT WHATEVER

An Orang Utan abandoned by its owner on a street in Taiwan grabbed a girl and kissed her repeatedly before being restrained by Police, it was reported yesterday. *Aberdeen Press and Journal* 29.5.96

WHITE MAN'S BURDEN

A mystery white tribe has been reported in Irian Jaya. Indonesian anthropologists are investigating sightings made by villagers in the Wirigar River area. The tribesmen are said to be tall and pale skinned and carry parrots on their shoulders which warn of strangers. (*Daily Mail* 1.7.96).

RELEASE THE BATS (B-B-B-B-B-B-BABY BATS)

A Male Savi's Pipistrelle, a species found in Britain only once previously was rescued from two cats in the backyard of a house in Wallasey, Merseyside. The creature, named Wallace, by Wildlife Rescue Officers in Liverpool, had strayed a long way from its normal habitat in the Mediterranean. Experts were trying to establish whether the animal was a vagrant, or "part of a small migrant population". *The Times* 13.3.96

animals & men

THE JOURNAL OF THE CENTRE FOR FORTEAN ZOOLOGY

Animals & Men — Issue Ten

This seems as good a place as any to introduce the subject of this issue's phone in quiz. We were very pleased with the response to the quiz in the last issue. The winner was Al Pringle from Cricket St. Thomas Wildlife Park in Somerset who correctly realised that our headline was a bastardisation of a song by John Otway and Wild Willie Barrett called *"Be careful of the flowers 'cos you know they're going to get you — yeah"*. Three other people got the answer right but too late alas. Commiserations to them and to the others who got the answer completely wrong! The quiz this issue is merely based around the headline to the above piece, the question is Who? why? what? where? The prize is a free one year subscription to 'Animals & Men'. By the way, for those of you who are still asking, the line *"Baal in silence dines on vulture soup"* which was our phone in quiz several issues ago, is from an opera called "Baal" by Berthold Brecht!

CROCODILE IN FINCHLEY.

Now we know where Lady Thatcher, once MP for Finchley, gets her flashy Crocodile-skin handbags. Bits of a decomposing crocodile carcass which measured nearly five foot in length were found in Dollis Brook, North London. An off-duty RSPCA Inspector was walking his dog when, Oscar the Labrador waded into the stream and appeared to pull the decomposing dead reptile from the bushes.

It was reported that the fragmented corpse was sent to London Zoo to discover what species the animal belonged to. (*Aberdeen Press and Journal 29.5.96*). We approached London Zoo, but we were unable to find anyone who could give us any information.

Aberrant crocodiles across parts of the United Kingdom are not a new phenomenon. Charles Fort was interested in them and several researchers have investigated the incidents without really reaching any conclusions. These historical accounts are particularly interesting, but it seems likely that the Finchley beast was merely an unfortunate pet which was dumped illegally, either because it had grown too large for its tank, or because it had died in captivity and its owners were unsure as how to dispose of the body.

All crocodiles, alligators and caimans are proscribed under the terms of the 1976 Dangerous Wild Animals Act, but they are surprisingly popular as pets. Disturbingly there does appear to be a black market trade in such things. At an exotic pet fair we were at recently one of our colleagues was approached on several occasions by people willing to pay high prices for a crocodile or alligator without the formality of having to obtain a license. Needless to say we were neither willing, nor able to comply with the requests, but the fact that the demand is there is disturbing in anyone's book!

PIC BY TONY SHIELS

GREAT SNAKES!

A nine-foot long Burmese Python was found in Campbell Park, Milton Keynes in March. Sid Mountstones found the (very) dead snake whilst walking his dog down the canal footpath. It was well away from houses and roads and no-one had admitted ownership. *Milton Keynes Citizen 4.4.96*

ANTS WITH ANGST

The Florida Ghost Ant, 1.33mm long and almost transparent has started to invade the UK. Three infestations of the species in Britain have been recorded to date, two in London and one in Birmingham, and experts fear that should the creatures infest a hospital, a serious infection risk could be posed. *Aberdeen Press and Journal 26.4.96*

ZOOFORM PHENOMENA

THE BEAST OF CHISWICK

Residents in Chiswick have been reporting sightings of a weird zooform phenomenon reminiscent of those reported in parts of the Mid West earlier this century. Loren Coleman's classic 'Mysterious America' contains several references to mysterious 'kangaroos' which ate meat and generally behaved in a most unkangaroolike manner.

The Editor recently wrote an article for 'Dead of Night' magazine which covered these and other 'unidentified hopping objects'. It was interesting therefore, to discover that a similar animal described as *"a demonic creature about two feet high with large haunches and long pointed ears"* was seen in 1994 by 25 year old Joy Persaud. The newspaper story (reprinted in TEMS NEWS #13) implied that other people had seen this 'creature' over a period of years.

A local man, Basil Hall, claimed that what the witnesses had seen was in fact an otter. But an RSPCA spokesman is quoted as saying that:

"There haven't been any otters seen living wild in

Animals & Men

THE JOURNAL OF THE CENTRE FOR FORTEAN ZOOLOGY

Issue Ten

London for the past few years and it is more likely to be a mink".

It is not for us to disagree with such an unimpeachable source but it does seem very unlikely that if, indeed Joy Persaud DID see what she claims, that any relatively small aquatic mustelid could be the cause of the sighting.

One should note, however not only that what Ms Persaud claims to have seen, whilst unlike any flesh and blood fauna likely to be reported from the area, is consistent with reports of zooform phenomena across the globe and even with the currently fashionable Chupacabras (SEE BELOW) reports from various parts of the world. It should also be noted that the RSPCA were probably wrong not only in their identification, but in saying that otters no longer exist in the London area. The Times (25.4.96) reported that an otter had been seen near Reading earlier this year, only 40 miles from London, and that the species was becoming more common across the country. The Reading animal, they said, was probably a straggler from a population from Hampshire. It is also difficult to reconcile The Times' claim that this animal was the first reported in the Thames for *"three decades"* with the RSPCA's claim that otters had not been seen in Chiswick for the *"past few years"*. Someone has got their facts wrong, and I don't think its 'The Thunderer'. I find it easier to believe in a teleporting Chupacabras!

WHERE THE GOAT SUCKS THERE SUCK....

Goat sucker fever is spreading across the USA and Mexico, where El Chupacabra now has its own page on the Internet. As usual, the price of cryptic fame is confusion, and one man's three foot, spiny-backed kangaroo becomes another's giant horned bat.

In the Mexican state of Sinaloa dozens of goats are said to have been found with their blood sucked dry and one human has allegedly been attacked. Farmers from Calderon village have formed vigilante squads to try and track down their flying 'goatsucker'. A rough sketch cobbled together by witnesses shows a bat-like creature, over a foot long, with two horn-like prongs protruding from a hair covered head.

Further south in Jalisco state, sheep and goats have been killed. The dead animals are all reported to have two toothmarks about a third of an inch apart, in the neck, and appear to have been drained of blood. Duran Larios, a farmer in the village of Tlajomulco, said 'it killed 15 of our sheep without leaving them a drop of blood'. Neighbour, Jose Angel Pulido Briseno said that one of the creatures had bitten him, and Hortencia Guadulupe Cuevas said she was attacked by a flying goatsucker with huge wings.

In the Hispanic neighbourhood of Sweetwater, South Miami, Florida the massacre of sixty nine assorted goats, chickens, geese and ducks was blamed on their local goat-sucker. Ron Magill, assistant curator at Metrodade Zoo, investigated. He found a hole dug under the fence, "a classic dog digging", together with dog prints and dog hair on the bottom of the fence. The 'vampire bites' were, he said, "classic canine punctures from dogs", and the animals had not been drained of blood, as he demonstrated with a knife to one goat's jugular. Magill says he is not a sceptic. He believes in UFOs and extraterrestrials - *'its just that in this case that was not it!'*

Cases continue however, with vampire-like attacks reported across South Florida. Descriptions of the beast responsible vary from a maroon gorilla to a huge flying creature which grabs its victims with a hook on the end of a long tail.

Meanwhile, the Chupacabra T-Shirt is on sale, and Jose 'Chemo' Soto, mayor of Canovanas (the Puerto Rican town where all this started) and leader of well publicised weekly monster hunts, turns out to be running for re-election. The truth is out there, but which bit is it?

(Aberdeen Press and Journal 3.5.96; Scotsman 7.5.96; Southampton Daily Echo 3.5.96; Dundee Evening Telegraph 3.5.96; St Petersburg Times 21.3.96).

EDITOR'S NOTE: 'Case' workers will note the significance of the initials of the Goat Sucker. Lexilinkers might note the similarity between 'Chemo' Soto, and Chemosit. Does any of this mean anything? Probably not!

OTHER STORIES

NOT FLAMING BUT DROWNING

Six firemen dug a two foot hole to rescue a hamster dropped in a sink-unit drain at Knodishall, Suffolk. In time-honoured fashion, the hamster thanked its rescuers with a hefty bite. (Daily Mail 29.5.96).

Soccer Fan Vicky Lowe claims the ghost of her hamster 'Miss Effie' saved Reading Football Club from relegation. Vicky buried 'Miss Effie' in the goalmouth at Reading's Elm-park ground, and is convinced the hamster's spirit allowed the team to win 3-0 against Wolves. Shame no-one

Club from relegation. Vicky buried 'Miss Effie' in the goalmouth at Reading's Elm-park ground, and is convinced the hamster's spirit allowed the team to win 3-0 against Wolves. Shame no-one thought of that at Wembley. (Aberdeen press and Journal).

AS A NEWT...

Ten year old Liz Faulkner, a pupil at Pencalenick School in Truro, found this bright yellow neotenic palmate newt. She had observed it, together with 'normal' specimens, on a number of occasions, in the pond in the school grounds. Mark Nicholson of the Cornwall Wildlife Trust said: "Neoteny has been recorded occasionally in Britain's newt species but is very rare in the palmate - I've never even seen a photo of a neotenous palmate newt". Neoteny, is of course the condition where an animal reaches adult size but retains its larval features, in the case of a newt, a tadpole like tail and external gills. Sadly, although this discovery has attracted a large amount of interest, there have been no further specimens.

MOTH MENACE

Property Management company Broadgate Estates has erected barriers around silver maple trees in Finsbury Avenue, near Liverpool Street Station in London to protect commuters from brown tailed moths. The larvae of the moth - Euproctis chryssorrhea - can strip trees bare in days, and their minute hairs can cause severe skin and eye irritation in humans. *Daily Mail 21.6.96*

(EDITORS NOTE: Infestations of this species during 1976 and 1978, as well as historical accounts, were noted in issues 20 and 29 of Fortean Times. Issue 20 noted that the swarms had been getting gradually worse since the mid 1950s. They noted that the mild winter of 1975 was generally thought of as a major causative factor in the expansion of the species.

Are the recent climate changes responsible for the infestations reported this year? Or have these been happening annually since FT first noted them and it is just that the Editorial team of 'Animals & Men' haven't noticed?).

Neotenous Palmate Newt. Pic. © Cornwall Wildlife Trust.

MYSTERY CATS

Highlands, Scotland.

An Inverness motorist claimed that his car was damaged when it struck "a big black scary cat larger than an Alsatian" near Culloden Moor in the last week.

Two tan coloured lioness-like cats were seen within six feet of a car at Elgin. Well lit by the headlights they were judged to be six feet long, including tail.

Lincolnshire.

Lesley and Doreen Dean watched an "eight foot long, black panther" as it apparently searched for prey on their twenty acre estate near Lincoln. They said "It was a magnificent creature, pure black with piercing eyes, and a tail as long as its body". (Daily Mail 22.5.96).

Buckinghamshire.

A 'huge cat' with a long tail ran across the road in front of motorist Graham Stringer at Newton Blossomville on 2nd June. (Milton Keynes Citizen 6.6.96).

The beast of Milton Keynes appeared to a hay fever sufferer in Westcroft on 11th June. Brenda Saville got up to make a cup of tea at 4.15 a.m and saw the animal from her window. She said "it was quite tall, about the size of a medium-sized dog, and very long". (Milton Keynes Citizen 13.6.96).

Artist Sue Reed saw a large cat-like animal walk across the road from her car near the archway leading to Stowe School, north of Buckingham. She watched for several minutes before it disappeared into a neighbouring field and described it as the size of an alsatian, with white colouring on its chest. (Buckingham and Winslow Advertiser 31.5.96).

Two weeks later, a big cat was seen at Gawcott, south of Buckingham. It ran out in front of Chris Walsh at 1.a.m on the 11th June. She said "It was big, black and staring with its mouth open". It stood about two feet at the shoulder. (Buckingham and Winslow Advertiser. 14.6.96).

NEWSFILE CORRESPONDENTS

Tom Anderson, Ian Sherred,
Wolfgang Schmidt, Mark Nicholson,
Tony 'Doc' Shiels, Darren Naish,
Joan Amos, Lionel Beer,
Dave and Penny Rowe
(congratulations), Robin from
'Lobster'.

*****

We are presently looking for regional correspondents and clipping collectors for each area not presently covered by our team. If you are interested in being a regional representative, then please telephone Alison on 01392 424811. We are also planning regular columns by representatives from different regions. We have already started with a regular column, starting this issue written by Aberdeen's Mr Entertainment; Tom Anderson. His musings on the odder side of Scottish zoology will appear in each issue.

We are also printing regular news from Richard Carter of The Loch Ness Society. We would like to run similar columns written by anyone involved in a specific field of research. We would be interested to hear from anyone with ideas about columns of this nature.

Finally, for the time being at least, the Newsfile will be compiled at the Editorial Office, so until further notice will you send all photocopies to us at the Exeter Address.

THE A-Z OF CRYPTOZOOLOGY
by Jan Williams

Emela-Ntouka:

Semi-aquatic, elephant sized beast, of the African Congo. Has a long, heavy tail, and a large horn on its snout with which it is said to disembowel elephants. Despite this aggressive behaviour, it is apparently a vegetarian.

Emmaville Panther:

Large cat-like creature reported frequently in the vicinity of Emmaville, New South Wales, Australia. Became notorious in the late 1950s when hundreds of sheep were mysteriously slain on stock farms in the area, though numerous sightings predate the Second World War. Most reports refer to a black, leopard-like cat, but sandy-coloured animals have also been seen. Emmaville is a 'window-area' where other strange events, including UFO sightings have occurred.

Filey, Sea Monster of:

Coastguard Wilkinson Herbert saw a thirty foot long monster on the beach at Filey Brig, North Yorkshire in 1934. It had an eight foot neck, huge eyes like saucers, and a mouth a foot wide. The black body had two humps and four short legs with flippers. The creature moved quickly into the sea. Fishermen had reported a monster three miles out to sea two weeks previously.

Flathead Lake Monster:

A huge, black creature seen in Flathead Lake, Montana, USA, on several occasions. Described by witness Ronald Nixon in 1963 as at leaste twnty-five feet long, with no fin on its back. Attempts to catch the monster with huge hooks baited with chickens met with no success.

Flixton Werewolf:

Legend states a werewolf with huge, shining teeth, crimson eyes, a terrible stench and a long tail which it uses to fell nocturnal travellers, haunts the area of Flixton, North Yorkshire.

Fur Bearing Trout:

Often shown at fairs, and exhibited in bars in the USA and Canada, the fur-bearing trout is said to be very rare and found only in deep and cold waters. Sadly, these very odd fish are forgeries, usually ordinary trout wrapped in Rabbit fur.

Wolf Scare
by Eric Sorensen

In Southern Sweden, in the small city of Ljunghusen, nurse Lena Sundberg claims to have been attacked by two wolves as she was working her garden. After some reading she has decided to identify them as wolves, even though they barked!

Even at the beginning of the last century reports such as this were rare, but were perhaps more widely believed. Yet, we must consider the stress of the situation. Perhaps the woman was subconsciously influenced by the fact that in 1984 a young wolf was observed in the vicinity. Occasional strays can come from the north, but there are often years between reports.

Swedish wildlife expert Olof Lisberg firmly denies the possibility of these animals being wolves, considering their behaviour during the attack, and the general shyness of wolves. He adds that wolves do not travel in pairs unless they are established in the area and this is not reported.

Personally, I think that wolves, if they could bypass the guns of the Reindeer-keeping Lapps in any numbers, could live discretely, and probably safely in Southern Sweden. Anyway, the old 'Wolf Scare' never dies, as this report has shown. Feral dogs are not known from Northern Europe to my knowledge, but recent years have seen a sort of 'arms race' with people wanting bigger and meaner dogs but devoting less time to their upbringing. Two big dogs running around would attack almost anything....

ANCIENT WHALES, SEA SERPENTS AND NESSIES PART 2: THEORISING ON SURVIVAL

Article Three in a series of Seven by

Darren Naish

"Perhaps there are acrodelphids still cruising the oceans, zeuglodonts browsing in lakes, lochs and fjords, the ancestors of these in tropical rivers, and even some 'first ancestors' on their banks". [1], (Fig. 1).

Well, perhaps. As explained in the first part of this article (2), extinct whales have long been bought 'back to life' by those seeking to explain the identities of various aquatic cryptids, and it remains for me here to review the instances where extinct whales of all kinds have been resurrected in the literature. The issues here are broad, and this is but an introduction.

To the cryptozoologist archaeocetes fall into two groups - the giant, long bodied basilosaurids ('zeuglodonts'), and the small, seal like protocetids ('pro-zeuglodonts' or 'pre-zeuglodonts'). Basilosaurids have been known since the 1830s, and have always deserved consideration in the cryptozoological literature - however just or unjust that may be - by virtue of their great size and apparent serpentiformity. Interpretations that initially lead to their treatment as such, as shown in the first part of this article, are certainly incorrect. Furthermore, a realistic case that these animals survived anywhere near recent times cannot be reconstructed: these animals aren't coelacanths (and with regard to the survival of large ancient vertebrates, *Latimeria* is a red herring in any case, excuse the pun...). The facts remain, however, that:

1. People have reported large, long bodied, aquatic cryptids of apparent cetacean affinity.

2. Zoologists of all stripes have speculated on archaeocete survival and evolution.

A brief historical review.

Heuvelmans [3] and Michell and Rickard [4], have provided excellent reviews of the sea serpent identities that have been proposed within the last couple of centuries. Archaeocetes - or, more specifically, the redundant name for *Basilosaurus*, *Zeuglodon* [5], clearly ranks up there with *Plesiosaurus* as a favourite sea monster candidate. Numerous examples can thus be provided of instances where those pondering the identity of an aquatic, long bodied cryptid have suggested that it might actually have been a surviving basilosaur. *Basilosaurus*, thus finds itself amongst those organisms so mistakenly beloved of cryptozoologists, the 'living fossils'. At its most extreme case, this scenario results in resurrection of *Basilosaurus* itself. In what is essentially a simplified re-write of Heuvelmans' monumental 1968 tome 'In the wake of the Sea Serpents', McEwan [6] suggests that some sea-serpents sound so much like Basilosaurus as to actually be Basilosaurus. His most controversial idea, yet hardly commented on as far as I am aware, is that the creature seen by Hans Egede off Greenland in 1734 was a rearing basilosaur!

Of course, the better known suggestion regarding this report is that the creature was a giant squid. In, however, his new book 'In Search of Prehistoric Survivors' [7], Shuker implies that he believes Egede's monster to be an archaeocete too. The arguments for and against a squid-identity for this sighting have been discussed in the literature (see [8]): I have nothing new to add. To briefly introduce lake serpents (discussed further below), an article published in 1982, and voicing the opinions of Dr. Roy Mackal, goes as far as classifying 'Ogopogo' and other Canadian lake monsters as 'related to *Basilosaurus cetoides*' [9]. Needless to say, the accompanying illustration is of a furiously wriggling, serpentine basilosaur.

Recognising that modern sea serpents aren't exact copies of this Eocene animal, Heuvelmans was most influential in suggesting that modern sea serpents are very much modified descendants of early whales (a sensible decision, given the 36 million years of missing time). Well known, and deservedly so, amongst cryptozoologists today is the conclusion of Heuvelmans that the very much disparate morphologies reported in

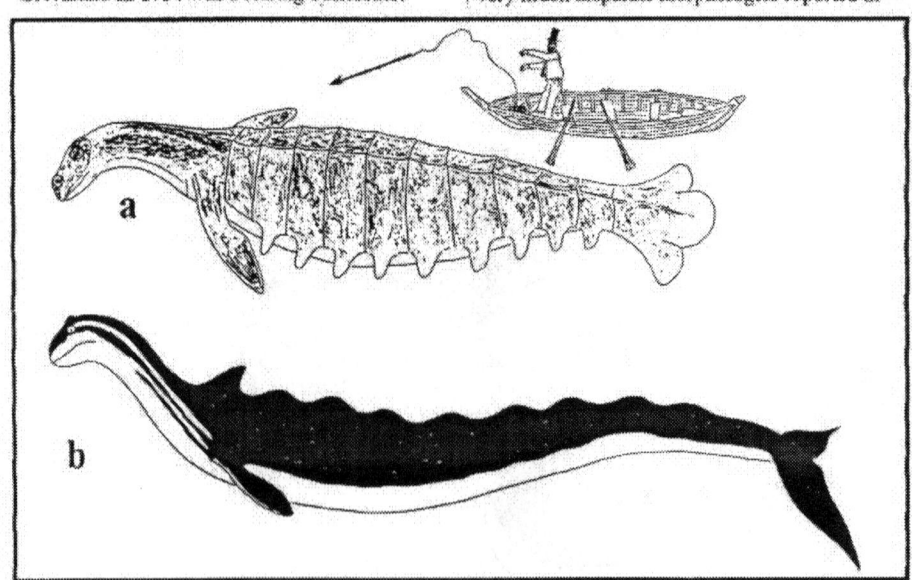

Fig. 2: (a) Aelian's cetacean centipede, referred to in earlier accounts as the 'many finned', as envisioned by Heuvelmans. (b) Many-humped sea-serpent. All three characters to scale. (a) and (b) are based on illustrations in refs [6] and [1].

-14-

'sea serpent' sightings are the result of the presence of a number of species of marine cryptids, and of the nine forms that Heuvelmans recognised, he deemed three to be modern-day archaeocetes. Of these, the 'Cetacean Centipede' ('*Cetioscolopendra aeliani*' [1(a)].), is a truly remarkable whale: equipped with numerous small lateral fins and an extensive covering of segmented bony plates. (Fig. 2a). Second is 'Many-humped' ('*Plurigibbosus novaeangliae*' [1(b)],), the animal mostly responsible for sightings of lines of humps (fig. 2b) - this species being particularly famous for the spate of sightings that occurred in Gloucester Bay, Massachusets, in and around 1817. I shall discuss the third form later in this article.

Enter Lake Monsters as Basilosaurs.

Both of Heuvelmans' animals, as do archaeocetes and all other whales, lack a neck of any significant length: in fact any creature described as having a long neck certainly cannot be any type of whale. This is relevant because it has often been suggested that the Lake Champlain monster, 'Champ', is an Archaeocete. The Sandra Mansi photograph, however, taken in 1977, clearly depicts a plesiosaur type creature (fig. 3a). Therefore, 'Champ' is no whale and neither are other lake monsters or sea-serpents with definite long necks. Paradoxically (for me, anyhow), Mackal has suggested that Mansi's photograph is of a Basilosaur [1(c), (b), (14)]. This is an extremely odd conviction - it is hard to imagine a large aquatic animal more different from a basilosaur than the object in the Mansi photograph. Basing my opinions on this photograph, I vehemently oppose notions of Champ-as-basilosaur. The story doesn't end there...

'Champ' has been made whale-like in at least one other instance: it has been proposed that the Mansi photograph actually depicts the fin of a small whale! Humpbacks (*Megaptera novaeangliae*) are the only whales - if not the only animals - with fins anything like the object in the Mansi photograph. Even there, the resemblance is poor as a humpback's fins do not bend over sharply at the tip (they are too stiff). Is it likely, in any case, that there are humpback whales in Lake Champlain? The idea that land-locked marine cetaceans may have contributed to, or be responsible for, lake monster sightings, is as appealing as it is unsubstantiated. [13]

'Champ' and a few of its cousins may not be the subjects of this article but other lake monsters are. Individual eye-witness accounts will not be referred to in this article because they would take up too much space (please consult other sources, eg. [13,17]) but we must consider a few sightings to witness the imposition of archaeocetes well into the cryptozoological Hall of Fame.

To put it another way, the idea that lacustrine as well as oceanic archaeocetes still form an exciting part of our fauna is augmented by eyewitness accounts. The arguments against this possibility I have presented previously [1,2] but in theory some of the odds are high: in less than thirty million years at least five other whale families have adapted to freshwater life and even marine whales can tolerate freshwater conditions. Versatile, unspecialised whales can be modelled for aquatic life in any number of environments, and this might be a reason for the success they seem to enjoy in cryptozoology - at the theoretical level of course. A possibility seems to exist that smooth backed 'rolling' lake monsters are whales, but aren't archaeocete. Maybe we still have yet to learn about some new type of elusive freshwater cetacean. [10]

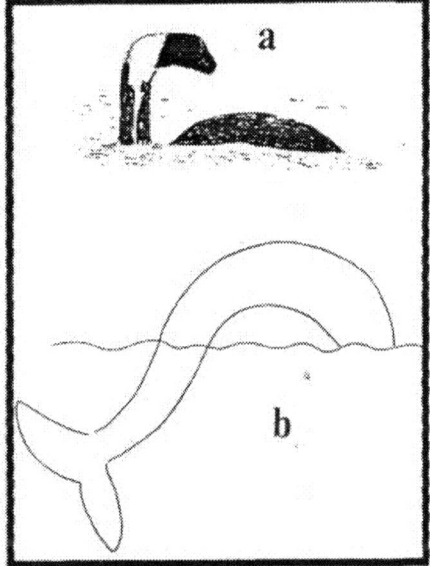

Fig. 3: (a) a diagrammatic representation of the plesiosaur-like object appearing in the photograph taken by Sandra Mansi on her visit to Lake Champlain in July 1977.
(b) the exceedingly whale-like tail of 'Ogopogo', as sketched by Mrs. B. Clarke in 1974. Please refer to text.
(b) is copied from Clark's sketch which is reproduced in ref. (19).

Whales with body armour.

But for the anatomical impossibility of serpentiform, wriggling, long bodied basilosaurs fit rather well the sea-serpent accounts given in the texts. McEwan even went as far as showing that the dark upper and white underparts of some many-humped sea-serpents were consistent with a cetacean identity, and consequently both Basilosaurus, and the 'many-humped' (which he calles 'multi-humped', incidentally) are restored accordingly in his book (fig. 4).

Not only for many-humped, but also for other sea serpents, however there exist yet more anatomical hurdles, if they are to achieve whaledom.

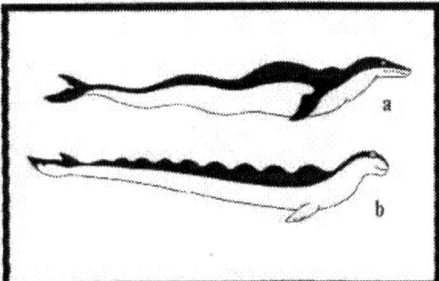

FIG. 4: McEwan's attempt to make:
(a) Basilosaurus look like a many-humped,
and
(b) many-humped look like a Basilosaurus.
Both after McEwan in [6].

Dermal armour might seem a feature utterly incompatible with a cetacean identity, but Heuvelmans and others have consistently referred to the scutes found in association with basilosaurid skeletons, and for a long time believed to be a primitive feature widespread amongst early whales. Some authors have even suggested that the tubercules found on the leading edge of the dorsal fin of the Black Porpoise (*Phocoena spinipinnis*) are relicts of this armour (e.g [22]). What we know of early cetaceans has come a long way in recent decades though, proving these assertions incorrect. It is now well known that the scutes sometimes found in association with archaeocete skeletons are actually from early leatherback turtles - archaeocetes, like living whales did not have any kind of bony armour at all. There is no evidence that the tubercules on the Black Porpoise are degenerate remnants of earlier structures, or retained at all from any ancient ancestors: rather they represent a recently evolved oddity of this species (these are called neomorphs).

The existence of armour in archaeocetes was referred to in the cryptozoological literature for longer than anywhere else - palaeozoologists had cast strong doubts on the existence of it as long ago as 1936. [20]. Seemingly, while 'armour' continued, as it does, to be reported on sea serpents, it tied in even neater with a proposed archaeocete identity.

Here we find the explanation for the peculiar armour-plating that covers the dorsal surface of Heuvelmans' 'Cetioscolopendra': his evolved basilosaurs have gone so far with their dermal scutes as to be totally encased in a rigid suit of it. Similarly, bumps and scales on the flanks of 'Plurigibbosus' have been explained as retained armour scutes, and, likewise, for freshwater serpents: on the basis of its amphibious habits and armoured back, Heuvelmans proposed an archaeocete identity for the South American Minhocao [22]. That this animal is also a burrower that allegedly grabs livestock from beneath the ground (it also has small 'horns'), should demonstrate beyond doubt that it is non-cetacean. [23].

While it is certainly evident, therefore, that there is no reason to *expect* armour in a basilosaur descendant, this does not make it an impossibility. The porpoises cited above have evolved their own dermal scutes, and it is well known that ground sloths and some other mammals have too. So this entire area of reasoning is something of a straw man! Even so, you still need the evolved basilosaur before you can have the neomorphic dermal scutes upon its back.

Tale of a whale's tail.

One of the lake monsters most likely to be considered as a surviving basilosaur is 'Ogopogo' of Lake Okanagan in British Columbia. Sometimes, 'Ogopogo' is described as having 'multiple dorsal fins' or some other form of spinal ornamentation. This indicates that what the witnesses saw was a giant sturgeon (an issue far too complex and controversial for me to remark upon here). Giant carnivorous eels [24], and a 'huge river otter', [25] [26]. have also been suggested as the identity behind 'Ogopogo', but as we shall see, these animals do not correlate with the morphology reported in sightings.

Amongst the North American lake monsters that lack the dermal scales of sturgeons, those with 'whiskers' or manes are evidently non cetacean too. Interestingly, these forms are often those exhibiting definite humps. However, smooth backed monsters resembling long, black eels [27] and exhibiting other whale-like features tally far better. In 1974, while swimming toward a raft in Lake Okanagan, Mrs. B. Clarke saw, and was actually bumped into by an animal that she estimated as 25-30 feet long. [28] Strongly suggesting that this animal was of cetacean nature is her description of its tail:

"...*forked and horizontal like a whales*". (Fig. 3b).

It is perhaps, fair judgement, that any aquatic cryptid with a horizontal, bifid tail be regarded a whale-like form. But things would be less interesting if they were that simple. Horizontal cetacean-style fluked tails have also been reported in lake monsters that also display humps and cranial appendages. [29]. (Fig.5a). Basing their conclusions on the photographs taken in 1937 of the Naden Harbour juvenile *Cadborosaurus* (a 3.2 metre long individual retrieved from the stomach of a sperm whale) Bousfield and LeBlond have recently discussed and illustrated horizontal fluke-like appendages on the tail of *Cadborosaurus* also. [31] (Fig 5b). They conclude that each 'fluke' is actually a degenerate hind limb, after comparing those elements visible in the photographs with those of a Triassic pachypleurosaur. [32]

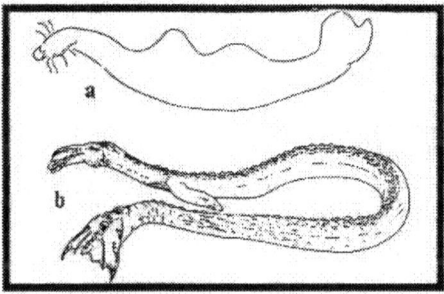

Fig. 5: (a) The humped creature seen in Lake Brompton, (Quebec) in 1976 by Mrs P. Robitaille. This sketch is based on hers, of which two versions appear on p.95 of ref. [30]. (b). Cadborosaurus as restored in [31].

They consequently term the structure a "Tail pseudo" Fluke". Interestingly, Heuvelmans, drew similar conclusions forwhat he called the 'false tail' of his Merhorse '*Halshippus*', [63] - in fact, as his creature may, in at least some cases, be the same as *Cadborosaurus* , he has drawn the same conclusions regarding fluke anatomy as have Bousfield and LeBlond. It is possible that Heuvelmans' comments regarding this structure in '*Halshippus*', were at least inspired by his allocation of this form to the Pinnepedia [63] .. but then that's another story!

It is therefore evident that a 'whale tail' is not unique to Cetacea: it may be characteristic of both serpentine and humped lake serpents, and the marine cadborosaurus too. This is hardly surprising: there are only so many ways a vertebrate can adapt its body for aquatic locomotion. Notably, non mammalian aquatic vertebrates have never evolved horizontal tail flukes, and that this design occurs in the cryptids discussed above strongly implies mammalian affinity. [34]

Lacustrine basilosaurs far and wide

Judging by descriptions, the monster of Montana's enormous Lake Flathead could well be considered an archaeocete (and one that must be cold adapted because this lake is fed by glacial meltwater!) [35] as could the rather aggressive Marakopa River monster from Wellington Province in New Zealand. [36] 'Winipogo' of Manitoba, and other 'long, dark, sinuous beasts sighted as far east as New Brunswick' [37], have long been interpreted similarly. In the news recently is the monster of Lake Van, Turkey: on the basis of its elongate body and dorsal fins, Shuker has suggested that this animal might also be a basilosaur [38]. As this beast has horns or ears, and is somewhat hairy, it's hard to accept this - it reminds me of the non discussed above [39], but confusingly if combines the serpentine morphology and the cranial appendages of what I consider to be two different types.

Note however that certain lake monsters, 'Ogopogo' included, are described as having 'alligator' heads. As we can see in the *Basilosaurus* reconstruction (figs. 1a and 6 in part 1 of this article), this is a fair description of the long jawed, small eyed head of a basilosaur (and look at fig.8). Creatures attributed with both alligatorine and serpentine features (and without dorsal scales) from certain Canadian lakes could even be seen as lake dwelling basilosaurs too, except in some cases the animals are quite small. I can understand it being irresistible to speculate that we might be dealing with dwarf forms, adapted to the lean conditions of smaller bodies of water. Mini lake monsters that I call Horse eels ('water horses' and 'peistes' are among their local names) have also been reported from small lakes in Ireland. [40]. In some descriptions these animals more than suggest a hint of cetacean. They are also capable of clumsy movement on land, hence their often overnight disappearances, and it is worth noting that terrestrial locomotion has been thought possible in basilosaurs by some workers - though a consensus nowadays would regard it as a blatant impossibility.

Important here is that most lake monsters, however, have become woven into local culture and folklore obscuring and confusing zoological identities (see [30]). As is also widespread amongst cryptozoological entities, it is very likely that a number of 'lake monsters' are composites: many of these bodies of water are very large and very productive. It is thus extremely reasonable, in my opinion, to argue that animals like large eels [41] may live alongside the two cryptic whale-tailed forms: the serpentine animals and the humped beasts, both of which we are concerned with here. It is unfortunate that any creature seen to appear above the surface is dubbed a 'lake monster', but such is the vicious circle of publicity.

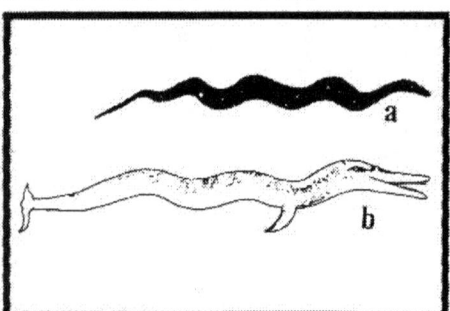

Fig. 6: (a) Swimming serpent image that can be seen on Inscription Rock, Agawa, Lake Superior. Compare this with (b), an attempt made by cetologist Slijper at restoring Basilosaurus. (a) is from a photograph that first appeared in Conway (43), and can also be seen on p.171 of ref. [30]. (b) after Slijper in [44].

Were basilosaurs truly the wriggly serpentine beasts they were once portrayed as, evidence that they may have played a part in the formation of ancient lake monster legends could be the Amerindian 'swimming serpent' images that can be seen on Inscription Rock at Agawa, Lake Superior (fig. 6a).

I was amazed at the resemblance between the form of these images and the old reconstructions of wriggling basilosaurs, such as that published by Slijper in 1962 (fig. 6b). Elements of folklore, stylised representations of real animals, or early attempts at reconstructing fossil remains? There is no way to ever know. In 1991, Michael Sword considered at length the zoological identity that might be behind the Sisuitl, a large, serpentine, alligator-headed, sea serpent featured on the totemic crests of Pacific Northwest Coast Amerindians [42]. Like several aquatic cryptids we have already seen, this form combines cetacean characteristics with cranial horns.

The resurrection of Eocene protocetids.

As mentioned at the beginning of this article, several different types of extinct whale are now metaphorically 'under the cryptozoological blanket'. While *Basilosaurus* may well win pride of place in standard texts, the ancestral protocetids usually get a mention too [43]. Perhaps most important of such considerations are the writings of Heuvelmans' with regard to the identity of his third evolved archaeocete: 'super otter'. Given the name *'Hyperhydra egedei'* by Heuvelmans [10], this is an Arctic Ocean marine mammal reaching thirty or so metres in length (fig. 7). 'Was an Arctic Ocean marine mammal' might be more appropriate, for sightings have not been reported since 1848.

Accounts reveal that *'Hyperhydra'* had a sinuous, flexible spine, a very long body, a small, blunt head, and two pairs of limbs. With certain of these features in mind, an archaeocete identity has therefore been superimposed and, as it has four limbs, descent away from the basilosaurids has been sought. Heuvelmans, and the authors who followed him, therefore chose protocetids as such ancestors. If this were so, *'Hyperhydra'* would be a drastically modified one: not only have these they have changed from a relatively stiff-bodied, truncated design to an extremely elongate, serpentine one. It is not my business to demolish such reasoning, for, in a hypothetical, unknown evolutionary lineage, literally anything can happen. As they stand, however, protocetids make poor models for *'Hyperhydra'* ancestors. As shown in the first part of this article, the idea that archaeocete whales could wriggle in the horizontal

Fig.7: 'Super-Otter' ('Hyperhydra'), as restored under the direction of Heuvelmans. Man and protocetid to scale. After illustration in [11].

plane is essentially a myth not borne out by structural and functional analyses. For a while, it was thought that there were long bodied, serpentine protocetids, [46] but such interpretations are now known to have been in error - all known protocetids are relatively short-bodied, seal-like mammals. There is no evidence for a trend towards serpentiformity, thus a hypothetical protocetid - 'Hyperhydra' lineage cannot be supported. And again we are faced with the problem of missing fossils, for the last known protocetids swam in Egyptian seas 38 million years ago. [47]

The crux of the pro-protocetid lobby, is the fact that four limbs are present in these modern sea-serpents. Small hind-limbs were reported in a basilosaurid in 1990 [48], and probably existed throughout this group [49] - some cetologists now think that hind limbs were retained by the earliest odontocetes and mysticetes too. [50]. This fact, the widespread presence of hind limbs in whales other than protocetids, therefore invalidates any special consideration of protocetids as 'Hyperhydra'

ancestors. Shuker [7]. therefore offered basilosaurids as the closest relatives of 'Hyperhydra'. Of course, as I have previously attempted to demonstrate, the case for basilosaurid survival and post-Eocene evolution is too bad for this to be offered as an alternative.

As they say, everyone's a sceptic: unfortunately, we are far from sure if these creatures ever existed in the first place.

But in the light of evidence, no matter how meagre, what can the cryptozoologist do but explore possibilities?

It is, perhaps ironic that the best evidence of any cryptid considered to be an archaeocete is of a relatively modest fresh-water animal from an island in the South Pacific. The story behind the 'migo' of New Britain's Lake Dakataua will now be quite familiar to A&M readers, and I do not need to repeat it here - an analysis is in progress and will be presented elsewhere [51]. At last, a firm footing on which to explore possibilities.

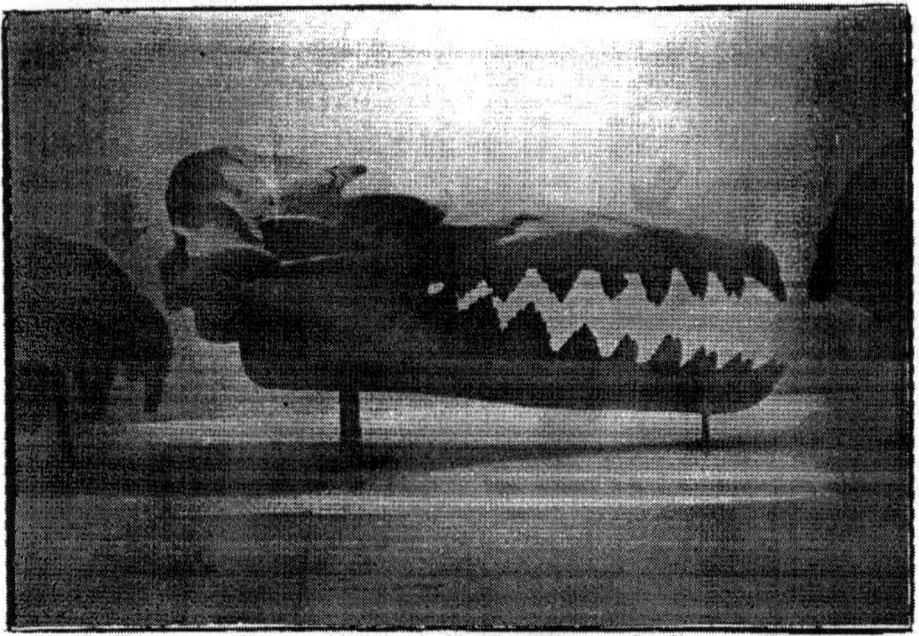

Fig. 8: The vaguely crocodilian skull of an Eocene basilosaur, *Basilosaurus isis*. Skulls such as this one are typically around 100cm in length. Photograph D.Naish.©

Acknowledgements.

This impossibly difficult two part article owes its completion to the assistance provided by a number of individuals. For their hospitality, many thanks to Jon, Alison and other livestock of the CFZ (particularly to Carruthers for 24 hour companionship). Thanks to Karl Shuker for useful discussion, Ewan Fordyce for information on the archaeocete fossil record, Gareth Dyke and Ian Harding for loans of various kinds, Ben Roesch for material and plenty of chat, and John Moore for comments. Special thanks to Jason Head for help with functional anatomy, and Craig Harris for getting my project off the ground. On the Case? Get Stuffed.

References and Notes.

1. SANDERSON, Ivan T. 1958. Follow the Whale (London).
2. NAISH, D.W. 1996. Ancient whales, sea serpents and nessies part one:pros and cons. Animals & Men #9: 16-23
3. HEUVELMANS, B. 1968. In the wake of the Sea Serpents. Rupert Hart-Davis (London).
4. MICHELL, J and RICKARD, R.J.M. 1982. Living Wonders. Thames and Hudson. (London).
5. The generic names Basilosaurus and Zeuglodon are often confused by cryptozoologists. Basilosaurus, created by Harlan in 1834, has priority over Zeuglodon (Owen, 1839). Owen invented the name Zeuglodon once it was proven that this animal was not a reptile, as Basilosaurus - 'King Reptile' obviously implies.
6. McEWAN, G.J. 1978. Sea Serpents. Sailors and Sceptics. Routledge and Kegan Paul (London).
7. SHUKER, K.P.N. 1995. In Search of Prehistoric Survivors. Blandford (London).
8. BRIGHT, M. 1989. There are giants in the sea. Robson Books (London).
9. MORELL, V. 1982. The myth and science of cryptozoology: on the trail of lost worlds and controversial species with Dr. Roy Mackal. Equinox. Sept/Oct 1982: 23-35.
10. Scientific names are not accepted without description of a type specimen and are invalid without them.
11. Bord, J. & BORD, C. 1991. From the Sea Serpent to the Super-Otter. In BROOKESMITH, P. (Ed). Creatures from Elsewhere. Black Cat (London), pp. 36-40.
12. In ref. 4 we read '(the Mansi photograph) is said to be the clearest yet of a monster in action and appears to show some kind of Zeuglodon'. (p.26).
13. COSTELLO, P. 1991. American lake monsters. In BROOKESMITH, P. (Ed). Creatures from Elsewhere. Black Cat (London), pp. 41-53.
14. GRANT, J. 1992. Monster Mysteries. The Apple Press (London).
15. Work in progress.
16. BORD, J. and BORD, C. 1985. Alien Animals. Panther (London).

17. WHITFARE, S and FAIRLEY, J. 1980. Arthur C Clarke's Mysterious World. Collins (London).
18. A possibility I hope to explore elsewhere.
19. WELFARE, S and FAIRLEY, J. 1993. Arthur C Clarke's A-Z of mysteries. Harper Collins (London).
20. BEDDARD, F.E. 1923. Mammalia. Macmillan and Co. (London). On pp. 342-3. 'the presence on the dorsal fin of a row of stoney tubercules' in Phocaena (now Phocoena) and Neomeris (now Neophocaena species is discussed as homologous with 'bony plates' (found) in connection with the remains of a Zeuglodont Cetacean (sic).
21. KELLOGG, A.R. 1936. A review of the Archaeoceti. Carnegie Inst. Washington Publ. 482: 1-366.
22. HEUVELMANS, B. 1995. On the Track of Unknown Animals. Kegan Paul International Ltd (London).
23. I have long considered the minhocao to be a cryptic giant caecilian, and am delighted to see that Karl Shuker favours a similar identity (in (7), pp. 147-8). This identity deserves further comment, and is yet another piece IN PREP.
24. PHILIP, D. 1987. On the trail of Ogopogo. Western Report. Aug. 17 1987.
25. ANON. 1989. Ogopogo may be big otter, scientists say. Toronto Star Sept. 24th 1989.
26. ANON. 1989. Ogopogo an otter monster? Toronto Sun Sept. 24th 1989.
27. One example of a report in which 'Ogopogo' is described as 'resembling a long black eel' is that of Harry Staines on seeing the animal in 1977. Reported in ref. 19 (pp. 118-119).
28. Reported on pp. 118-119 of ref. (19), (where Clark's sketch can be seen too), and discussed on pp. 100-101 of ref. 7. First reported in GREENWELL, J.R. 1987. Close Encounter in Lake Okanagan Revealed. ISC Newsletter 6 (spring): 1-3.
29. True of the Lake Brompton Monster, discussed on pp. 93-8 of ref.30.
30. MEURGER, M. and GAGNON, C. 1988. Lake Monster Traditions. Fortean Tomes (London).
31. BOUSFIELD, E. and LeBLOND, P.H. 1995. An account of Cadborosaurus willsi, new genus, new species, a large aquatic reptile from the Pacific coast of North America. Amphipacifica 1 (supplement 1): 3-25.
32. Bousfield and LeBlond refer to Pachypleurosaurus as a nothosaur. It has become evident that 'nothosaurs' do not represent a single group of closely related marine reptiles: the true nothosaurs are close to the plesiosaurs, whilst Pachypleurosaurus, as part of the Pachypleurosauria, represents a distant lineage.
33. The group name used for seals, sea-lions and walruses. They may not be a natural group, but this is very controversial.
34. With respect to Cadborosaurus, this is an opinion similarly presented in DASH, M. 1993. The Dragons of Vancouver. Fortean Times 70: 46-48. Dash describes the report of William Hagelund, a former sea-captain who, in 1968, allegedly caught a baby 'caddy'. Hagelund's sketch features a flukcd tail that Dash describes as 'characteristically mammalian'. (p.46).
35. SHUKER, K.P.N. 1995. New Britain's lake Monster. Fortean Times 82: 38-39.
36. Furthermore, if this animal's existence could be proven, it would provide substantial food for biogeographical thought. New Zealand has been isolated for about 80 m.a and has a unique endemic fauna.
37. OHLENDORF, P. 1982. A hunt for cryptic beasts. Macleans Feb. 22nd 1982.
38. SHUKER, K.P.N. 1996. Turkish delight. Wild about Animals 8 (2): 15
39. It is worth pointing out that these animals are not the same as another group of lake dwelling mammals; the water 'horses' and 'cows' of Scandanavia. These are little or nothing to do with whales and most probably represent sightings of known mammals in unfamiliar circumstances.
40. BORD, J. and BORD, C. 1991. Creatures of the Irish Lakes. In BROOKESMITH, P. (Ed). Creatures from Elsewhere. Black Cat (London), pp. 71-80.
41. ARNOLD, N. 1995. Loch Ness - a cauldron of definites and possibilities. In DOWNES, J. (ed). CFZ Yearbook 1996. STPATZ (Exeter) pp. 127-131.

42. SWORD, M.D. 1991. The Wasgo or Sisiutl. A cryptozoological Sea-Animal of the Pacific Northwest coast of the Americas. Journ. Sci. Exploration 5: 85-101
43. CONWAY, T. 1985. Halley's Comet legends among the Great Lakes Ojibwa Indians. Archaeoastronomy 8: Jan-Dec (not seen).
44. SLIJPER, E.J. 1962. Whales. Hutchinson (London).
45. The name 'protocetid' is a convenient term that, strictly speaking, applies to several groups of early whales of various affinity. The name pakicetid has recently been used for the earliest forms, Pakicetus and Nalacetus (a new genus in press), in THEWISSEN, J.G.M., ROE, L.J., O'NEIL, J.R., HUSSAIN, S.T., SAHNI, A. and BAJPAI, S. 1996. Evolution of cetacean osmoregulation. Nature 381:379-380.
46. DECHASEAUX, C. 1961. Cetacea. In PIVETEAU, J. Traite de Paleontologie VI Vol I. Masson et cie (Paris), pp. 831-886.
47. STUCKY, R.K. and McKENNA, M.C. 1993. Order Cetacea Brisson, 1762. In BENTON, M.J. (ed) The Fossil Record 2. Chapman and Hall (London), pp. 761-762.
48. GINGERICH, P.D., HOLLY SMITH, B, and SIMONS, E.L. 1990. Hind limbs of Eocene Bailosaurus: Evidence of feet in whales. Science 249: 154-157.
49. FORDYCE, R.E and BARNES, L.G. 1994. The evolutionary history of whales and dolphins. Annu. Rev. Earth Planet. Sci. 22: 419-55.
50. MCAULIFFE, K. 1994. When Whales had Feet. Sea Frontiers 40 (1): 20-32.
51. NAISH, D.W. In prep. An analysis of the migo footage (real title being kept secret). To be published in CFZ Yearbook 1997.

EDITOR'S NOTE: Cryptozoology and its allied disciplines within forteana are, by their very nature controversial subjects. As both a fortean and a zoologist (and probably many other things besides), I feel that the controversy is something to be encouraged. We have printed controversial articles before, but this one, is potentially the most controversial article we have yet included.

Darren Naish is to be congratulated for his meticulous research in producing this work. He has, however, made assertions which contradict other major works on the subject, many of them written by contributors and subscribers to this magazine. As Editor I welcome responses to this article by any of the authors he has cited, or indeed from anyone else and will print whatever we are sent, probably in the 1997 Yearbook, in the interests of encouraging an open and scientific dialogue.

SPOTTING CATS WITH SPOTS

In recent years there have been a number of instances of mysterious spotted cats being shot by farmers and 'sportsmen' in the UK. Many of these have been identified as specimens of the Asian Leopard Cat (F. bengalensis), but recent advances in the pet keeping world have also produced spotted cats. Mrs Anita Cox, a breeder of such animals and veteran zoologist and zoo keeper Clinton Keeling describe the two creatures. They hold radically opposing viewpoints on the matter. At the Centre for Fortean Zoology we are remaining steadfastly neutral, but invite further comments from people on both sides of the metaphorical fence:

THE BENGAL CAT
by Anita Cox

An attempt by breeders initially in the U.S.A. to duplicate as far as possible, the luxurious beauty of the small wild Asian leopard cat (F. bengalensis), Bengals are therefore hybrids, the result of crossing domestic queens with the Asian leopard cat. The aim being to get eventually a wild replica but with gentle domestic temperament.

The male leopard cat will not mate with a domestic

A BENGAL CAT. BRED AND PHOTOGRAPHED BY MRS ANITA COX

unless it has been raised with them. The first generation males from this outcross, being hybrids, are always sterile.

The spotting patterns on kittens seems to flow horizontally, is well defined and can be large spots, and even rosettes. Good examples of the breeds have pelts rather than coats, the fur being short but very plush and like silk; sometimes one gets gold dusting on the tips of the hair. These hybrids tend to be larger then most domestic cats, vigorously heathy but as yet there is much variation in the type especially the head and ear shape. They adore playing in water, are quite vocal, some sounding quite raspy and guttural. At present, breeders are attempting to mate these hybrids back to Asian leopard cats to increase the gene pool and better fix the gorgeous pelts and other attributes whilst at all times essaying to maintain sweetness of temperament.

THE LEOPARD CAT
(Felis bengalensis)
by Clinton Keeling.

The leopard cat is one of the smaller of the thirty-seven or so species of Cats, so therefore it's a subject the zoologist or naturalist dreads writing about. Yes, these and other creatures such as most Mongooses, many rodents, the majority of Pheasant species and so on, for the very simple reason their behaviour is so unremarkable that there's precious little to say about them.

Most of the smaller Cats just sleep by day in rock crevices or in hollow trees, come out at night to prey on small mammals and birds and then, when the sun comes up, go back to sleep again. So try to write interestingly about such animals if you will, or can. Talk about seeking to make bricks without straw...

However, I've been asked for an article about the Leopard Cat, so devotion to duty compels me to see what I can do - although don't expect too much, as there's pretty little that's out of the ordinary to hold forth about where it's concerned.

As it's found over a vast area - from India, Assam and Burma, to China, and out as far as the Philippines, then southwards to the Malay Peninsular and a number of islands - there's bound to be a considerable degree of geographical colour variation, but what might be termed a typical pecimen is about the size of a domestic Cat with short, smooth fur; the ears are rather pointed and the eye greyish-yellow; the ground colour is brownish-yellow, with white on the cheeks, and liberally streaked and spotted with dark-brown and black. In many specimens the markings form almost a dorsal line, and almost invariably the tail is banded.

The first 'British' specimen, of which we have proof (i.e., some earlier ones in menageries or privately-owned might have gone unrecorded) arrived at the London Zoological Garden in 1833, and just by chance it turned out to be a very wild and unfriendly (probably nervous) individual that resisted all attempts by its keepers to get on good terms with it. Consequently this one animal gave the species its earlier reputation for hostility, if not downright ferocity, which we now know to be quite unjustified. The fact remains, however, that in the wild it frequents forested regions and, preferring the seclusion they provide, is inclined to avoid human villages and other settlements, unlike other wild Cats.

As I said earlier, there's precious little that's out of the ordinary about the Leopard Cat, but note well that I didn't say there was nothing out of the ordinary about it - as a scientist I don't use words lightly. In fact there are two points about it worth reporting here.

First, over recent years there's been a considerable amount of crossing or hybridising it with the ordinary domestic Cat - for reasons known only to the Almighty and those who produce these violations of nature. Like all serious naturalists I greatly disapprove of this practice and forsee various problems to come in the future. Mark My words.

Then, we come upon a real mystery that will probably never be explained, and which in a way lifts the Leopard Cat out of its behavioural doldrums and places it in a category (not intended as a pun) all of its own.

In every species what is known as the 'type specimen' is the first individual to be observed or collected and scientifically described. Fine, so what about the type specimen of our subject? Simply that it was found swimming, miles from the nearest land, in the Bay of Bengal - hence its scientific name, as 'ensis' in such nomenclature means 'from'. There's doubtless an interesting story as to how this situation (I suppose if I were a trendy I'd say 'scenario') came about, but it will forever remain one of Nature's many unsolved puzzles.

EDITOR'S NOTES:

1. For a listing of all Leopard Cats (and specimens of other species killed or captured) in the UK consult the paper by Dr. Karl P.N.Shuker in Fortean Studies Volume 2.

2. As regular readers will know, we are presently engaged in a study of the Fortean Zoology of Hong Kong, and it may be of interest to note that the Leopard

Cat is the only endemic cat species still living in the territory. It is also worth noting that on at least one occasion in our records a natural (rather than artificially contrived) cross-breeding between this species and a domestic cat has taken place, in Hong-Kong.

3. The taxonomy of the species is also controversial. Whilst it was described as *Felis bengalensis* many zoologists place it, and four other species of Asian wild cat in a seperate genus: *Prionailurus*, making the nomenclature for this specis *P.bengalensis*. Richard Green (1991) lists eleven sub-species.

NORTH OF THE BORDER

Scottish News from Tom Anderson

November 24th 1995 saw the introduction of the deer bill, designed to give a goverment quango compulsary powers to cull red deer, specially hinds.

There has been a massive increase in the herds, now numbering 350,000, the largest figure since 1945. In those days it was due to stalkers being recruited as snipers in the infantry. to-days problems are put down to mis-management. An estimated cull of 100,000 is thought necessary to redress the balance of deer to acreage. The new law would allow all terrain vehicals and helicopters to drive the herds toward the "*killing grounds*". This was the method used against the mustang herds in the mid-west until public pressure stopped it. Animal concern claim the existing birth control pellet to be both more effective and less contentious.

At present a red stag costs around £800 for the stalk, services of a ghillie etc.

Add on accomodation, transport, clothing, ammunition, air fares (most shooters are foreign) and it is a sizeable industry. If he's successful the shooter pays £300 for the head and the estate keeps the meat, worth £150. The hind, having virtually no trophy value, is worth £90. Mean body weight is down in most herds and in some areas starvation is rife. Only the remoteness from the public view has stopped a national protest. As there is no political mileage involved (how many socialists have rural/highland seats?) the bill would seem to have a free passage to legislation.

Tayside police, convinced by a score of sightings over the last sixteen months, are collating all relevant information to establish a pattern of movements and population. Their wildlife officer said most reports were of a 'Black Panther' type:

"..*with all these people phoning in saying they are seeing a large feline (sic), the law of averages means there probably is a large feline (sic)*"..

'Eh? Ed.)'

Examined sheep kills apparently rule out dogs or foxes as:

"*Whatever did it had quite a bit of power behind it*".

Senior zoology lecturer at Dundee University, Dr. John Reilly, however, is "very sceptical", despite one cat appearing in someone's back garden and another (or perhaps the same animal), seen strolling the Esplanade at Broughty Ferry. No date is obtainable for this last incident, but the only possible for explanation for a big cat to venture into a densely populated built up area like this would be if it heard the seal pups which lie up there in some numbers at low tide. If true this would make an interesting addition to a felid diet.

N.B. Dr. Reilly recently returned from the Congo where he was studying dwarf crocodiles (of which he is inordinately fond) in the course of which he saved the life of a German colleague with an infected foot, using a cigarette lighter and a razor blade.

THE 'PREDICTED' MOTH OF MADAGASCAR: AN ILL-KNOWN SUCCESS OF CRYPTOZOOLOGY.

by

Michel Raynal

Cryptozoology is not only interested in giant unknown animals, as misinformed people (including some cryptozoologists) believe. Of course, living brontosaurs strike our imagination, but little unknown animals should not be neglected (and in fact their existance is often much more likely than these "monsters"). Interestingly, one of the most remarkable victories of a true cryptozoological mind, concerns a very little animal - a moth! - though it is unknown to most cryptozoologists...

In 1862, the famous naturalist Charles Darwin published a book on the evolutionary biology of orchids. 'On the various contrivances by which British and foreign Orchids are fertilised by insects'. Studying the angraecoids, he remarked that they were pollinisated by specific insects. One of these orchids from Madagascar, *Angraecum sesquipedale*, had nectaries eleven and a half inches long, with only the lower inch and a half filled with nectar. From the structure of this orchid, Darwin "predicted" the existence of an unknown moth:

"It is, however, suprising that any insect should be able to reach the nectar: our English sphinxes have probosces as long as their bodies; but in Madagascar there must be moths with probosces capable of extention to a length of between ten and eleven inches!"

Darwin then made an experiment. He took a cylinder, one-tenth of an inch in diameter, and pushed it down through the cleft of the rostrellum:

"By this means alone I succeeded in each case in withdrawing the pollinia : and it cannot, I think be doubted that a large moth must thus act; namely, by driving its proboscis up to the very base, through the cleft of the rostrellum, so as to reach the extremity of the nectary; and then withdrawing its proboscis with the pollinia attached to it."

This insect would, of course affect the fertilization of the orchid, and Darwin concluded to the survival of this moth from ecological evidence:

"The pollinia would not be withdrawn until some huge moth, with a wonderfully long proboscis, tried to drain the last drop. If such great moths were to become extinct in Madagascar, assuredly the *Angraecum* would become extinct."

In a letter published in the June 12, 1873, issue of Nature, W.A Forbes asked if readers were aware of such moths in Madagascar, and he proposed an identification:

"They would probably be Sphingidae of some kind, as no other moths would combine sufficient size and length of proboscis".

Herman Muller, in the July 17 issue of the same year, mentioned that his brother had caught in Brazil a sphinx:

"the proboscis of which has a length of about 0.25 metres".

demonstrating that Darwin's moth was not at all impossible.

In the second edition of his book (1877), the 'Father of Natural Selection' remarked:

"This belief of mine has been ridiculed by some entomologists, but we know from Fritz Muller that there is a sphinx-moth in south Brazil which has a proboscis of nearly sufficient lenght, for when dried it was between ten and eleven inches long. When not protruded it is coiled up into a spiral of at least twenty windings.".

Meanwhile, Alfred Russel Wallace, the 'Father of Biogeography', commented at greater length on this orchid in his book 'Contributions To The Theory Of Natural Selection' (1871), and he came to the same conclusion:

"I may here mention that some of the large sphinx moths of the tropics have probosces as long as the nectary of *Angraecum sesquipedale*. I have carfully measured the proboscis of a specimen of *Macrosilia cluentius* [= *Cocytius cluentius*] from south America, in the collections of the British museum, and find it to be nine inches and a quarter long! One from tropical Africa (*Macrosilia morgani*) [= *Xanthopan morgani*] is seven inches and a half [...] That such a moth exists in Madagascar may be safely predicted; and naturalists who visit that island should search for it with as much confidence as astronomers searching for the planet Neptune, and I venture to predict they will be equally successful."

This remark alluded to German astronomer Galle, who had searched for, and found, Neptune, after French mathematician Le Verrier predicted its existence and position. from calculations on the orbit of Uranus, then last known planet of the solar system - a well- known case in the history of sciences, often mentioned for its significance in epistemology.

And the idea of a close relation with the large sphingid of tropical Africa, *Xanthopan morgani*, which has a proboscis about 20cm, was quite judicious and prophetic. This "cryptolepidoptere" was actually found and described 41 years after Darwins prediction: it belonged to that very species, but it was a new sub-species, with Rothschild and Jordon named *Xanthopan morgani praedicta* in 1903. i.e. "predicted", which is fully justified. This insect has a wing span of 13 to 15 cm, of the colour of a dead leaf and its proboscis is actually 25 cm (ten inches) long.

History seems to be repeating itself: American entomologist Gene Kirsty, of the Mount St Josephs of Ohio college in cincinnati, rescently made an hypothesis similar to Darwins prediction. Another Madagascar orchid, *Angraecum longicalcar*, has a rostrellum still deeper then that of *A.sesquipedale*: about 16 inches (40 cm). Consequently, Gene Kirsty predicted in the American Entomologist of Winter 1991 the existence of another unknown large in Madagascar, with a proboscis 15 inches (38 cm) long! Let us hope that we will not have to wait 41 years before this new predicted moth will be found...

Front cover Photograph: The star orchid *Angraecum sesquipedale* and the predicted moth *Xanthopan morgani praedicta*. (Copyright Marcel LECOUFLE).

BIBLIOGRAPHY.

ANGIER, Natalie. 1992. *May be elusive but moth with 15 inch tongue should be out there*. The New York Times (January 14).

DARWIN, Charles. 1862. *On the Various Contrivences by which British and forign Orchids are Fertilised by insects, and on the good effects of intercrossing*. London, John Murray:197-203.

DARWIN Charles. 1877. *The Various Contrivances by which Orchids are fertilised by insects*. London John Murray:162-166.

FORBES. W.A. 1873. *Fertilisation of Orchids*. Nature, vol.8:121.

KRITSKY, Gene. 1991. *Darwin's Madagascan hawk moth prediction*. American Entomologist, vol. 37 [# 4]:206-210 (winter).

MULLER, Herman. 1873. *Proboscis capable of sucking the nectar of Angraecum sesquipedale*. Nature vol.8:223.

RAMSEY, Carl T. 1965 *Darwin and the star orchid of Madagascar*. American Orchid Society Bulletin, vol. 34: 1056-1062 (December).

ROTHSCHILD, Walter, & Carl JORDAN. 1903. *A revision of the Lepidopterous family Sphingate*. London and Aylesbury, Hazell, Watson and Viney:30-32.

WALLACE, Alfred Russel 1871. *Contributions to the Theory Of Natural Selection*. London, Macmillan, 2nd edition:272-275.

WALLACE. A.R.1867 *Creation by law*. Quarterly Journal of science, vol.4:470-488.

*****

Of Moose, Men and Monsters.

by Lars Thomas

About 400 km north of Stockholm in Sweden lies a mighty lake. So large in fact, that it just called Storsjon (The great lake). For many years this has been the Swedish equivalent of Loch Ness, the home of a lake monster known as *Storsjoodjuret* (The Great Lake Monster).

On an old runestone on the banks of the lake can be seen, what local legend calls the oldest depiction of the sea-monster. A long dragon-like animal circling the stone, biting its own tail. Although the image is very clear, the connection with the lake-monster is at best far fetched. The animal is probably *Jormungandr*, the Midgard snake of Nordic mythology, which encircled the world.

The story of the Storsjo-monster starts in the 1890's, when a series of reports in local newspapers caught the attention of Dr. Peter Olsson, a local naturalist and science teacher.

He started collecting sightings and studying the monster people claimed they were seeing. The oldest sighting he was able to find was from 1820, but later researchers found stories even older. An old legend, written down by a priest in 1635 tells the story of two trolls creating the monster, which suggests that the creature was well known even then.

In 1894 several wealthy local people made an effort to catch the monster. They had several large traps made, and hired a very experienced Norwegian whaler to catch the animal. The traps, which can be seen at the museum in Ostersund at the lake today, never caught anything, and the whaler spent an entire year at the lake, without even seeing the monster. Since then there has been no further serious attempt to catch the animal, and in 1986 the animal was declared a protected species.

The Storsjomonster is in many ways a typical lake-monster. It has been variously described as looking like an upturned boat, a string of humps, or like an animal with a long thin neck, and a small dog-like or a larger horse-like head. The size varies from 3 to 14 meters according to witnesses.

In two very important aspects, the Storsjo-monster does vary strikingly from other lake monsters. It apparently prefers the very narrow parts of the lake close to the most populated areas, and it has very large, prominent, white or pale ears, compared by some witnesses to sails, fins or bat wings. Not all sightings mention the ears, but those that do are all from late summer, or early autumn. This is a rather strange coincidence. It could, however easily be explained if the lake-monsters with the white ears were swimming moose, and not lake monsters at all.

In late summer and early autumn, the moose antlers are clean of velvet, and look like large, pale fins, sails or bats wings. Most of the local eyewitnesses would probably say, that they know perfectly well what a moose looks like, after all there are plenty of moose in the woods around lake Storsjon. Exactly! What most people don't know, however, is the fact that moose are very strong and powerful swimmers. They can swim several miles. Every now and then an animal will even swim from Sweden to Denmark.

Sweden showing Lake Storsjon

At the narrowest part, this means a swim of at least four kilometers through very strong currents. The actual distance is probably even larger, since the shortest distance is between two heavily populated areas that the moose would probably avoid. Moose are also good divers. They can dive to a depth of four or five metres, and stay down for one or two minutes, munching on aquatic plants.

A good part of the sightings in the narrow parts of lake Storsjon, and definitely the sightings of the lake-monsters with big ears, are probably nothing more than moose swimming from one lake-bank to the other. And, I have no doubt, scaring the life out of people in small boats or walking along the banks, when they suddenly appear from the depths of the lake, wet and shin. y, with bundles of aquatic plants hanging from their neck or mouth. It is not surprising, that people do not recognise a moose in a situation like that, and it is no surprise either, that the moose sinks back into the water and disappears as quickly as possible.

REFERENCES:

Bord, Janet and Colin: *Alien Animals* Granada London 1980.

Costello, Peter: *In search of Lake Monsters* Coward, McCann and Geoghegan, New York 1974

McDonald, D and P.Barrett: *Mammals of Britain and Europe* Harper Collins, London 1993

Oscarsson, Ulla: *Storsjoodjuret* Jamtlands lans Museum. Ostersund 1986

Svedjeland, Knut: *Storsjoodjuret* S-Forlaget, Ostersund 1959.

AVAILABLE NOW

"*The Smaller Mystery Carnivores of the West Country*"

by Jonathan Downes

117pp Many illustrations
£7.50

The Derry

by

Sunila Sen-Gupta

Editorial Note: Every culture on earth has created its own individual zoomythology, to fulfill a specific cultural function. These functions are diverse, and often subtle, and it is our belief that they deserve study as much as do the more tangible creatures in the fortean zoological bestiary. Creatures like 'The Brentford Griffin', for example, are a sociological zoomyth. They are neither based on a specific cultural mythology from history, nor on a zoological reality, but are 'real' in sociological terms, and deserve study.

It is unwise, we believe, to assume that each zoo-myth has its roots in a living, breathing cryptid just waiting to be discovered. Some zoomyths were created for spiritual, financial or even political reasons, and some, like the Swiss 'Derry' have a more subtle sociological function.

Any reader who has ever worked on a building site in Britain, as I did for a few months as a teenager, will be familiar with the ritual which takes place on the first morning of one's employment when the unwary are sent to the foreman's office to collect a piece of mythical equipment called 'a long weight'.

There are several variants on this theme. In Scotland, visiting foreigners have often been sent on a 'haggis hunt', having been told that the haggis is a mythical beast which lurks in the heather of the local moorlands, and no doubt every other culture has its similar mechanism for expressing cultural solidarity by teasing outsiders in a light-hearted manner. The Derry is one of these zoomyths. It is a 'creature' unheard of outside Switzerland, and we are indebted to our Swiss correspondent for enlightening us on the matter...

NERVOUS TWITCH

The Nervous Twitcher takes her regular look at all thats most wierd in the world of our feathered friends...who WAS that masked ornithologist?

CRIME AND PUNISHMENT

Several tales of stolen and smuggled birds have filtered through in the last few months. A man was caught at an unnamed airport recently trying to smuggle 10 fighting cocks and two brood hens. Some of the birds woke up from a drugged sleep and started to crow loudly, giving the game away. The chickens had been hidden inside a large shipping carton by Florante Pascua, a Philippino-American from Guam. *ITV TELETEXT 18.3.89*

Two very rare yellow shouldered Amazon Parrots recently reared a brood of four youngsters. The two birds, Ken and Barbie, had been separately kidnapped from their native Venezuala and smuggled out. Barbie was picked up at Heathrow customs and Ken was found in Amsterdam. The happy couple have now set up home at Paradise Park, Hayle in Cornwall, where they will play an important part in a breeding programme designed to help the species survive. *DAILY MAIL Jan 12.95*

A blue fronted Amazon was stolen with personal possessions from a house in Hale, Cheshire. The owner Julie Rollings, sent out a desperate plea via a newspaper advertisement for his safe return but heard nothing for nine days. Then one day she had a strange 'phone call from a woman who told Julie to be at the car park of the George and Dragon pub in Altrincham at a certain time *'Be there and you can have your parrot back'* she said, *'but no questions asked'*. Eventually a taxi turned up and the sole passenger was Silver, her lost parrot! It sounds like a plot from a bad B Movie but at least it had a happy ending! *Daily Mail 23.2.95*

SOCK IT TO ME MAMA

A ten day old vulture called *'Bert'* is currently being reared by....an old sock! He was abandoned at an early age and zoo keepers at Whipsnade are using the makeshift puppet to help feed Bert and to make him think that it is another vulture. *BBC TELETEXT NEWSROUND 23.2.95*

WHITHER SHALL YE WANDER?

I can't think of many worse things than slicing off your own finger with a chisel, but one of them must be when the finger you've just sliced off gets eaten by your pet geese! That's exactly what happened to handyman David Bidmead from Crawley when he was doing a spot of DIY. *Northampton Chronicle 22.3.95*

DON'T BE SILLY

Is this an urban myth, a practical joke or real life? *The Daily Mail* reported in 1993 that hundreds of tiny wooly jumpers had been knitted by volunteers to help save oiled seabirds. People, it is claimed, believed that the jumpers would help soak up the oil and keep them warm. Apparently the RSPCA were inundated with them. If this story had appeared on the first of April I could understand but it appeared on the 20th February. Any thoughts?

LETTERS

Opinions expressed are those of the individual writer and not necessarily those of this Magazine.

As has been the case since the editor's father first mooted the idea of a letters page last summer the crypto post bag has been overflowing with your missives on all subjects Crypto not to mention Zoological.

EASY AS A B C?

Dear Sir,

Regarding cats: Zoologist Dr. Ingvald Lieberkind in his Danish Encyclopaedia *'Dyrenes Verden'* from the mid sixties lists the following big cat crossbreeds:

Lion/Tiger
Lion/Leopard
Lion/Jaguar

and between the domestic cat and:

Felis chaus
F. Silvestris
F.s.ocreata
F.s.ornata
F.s.cafra
F.lynx

The latter fits some descriptions of Alien Big Cats (ABC's). Other than that he also listed a cross between Puma and Leopard (two different genera).

It seems that cats are in general so close genetically that 'anything goes', and this fact could for the moment be a necessity in a thinly spread population. Some of this offspring should be considered sterile though, but we just might be so lucky as to watch a 'species' in the making; nature working from scratch. A topic for future investigation would be an independent library of hair types for reference purposes. A zoo would probably be helpful. The library should contain pictures of hair types, including individual variation, protein profile and possibly DNA profile. Considering the interest from the police in this matter they will help.

By the way: We should not expect to keep the big cats forever. The moment the ABC's (or should we say the BBC's) get their official confirmation we could lose them. England can live with in the region of 5, 000 people killed in traffic per year and (multiplied from Denmark) more than 100, 000 dog bites, but man is an irrational animal. The moment a threat is perceived from ABC's, real or imagined, the devil is loose. This problem has to be dealt with along the way. My feelings are therefore mixed with worry, but that must be the eternal problem of cryptozoology. Personally, regarding ABC's, the British fauna needs a medium sized or big predator, whether cat or wolf. Some purists may argue but the present state of the ecosystem with nothing bigger than a fox or a badger is un-natural.

Eric Sorensen
Denmark

Hopefully the boar won't become just a delicacy for gourmets although those who live near Romney Marsh believe that the animals should be wiped out as soon as possible. The confrontations have been few and far between and like most creatures, the boar will only attack when provoked. However, a fifty pound peccary on the loose proved to be more of a stranded creature when it attacked a man and his three well built dogs which included a rottweiler. The peccary had been on the run for a full week and caused extreme damage to the dogs. Eventually the animal was tempted back to the park it has escaped from.

A few other boars have been sighted in the area as well as Herne Bay and other parts of Kent. Two of the original Romney Marsh escapees may well be responsible for the family but let's hope they are given enough time to breed healthily. Even a few cross breeds may be formed and the boar situation may become as interesting as the big cat situation.

Of course, the hunters will never cease but we can hope that not all creatures can be extinguished. There are enough zoo's, farms and parks in Kent and knowing the nature of the wild boar there is always a chance that a few may escape. As we know, these creatures were once part of the furniture but nowdays a three hundred pound boar tends to make a few people a little uncomfortable. 'Beaky' the fifty pound peccary had already done too much damage in most peoples eyes so it is going to take a drastic change in people's attitudes before any sort of reintroduction programme can be discussed. It is time to recognize that wild boar do exist in small numbers in the south of England, and we should treasure them and hopefully look after them otherwise another chapter in Britains wildlife will be closed forever. A two hundred year absence is a heck of a long time but when the caged boars start mating I'm pretty sure that a few lusty visitors with unfamiliar grunts will be homing in.

Although the population of boar is small, it is livly and judging by the size of some of them it could be said that we have another monster in our stable. Something that will no doubt fuel the hunters and feed the resteraunts. And for every snorting creature that makes the dish let's hope another is born and that Britan can permenantly regain one of its true natives.

NOW THAT'S WHAT I CALL CRYPTO
(Selections from a mythical compilation LP)
by Neil Nixon

The Neutrons - 'Mermaid and Chips'.

Tinkling pianos, early synth effects, choral backing vocals and a lead singer who combines a choirboy vocal line with a hint of strain and throatiness. Yup, we're in obscure prog. rock heaven and the lyrics are a wonderfully arty mish mash of the mundane and the mythical. In the opening line we're on 'Swansea peir' - soon we're spiritred away to Tintagel. We sped the whole track seeking a beauty who is never defined because, as the singer says, 'Every time I get a bit closer I seem to get a little bit near'!!.

So much the better if it sounds like a bizarre dream, we're chasing a mermaid here, and after a few trippy keyboard tinkles we find ourselves in the Glasgow snow and reach the end of our search. As per usual in the great crypto quest we get a tantalising fragment of proof. In this case its nothing more than 'broken shells'.

Sound wise, it leans on Genesis, takes in the odd eclectic musical reference and creates its own peculiar world. 1996 it ain't. This gem resides on the ultra rare 'Black Hole Star' album by the Neutrons, originally released in 1974. You've probably got more chance of finding a real mermaid these days. If you want to sample fortean music of invention, ideas and melodic overkill you could spend £10.00, ten years and about 10,000 road miles hunting 'The Neutrons' out of a second hand shop. Then again, you could check out the latest CD by The Amphibians from Outer Space... (I've heard of them somewhere..Ed).

Guiafairo - The fear that flies by night.

by Owen Burnham

In the forest regions of West Africa there re many beliefs concerning the afterlife, the gods of nature and animal ancestor spirits. These are the entities that populate the skies, trees, rivers and soils of the continent and they exact a powerful influence on the beliefs and lives of the human inhabitants of the area.

One of the most mysterious and terrifying of these 'things that fly by night' is the notorious guiafairo of the savannahs, especially where there are rocky outcrops rising above the plains. Such places abound in West Africa and the guiafairo is seen as a menace in all such areas.

Naming the guiafairo is one thing, describing it is another. All that is clear from each and every account is its stealthy flying ability and the nauseating smell it brings with it. In colour it is said to be grey, 'with the face of a man', and some accounts speak of wings, whilst others merely suggest flight - how else could it come through locked doors? The grey phantasmal shape of the guiafairo is again debateable, because in some cases it appears to be a spirit entity and in others a creature of ghostly greyish black flesh. One thing is clear, those who have encountered the grey, suffocating fear that is the guiafairo never forget it, and in many cases death, from some malaise, occurs a short time after. It is a creeping, paralysing death, like the fear itself, and there is no remedy, no escape and no hope.

By day the guiafairo is said to haunt the hollow trees and rocky outcrops (with their caves) that exist in the hot lands of West Africa. Since no-one seems prepared to verify the lair of the guiafairo nothing can be confirmed. It is a grey entity which appears and disappears at will and only the power of an extreme good-luck charm appears to offer any peace to the people who share its territory. Only rarely does the visiting entity leave a trace of its presence - its smell, or the marks of its clawed feet on dirt floors. These are the only signs of the marauder, the fear that comes by night and steals the souls of its victims. This is guiafairo- the fear that comes by night.

EDITOR'S NOTE: Our interest in Owlman type phenomena is well known, and it seems apparent that this entity is similar if not identical to that reported from the area of Falmouth Bay surrounding Mawnan Old Church. We welcome information on similar 'creatures' from around the world.

LETTER FROM THE LOCH-SIDE

by Richard Carter
(of the Loch Ness Society).

I've just returned from a week at the loch and thought you might be interested in something that crossed my mind while sat watching the water. I've seen other people's Nessie.

While sat watching the Loch I was studying a wake from a boat that passed about 10 minutes before, when I wondered how many people had seen the same thing and believed that they had glimpsed the monster. It was then that I started to think just how sceptical one has to be to believe in something like the Loch Ness Monster. I've seen a Gosander with her young run down the middle of the Loch then seemingly just vanish when they stop. Wind slicks shoot across the loch which at first glance look like the shadow of some large beast just under the surface. Ducks seen on a mirror calm loch can be distorted into something of giant size with a terrific wake spreading out. Even the small fishing boats seen on the loch can, under the right conditions take on unusual shapes.

Great Northern Divers can be seen on the Loch as they sit so low in the water with their head and neck sticking out. I'll bet more than a few people out there have seen their 'nessie'. Otters live around the Loch but are rarely seen by people. When they are ... how big would a five foot otter look like to someone who's never seen one before?

I'm not trying to say that Nessie is a case of mistaken objects. Just that, to watch for a sighting you must be aware of what could be misinterpreted for a sighting. When eventually I have MY Nessie sighting, because I am in the right place at the right time, I know that I will have seen the Nessie of Loch Ness and not the 'nessie' of my mind's eye (I hope).

EDITOR'S NOTE: This is the first in a regular series of bulletins aimed at keeping the Animals & Men readership up to date with events at Loch Ness. Richard can be contacted at:

5 Dirker Drive
Marsden
Huddersfield
HD7 6AP

HELP

This is the section of 'Animals & Men' where we, and you appeal for assistance in various research projects. There are several expeditions in the pipeline at the moment, and at least one needs some assistance:

"Dear Mr Downes,

I am planning an expedition into the North of Tasmania in the summer of 1997 to search for the Thylacine or Marsupial Wolf.

In 1979 Jim Sayles claimed to have attracted a Thylacine by imitating the distress calls of small animals. Can anyone tell me where I could get hold of a tape recording of the distress calls of wombats, wallabies and other prey species. Failing that an old fashioned hunter's "Varmint Caller"?

Sayles also marked his, and his equipment scent with Eucalyptus Oil. If you have any readers in Tasmania, maybe they know a good place to get large quantities?

Finally where could I get hold of a cast, or a copy of the cast of a Thylacine's footprint for use as reference.

Thanks for your help.
Richard Freeman".

We would suggest that you approach the National Sound Archive (0171 412 7440) for recordings of the animals that you require. They were helpful a few years ago when certain researchers on Bodmin Moor wanted the sound of a female puma in oestrus, and they may well be able to help you. Another good starting point would be the librarian at the Institute of Commonwealth Studies (0171 580 5876) who have been helpful to us recently. As for the rest, at the risk of sounding like a fortean Esther Rantzen, it is over to the 'Animals & Men' readership.

Richard can be contacted c/o the Editorial Address.

HELP EXTRA: A STRANGE FISH INDEED
by Michael Goss

(Editor's Note: It is always exciting when we are able to solve a mystery. In the HELP column of issue three, and again in the last issue, we appealed for information about a pair of peculiar carcasses washed up on an Essex beach. Veteran fortean Michael Goss picked up a copy of issue 9 at the Unconvention. On June 12 he wrote the following letter to me.)

The strange aquatic creature mentioned in Animals & Men #9 (p.38) was almost certainly the angler fish washed ashore at Canvey Island on 29th November 1953, *"where it created no end of a stir, and who could wonder at it?"*. This information comes from 'Beachcomber' in his regular natural history column for the 'Southend Standard' of Thursday 3rd December following, where it acted as an excuse for a fairly whimsical piece on angler fish and their nightmarish grotesqueness in general. Fluent as he was on the subject, 'Beachcomber' failed to provide any further details of the Canvey specimen, but luckily the 'Canvey News and Benfleet Recorder' put the fish on the front page of its Friday (4 December 1953) issue as a small photo and caption story-with more details on page 3. This states that Museum authorities (sic.) were to be consulted about this *'Fish with teeth and toes'* which 12-year-old Jacqueline Ward had found the previous Sunday on the beach; it weighed 30lbs and was 2ft. g inches long by 15 inches wide with *'protruding eyes, a tongue and teeth. In the centre of the back are two 'feet' complete with toes"*. In point of fact, a former Leigh fisherman had already identified it as a "pocket" or "fiddle" fish: the latter also being noted in "Beachcomber's" article as one of the popular names for the angler fish.

The page 1 photo leaves absolutely no doubt that the creature was a fish and there is equally no doubt that everyone concerned recognised it as one. Nor was there much ambiguity about the "Fish with feet..." that the Rev. Joseph Overs found on a Canvey beach on Tuesday 10 August the next year. Reporting that he had described it as *"four feet long with staring eyes and a large mouth ... on its stomach, it had two feet, each with five toes...."*, the 'Canvey News and 0Benfleet Recorder' for 13 August 1954 reminded readers that:

HELP EXTRA: CONTINUED...

"A peculiar fish was found in almost the same place last year and identified as a pocket or 'fiddler' fish'. Patently, and allowing for the fact that the fins and other appendages of the angler fish can be mistaken for 'feet' or similar, this latest arrival belonged to the same family.

For me the biggest mystery about this story lies in the way that it came to be presented as a mystery. My first acquaintanceship with it came from an article in either 'Weekend' or 'Titbits' - more probably the latter - some time between 1978-80, where it was told in what (if memory serves) was very similar wording to the account sent to 'Animals & Men'. I assumed that it had been lifted from some 'Amazing but True' kind of source, as were most of the Fortean-style articles that crept into popular magazines for this period ... but I never managed to track that source down. Nor can I find it in any of my cryptozoological ones.

The writer seems to have taken a strictly local piece of news and blown it up into a major mystery with pronounced cryptoconspiratorial overtones (which, need I say, are totally alien to the press reports I have seen). From clues like the way the author writes of the 'British Canvey Islands', I conclude the author was unfamiliar with the place ... and expected his readers to be unfamiliar with it, too.

Then there is the determined effort to present the story in the context of the Devil's Hoofprints. Any resemblance to accounts of other beached enigmas - the Tasmanian globster of 1960, for example - may be accidental. All things considered, I'd guess this account came from an American source of the late 50's or early 60's: Fate perhaps, though I can't find it in the incomplete run of that magazine which I own. But it may well be that the author had some other (English) source which provided data not found in any of the press reports.

Quite Remarkable, to borrow from a much-imitated soccer commentator, that a story which got very little coverage even in a paper serving folk in a small corner of Essex for whom it ought to have been a significant event should get this kind of celebrity. But then, as an old man once told me, 'Stranger things have happened on Canvey Island'.

ODD ORNITHOLOGY
by ALISON DOWNES

SNOW JOKE!

A pair of rare Arctic snowy owls were seen in Scotland recently. They were thought by excited twitchers to be considering breeding there, but the RSPB confirmed that they were just 'passing through'. *(Newsround BBCTV Teletext 8.7.96)*

BORNE FROM THE USA

More rare visitors, this time from the USA, have been seen on the Isle of Wight. A rose breasted grosbeak was blown off course during its autumn migration, last year. It is a large, finch like bird which has only been recorded in the UK 23 times. Other American birds were also seen during that month. Teletext on 3 *(ITV) p.340. 1.11.95*

RINGNECK ROUNDUP

A government survey is being carried out by the Central Science Laboratory on the feeding habits of Britain's colonies of wild ringneck parakeets. MAFF is worried that the birds may become a pest. The Times newspaper recently reported that they were *"ousting jackdaws, owls and kestrels from their nests"* and this appears to have no foundation in truth.

There are now estimated to be up to 5,000 birds living in colonies around the UK, from the west country to Argyllshire in Scotland. The biggest single colony is at Walton on Thames in Surrey, but there are also many large groups around the London area.

The parakeets are feeding off nuts, bark, flowers, and orchard fruit, and have even been seen on bird-tables. *(Cage and Aviary Birds 27.4.96)*.

BERT THE VULTURE
(slight return)

Regular readers will be glad to hear that Bert the vulture, who was reared by an old sock, (see A&M5), has been taught to fly..eventually! His keepers were forced to resort to throwing him out of a hot air balloon! If it works....

LETTERS

THE EDITOR WELCOMES LETTERS FOR PUBLICATION ON ANY SUBJECT OF INTEREST TO THIS MAGAZINE. HE RESERVESTHE RIGHT TO EDIT LETTERS FOR REASONS OF SPACE. HE WOULD, HOWEVER, LIKE TO POINT OUT THAT ALL OPINIONS MADE IN LETTERS OR INDEED ARTICLES ARE THOSE OF THE AUTHOR AND NOT NECESSARILY THOSE OF THE EDITOR, ANIMALS & MEN, OR THE CENTRE FOR FORTEAN ZOOLOGY

THE KILLING JOKE 1

Dear Mr Downes,

I found the article 'On Collecting a Cryptid' interesting, as I have just finished re-reading a book that deals in part with that very question, i.e. should a specimen of an 'unknown' animal be collected just to prove that it does indeed exist and is now 'known'.

The book in question is "Emma Tupper's Diary" by Peter Dickinson, a novel published in 1971 by Victor Gollancz. It deals with the existence, in a fictitious Scottish Loch of a relict colony of Plesiosaurs. Over millions of years they have adapted to a cold water environment, fresh water etc, by becoming smaller and specialised, so much so that any major change to their environment could prove fatal. They are only hanging on by a thread as it were, by the fact of the Loch's isolation, very few farms in the surrounding area, so no pollution - nitrates draining into the Loch etc. The Loch itself is privately owned by a family who's head is aware of the situation and seeks to keep it that way.

When the Ice Ages came, the creatures retreated to a huge cave in the surrounding rocks, heated by hot springs. With this refuge as a base, they could then forage out under the ice-cap to hunt. They became so adapted to dark conditions, that now they're photosensitive, only venturing out on the darkest nights. Also, they could afford to become smaller as they had the heated cave to fall back on.

Towards the end of the book there is a family meeting to preside over the fate of the creatures, and this is where the connection with the article by Prof. Krantz comes in. The first argument against 'discovery' of these relict plesiosaurs is that they are only just 'hanging on' even though they look so strong and healthy. Any small change in the environment could prove fatal. Investigating scientists, however careful, could perhaps infect the creatures with bacteria from the breaths, for example, as they study the creature's nesting cave.

The head of the clan has this final word to say:

"*the question is whether it is better for your creature to subsist in its own strange way, unknown. Or whether it is better to have it thoroughly studied, and probably, in the process kill it dead. It would then be KNOWN; you could find accounts of it in libraries, casts and skeletons in natural history museums. But it would be extinct, as the Dodo is, and the Oryx and the Tiger almost are. Are you prepared to choose?"*

I think those words, even after 20 odd years are still relevant. Do we really want to know everything about the Loch Ness creature, even if it means future generations can see the thing displayed in a 'Loch Ness Museum' but the Loch itself would have lost its centuries old aura of mystery and wonder. No-one will ever again see those mysterious humps and necks cruising along the dark waters.

That could never happen? Tell that to the Dodo, and all the other victims of Man's rapaciousness set out in Peter Verney's 1979 book "*Homo Tyrranicus: Man's war against animals*". Round about 1830, when it became obvious to the directors of museums worldwide that the Great Auk was on the verge of extinction, what did they do? Band together in an effort to preserve and protect the last remaining survivors?

No. Museums that had no specimens of the Great Auk in their collections sent out expeditions to scour the northern seas for any stragglers that remained. On the island of Eldey the last remaining colony of fifty animals were hunted down and slaughtered to provide museum exhibits. In 1844 the very last known specimen was killed to satisfy the vanity of an Icelandic bird collector.

But that couldn't happen now, could it? Tell it to all the rhinos killed so that some rich arab can swank it up over another rich arab because he's got a rhino horn hilt on his ceremonial dagger, and the other one hasn't. This is happening NOW!

Yours faithfully,

Colin Mather,
Wigan.

THE KILLING JOKE 2

Dear Mr Downes,

I would like to comment on the article 'On Collecting a Cryptid' by Grover Krantz.

In 1989 I was asked by a Dutch television station to comment on a film concerning the hunt for Bigfoot. At first I did not like this too much as I am not specialised in Bigfoot but more in the Loch Ness phenomena. However, when I saw the short film I found it necessary to comment as Prof. Krantz was promoting the killing of one, and probably more, as scientists are not that easily convinced of the existence of these animals.

Personally, I do not like this way of getting proof. It may satisfy the scientist's hunger for a big achievement, but I don't think it will do the 'animals' themselves any good. The big idea is always that it needs identification to get protected, but I don't see any big scientists acting on this protection. Even though they must have a lot of influence, they leave it to others.

In the article Prof. Krantz again comes up with his killing theories, this time in regards to the Loch Ness phenomena. Sending out whalers to harpoon one. These whalers, he hopes are "hopefully unemployed". He seems concerned for the whales, but also feels that harpooning a Nessie will be O.K. We all know what it means to kill in the name of science; just look at the animals who use this pretext to hunt the whales into extinction. I would like to point out to Prof.Krantz that the local by law protecting the Loch Ness phenomena, still appears to be active.

I also contacted the Departments of Wildlife in Oregon, Washington State and British Columbia concerning the hunt for Bigfoot and even though Washington State and British Columbia stated that they were not in a position to forbid this; Oregon State passed a resolution to protect the Bigfoot against hunting. Mr William I. Haight, Chief of Non-Game Wildlife Management, stated to me in a letter of 26.10.1989:

"Whilst this action does not carry the same enforcement and penalty provisions as a state statute, it did send a message to would be Bigfoot hunters that killing of one of these animals in Oregon would not be tolerated. Should Prof. Krantz attempt to propose such an action in this state, I assure you that the idea will be discouraged".

So, Prof. Krantz, in my opinion, should be more careful with his promotion of hunting.

I would also like to comment on the letter by Mr. Michael Playfair, Leicestershire, in which it was, to my humble meaning, rightly stated that there seems to be a tradition of monster sightings there. However, I always found the Alexander Graham statement a little doubtful as he mentions a River Enrick entering Loch Lomond. There is a River Enrick entering Urquhart Bay, Loch Ness. Is there actually one entering Loch Lomond as well? I could not find it on any map?

Yours faithfully,

Martien 't Mannetje,
Rockanje,
The Netherlands.

ALAN MOORE KNOWS THE SCORE

Dear Mr Downes,

In response to your request for cryptozoological related comics, I remember one story concerning the yeti. It was published in 1979 or 1980 in Marvel UK's 'Dr Who Monthly'. (Come to think of it, back then it was a weekly). The artist was Dave Gibbons, and I think the writer was the renowned Alan Moore (of 'Swamp Thing' and 'The Killing Joke') fame).

The story concerned a cryptozoological expedition in search of the yeti. The yeti turn out to be robot replicas, much the same as in the two Dr. Who yeti adventures. They are controlled by the Great Intelligence, a disembodied entity that possesses the expedition's Sherpa guides.

At the end of the story a Buddhist monk leads an army of real yetis to the rescue. The genuine articles tear apart their robot replicas. The robot yetis are dumpy creatures with round hips and a featureless head with no neck. The real yetis look like huge, hairy apes much as the real ones are supposed to. The exception are their heads. They are too round (not conical as the real yetis are supposed to be), and their eyes are much too round and large like those of a Bush Baby.

In issue three you printed a letter from a 'retired Colonial Officer' concerning the apparent immunity of a Nigerian man to Scorpion venom. The arachnid in question is described as 'large and black'. This sounds very like the Imperial Scorpion. This species has venom no more potent than a Bumble Bee's. It could sting a man many times with only discomfort ensuing. Generally, scorpions with large claws crush their prey, and the venom is only a secondary line of attack. Look out for scorpions with slender claws, however, they are the deadly ones.

Yours sincerely,

Richard Freeman.
Nuneaton.

EDITORIAL INTERJECTION: Because, as I type this, it is a beautiful summer day, I am watching the Men's Single's Final at Wimbledon, and I am feeling generally frivolous, here is a second 'phone in quiz'. The headline to this letter! Who, Why, When? The winner gets a free year's subscription to A&M. The first person to sing the relevant passage to us down the telephone also gets a free copy of my new book.

NEGATIVE FEEDBACK

I read with genuine sadness of our noble Editor's largely fruitless struggle to persuade numerous other organisations to co-operate with us via the medium of copies of 'Animals & Men' - but to be perfectly frank I cannot say I'm surprised.

One of the truest sayings is 'a chain is as strong as its weakest link', and I am going to grasp the nettle and say that quite a lot of what goes into this otherwise excellent publication does the Centre for Fortean Zoology no good at all.

Yes, I feel the cause of this rejection is in your hands at this moment. Just read it carefully and objectively - and honestly ask yourself what sort of an impression it might give to someone who might not know us.

On the one hand there are such excellent, valuable and important articles as those on extinct Whales and the Congo Peacock, that could well grace any scientific journal on this planet, whilst on the other there's sheer, utter, rot, such as 'Now that's what I call Crypto', in which the author tries desperately, and unsuccesfully to be funny.

Someone gives his address as 'somewhere' - which would be fine in a Student's rag magazine, but not in one that seeks to be taken seriously - and I'm sincerely sorry to note that the Editorial Staff does not take it's work as seriously as it might: I mean, just read the very first part on the inside of the cover, beginning with "This" and ending in "Crew", and I think you'll see what I mean.

Yes, in my own magazine, 'Mainly about Animals', I write in a very free, friendly and informal manner, but out of respect for its readers I firmly refrain from mateyness, cosyness, cameraderie, bonhomie, - call it what you will - simply because I don't think it's a good thing under the circumstances. I think I've been proved right, too, by the lack of response from those other societies.

I've been a cryptozoologist since before most of 'Animals & Men' readers were even thought of and take the subject very seriously (although not ponderously or heavily). As things stand I cannot help feeling that many open-minded people must wonder whether it's an important and highly specialised science, or a haven and forum for offbeat oddballs.

Clinton Keeling.

EDITORIAL RESPONSE:

To answer Clinton's last statement first (in my best surrealchemical manner): It's both! One person's definition of 'offbeat oddball' however is another person's definition of freethinker, and yet another person's 'dangerous lunatic'. Cryptozoology is a "serious and specialised science", and has been for well over forty years (as Clinton says, before even I was thought of), but Cryptozoology is only part of what we deal with. Fortean Zoology is a completely different kettle of coelacanth's (I know because I invented it!) It is an outrageous and ridiculous discipline, in which Cryptozoology, the study of folklore, large chunks of sociology, theology and anthropology, and many other accepted branches of the natural sciences go hand in hand with Lexilinking and Surrealchemy in search of the truth behind various, seemingly insoluble mysteries.

To answer the other comments, however. Our readership, which presently has a growth rate of something in the region of 65% a year range in age (that I know of) between 12 and 84. We try to include editorial content for both age groups as well as everything in-between. We have always stressed the importance of 'mystery animals' as culture icons. 'Now that's what I call crypto' is a light-hearted attempt to list various pieces of rock music dealing with the subject. As such, I feel that it is successful.

'Gavin' is the pseudonym used by the 1989 Owlman witness. In view of his, almost unique, and surreal experience, as well as his anonymity, to give his address as 'somewhere' seems perfectly appropriate.

I would like to stress that Clinton Keeling, both as a zoologist, a writer and a human being is someone for whom I have a lot of respect. I may not always agree with him but that is my privilege, as it is his to disagree with me. The fact that this magazine provides a forum for two such disparate writers as him and myself to write, under the same metaphorical roof as writers as diverse as Shuker, Shiels, Heuvelmans and Naish, can only, I feel be a good thing.

NEGATIVE FEEDBACK 2.

Excerpts from a much longer letter....

Re the reported lack of interest you claimed from various natural history societies, it comes as no surprise to me, nor, I expect to you.

From my experience, for what its worth, these groups are the last vestiges of the Victorian amateurism, with its inherent myopic view of anything outside its narrow borders. Composed of retired people, led by a local academic of advanced years, they have a predelicition for songbirds and wildflowers. They can only cope with a sanitised view of things, never mind anything vaguely fortean.

I can remember at primary school being asked by our teacher, one of the above, to name animals for some test or other. I said 'Echidna', being a smartarse kind of kid. She informed me no such thing existed.

That taught me more than she had intended...

Tom Anderson,
Aberdeen.

(EDITORIAL NOTE: I had practically the same experience with the words 'Caecilian' and 'Amphiuma'. If they don't exist, I wonder what is swimming around in that tank outside my bedroom door?

Our main are of argument is the lack of cooperation we have had from some 'small-town' natural history societies and from a few, but by no means all the internationally known museums.
When I started cryptozoological research in 1978, I had a long, happy and fruitful relationship with various scientists at the British Museum (Natural History). They then felt that their remit included assisting with serious research by members of the general public. In recent years, some staff at this and other museums, have been exceedingly rude to both Alison and myself, as well as other members of our organisation. They have also refused to help us in even the most simple areas of research without charging us ridiculous sums of money. I find this attitude immeasurably sad, and feel convinced that much valuable research is not taking place because of these draconian costs. What was once a national treasure house is now a source for national shame!

As far as the lack of interest we have received from regional natural history societies, Tom Anderson's hypothesis is probably right. More prosaically, however, some of these societies combine their lack of imagination with a lamentable lack of manners. Over the past few weeks we have met representatives from some regional naturalists' societies who have just greeted our attempts at 'bridge building' with deliberate rudeness! (That was without actually seeing the magazine). We have/do collaborate(d) successfully with scientists from Exeter University, The Royal Albert Memorial Museum, Plymouth Museum, The National Museums of Scotland, The University of Hong Kong, and a number of other museums, Universities and Zoos worldwide. We are taken seriously by publishing firms, TV companies, and newspapers/magazines with an international distribution. To date, although there are a number of organisations who have refused to collaborate with us this is their loss rather than ours! There is no-one to date whose refusal has caused me more than momentary annoyance. JD.).

BOOK REVIEWS

'The Lost Birds of Paradise' by Errol Fuller 160pp (Swan Hill) £30.00

One of the nice things about running a magazine like 'Animals & Men' is that you come across books that you would otherwise, almost certainly, never have read. This book is a perfect example. From the author of the best book I have ever read about Extinct Birds, this book examines the specific status of nineteen species of Birds of Paradise - some known only from a single specimen. Whereas forty three species of these birds are generally known to science, these extra nineteen - the 'lost' Birds of Paradise turn out to be a tantalising miscellany of hybrids, aberrations with the occasional hint of a new species. The number of putative hybridisations between the species is interesting. It seems that, especially amongst some of the Riflebirds such genetic mix-and-matching is more common than would otherwise be supposed.

Although the scholarship of this book cannot be faulted, it is as a series of meticulously crafted 'detective stories' that it is most successful. As an afficianado of such things I find the narrative, which intertwines continuously with the life story of the tortured but brilliant Baron Rothschild, once the owner of what was perhaps the biggest private collection of Natural History specimens nothing short of enthralling. As a child my Grandfather used to tell me stories about Rothschild and his exploits, and this book offers up, amongst the wealth of ornithological detail precious vignettes and insights into his unique life.

This book is masterfully written and lavishly illustrated with many photographs, prints and drawings. It is an essential item for the library of anyone interested either in birds or in cryptozoology.

'Rumours of Existence' by Matthew Bille (Hancock House)

A new book on general cryptozoology from the editor of the excellent news-sheet 'Exotic Zoology'. This book manages, not only to cover well known cryptids (if that is not a contradiction in terms), in a fresh and interesting way, but also includes a wealth of exciting and interesting information that I, for one, have not come across elsewhere.

It is divided into three sections: 'Recent Discoveries', 'Presumed Extinct' and 'The Mystery Animals'. It is hard to know which sections to single out for particular praise. In order to try and make up my mind I leafed through the contents page which prompted me to want to read the book all over again! You can't really praise a book higher than that!

'Hills and Streams - An Ecology of Hong Kong' by David Dudgeon and Richard Corlett (Hong Kong University Press 234pp. Price on Application to us).

Regular readers will be aware of my longstanding interest in the zoology of Hong Kong, and of our ongoing study into the Fortean Zoology of the territory. For those who do not understand the fascination that I have with the subject, this book may enlighten them to a degree at least. It is a scholarly but gripping insight into the ecology of a landscape almost entirely shaped by man. The original forestation was destroyed several centuries ago, and whilst the British Administration fostered a reforestation programme starting in the years previous to the first world war, most of this secondary growth was destroyed during the Japanese occupation of 1941-5.

The reforestation began again after the war, and as the countryside has slowly recovered so has its zoology. This is the story of the recovery and provides some essential signposts to indicate what may happen over the next hundred years.

'Sasquatch Bigfoot - The Continuing Mystery' by Thomas N. Steenburg (Hancock House 127pp $11.95US)

An engaging account of one man's search for the reclusive Canadian man-beast. One of the most likeable things about this book is that it is nearly all from eyewitness accounts researched personally by the author.

It could be argued that this is also one of the drawbacks of the book, in that the better known cases are not included. Unlike the bulk of the material presented here they are available elsewhere.

This is not the definitive work on the subject. That honour goes either to John Green (see below) or to Grover Krantz, but it is a nice collection of interviews and research notes which makes a useful addition to the 'man-beast' section in our cryptozoological library.

'Sasquatch - The Apes Amongst Us' by John Green (Hancock House 492pp)

A timely re-print of what, by anyone's standards is one of the classic works on the subject. This book contains all that you could possibly want to know about the larger BHM phenomena of the North American continent. If I have any reservations at all about it, it is that it treats the phenomena within a purely zoological frame of reference, and whilst I have little doubt that there is a conventional cryptozoological element to the Bigfoot and Sasquatch reports of the last four decades, I am equally certain that a large number of these phenomena are zooform in nature.

It is, however churlish to reject the immense amount of work which has gone into this book purely on those grounds, and therefore I have no hesitation whatsoever in recommending it.

'According to the Evidence' by Erich von Daniken £9.99
'Signs of the Gods' by Erich von Daniken £7.99
'Journey into Supermind' by Dr. Richard Lawrence £8.99
'The Lost world of Agharti' by Alec Maclellan £7.99
'The Bermuda Triangle' by Charles Berlitz £8.99
'Zolar's encyclopaedia of ancient and forbidden knowledge' £9.99

"Hey guys", said the eager and fresh-faced publicity director at the Monday morning Board Meeting. "You must have seen how the X Files is the most popular programme on TV these days....Strange phenomena are this year's thing ... well, why don't we reissue some of these ever so groovy books on the subject?"

The answer should have been, "...Because they are outdated nonsense which you can pick up at any car boot sale for 50p a time!".

Of course nobody dared say this to the fresh-faced publicity director so the company, (whose name I am leaving out because I am probably being libellous), went ahead and reprinted the books listed above (if this 'knowledge' - and I use the word reservedly - is that ancient and forbidden why is it included in tacky paperbacks?), and sent out unsolicited packages of six or seven books to any publication they could find with even the most tenuous links to the paranormal.

We, as the fresh-faced publicity director should have known, are a magazine about cryptozoology and its allied disciplines, and only very occasionally give any space to blatantly commercial twaddle of no scientific or fortean significance (and then only when it is amusing). We therefore took the lot down to the car boot sale where we swapped them for a CD by Scott Walker, a broken fish tank, and an electric kettle and promptly forgot about the whole matter.

'Monster Monster - A Survey of the North American Monster Scene' by Betty Sanders Garner (Hancock House 190pp $12.95US)

The worst thing about this book is the title and the tacky picture of a 'nessie' type creature on the front cover. The packaging doesn't really do the contents justice because it is a cheerful round up of various North American cryptids which presents both well known and more obscure cases in an eminently readable and approachable style.

'On the Track'... it ain't, but although not essential by any means it is a satisfying addition to the library.

The chapter on the White River Monster is particularly good. On the whole the coverage of aquatic phenomena here is better than either the BHM coverage or the (very brief) look at the Texas 'Big Bird' reports. It is, however worth buying, or at least borrowing.

'The Book of the Unicorn' by Nigel Suckling. (Paper Tiger 128pp £12.95).

I am not a great fan of Paper Tiger's whimsical 'hippy' art books. Artwork which looked great on a 'Yes' LP in 1972 has, I believe, little or no relevance to the serious fortean researcher, and, now the smell of incense, and the sounds of temple bells (not to mention temple balls - snigger), has faded the new-agey culture they present is aesthetically fairly displeasing in 1996. This book, however, is undeniably attractive, and could well be seen as a counterpart to Karl Shuker's excellent Dragon book of last year. The illustrations are a little bit too Patrick Woodruffe/Roger Dean for my liking, but the text is neatly written and includes an account of Dr Dove's 1930's experiments on bull calves, as well as the more familiar Biblical and mythological references. Much to my surprise, I even got quite enthusiastic about things unicornian by the end of the book, and despite the hippy drawings, I can honestly reccomend it!

'LOCH NESS - The Tour' by Richard Carter (Carterways 32pp £1.50)

This particularly engaging little booklet is written by one of the founder members of The Loch Ness Society. For half the price of a packet of cigarettes you get one man's viewpoint of the best places to visit in the vicinity of Loch Ness.

You are told where the best spots are if you want to see spawning salmon, a little bit about Aliester Crowley's sojourn at Boleskine House (but nothing about Jimmy Page's much longer residence at the same place), a guide to some of the local wildlife and the best places to go to see them.

There is, of course, a brief history of 'Nessie' sightings, but, refreshingly it is the other sights and sounds of the area which make up the bulk of the information on offer. There are a number of useful telephone numbers and route planning instructions, and I can truthfully say that this is one of the NICEST books on Loch Ness that has ever come our way.

'CADBOROSAURUS -Survivor from the Deep' by Paul LeBlond and Edward Bousfield. 134pp.

This is one of the most remarkable books on a single facet of cryptozoology that I have read in many years. Following on from their acclaimed paper for Amphipacifica last year, this is an extraordinary piece of research which paints a convincing picture of an extraordinary cryptid - a reptile with 'mammalian traits'. Even a hard core sceptic like your editor is convinced wholehear6edly.

The important thing now is for Bousfield and LeBlonde to get funds enough to continue their work and get the conclusive proof that they so unquestionably deserve. In this case at least the truth really IS out there!

COMING SOON

Later this year. The Centre for Fortean Zoology will be publishing some more books. Reprint volumes of '*The Shiels Effect*' and '*The Cantrip Codex*' by Tony 'Doc' Shiels, '*The Owlman and Others*' by Jonathan Downes and the CFZ Yearbook 1997 are all expected in October.

Not to be confused with the yearbooks are planned book format reprints of the first four issues of 'Animals & Men' which, hopefully will also be issues before Christmas.

We are still hoping to issue the first of our Supplements, a collection of information on the out of place birds of the last twelve months, sometime this year.

At present, apart from the back issues, which will no longer be available when the reprint volumes are published, we have three books available.

THE CFZ YEARBOOK 1996. £10.00
Nearly two hundred pages of research papers and long articles by a variety of contemporary cryptozoologists, including Dr Karl Shuker, Tony 'Doc' Shiels, Jonathan Downes, Francois de Sarre, Tom Anderson, Richard Muirhead, Clinton Keeling and many more. Well illustrated with drawings and maps.

MORGAWR: THE MONSTER OF FALMOUTH BAY by A Mawnan-Peller £1.50

Timely reprint of the 1976 original with a new introduction by Tony 'Doc' Shiels, and an essay by Jonathan Downes, plus the complete text of the original.

THE SMALLER MYSTERY CARNIVORES OF THE WEST COUNTRY by Jonathan Downes £7.50.

A fascinating guide to some of the lesser known mammalian cryptids of the south western peninsular of the British Isles. Over a hundred pages. Lavishly illustrated with photographs, maps and drawings. Introduction by Dr Karl P.N.Shuker.

WE ARE ENTIRELY SELF FINANCING AND RELY ON SALES TO CONTINUE SO PLEASE SUPPORT US BY BUYING OUR PUBLICATIONS.

PERIODICAL REVIEWS

We welcome an exchange of periodicals with magazines of mutual interest although because we now exchange with so many magazines we have been forced, much against our fortean methodology, to categorise them.

CRYPTOZOOLOGY AND ZOOMYTHOLOGY

DRAGON CHRONICLE, The dragon trust, PO Box 3369, London SW6 6JN. A fascinating collection of all things draconian which now appears four times a year. Now A4 and Glossy...how do they DO it?

THE BRITISH COLUMBIA CRYPTOZOOLOGY CLUB NEWSLETTER, 3773 West 18th Avenue, Vancouver, British Columbia, Canada. V6S 1B3. Excellent and well put together, and they are now on the Internet as well!

CREATURE RESEARCH JOURNAL, Paul Johnson, 721 Old Greensburg Pike, North Versailles, PA 15137-1111 USA. New issue devoted to Pennsylvania Bigfoot reports 1994-5.

CRYPTOZOOLOGIA, Association Belge d'Etude et de Protection des Animaux Rares, Square des Latins 49/4, 1050 Bruxelles, Belgium. A French language magazine published by the Belgian society for Cryptozoology.

CRYPTOZOOLOGY REVIEW, 137 Atlas Ave, Toronto, Ontario. Canada. M6C 3P4. Excellent new publication on cryptozoology. Includes fascinating article on a cryptic polychaete from St Lucia.

EXOTIC ZOOLOGY, 3405 Windjammer Drive, Colorado Springs, CO80920 USA. A free newsletter from the author of 'Rumours of existence'. Useful round up of information on new and rediscovered species.

FRINGE SCIENCE

SCIENCE FRONTIERS, Sourcebook POroject, PO Box 107, Glen Arm, MD21057. Newsletter of William Corliss' invaluable Sourcebook Project. Fascinating snippets of useful information. Their latest book, by the way 'Mammals Vol. 1' will be reviewed in A&M#11.

NEXUS 55 Queens Rd, E. Grinstead, West Sussex RH19 1BG. Intelligent look at the fringes of science. Well put together. Very impressive.

FORTEAN/EARTH MYSTERIES/FOLKLORE

TEMS NEWS, 115 Hollybush Lane, Hampton, Middlesex, TW12 2QY. An entertaining collection of odds and sods and generally weird stuff. A magazine I always enjoy reading. Reccomended.

HAUNTED SCOTLAND, Mark Fraser, 35 South Dean Rd, Kilmarnock,Ayrshire, Scotland. KA3 7RD. This has been an enjoyable and bizarre newsletter covering weirdness from north of the border. Soon to be a magazine per se, we await the first issue eagerly.

COVER UP, David Coleman, 39 Limefield Crescent, Bathgate, West Lothian, Scotland. EH48 1RF. The magazine of the Lothian Unexplained Phenomena Research group. UFOs, animal mutilation, ghosts etc. This is a useful addition to the scene and the editor should be congratulated for his hard work.

DELVE, Gene Dyplantier, 17 Shetland St. Willowdale, Ontario. Canada.M2m 1X5. Fortean magazine. New issue includes an article on the flying snake of Namibia.

3rd STONE, PO Box 258, Cheltenham, GL53 1HR. Magazine of the Gloucester Earth Mysteries Group. Wittily and intelligently put together.

DEAD OF NIGHT, 156 Bolton Road East, Newferry, Wirral. Merseyside, L62 4RY. An amusing and intelligently put together Fortean magazine. Great article about Crowley/Boleskine. My favourite fortean journal.

ZOOLOGY/NATURAL HISTORY

SOUTH WEST HERPETOLOGICAL SOCIETY NEWSLETTER, Frank Gibbons, Acanthus, 59 St Marychurch Rd, Torquay, Devon. Entertaining and informative newsletter from a thriving organisation. Contains some quasi fortean oddments.

BIPEDIA, Francois de Sarre, C.E.R.B.I, 6 Avenue George V. 06000 Nice, France. Issue twelve of this scholarly magazine is now available. Written partly in French, partly in English, it explores the obscure, but fascinating theory of Initial Bipedalism, and its allied disciplines.

MILTON KEYNES HERPETOLOGICAL SOCIETY 15 Esk Way, Bletchley, Milton Keynes. Excellent A5 magazine containing handy hints, informative articles and news of what appears to be an exciting organisation.

MAINLY ABOUT ANIMALS, 13 Pound Place, Shalford, Guildford, Surrey GU4 8HH. Veteran Zoologist Clinton Keeling edits this wonderful A5 magazine which is, as the title says, mainly about animals. This is a genre of magazine that I and many others feared was lost forever and it comes with your editor's highest reccomendation.

ESSEX REPTILES AND AMPHIBIANS SOCIETY, 6 Chestnut Way, Tiptree, Colchester, Essex, CO5 ONX. Another excellent and lively regional reptile society.

NATIONAL ASSOCIATION OF PRIVATE ANIMAL KEEPERS, 8 Yewlands Walk, Ifield, Crawley, West Sussex. RH11)QE. Useful publication including a wealth of information about wild animal husbandry. This is an organisation which, especially in the present political climate needs your support.

THE MANE, Wild Equid Society, Flat,19, 119 Haverstock Hill, London NW3 4RS. Fascinating journal about wild horses and their relatives. Includes much of interest to the cryptozoologist.

MISCELLANEOUS

NETWORK NEWS, P.O BOX 2, LOSTWITHIEL, CORNWALL PL22 0YY. Anarchism, Earth mysteries, weirdness, and even a little cryptozoology. This is the sort of monumentally groovy collection which should be encouraged. Issue 10 is the 'Sex Magic Sacrifice' issue by the way...

FOAFTALE NEWS, Department of Folklore, Memorial University of Newfoundland, St Johns, Newfoundland, CANADA. A1B 3X8. Academic approach to contemporary folklore. Essential.

PENDRAGON, Smithy House, Newton by Frodsham, Cheshire WA6 6SX. A scholarly and massively entertaining magazine on things Arthurian. Manages to keep an entertaining balance between literature and history. Highly reccomended.

LOBSTER, 214 Westbourne Avenue, Hull, HU5 3JB.It is nice to see a conspiracy theory magazine with a UK bias which means that it is not overly obsessed with JFK. The articles on the MI6 involvement in the 1953 coup in Iran in issue 30 was especially good, and the same issue even mentioned Arthur Ransome, which as our Sussex reps will tell you can only endear them in the eyes of the A&M editor!

animals&men
THE JOURNAL OF THE CENTRE FOR FORTEAN ZOOLOGY

Cartoon by Mark North

THE CENTRE FOR FORTEAN ZOOLOGY

The Centre for Fortean Zoology is the world's only professional and scientific organisation dedicated to research into unknown animals. Although we work all over the world, we carry out regular work in the United Kingdom and abroad, investigating accounts of strange creatures.

THAILAND 2000
An expedition to investigate the legendary creature known as the Naga

SUMATRA 2003
'Project Kerinci'
In search of the bi-pedal ape Orang Pendek

MONGOLIA 2005
'Operation Death Worm'
An expedition to track the fabled 'Allghoi Khorkhoi' or Death Worm

Led by scientists, the CFZ is staffed by volunteers and is always looking for new members.

To apply for a <u>FREE</u> information pack about the organisation and details of how to join, plus information on current and future projects, expeditions and events.

Send a stamp addressed envelope to:

THE CENTRE FOR FORTEAN ZOOLOGY
MYRTLE COTTAGE, WOOLSERY,
BIDEFORD, NORTH DEVON EX39 5QR.

or alternatively visit our website at: w w w . c f z . o r g . u k

Other books available from
CFZ PRESS

THE OWLMAN AND OTHERS - 30th Anniversary Edition
Jonathan Downes - ISBN 978-1-905723-02-7

£14.99

EASTER 1976 - Two young girls playing in the churchyard of Mawnan Old Church in southern Cornwall were frightened by what they described as a "nasty bird-man". A series of sightings that has continued to the present day. These grotesque and frightening episodes have fascinated researchers for three decades now, and one man has spent years collecting all the available evidence into a book. To mark the 30th anniversary of these sightings, Jonathan Downes, has published a special edition of his book.

DRAGONS - More than a myth?
Richard Freeman - ISBN 0-9512872-9-X

£14.99

First scientific look at dragons since 1884. It looks at dragon legends worldwide, and examines modern sightings of dragon-like creatures, as well as some of the more esoteric theories surrounding dragonkind. Dragons are discussed from a folkloric, historical and cryptozoological perspective, and Richard Freeman concludes that: "When your parents told you that dragons don't exist - they lied!"

MONSTER HUNTER
Jonathan Downes - ISBN 0-9512872-7-3

£14.99

Jonathan Downes' long-awaited autobiography, *Monster Hunter*... Written with refreshing candour, it is the extraordinary story of an extraordinary life, in which the author crosses paths with wizards, rock stars, terrorists, and a bewildering array of mythical and not so mythical monsters, and still just about manages to emerge with his sanity intact.......

MONSTER OF THE MERE
Jonathan Downes - ISBN 0-9512872-2-2

£12.50

It all starts on Valentine's Day 2002 when a Lancashire newspaper announces that "Something" has been attacking swans at a nature reserve in Lancashire. Eyewitnesses have reported that a giant unknown creature has been dragging fully grown swans beneath the water at Martin Mere. An intrepid team from the Exeter based Centre for Fortean Zoology, led by the author, make two trips – each of a week – to the lake and its surrounding marshlands. During their investigations they uncover a thrilling and complex web of historical fact and fancy, quasi Fortean occurrences, strange animals and even human sacrifice.

**CFZ PRESS, MYRTLE COTTAGE,
WOOLFARDISWORTHY BIDEFORD,
NORTH DEVON, EX39 5QR
w w w . c f z . o r g . u k**

Other books available from
CFZ PRESS

ONLY FOOLS AND GOATSUCKERS
Jonathan Downes - ISBN 0-9512872-3-0

£12.50

In January and February 1998 Jonathan Downes and Graham Inglis of the Centre for Fortean Zoology spent three and a half weeks in Puerto Rico, Mexico and Florida, accompanied by a film crew from UK Channel 4 TV. Their aim was to make a documentary about the terrifying chupacabra - a vampiric creature that exists somewhere in the grey area between folklore and reality. This remarkable book tells the gripping, sometimes scary, and often hilariously funny story of how the boys from the CFZ did their best to subvert the medium of contemporary TV documentary making and actually do their job.

WHILE THE CAT'S AWAY
Chris Moiser - ISBN: 0-9512872-1-4

£7.99

Over the past thirty years or so there have been numerous sightings of large exotic cats, including black leopards, pumas and lynx, in the South West of England. Former Rhodesian soldier Sam McCall moved to North Devon and became a farmer and pub owner when Rhodesia became Zimbabwe in 1980. Over the years despite many of his pub regulars having seen the "Beast of Exmoor" Sam wasn't at all sure that it existed. Then a series of happenings made him change his mind. Chris Moiser—a zoologist—is well known for his research into the mystery cats of the westcountry. This is his first novel.

CFZ EXPEDITION REPORT 2006 - GAMBIA
ISBN 1905723032

£12.50

In July 2006, The J.T.Downes memorial Gambia Expedition - a six-person team - Chris Moiser, Richard Freeman, Chris Clarke, Oll Lewis, Lisa Dowley and Suzi Marsh went to the Gambia, West Africa. They went in search of a dragon-like creature, known to the natives as `Ninki Nanka`, which has terrorized the tiny African state for generations, and has reportedly killed people as recently as the 1990s. They also went to dig up part of a beach where an amateur naturalist claims to have buried the carcass of a mysterious fifteen foot sea monster named 'Gambo', and they sought to find the Armitage's Skink (Chalcides armitagei) - a tiny lizard first described in 1922 and only rediscovered in 1989. Here, for the first time, is their story.... With an forward by Dr. Karl Shuker and introduction by Jonathan Downes.

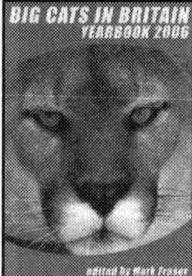

BIG CATS IN BRITAIN YEARBOOK 2006
Edited by Mark Fraser - ISBN 978-1905723-01-0

£10.00

Big cats are said to roam the British Isles and Ireland even now as you are sitting and reading this. People from all walks of life encounter these mysterious felines on a daily basis in every nook and cranny of these two countries. Most are jet-black, some are white, some are brown, in fact big cats of every description and colour are seen by some unsuspecting person while on his or her daily business. 'Big Cats in Britain' are the largest and most active group in the British Isles and Ireland This is their first book. It contains a run-down of every known big cat sighting in the UK during 2005, together with essays by various luminaries of the British big cat research community which place the phenomenon into scientific, cultural, and historical perspective.

CFZ PRESS, MYRTLE COTTAGE,
WOOLFARDISWORTHY BIDEFORD,
NORTH DEVON, EX39 5QR
w w w . c f z . o r g . u k

Other books available from
CFZ PRESS

ANIMALS & MEN - Issues 1 - 5 - In the Beginning
Edited by Jonathan Downes - ISBN 0-9512872-6-5

£12.50

At the beginning of the 21st Century monsters still roam the remote, and sometimes not so remote, corners of our planet. It is our job to search for them. The Centre for Fortean Zoology [CFZ] is the only professional, scientific and full-time organisation in the world dedicated to cryptozoology - the study of unknown animals. Since 1992 the CFZ has carried out an unparalleled programme of research and investigation all over the world. We have carried out expeditions to Sumatra (2003 and 2004), Mongolia (2005), Puerto Rico (1998 and 2004), Mexico (1998), Thailand (2000), Florida (1998), Nevada (1999 and 2003), Texas (2003 and 2004), and Illinois (2004). An introductory essay by Jonathan Downes, notes putting each issue into a historical perspective, and a history of the CFZ.

THE BLACKDOWN MYSTERY
Jonathan Downes - ISBN 978-1-905723-00-3

£7.99

Intrepid members of the CFZ are up to the challenge, and manage to entangle themselves thoroughly in the bizarre trappings of this case. This is the soft underbelly of ufology, rife with unsavory characters, plenty of drugs and booze." That sums it up quite well, we think. A new edition of the classic 1999 book by legendary fortean author Jonathan Downes. In this remarkable book, Jon weaves a complex tale of conspiracy, anti-conspiracy, quasi-conspiracy and downright lies surrounding an air-crash and alleged UFO incident in Somerset during 1996. However the story is much stranger than that. This excellent and amusing book lifts the lid off much of contemporary forteana and explains far more than it initially promises.

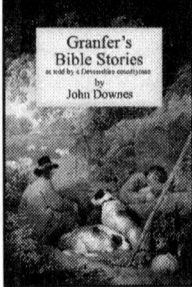

GRANFER'S BIBLE STORIES
John Downes - ISBN 0-9512872-8-1

£7.99

Bible stories in the Devonshire vernacular, each story being told by an old Devon Grandfather - 'Granfer'. These stories are now collected together in a remarkable book presenting selected parts of the Bible as one more-or-less continuous tale in short 'bite sized' stories intended for dipping into or even for bed-time reading. `Granfer` treats the biblical characters as if they were simple country folk living in the next village. Many of the stories are treated with a degree of bucolic humour and kindly irreverence, which not only gives the reader an opportunity to re-evaluate familiar tales in a new light, but do so in both an entertaining and a spiritually uplifting manner.

FRAGRANT HARBOURS DISTANT RIVERS
John Downes - ISBN 0-9512872-5-7

£12.50

Many excellent books have been written about Africa during the second half of the 19th Century, but this one is unique in that it presents the stories of a dozen different people, whose interlinked lives and achievements have as many nuances as any contemporary soap opera. It explains how the events in China and Hong Kong which surrounded the Opium Wars, intimately effected the events in Africa which take up the majority of this book. The author served in the Colonial Service in Nigeria and Hong Kong, during which he found himself following in the footsteps of one of the main characters in this book; Frederick Lugard – the architect of modern Nigeria.

CFZ PRESS, MYRTLE COTTAGE,
WOOLFARDISWORTHY BIDEFORD,
NORTH DEVON, EX39 5QR
www.cfz.org.uk

Other books available from
CFZ PRESS

THE SMALLER MYSTERY CARNIVORES OF THE WESTCOUNTRY
Jonathan Downes - ISBN 978-1-905723-05-8

£7.99

Although much has been written in recent years about the mystery big cats which have been reported stalking Westcountry moorlands, little has been written on the subject of the smaller British mystery carnivores. This unique book redresses the balance and examines the current status in the Westcountry of three species thought to be extinct: the Wildcat, the Pine Marten and the Polecat, finding that the truth is far more exciting than the currently held scientific dogma. This book also uncovers evidence suggesting that even more exotic species of small mammal may lurk hitherto unsuspected in the countryside of Devon, Cornwall, Somerset and Dorset.

STRENGTH THROUGH KOI
They saved Hitler's Koi and other stories

£7.99

Jonathan Downes - ISBN 978-1-905723-04-1

"For years I have augmented my income by working as a `hack` writer, penning throwaway articles for anyone who will pay me. Regularly, I would get the bus into Exeter City Centre, and sneak into W.H.Smiths and peruse the magazines for sale, and make a surreptitious list of any new publications whom I could approach to buy an article from me. One day in the late winter, I was doing just this when I found a copy of a magazine called Koi Carp. With my tongue firmly in cheek, I telephoned them, and asked whether they would be interested in an article - or even a series of articles - about the fortean aspects of their hobby. Much to my surprise and gratification they accepted, and so I started work on my first article. I had been so used to working for fly-by-night publications, that I had stopped taking a long-term view of my writing work. I was lucky if a series I wrote lasted three issues, so the fact that I knew next to nothing about the fortean aspect of koi carp-keeping didn't really matter. However, on this occasion, I was hoist by my own petard, as the series carried on for nearly two years! After six or seven issues, I bit the bullet, and started to employ the old journalistic adage that one should never let the truth get in the way of a good story. Some of the stories that follow are true. Some are mostly true, others have a germ of truth, and even the ones that I made up are based on true events. I think my proudest moment as a journalist came after the publication of "They Saved Hitler's Koi", when Simon Wolstencroft, an old friend of mine, and then editor of a sister-magazine to the one for which I was working, sent me the following email. 1. How did you think you would get away with having this printed? 2. How did you get away with it? For goodness sake, don't read these stories looking for any firm insights into the history and culture of koi keeping, but I hope that they may give you some little amusement, because that was the spirit in which they were written."

**CFZ PRESS, MYRTLE COTTAGE,
WOOLFARDISWORTHY BIDEFORD,
NORTH DEVON, EX39 5QR
w w w . c f z . o r g . u k**

www.ingramcontent.com/pod-product-compliance
Lightning Source LLC
Chambersburg PA
CBHW062205080426
42734CB00010B/1791